SATISFACTION GUARANTEED OR DOUBLE YOUR FROWN BACK

BUILDS GLADNESS OF HEART

A COLLECTION OF **100% WHOLE GRIN**

ROSE IS ROSE COMICS

PROVIDES 100% OF ESSENTIAL DAILY SMILES

THIS CONTAINER IS NEVER EMPTY

ROSE IS ROSE ®

CREATED BY PAT BRADY, BY DON WIMMER

SINCE 1984 WHOLESOME GOODNESS FOR THE ENTIRE FAMILY

BEST IF READ BY APRIL 15, 2284

NET WT.12 OZ.(1.09 Kg.)

**Andrews McMeel
Publishing,LLC**

Kansas City

08 09 10 11 12 SDB 10 9 8 7 6 5 4 3 2 1

ISBN-13: 978-0-7407-7094-4
ISBN-10: 0-7407-7094-2

Library of Congress Control Number: 2007937788

www.andrewsmcmeel.com

Cover design and cover art by Pat Brady

ATTENTION: SCHOOLS AND BUSINESSES

Andrews McMeel books are available at quantity discounts with bulk purchase for educational, business, or sales promotional use. For information, please write to: Special Sales Department, Andrews McMeel Publishing, LLC, 4520 Main Street, Kansas City, Missouri 64111.

Other *Rose is Rose*® Books

She's a Momma, Not a Movie Star

License to Dream

Rose is Rose 15th Anniversary Collection

The Irresistible Rose is Rose

High-Spirited Rose is Rose

Rose is Rose Right on the Lips

Rose is Rose Running on Alter Ego

Red Carpet Rose

The Enchanting Rose

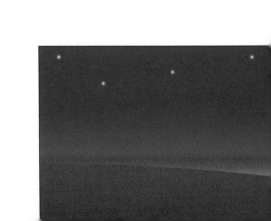

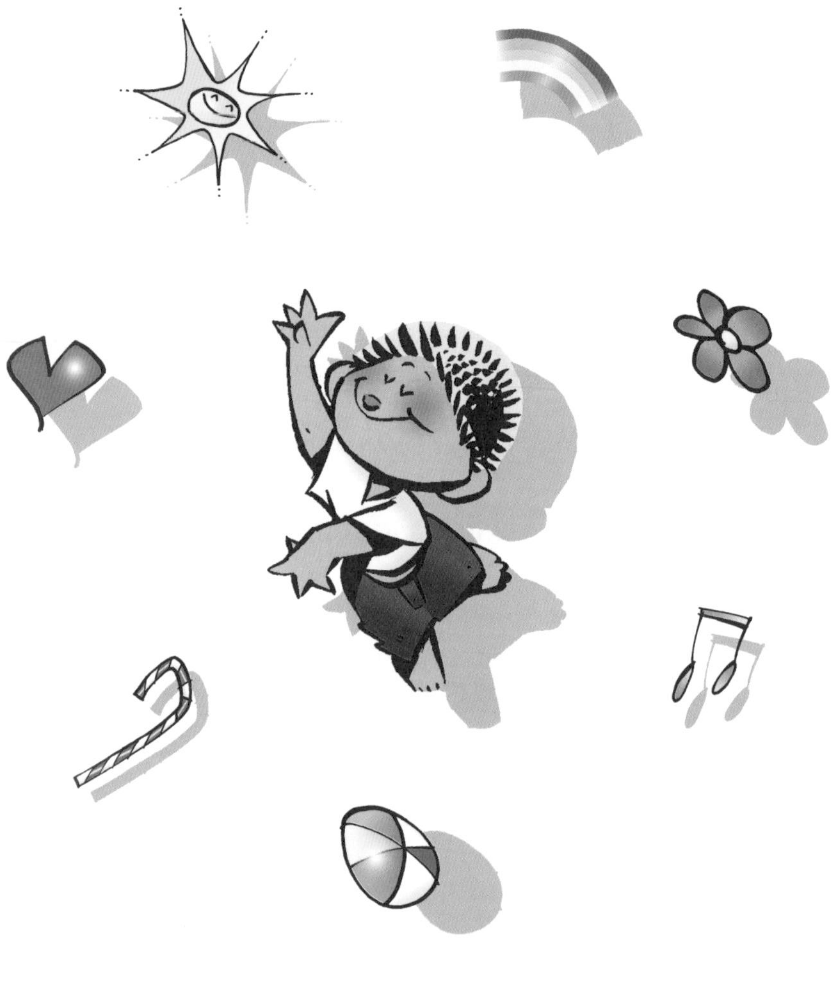

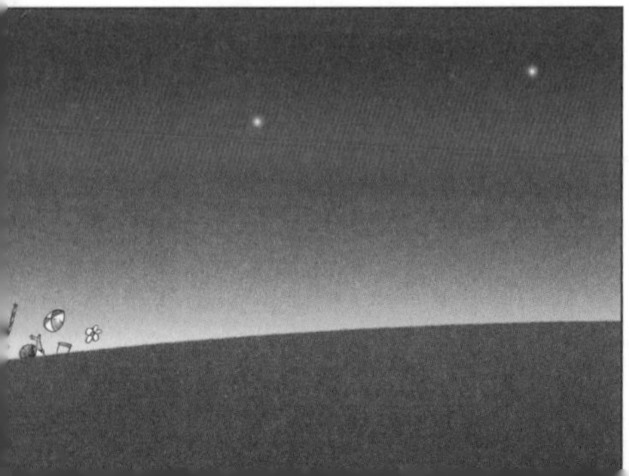

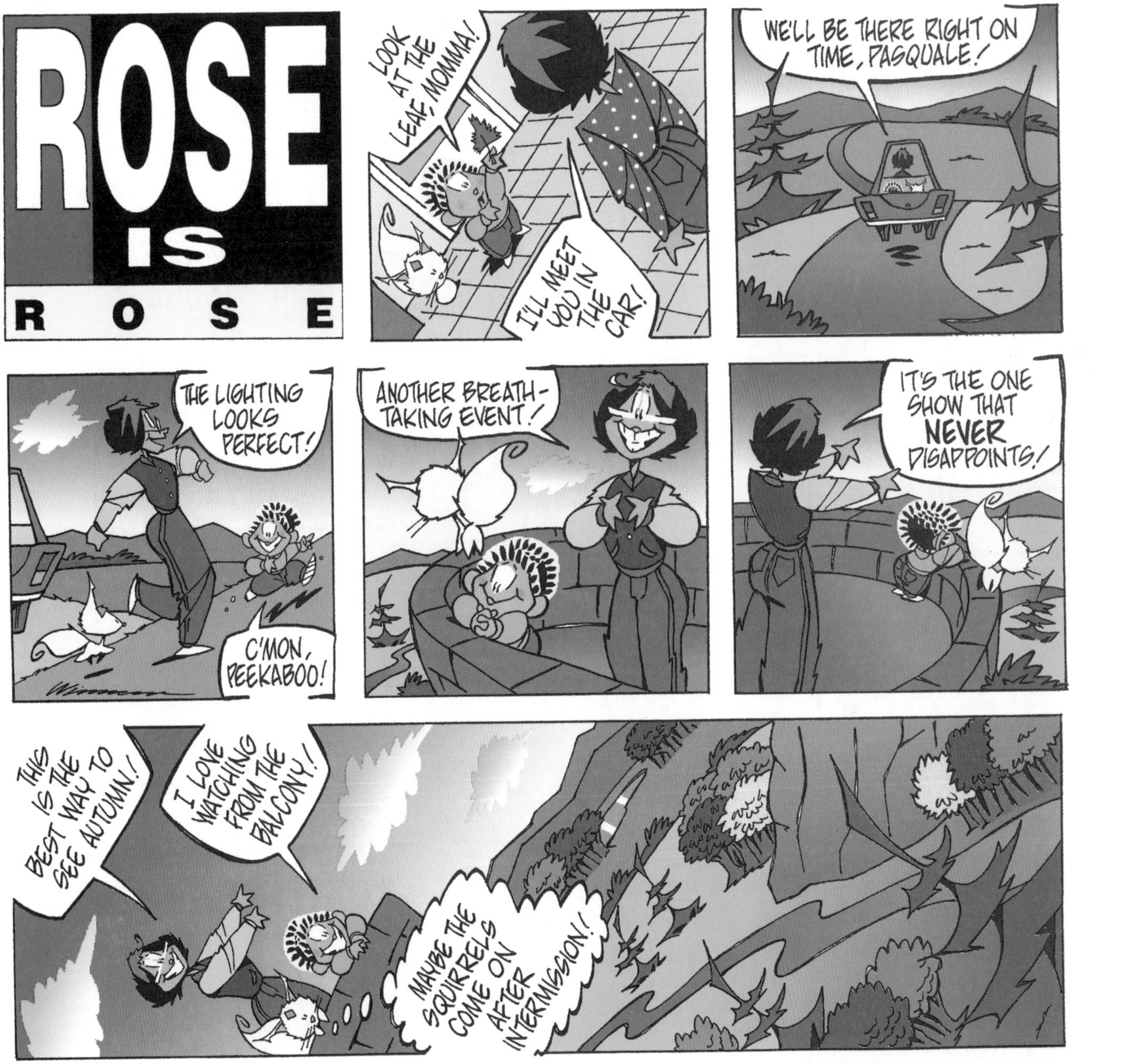
ROSE IS ROSE
LOOK AT THE LEAF, MOMMA!
I'LL MEET YOU IN THE CAR!
WE'LL BE THERE RIGHT ON TIME, PASQUALE!
THE LIGHTING LOOKS PERFECT!
C'MON, PEEKABOO!
ANOTHER BREATH-TAKING EVENT!
IT'S THE ONE SHOW THAT NEVER DISAPPOINTS!
THIS IS THE BEST WAY TO SEE AUTUMN!
I LOVE WATCHING FROM THE BALCONY!
MAYBE THE SQUIRRELS COME ON AFTER INTERMISSION!

FLIP THE PAGE CORNERS FROM FRONT TO BACK AND WATCH BOTH SIDES TOGETHER!

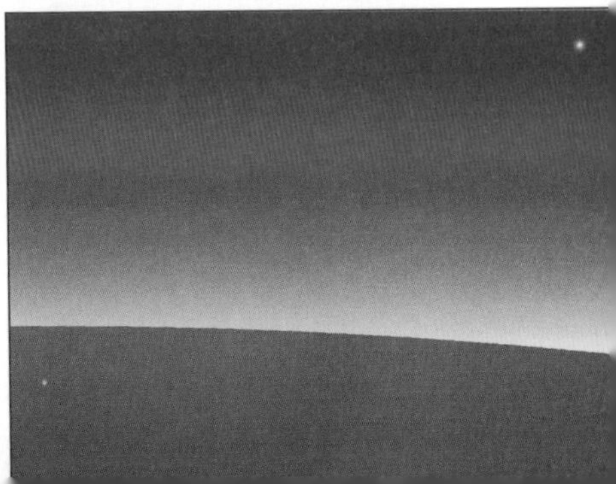

MOMMA, CAN WE GET MY BACK-TO-SCHOOL SUPPLIES TODAY?
SURE!
BOUNCE
PULL
TUG
ZIP
I'D LIKE TO FINISH MY COFFEE AND CHANGE!
GOOD! YOU USUALLY DON'T SHOP IN YOUR PAJAMAS!

WE'RE GOING TO THE MALL, CLEM... YOU'RE WELCOME TO JOIN US!
YIPPEE!
SURE, AUNTIE ROSE! THAT SOUNDS LIKE FUN!
SO... WHAT ARE WE SHOPPING FOR?
SCHOOL SUPPLIES!
MOMMA, WHY DID CLEM SUDDENLY CHANGE HIS MIND ABOUT GOING WITH US?
BACK-TO-SCHOOL SHOPPING ISN'T EVERYONE'S IDEA OF A GOOD TIME!

THAT'S EVERY ONE WE HAVE IN STOCK!
HIGHLIG
WE'LL ORDER MORE FROM YOUR WEB SITE!
YOU MUST BE A DILIGENT STUDENT TO NEED SO MANY HIGHLIGHTERS!
THEY'RE NOT FOR ME, SIR!
UH... YES, THE HIGHLIGHTERS ARE FOR ME!
NOW CAN WE DO MY SUPPLY LIST, MOMMA?!
I SHOULD HAVE RECOGNIZED THE SIGNS! I'VE BEEN A ZEALOUS HIGHLIGHTER FOR YEARS!

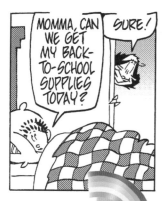

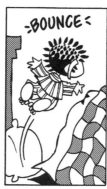

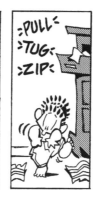

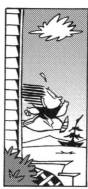

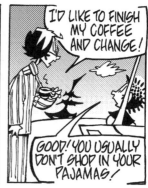

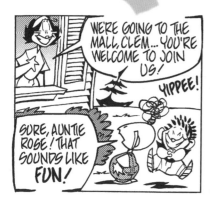

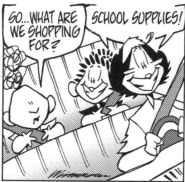

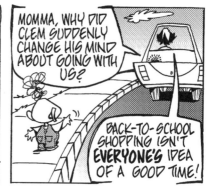

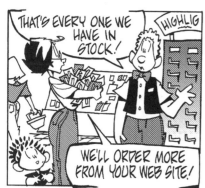

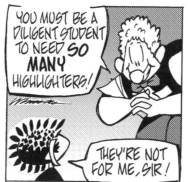

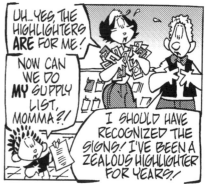

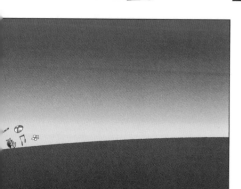

RRRR
RRRR
OOPS! I GOT CARRIED AWAY WITH THE TRIMMING!
OH, WELL... IT'LL GROW BACK!
HE FEEDS ME THE **SAME** LINE AFTER **EVERY** HAIRCUT!

IT'S OUT THERE, ROSE... THE LAST UNINHABITED ISLAND... BEAUTY... ISOLATION... UNSPOILED BY CIVILIZATION...
THE **ULTIMATE** GETAWAY!
ALL WE HAVE TO DO IS FIND IT!
IT DOESN'T SOUND LIKE A "**WE**" KIND OF PLACE!

IT'S HARD TO IMAGINE THAT ONE DAY MIMI WON'T NEED AN AFTERNOON NAP, ABBY!
I KNOW, ROSE!
I BELIEVE **I'M** PREPARED FOR THAT DAY...
IT'LL BE A WAKE-UP CALL FOR CORKY!

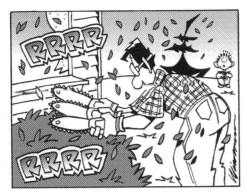

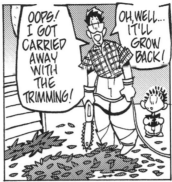

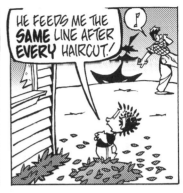

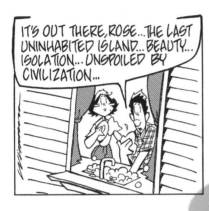

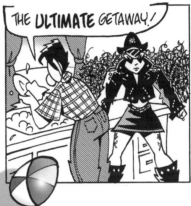

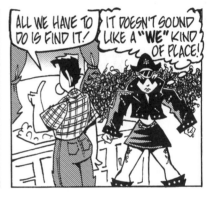

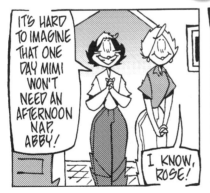

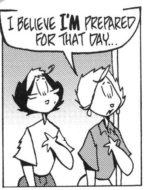

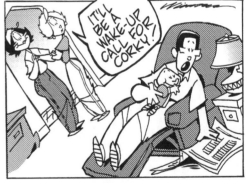

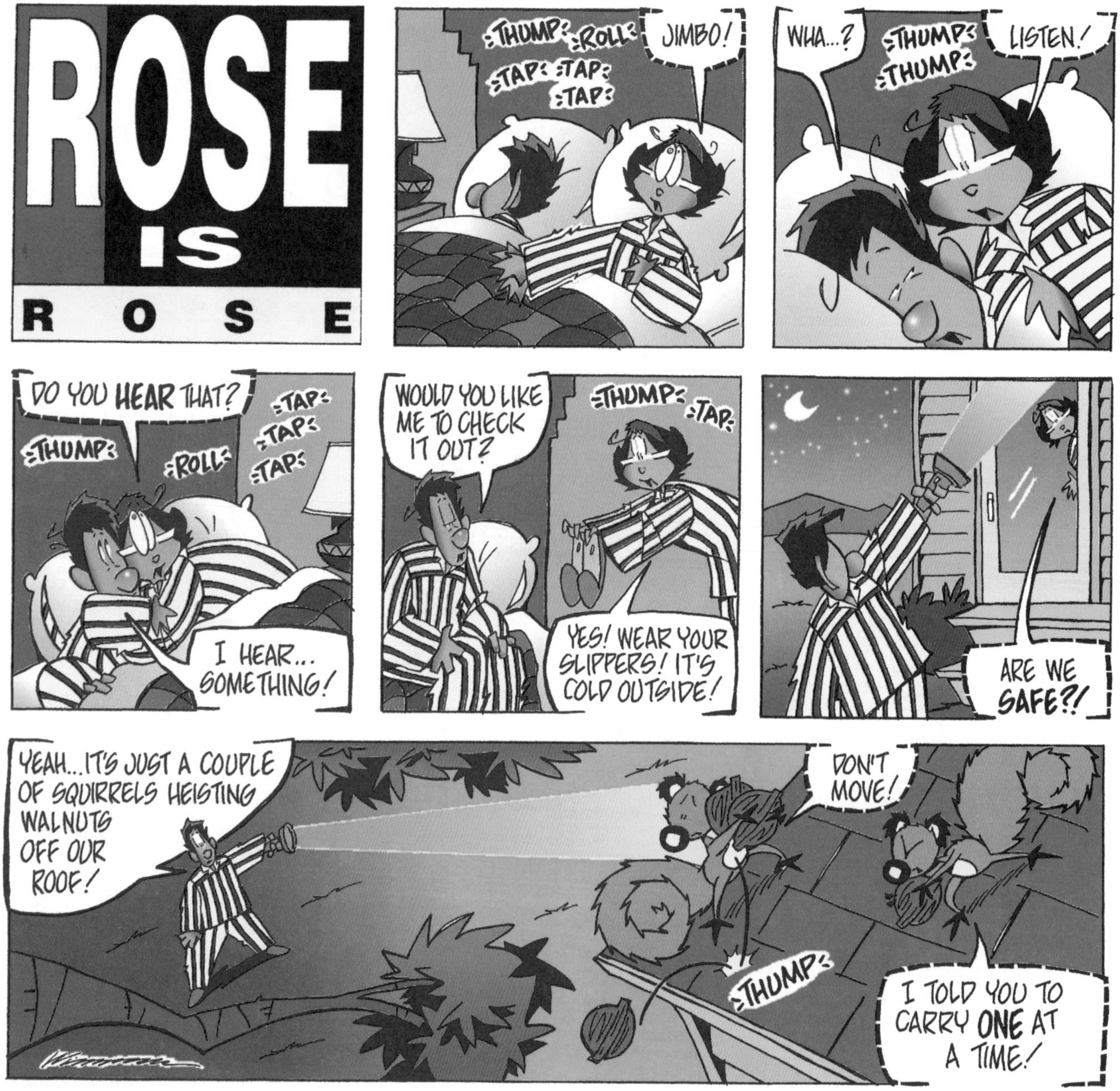
ROSE IS ROSE
THUMP
ROLL
TAP
TAP
TAP
JIMBO!
WHA...?
THUMP
THUMP
LISTEN!
DO YOU HEAR THAT?
THUMP
ROLL
TAP
TAP
TAP
I HEAR... SOMETHING!
WOULD YOU LIKE ME TO CHECK IT OUT?
THUMP
TAP
YES! WEAR YOUR SLIPPERS! IT'S COLD OUTSIDE!
ARE WE SAFE?!
YEAH...IT'S JUST A COUPLE OF SQUIRRELS HEISTING WALNUTS OFF OUR ROOF!
DON'T MOVE!
THUMP
I TOLD YOU TO CARRY ONE AT A TIME!

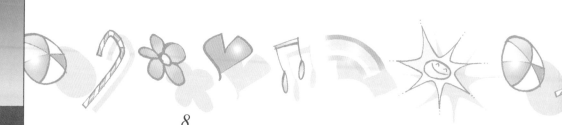

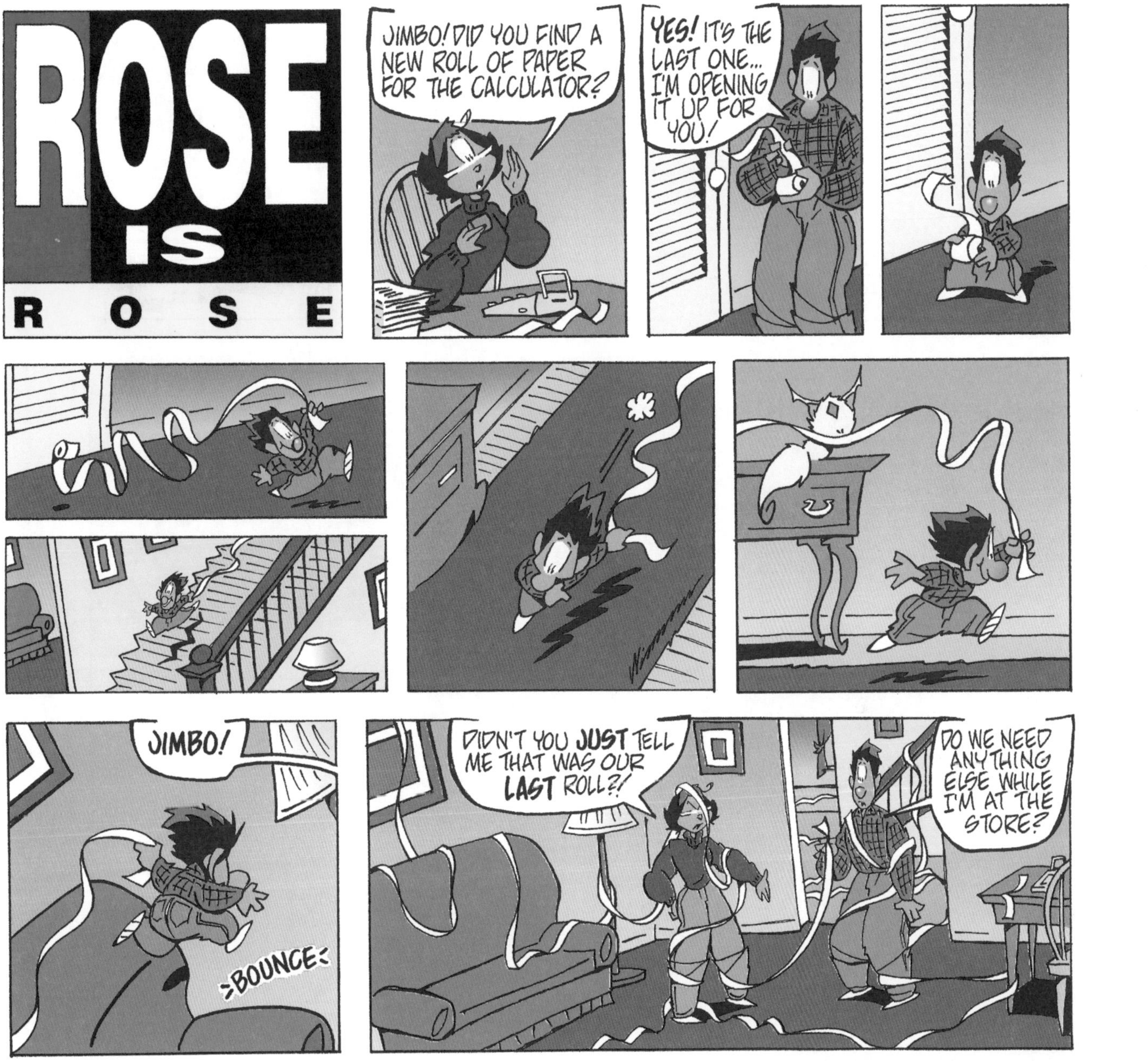
ROSE IS ROSE
JIMBO! DID YOU FIND A NEW ROLL OF PAPER FOR THE CALCULATOR?
YES! IT'S THE LAST ONE... I'M OPENING IT UP FOR YOU!
JIMBO!
>BOUNCE<
DIDN'T YOU JUST TELL ME THAT WAS OUR LAST ROLL?!
DO WE NEED ANYTHING ELSE WHILE I'M AT THE STORE?

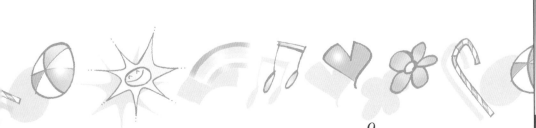

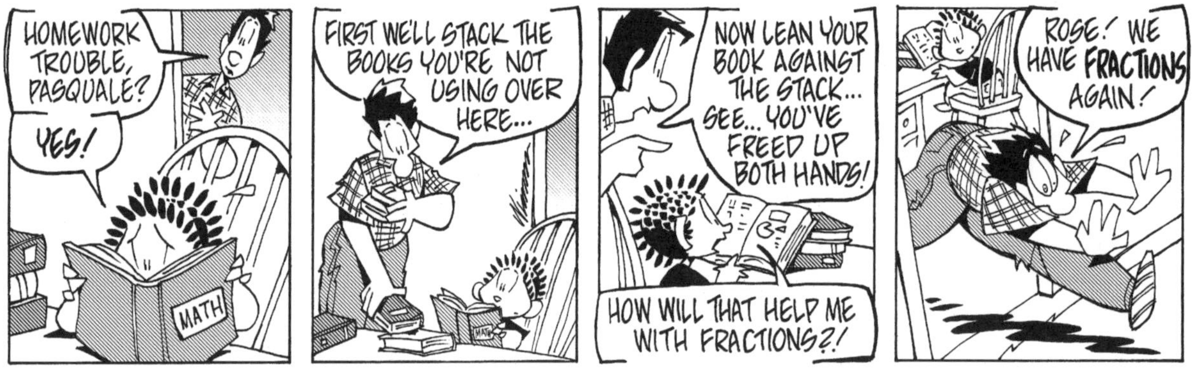
HOMEWORK TROUBLE, PASQUALE?
YES!
MATH
FIRST WE'LL STACK THE BOOKS YOU'RE NOT USING OVER HERE...
NOW LEAN YOUR BOOK AGAINST THE STACK... SEE... YOU'VE FREED UP BOTH HANDS!
HOW WILL THAT HELP ME WITH FRACTIONS?!
ROSE! WE HAVE **FRACTIONS** AGAIN!

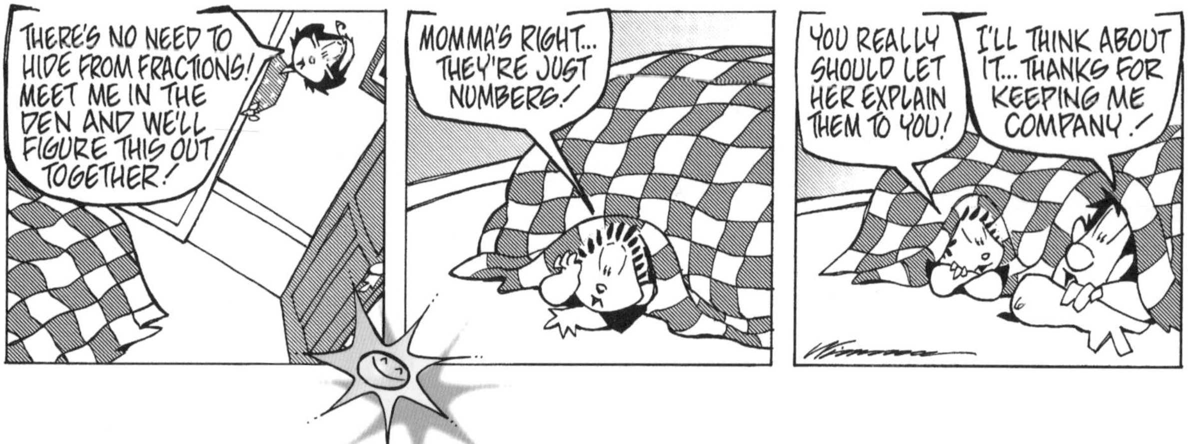
THERE'S NO NEED TO HIDE FROM FRACTIONS! MEET ME IN THE DEN AND WE'LL FIGURE THIS OUT TOGETHER!
MOMMA'S RIGHT... THEY'RE JUST NUMBERS!
YOU REALLY SHOULD LET HER EXPLAIN THEM TO YOU!
I'LL THINK ABOUT IT... THANKS FOR KEEPING ME COMPANY!

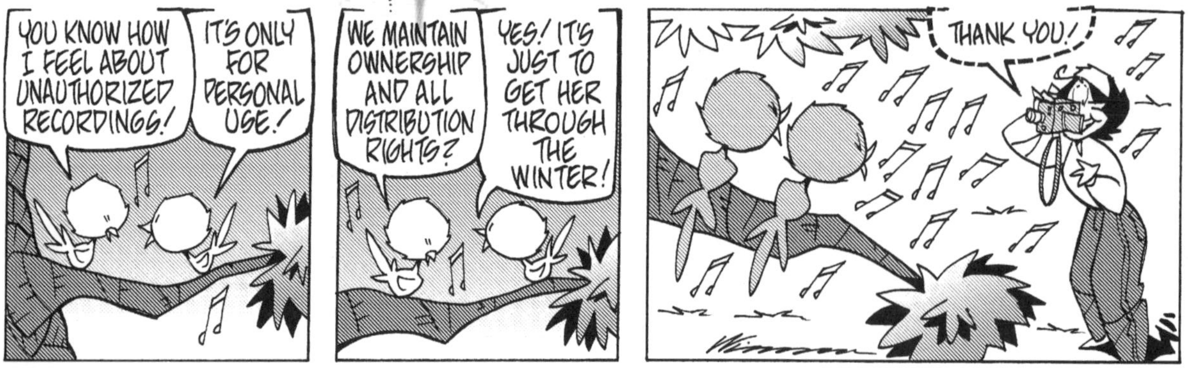
YOU KNOW HOW I FEEL ABOUT UNAUTHORIZED RECORDINGS!
IT'S ONLY FOR PERSONAL USE!
WE MAINTAIN OWNERSHIP AND ALL DISTRIBUTION RIGHTS?
YES! IT'S JUST TO GET HER THROUGH THE WINTER!
THANK YOU!

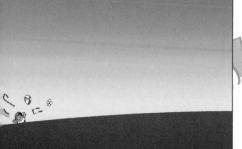

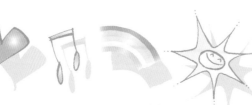

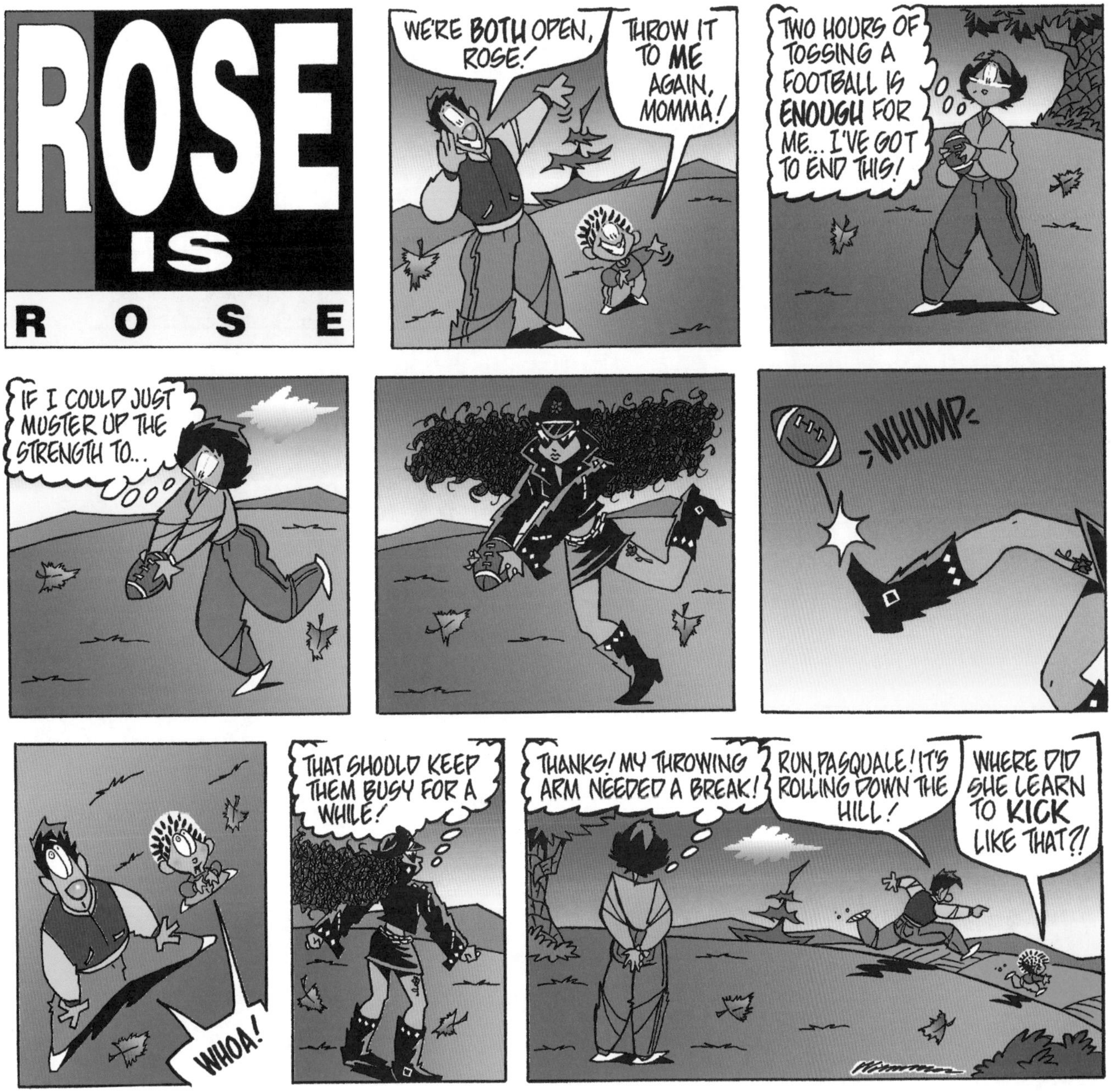
ROSE IS ROSE
WE'RE BOTH OPEN, ROSE!
THROW IT TO ME AGAIN, MOMMA!
TWO HOURS OF TOSSING A FOOTBALL IS ENOUGH FOR ME... I'VE GOT TO END THIS!
IF I COULD JUST MUSTER UP THE STRENGTH TO...
WHUMP
WHOA!
THAT SHOULD KEEP THEM BUSY FOR A WHILE!
THANKS! MY THROWING ARM NEEDED A BREAK!
RUN, PASQUALE! IT'S ROLLING DOWN THE HILL!
WHERE DID SHE LEARN TO KICK LIKE THAT?!

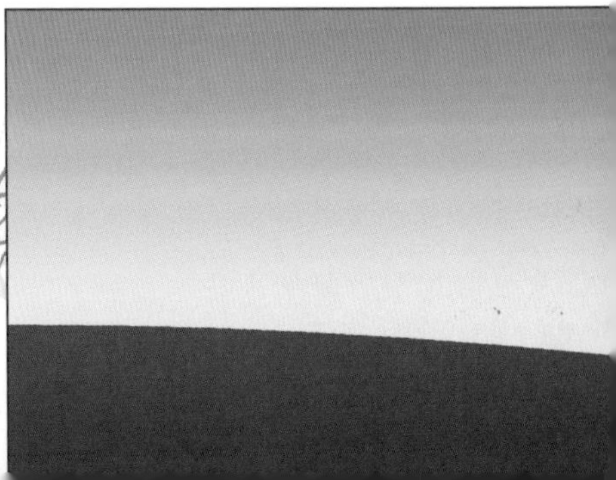

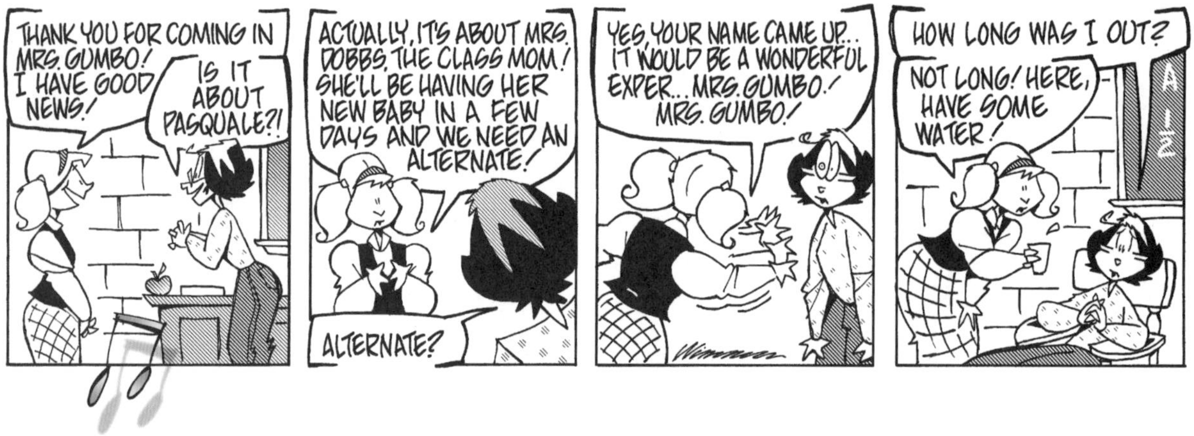
THANK YOU FOR COMING IN MRS. GUMBO! I HAVE GOOD NEWS!
IS IT ABOUT PASQUALE?!
ACTUALLY, IT'S ABOUT MRS. DOBBS, THE CLASS MOM! SHE'LL BE HAVING HER NEW BABY IN A FEW DAYS AND WE NEED AN ALTERNATE!
ALTERNATE?
YES, YOUR NAME CAME UP... IT WOULD BE A WONDERFUL EXPER... MRS. GUMBO! MRS. GUMBO!
HOW LONG WAS I OUT?
NOT LONG! HERE, HAVE SOME WATER!
A 1 2

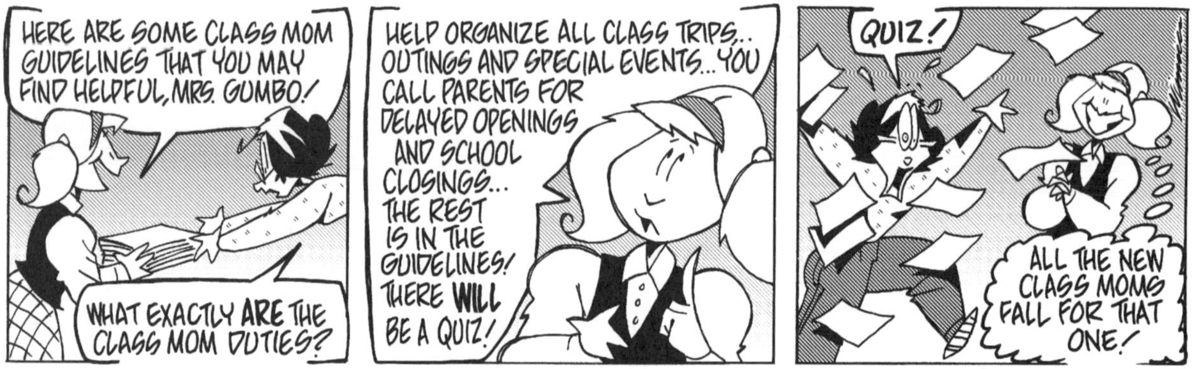
HERE ARE SOME CLASS MOM GUIDELINES THAT YOU MAY FIND HELPFUL, MRS. GUMBO!
WHAT EXACTLY **ARE** THE CLASS MOM DUTIES?
HELP ORGANIZE ALL CLASS TRIPS... OUTINGS AND SPECIAL EVENTS... YOU CALL PARENTS FOR DELAYED OPENINGS AND SCHOOL CLOSINGS... THE REST IS IN THE GUIDELINES! THERE **WILL** BE A QUIZ!
QUIZ!
ALL THE NEW CLASS MOMS FALL FOR THAT ONE!

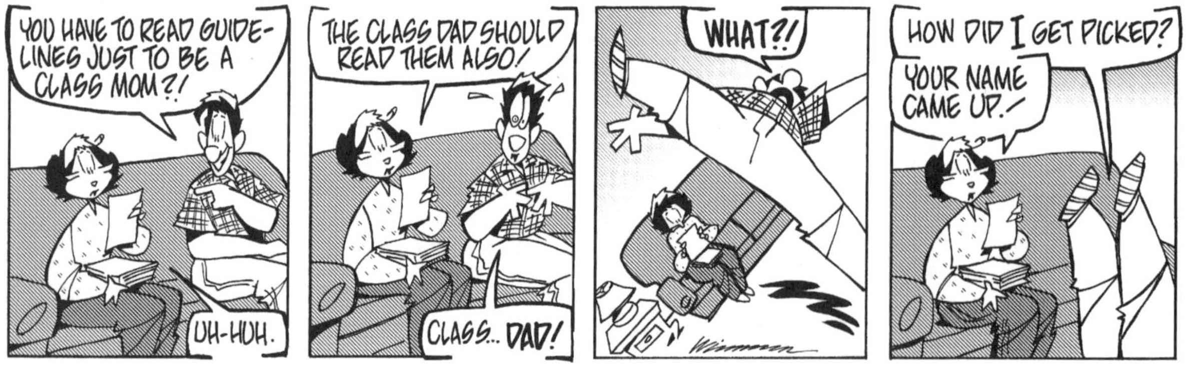
YOU HAVE TO READ GUIDE-LINES JUST TO BE A CLASS MOM?!
UH-HUH.
THE CLASS DAD SHOULD READ THEM ALSO!
CLASS... **DAD!**
WHAT?!
HOW DID I GET PICKED?
YOUR NAME CAME UP.

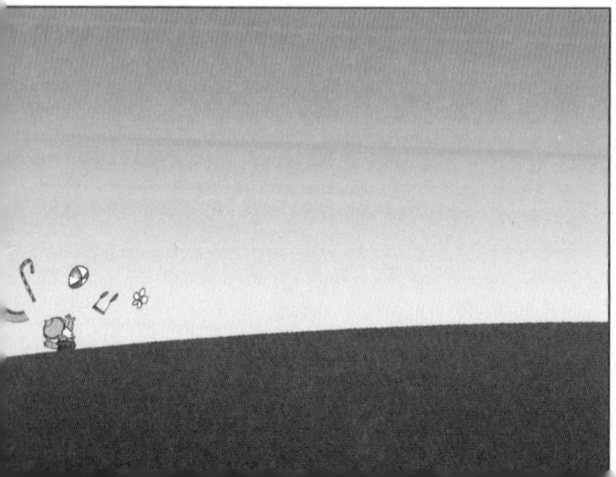

YOUR FIRST ORDER OF BUSINESS AS CLASS MOM IS TO HELP ME DECIDE ON OUR FALL CLASS TRIP, MRS. GUMBO!
ME?! DECIDE ON A TRIP?
WE'LL RIDE DAY AND NIGHT... ONLY STOPPING FOR FOOD AND SUNSETS!
WELL...
Xx Yy Zz
LET'S START WITH PARKS, MUSEUMS AND PETTING ZOOS!
OH, YES! THEY SOUND NICE, TOO!

PASQUALE, WOULD YOU INTRODUCE OUR SPECIAL GUEST!
PLEASE WELCOME OUR NEW CLASS MOM... MY MOMMA!
HELLO, I'M MRS. GUMBO...
SHE'S GOT BROWNIES!
SHE'LL DO FINE!
YOU ROCK, MRS. GUMBO!
OKAY! OKAY! THERE'S PLENTY FOR EVERY-ONE!
YIPPEE

YOU'VE CONVINCED ME THAT WE DESERVE A LITTLE TIME FOR OUR-SELVES, ROSE!
BECAUSE IT'S TRUE, ABBY!
BUT HOW WILL YOU CONVINCE THE REST OF OUR WORLD?
~SIP~
IGNORE THEM!

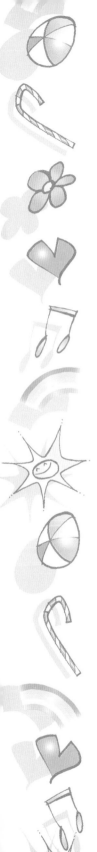

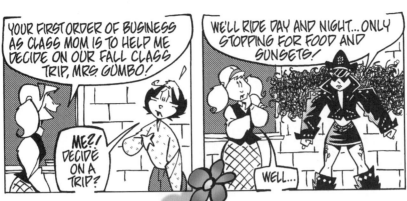

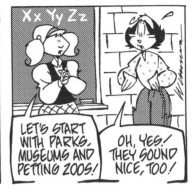

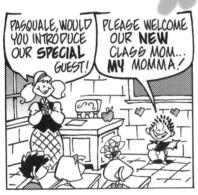

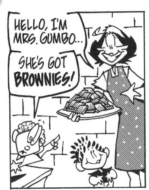

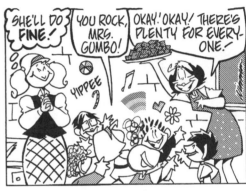

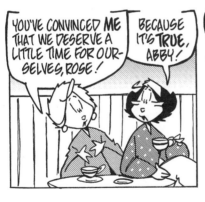

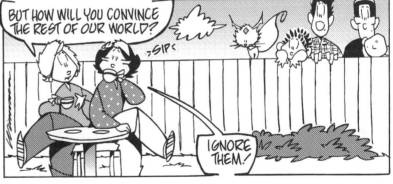

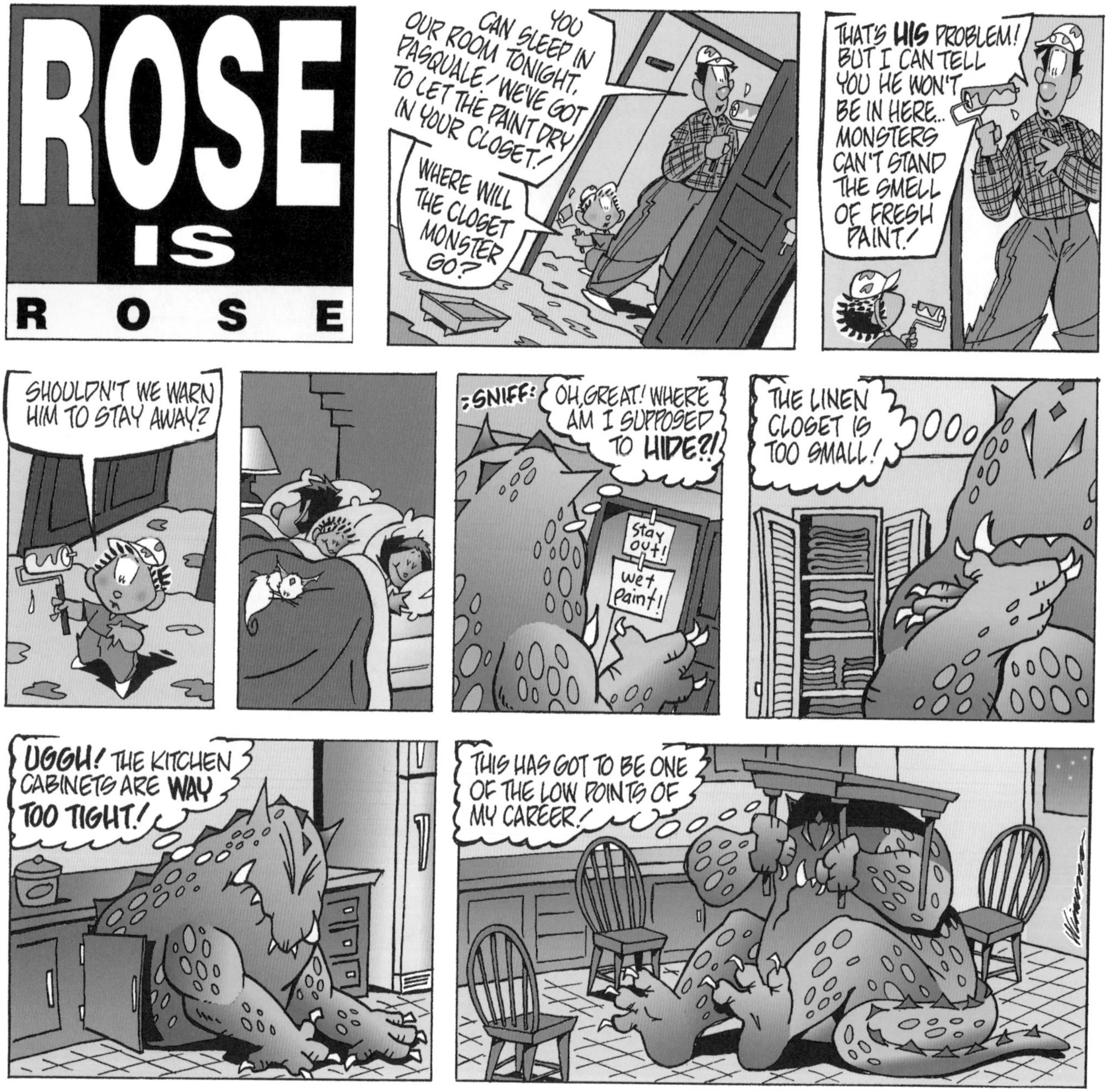
ROSE IS ROSE
YOU CAN SLEEP IN OUR ROOM TONIGHT, PASQUALE! WE'VE GOT TO LET THE PAINT DRY IN YOUR CLOSET!
WHERE WILL THE CLOSET MONSTER GO?
THAT'S HIS PROBLEM! BUT I CAN TELL YOU HE WON'T BE IN HERE... MONSTERS CAN'T STAND THE SMELL OF FRESH PAINT!
SHOULDN'T WE WARN HIM TO STAY AWAY?
:SNIFF:
OH, GREAT! WHERE AM I SUPPOSED TO HIDE?!
stay out!
wet paint!
THE LINEN CLOSET IS TOO SMALL!
UGGH! THE KITCHEN CABINETS ARE WAY TOO TIGHT!
THIS HAS GOT TO BE ONE OF THE LOW POINTS OF MY CAREER!

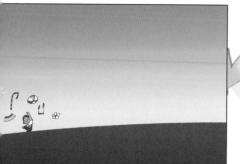

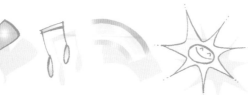

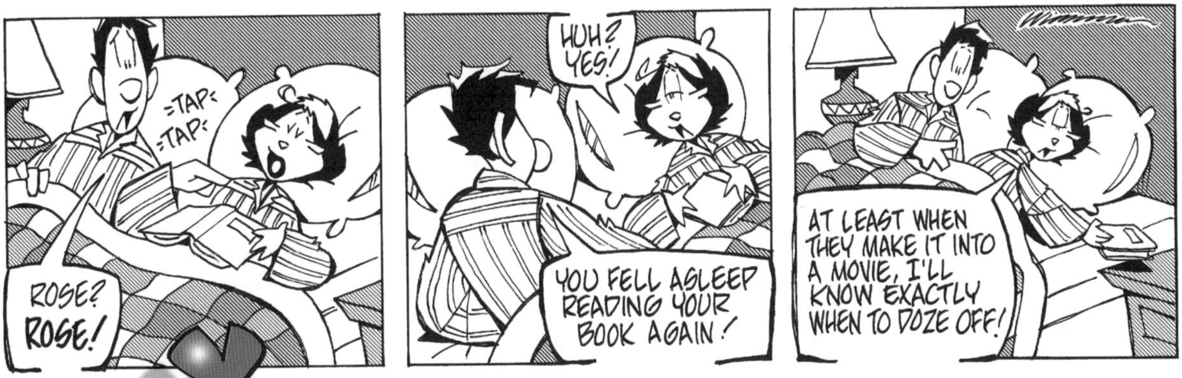
ROSE? ROSE!
TAP TAP
HUH? YES!
YOU FELL ASLEEP READING YOUR BOOK AGAIN!
AT LEAST WHEN THEY MAKE IT INTO A MOVIE, I'LL KNOW EXACTLY WHEN TO DOZE OFF!

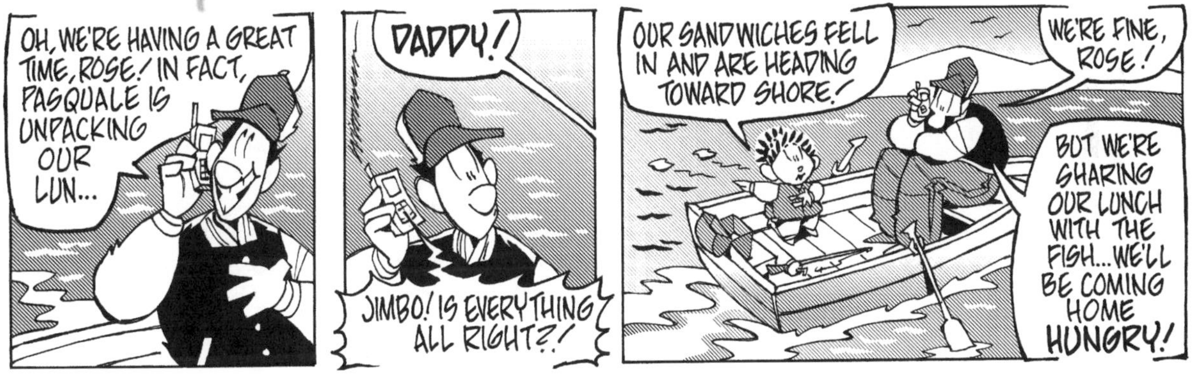
OH, WE'RE HAVING A GREAT TIME, ROSE! IN FACT, PASQUALE IS UNPACKING OUR LUN...
DADDY!
JIMBO! IS EVERYTHING ALL RIGHT?!
OUR SANDWICHES FELL IN AND ARE HEADING TOWARD SHORE!
WE'RE FINE, ROSE!
BUT WE'RE SHARING OUR LUNCH WITH THE FISH...WE'LL BE COMING HOME HUNGRY!

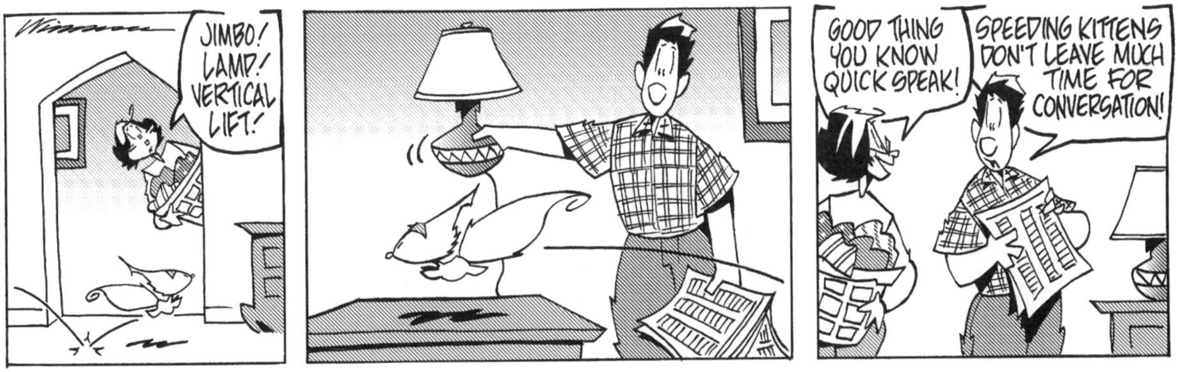
JIMBO! LAMP! VERTICAL LIFT!
GOOD THING YOU KNOW QUICK SPEAK!
SPEEDING KITTENS DON'T LEAVE MUCH TIME FOR CONVERSATION!

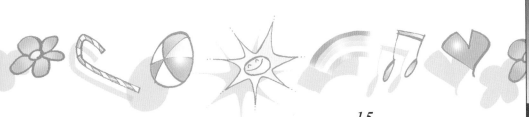

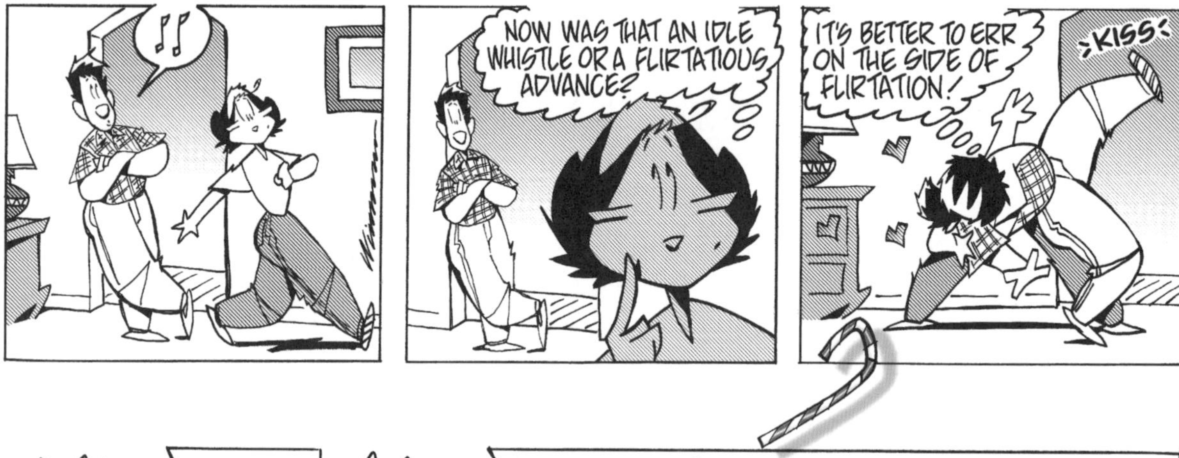
NOW WAS THAT AN IDLE WHISTLE OR A FLIRTATIOUS ADVANCE?
IT'S BETTER TO ERR ON THE SIDE OF FLIRTATION!
KISS

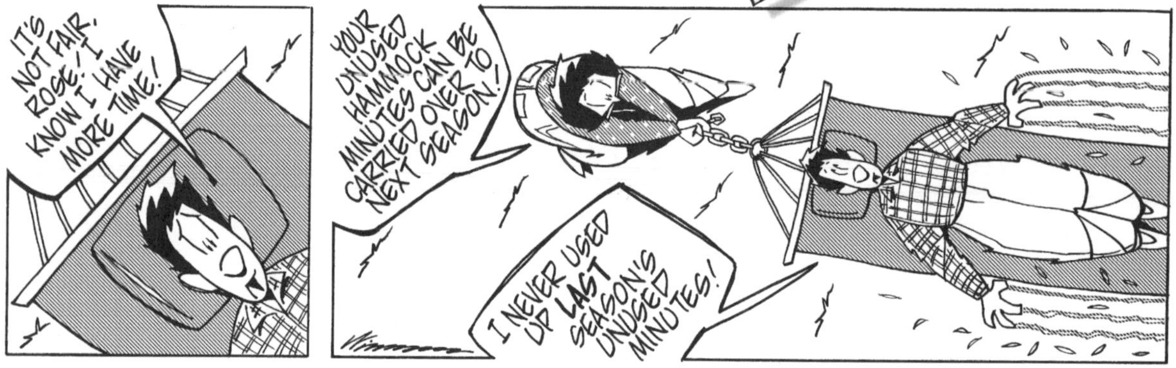
IT'S NOT FAIR, ROSE! I KNOW I HAVE MORE TIME!
YOUR UNUSED HAMMOCK MINUTES CAN BE CARRIED OVER TO NEXT SEASON!
I NEVER USED UP **LAST** SEASON'S UNUSED MINUTES!

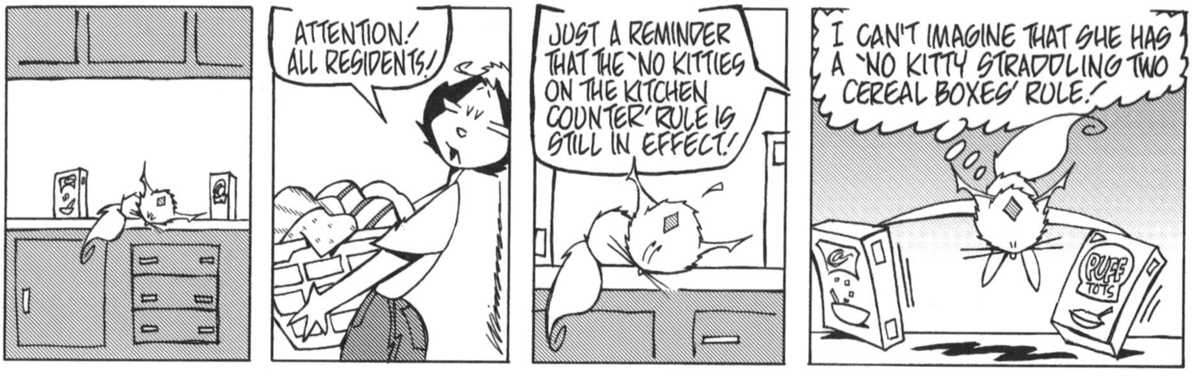
ATTENTION! ALL RESIDENTS!
JUST A REMINDER THAT THE 'NO KITTIES ON THE KITCHEN COUNTER' RULE IS STILL IN EFFECT!
I CAN'T IMAGINE THAT SHE HAS A 'NO KITTY STRADDLING TWO CEREAL BOXES' RULE!
RUFF TOTS

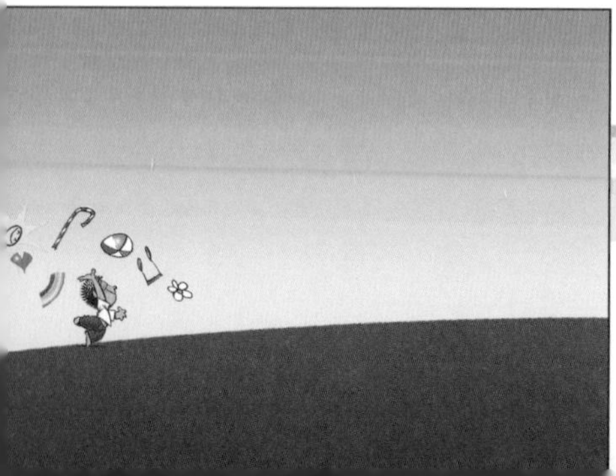

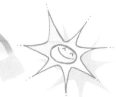

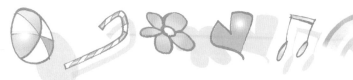

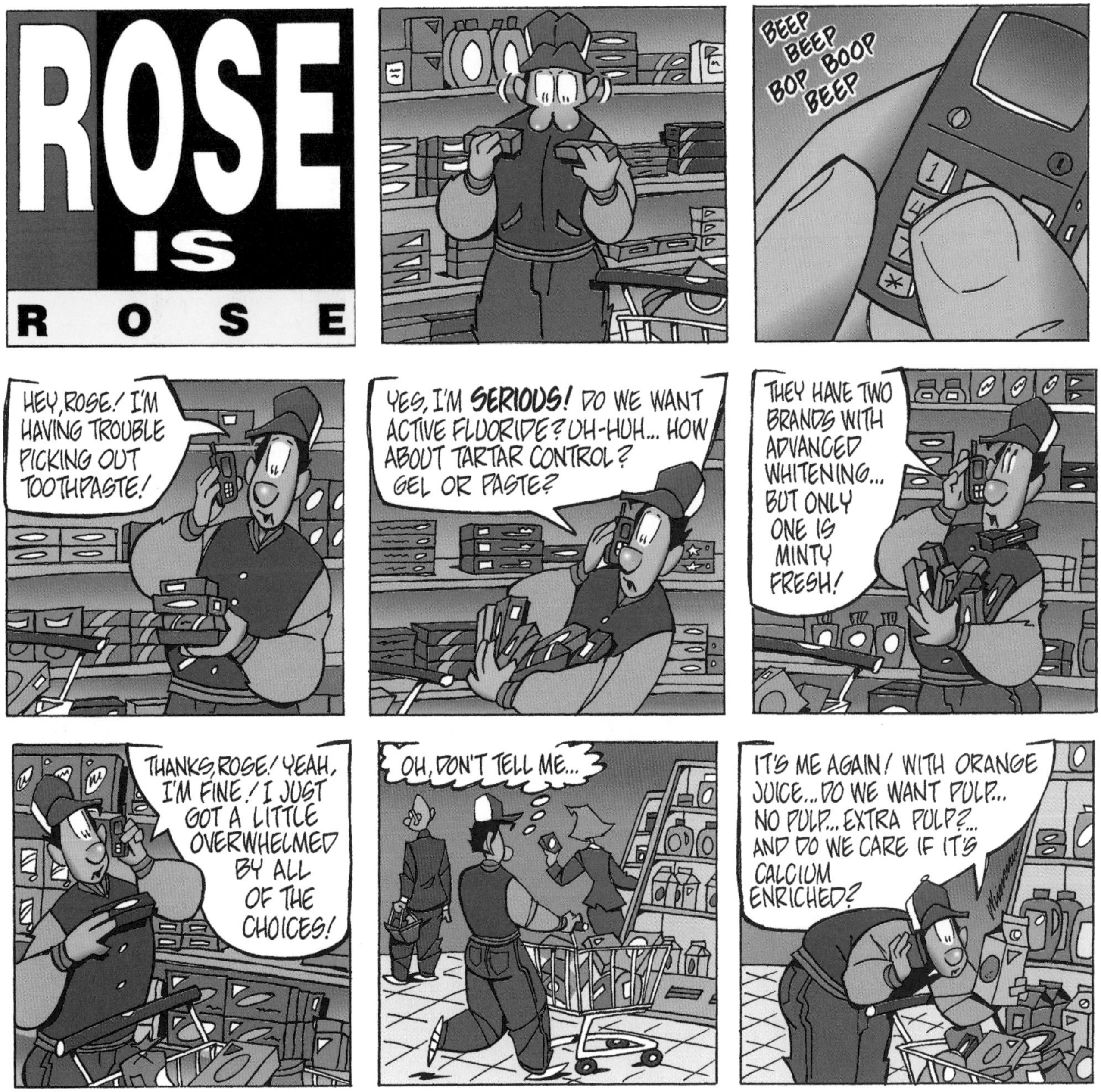
ROSE IS ROSE
BEEP BEEP BOP BOOP BEEP
HEY, ROSE! I'M HAVING TROUBLE PICKING OUT TOOTHPASTE!
YES, I'M **SERIOUS!** DO WE WANT ACTIVE FLUORIDE? UH-HUH... HOW ABOUT TARTAR CONTROL? GEL OR PASTE?
THEY HAVE TWO BRANDS WITH ADVANCED WHITENING... BUT ONLY ONE IS MINTY FRESH!
THANKS, ROSE! YEAH, I'M FINE! I JUST GOT A LITTLE OVERWHELMED BY ALL OF THE CHOICES!
OH, DON'T TELL ME...
IT'S ME AGAIN! WITH ORANGE JUICE... DO WE WANT PULP.. NO PULP... EXTRA PULP?... AND DO WE CARE IF IT'S CALCIUM ENRICHED?

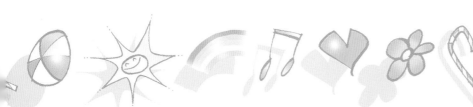

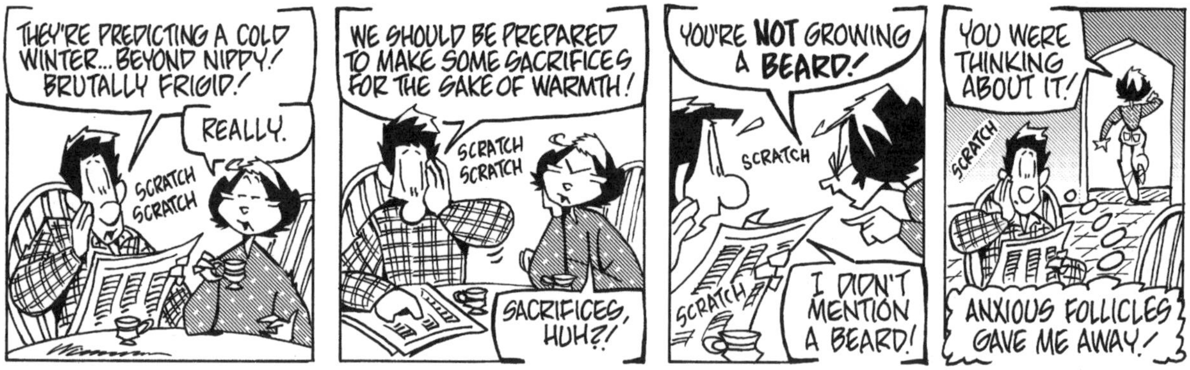
THEY'RE PREDICTING A COLD WINTER... BEYOND NIPPY! BRUTALLY FRIGID!
REALLY.
SCRATCH SCRATCH
WE SHOULD BE PREPARED TO MAKE SOME SACRIFICES FOR THE SAKE OF WARMTH!
SCRATCH SCRATCH
SACRIFICES, HUH?!
YOU'RE **NOT** GROWING A **BEARD!**
SCRATCH
SCRATCH
I DIDN'T MENTION A BEARD!
YOU WERE THINKING ABOUT IT!
SCRATCH
ANXIOUS FOLLICLES GAVE ME AWAY!

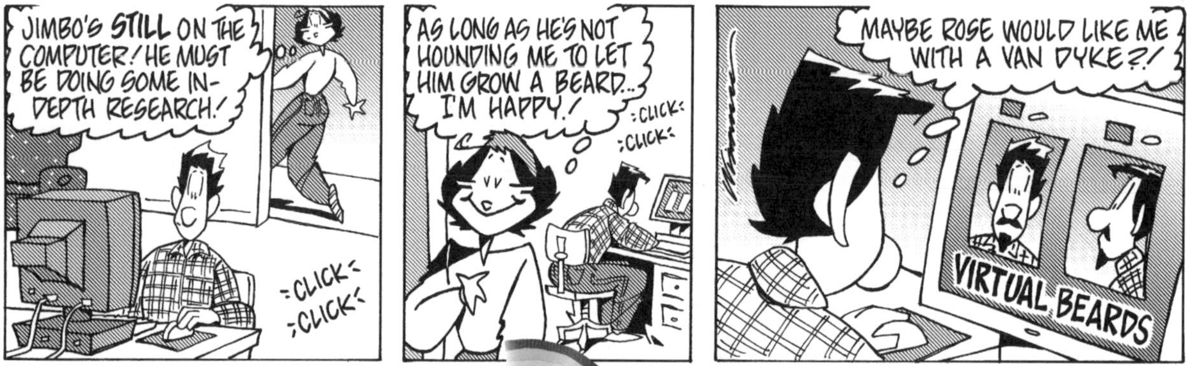
JIMBO'S **STILL** ON THE COMPUTER! HE MUST BE DOING SOME IN-DEPTH RESEARCH!
CLICK CLICK
AS LONG AS HE'S NOT HOUNDING ME TO LET HIM GROW A BEARD... I'M HAPPY!
CLICK CLICK
MAYBE ROSE WOULD LIKE ME WITH A VAN DYKE?!
VIRTUAL BEARDS

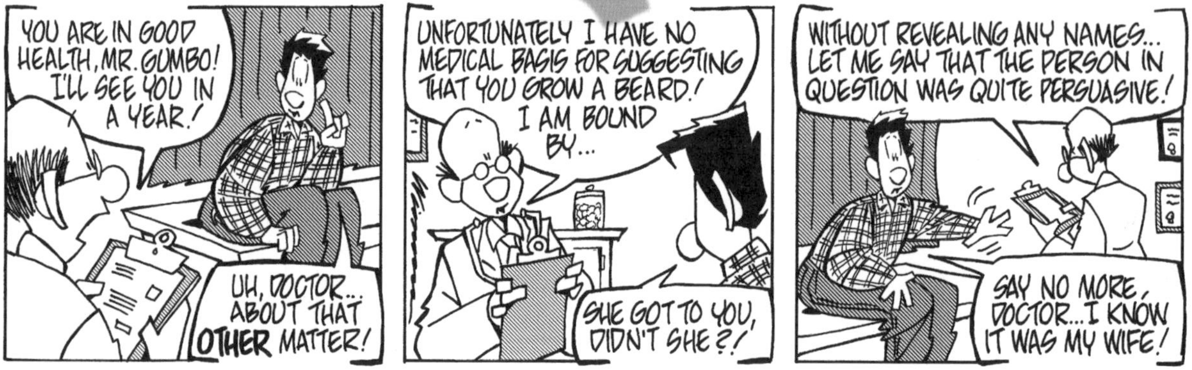
YOU ARE IN GOOD HEALTH, MR. GUMBO! I'LL SEE YOU IN A YEAR!
UH, DOCTOR... ABOUT THAT **OTHER** MATTER!
UNFORTUNATELY I HAVE NO MEDICAL BASIS FOR SUGGESTING THAT YOU GROW A BEARD! I AM BOUND BY...
SHE GOT TO YOU, DIDN'T SHE?!
WITHOUT REVEALING ANY NAMES... LET ME SAY THAT THE PERSON IN QUESTION WAS QUITE PERSUASIVE!
SAY NO MORE, DOCTOR... I KNOW IT WAS MY WIFE!

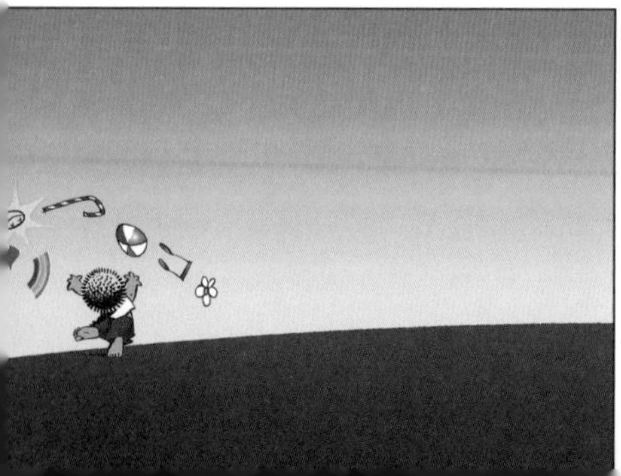

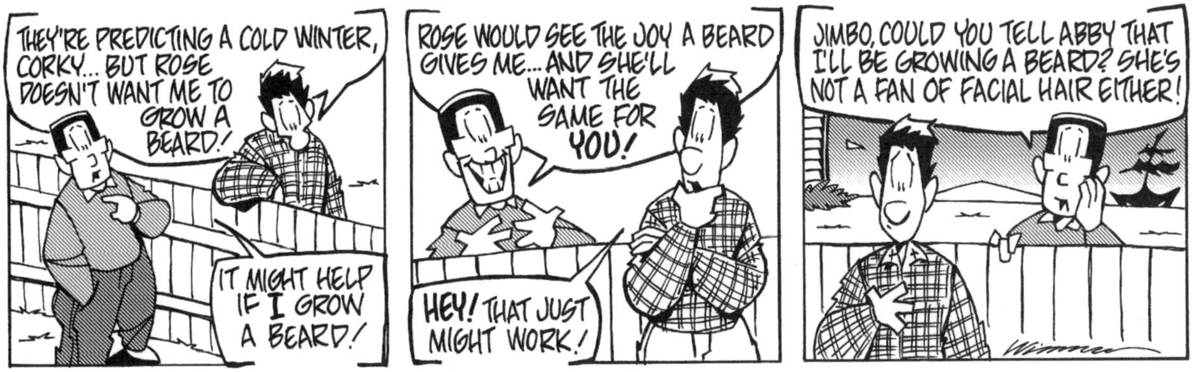
THEY'RE PREDICTING A COLD WINTER, CORKY... BUT ROSE DOESN'T WANT ME TO GROW A BEARD!
IT MIGHT HELP IF I GROW A BEARD!
ROSE WOULD SEE THE JOY A BEARD GIVES ME... AND SHE'LL WANT THE SAME FOR YOU!
HEY! THAT JUST MIGHT WORK!
JIMBO, COULD YOU TELL ABBY THAT I'LL BE GROWING A BEARD? SHE'S NOT A FAN OF FACIAL HAIR EITHER!

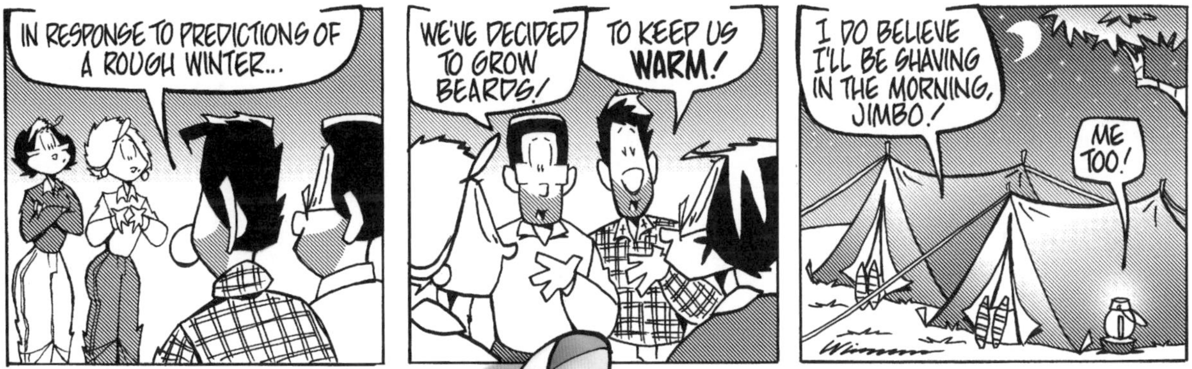
IN RESPONSE TO PREDICTIONS OF A ROUGH WINTER...
WE'VE DECIDED TO GROW BEARDS!
TO KEEP US WARM!
I DO BELIEVE I'LL BE SHAVING IN THE MORNING, JIMBO!
ME TOO!

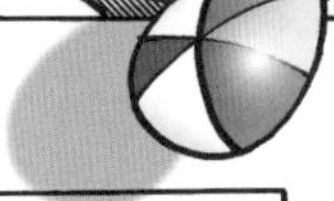

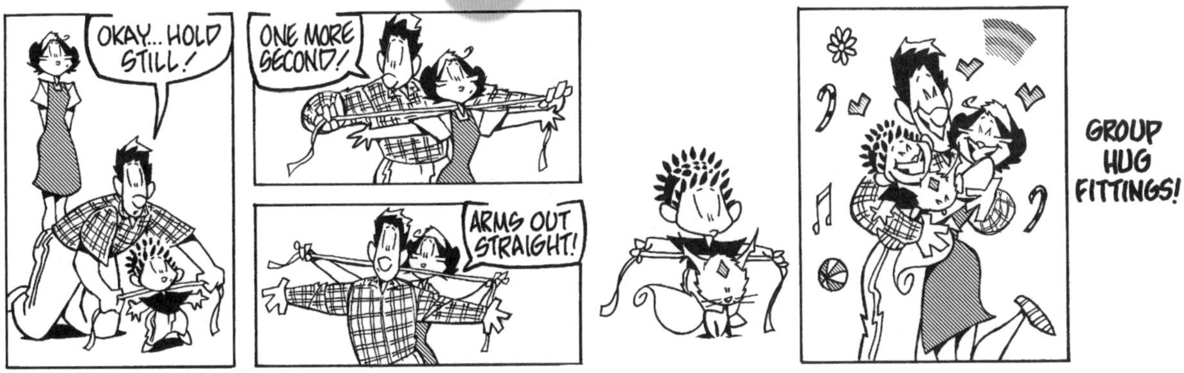
OKAY... HOLD STILL!
ONE MORE SECOND!
ARMS OUT STRAIGHT!
GROUP HUG FITTINGS!

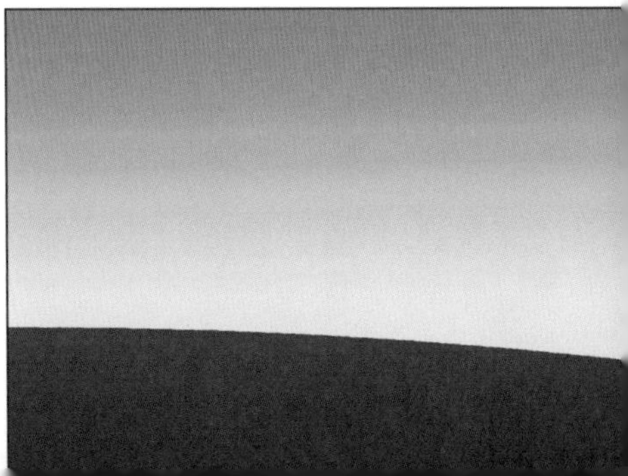

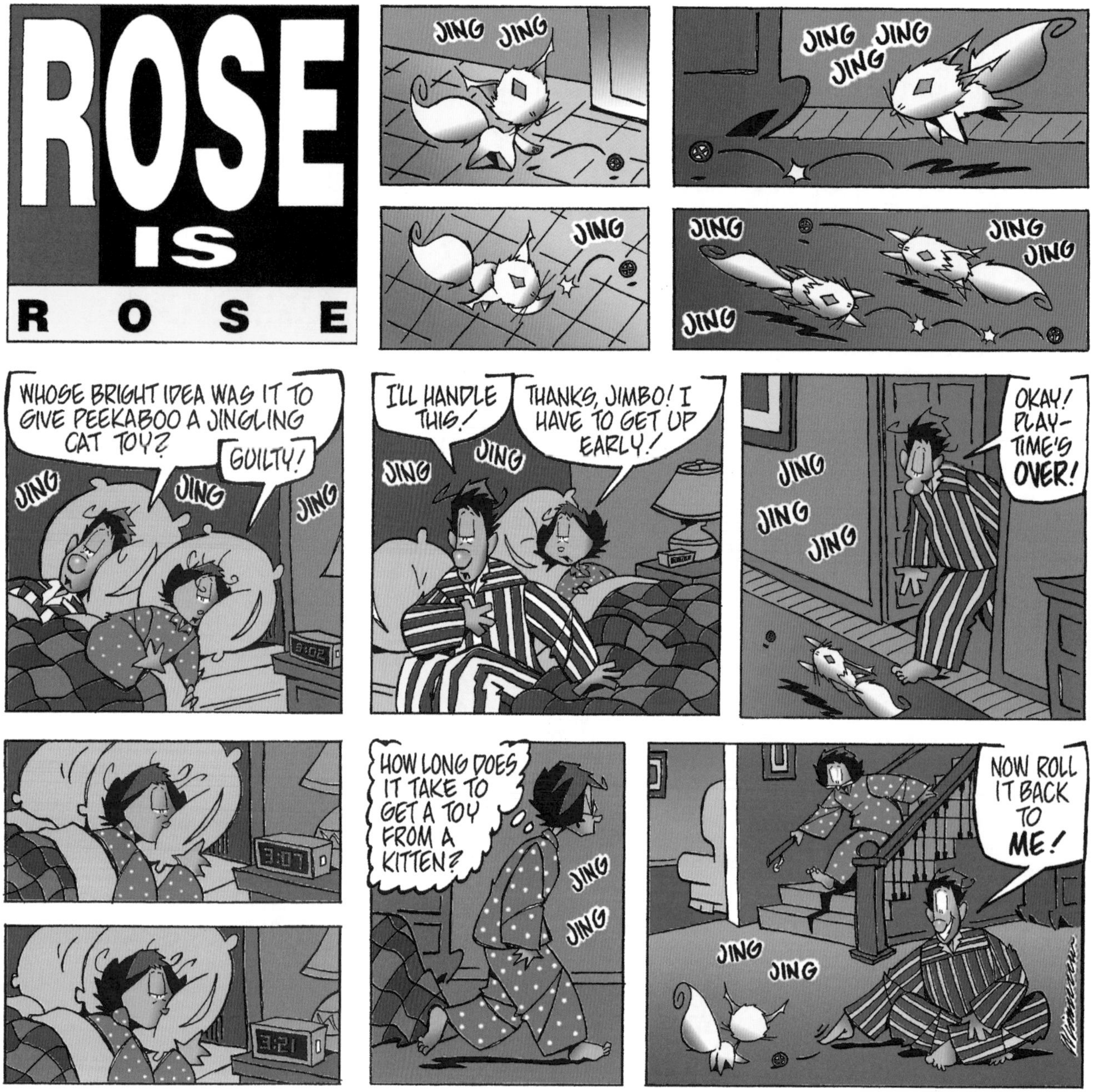
ROSE IS ROSE
JING JING
JING JING JING
JING
JING JING JING JING
WHOSE BRIGHT IDEA WAS IT TO GIVE PEEKABOO A JINGLING CAT TOY?
GUILTY!
JING JING JING
I'LL HANDLE THIS!
THANKS, JIMBO! I HAVE TO GET UP EARLY!
JING JING
OKAY! PLAY-TIME'S OVER!
JING JING JING
HOW LONG DOES IT TAKE TO GET A TOY FROM A KITTEN?
JING JING
NOW ROLL IT BACK TO ME!
JING JING

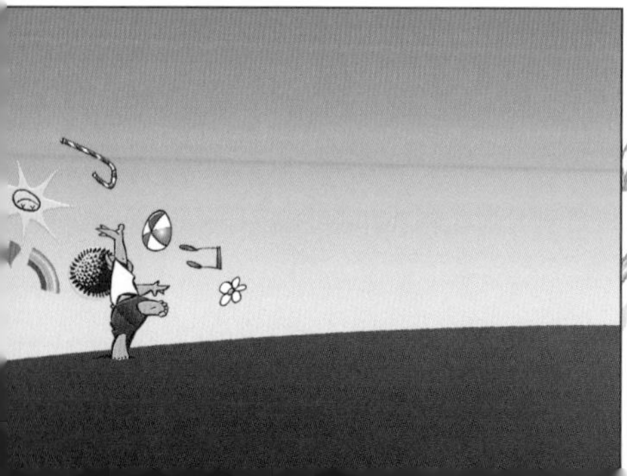

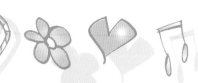

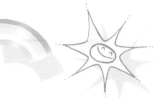

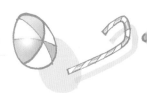

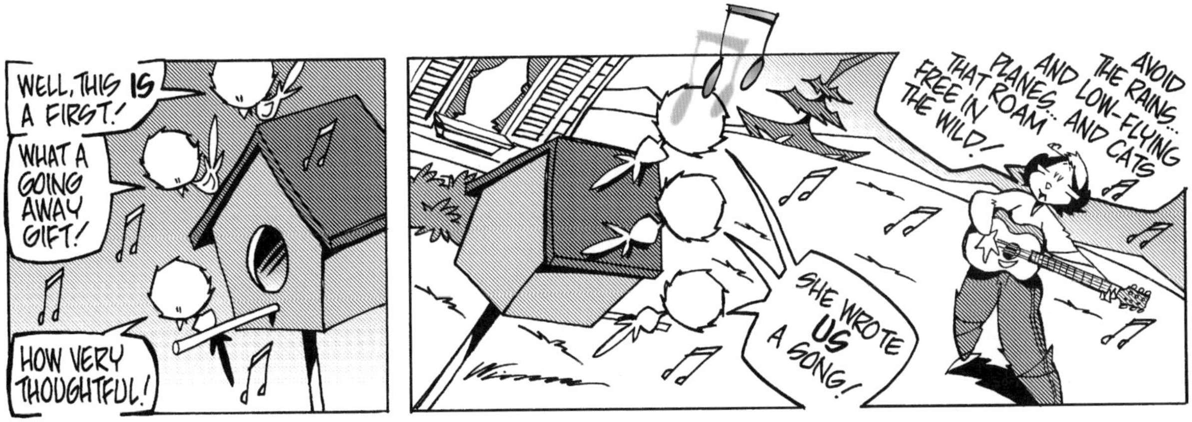
WELL, THIS IS A FIRST!
WHAT A GOING AWAY GIFT!
HOW VERY THOUGHTFUL!
AVOID THE RAINS... AND LOW-FLYING PLANES... AND CATS THAT ROAM FREE IN THE WILD!
SHE WROTE US A SONG!

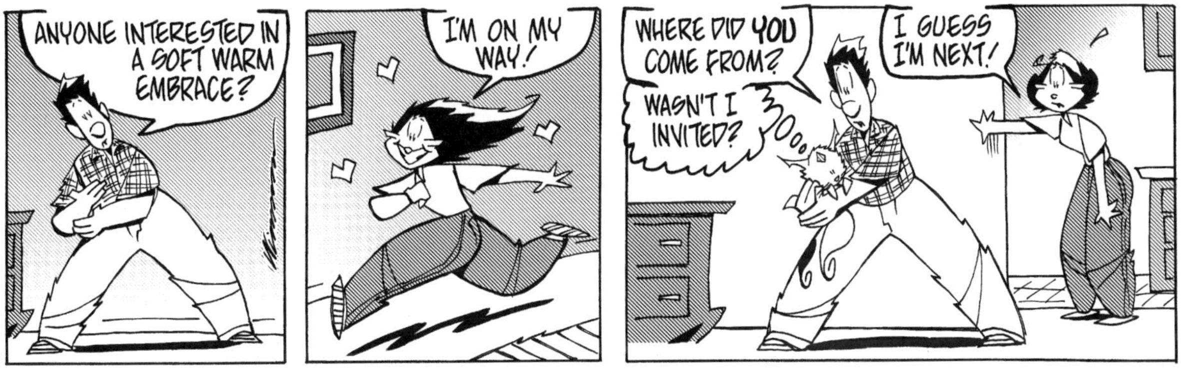
ANYONE INTERESTED IN A SOFT WARM EMBRACE?
I'M ON MY WAY!
WHERE DID YOU COME FROM?
WASN'T I INVITED?
I GUESS I'M NEXT!

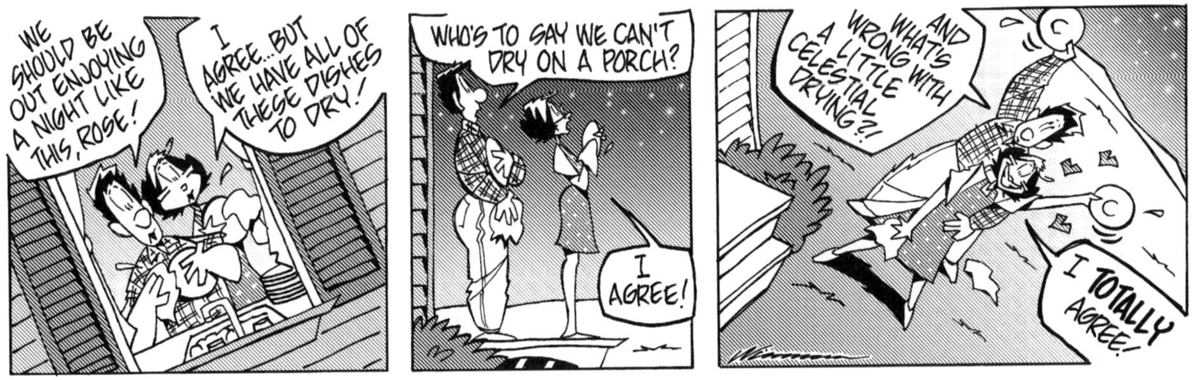
WE SHOULD BE OUT ENJOYING A NIGHT LIKE THIS, ROSE!
I AGREE... BUT WE HAVE ALL OF THESE DISHES TO DRY!
WHO'S TO SAY WE CAN'T DRY ON A PORCH?
I AGREE!
AND WHAT'S WRONG WITH A LITTLE CELESTIAL DRYING?!
I TOTALLY AGREE!

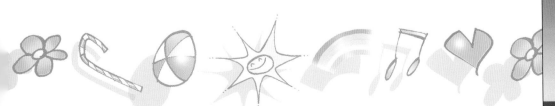

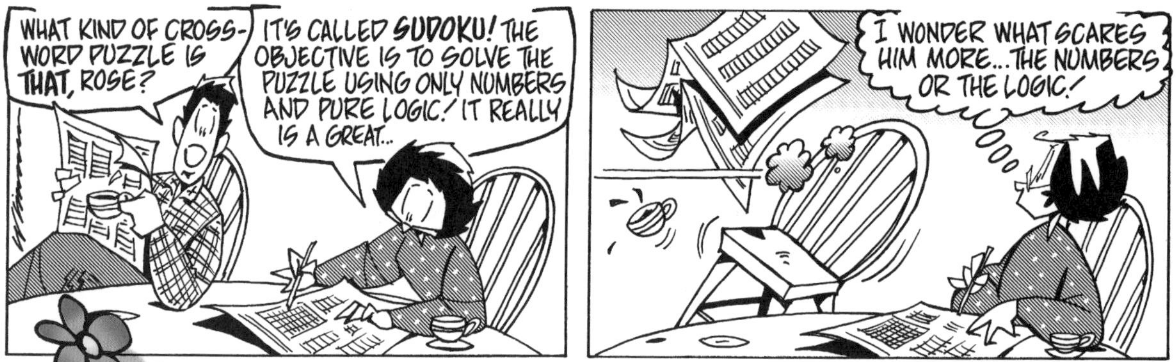
WHAT KIND OF CROSS-WORD PUZZLE IS **THAT**, ROSE?
IT'S CALLED **SUDOKU**! THE OBJECTIVE IS TO SOLVE THE PUZZLE USING ONLY NUMBERS AND PURE LOGIC! IT REALLY IS A GREAT...
I WONDER WHAT SCARES HIM MORE... THE NUMBERS OR THE LOGIC!

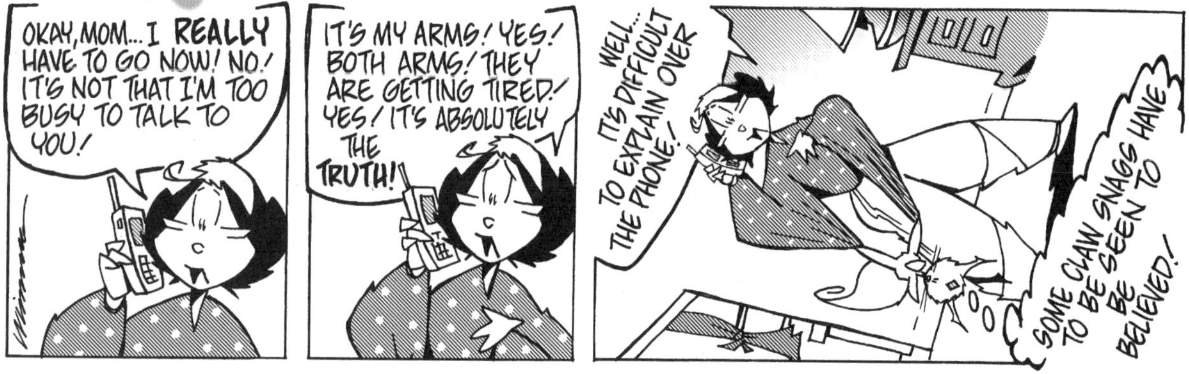
OKAY, MOM... I **REALLY** HAVE TO GO NOW! NO! IT'S NOT THAT I'M TOO BUSY TO TALK TO YOU!
IT'S MY ARMS! YES! BOTH ARMS! THEY ARE GETTING TIRED! YES! IT'S ABSOLUTELY THE **TRUTH**!
WELL... IT'S DIFFICULT TO EXPLAIN OVER THE PHONE!
SOME CLAW SNAGS HAVE TO BE SEEN TO BE BELIEVED!

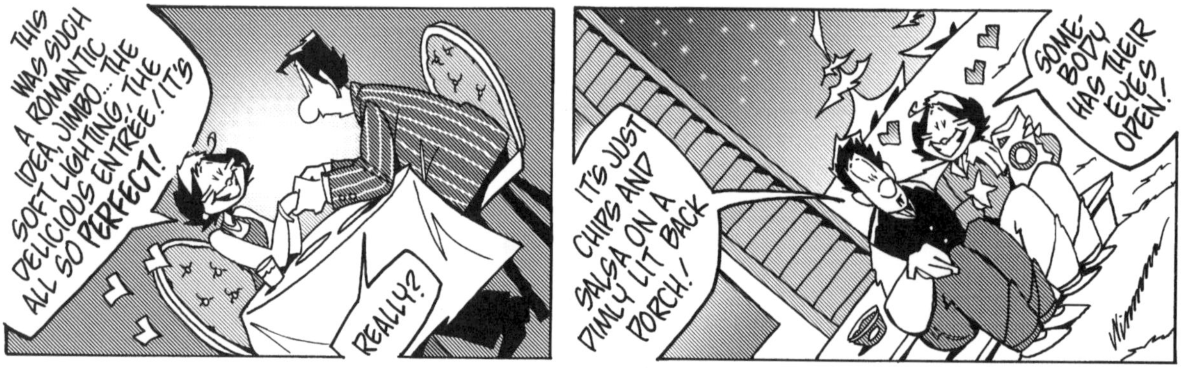
THIS WAS SUCH A ROMANTIC IDEA, JIMBO... THE SOFT LIGHTING, THE DELICIOUS ENTRÉE! IT'S ALL SO **PERFECT**!
REALLY?
IT'S JUST CHIPS AND SALSA ON A DIMLY LIT BACK PORCH!
SOME-BODY HAS THEIR EYES OPEN!

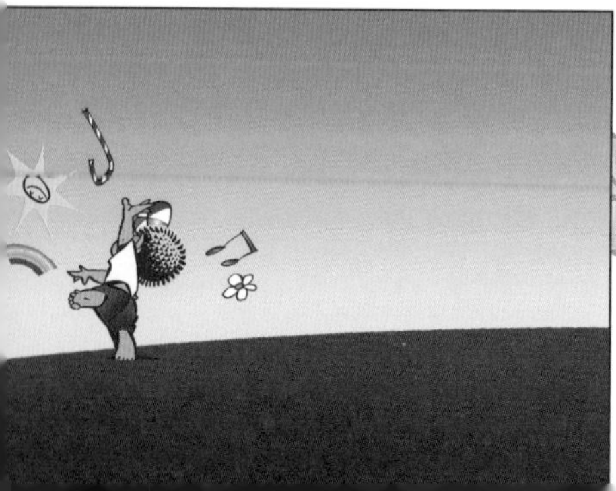

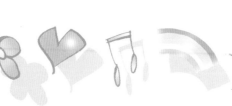

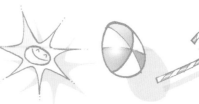

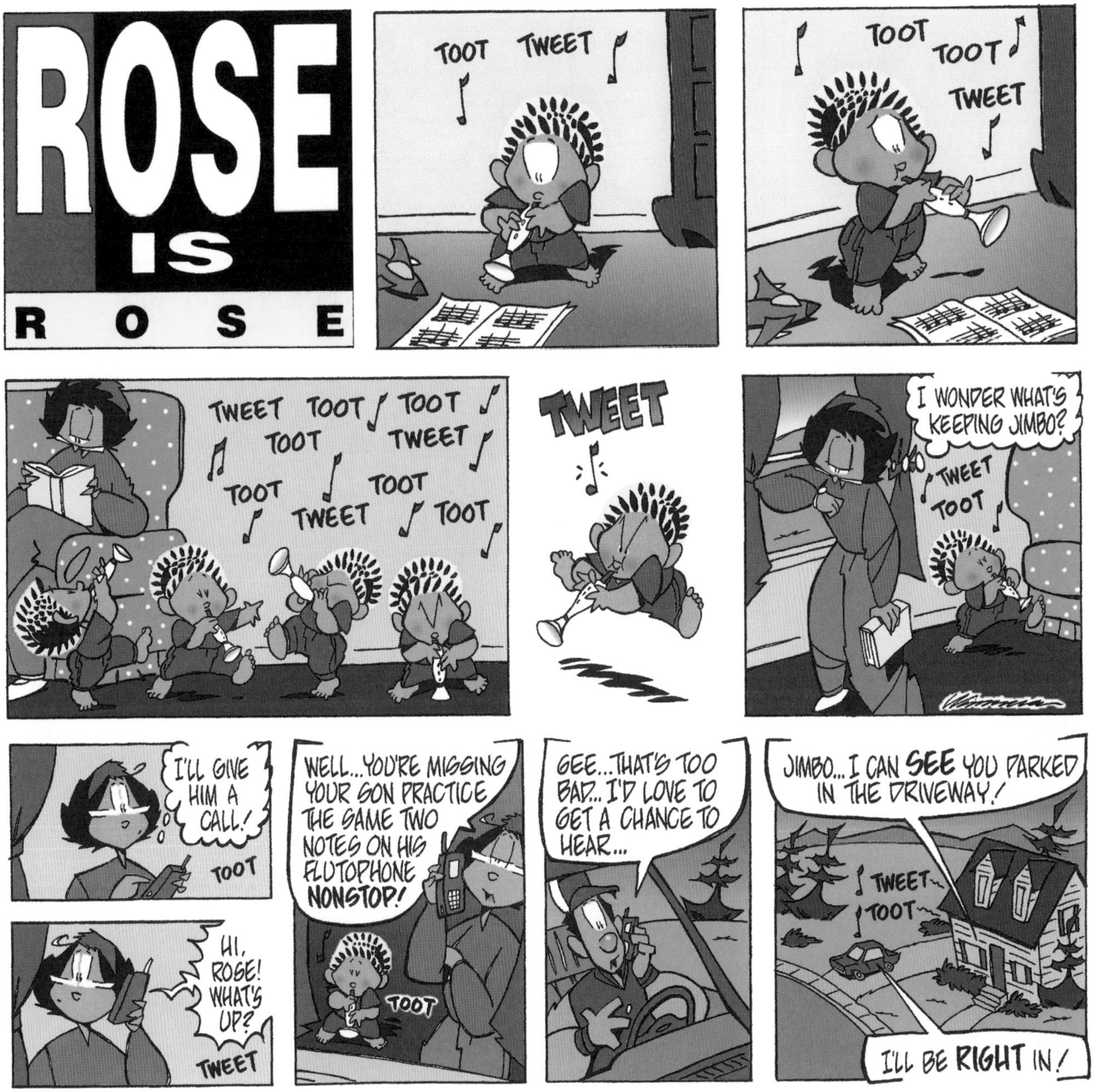
ROSE IS ROSE
TOOT TWEET
TOOT TOOT TWEET
TWEET TOOT TOOT TOOT TWEET TOOT TOOT TWEET TOOT
TWEET
I WONDER WHAT'S KEEPING JIMBO?
TWEET TOOT
I'LL GIVE HIM A CALL!
TOOT
HI, ROSE! WHAT'S UP?
TWEET
WELL...YOU'RE MISSING YOUR SON PRACTICE THE SAME TWO NOTES ON HIS FLUTOPHONE NONSTOP!
TOOT
GEE...THAT'S TOO BAD...I'D LOVE TO GET A CHANCE TO HEAR...
JIMBO...I CAN SEE YOU PARKED IN THE DRIVEWAY!
TWEET TOOT
I'LL BE RIGHT IN!

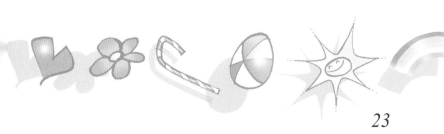

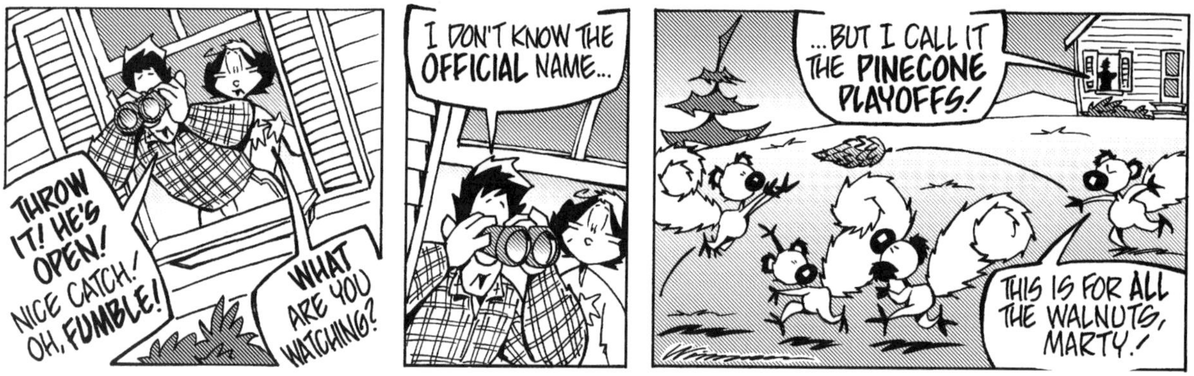
THROW IT! HE'S OPEN!
NICE CATCH! OH, FUMBLE!
WHAT ARE YOU WATCHING?
I DON'T KNOW THE OFFICIAL NAME...
...BUT I CALL IT THE PINECONE PLAYOFFS!
THIS IS FOR ALL THE WALNUTS, MARTY!

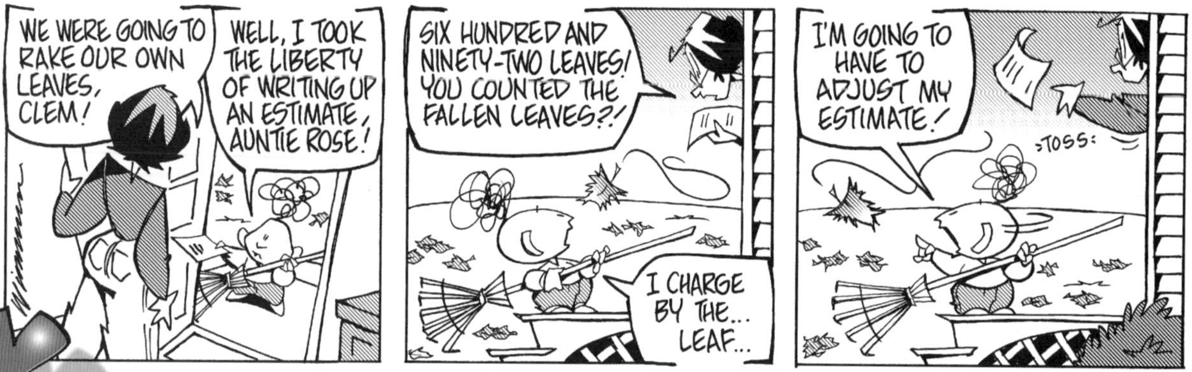
WE WERE GOING TO RAKE OUR OWN LEAVES, CLEM!
WELL, I TOOK THE LIBERTY OF WRITING UP AN ESTIMATE, AUNTIE ROSE!
SIX HUNDRED AND NINETY-TWO LEAVES! YOU COUNTED THE FALLEN LEAVES?!
I CHARGE BY THE... LEAF...
I'M GOING TO HAVE TO ADJUST MY ESTIMATE!
:TOSS:

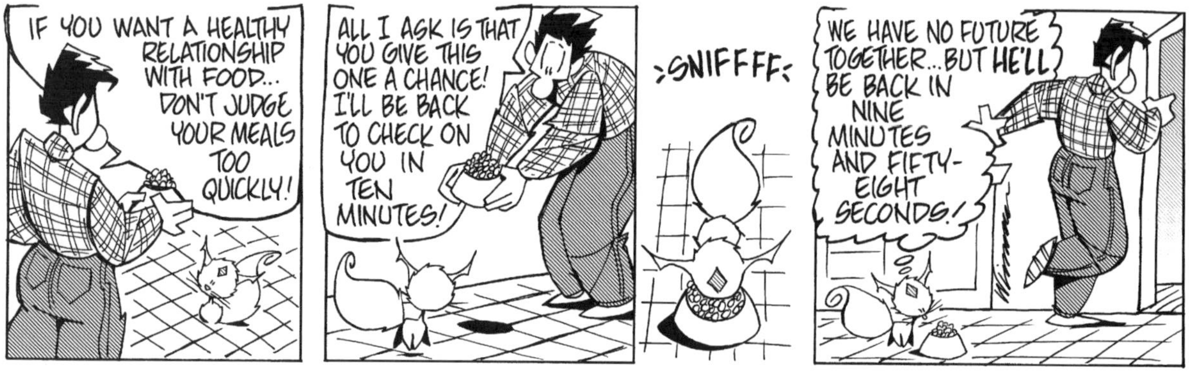
IF YOU WANT A HEALTHY RELATIONSHIP WITH FOOD... DON'T JUDGE YOUR MEALS TOO QUICKLY!
ALL I ASK IS THAT YOU GIVE THIS ONE A CHANCE! I'LL BE BACK TO CHECK ON YOU IN TEN MINUTES!
:SNIFFFF:
WE HAVE NO FUTURE TOGETHER...BUT HE'LL BE BACK IN NINE MINUTES AND FIFTY-EIGHT SECONDS!

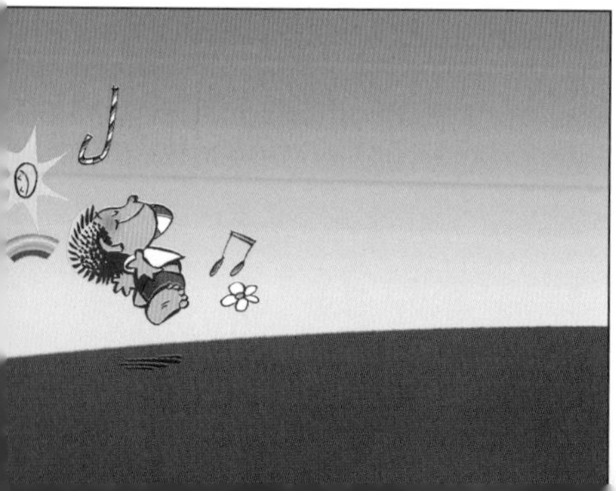

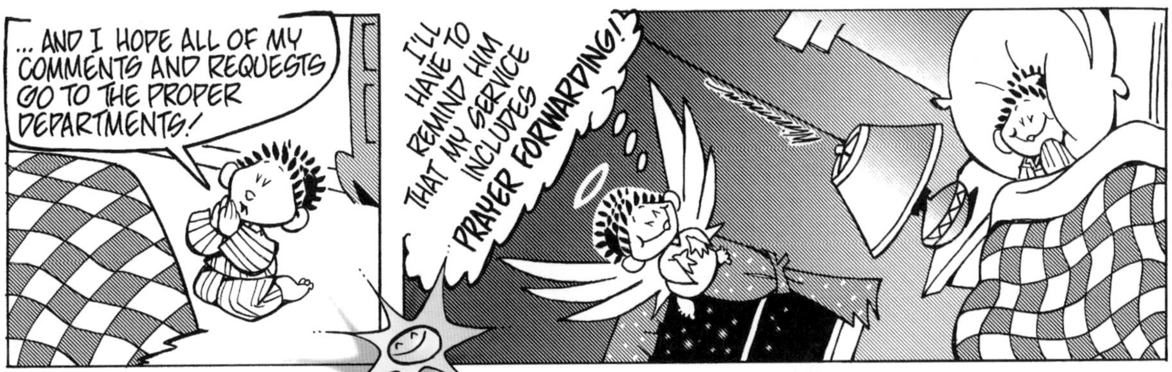
... AND I HOPE ALL OF MY COMMENTS AND REQUESTS GO TO THE PROPER DEPARTMENTS!
I'LL HAVE TO REMIND HIM THAT MY SERVICE INCLUDES PRAYER FORWARDING!

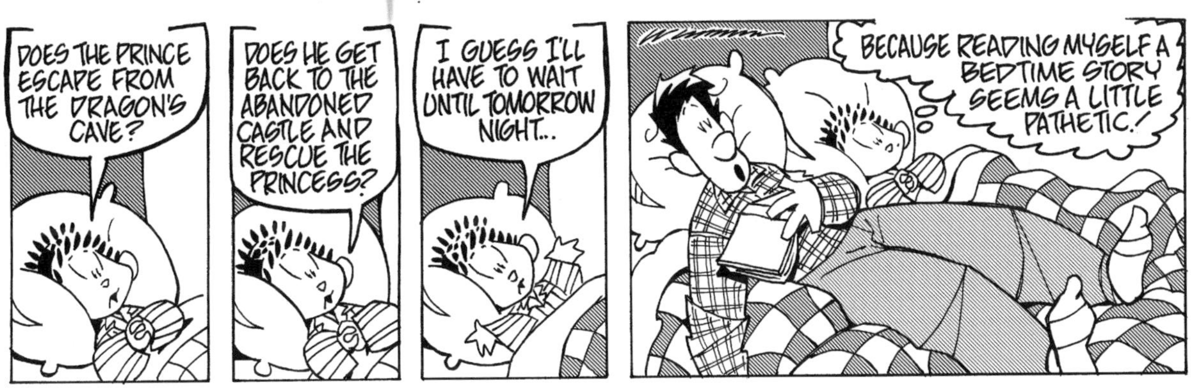
DOES THE PRINCE ESCAPE FROM THE DRAGON'S CAVE?
DOES HE GET BACK TO THE ABANDONED CASTLE AND RESCUE THE PRINCESS?
I GUESS I'LL HAVE TO WAIT UNTIL TOMORROW NIGHT...
BECAUSE READING MYSELF A BEDTIME STORY SEEMS A LITTLE PATHETIC!

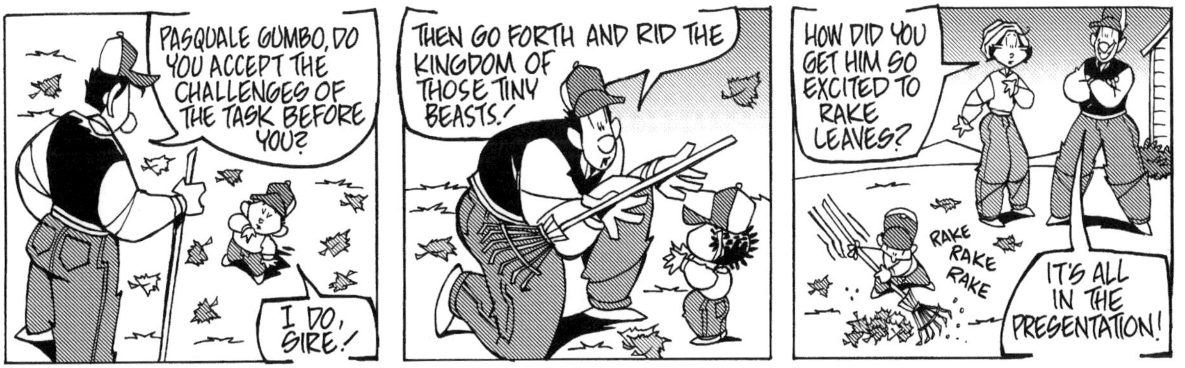
PASQUALE GUMBO, DO YOU ACCEPT THE CHALLENGES OF THE TASK BEFORE YOU?
I DO, SIRE!
THEN GO FORTH AND RID THE KINGDOM OF THOSE TINY BEASTS!
HOW DID YOU GET HIM SO EXCITED TO RAKE LEAVES?
RAKE
RAKE
RAKE
IT'S ALL IN THE PRESENTATION!

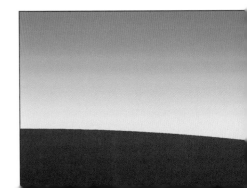

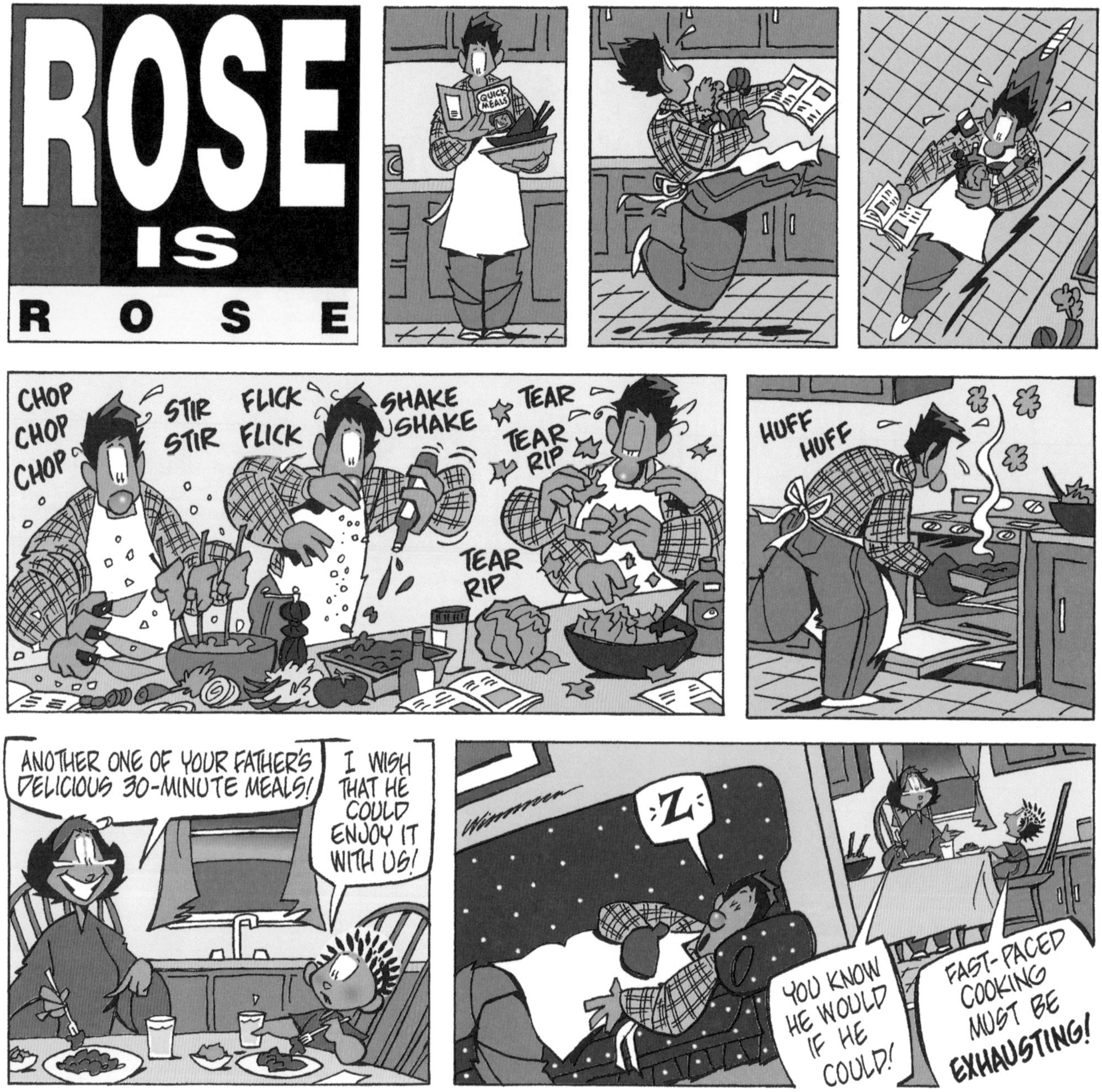
ROSE IS ROSE
QUICK MEALS
CHOP CHOP CHOP
STIR STIR
FLICK FLICK
SHAKE SHAKE
TEAR
TEAR RIP
TEAR RIP
HUFF HUFF
ANOTHER ONE OF YOUR FATHER'S DELICIOUS 30-MINUTE MEALS!
I WISH THAT HE COULD ENJOY IT WITH US!
Z
YOU KNOW HE WOULD IF HE COULD!
FAST-PACED COOKING MUST BE EXHAUSTING!

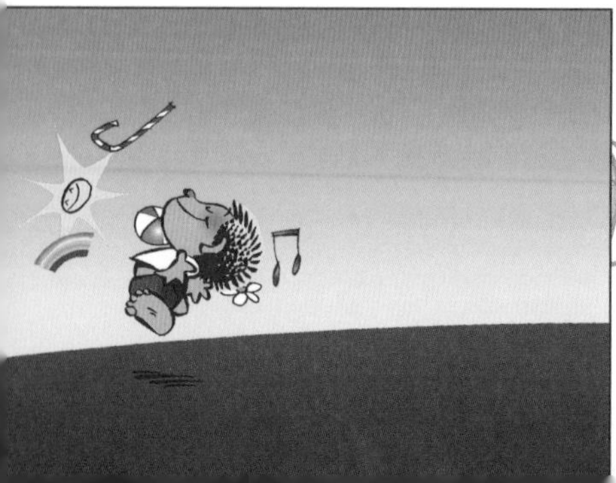

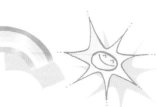

I'VE LEFT YOU SOME WALNUTS!
I'M NOMINATING THAT KID FOR SQUIRRELHOOD!

WHAT ARE THEY DOING?
IT'S OBVIOUS THAT THEY'RE GATHERING FOOD TO STORE FOR WINTER!
HIDE THE WALNUTS! AFTER A FEW DAYS OF THAT DIET... THEY'RE GOING TO BE MIGHTY HUNGRY!

WHAT KIND OF CONTEST IS THIS, CLEM?
A LUCKY LEAF IS HIDDEN IN MY YARD... FIND THE LEAF AND YOU WIN!
Lucky Leaf Contest
PARTICIPANTS GATHER AS MANY LEAVES AS THEY WANT AND PUT THEM IN BASKETS! OBVIOUSLY THE MORE LEAVES YOU CAN COLLECT... THE BETTER YOUR CHANCES!
AND WHAT KIND OF PRIZE DO WE WIN?
I WOULD THINK THE LUCKY LEAF IS A PRETTY GOOD PRIZE!
I THINK I'VE GOT IT!
UH-UH! I DO!

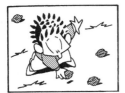

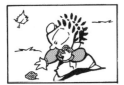

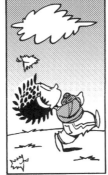

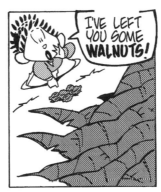

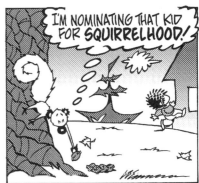

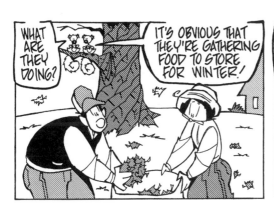

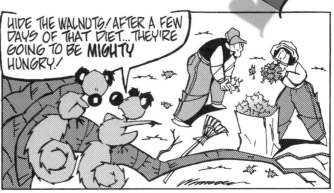

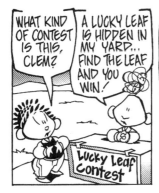

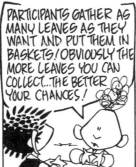

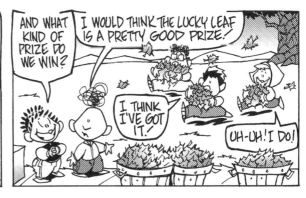

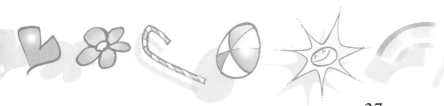

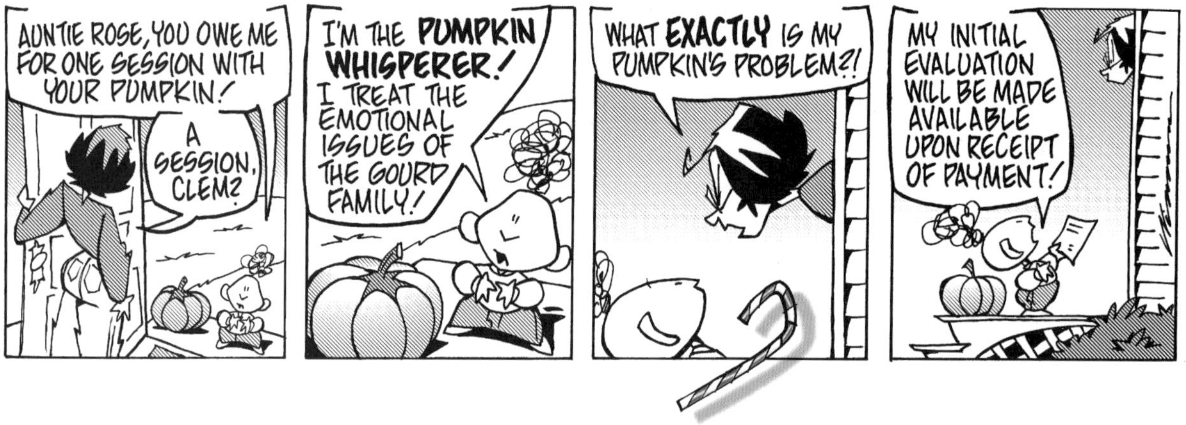
AUNTIE ROSE, YOU OWE ME FOR ONE SESSION WITH YOUR PUMPKIN!
A SESSION, CLEM?
I'M THE **PUMPKIN WHISPERER**!
I TREAT THE EMOTIONAL ISSUES OF THE GOURD FAMILY!
WHAT **EXACTLY** IS MY PUMPKIN'S PROBLEM?!
MY INITIAL EVALUATION WILL BE MADE AVAILABLE UPON RECEIPT OF PAYMENT!

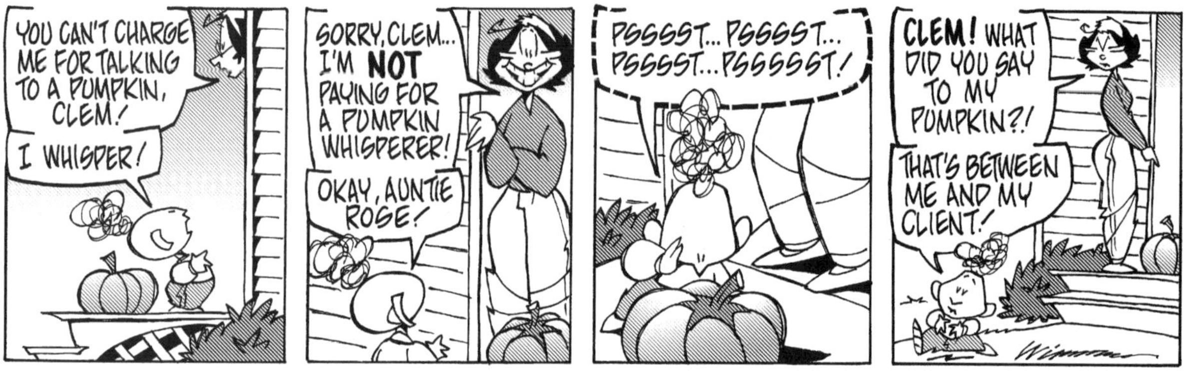
YOU CAN'T CHARGE ME FOR TALKING TO A PUMPKIN, CLEM!
I WHISPER!
SORRY, CLEM... I'M **NOT** PAYING FOR A PUMPKIN WHISPERER!
OKAY, AUNTIE ROSE!
PSSSST... PSSSST... PSSSST... PSSSSST!
CLEM! WHAT DID YOU SAY TO MY PUMPKIN?!
THAT'S BETWEEN ME AND MY CLIENT!

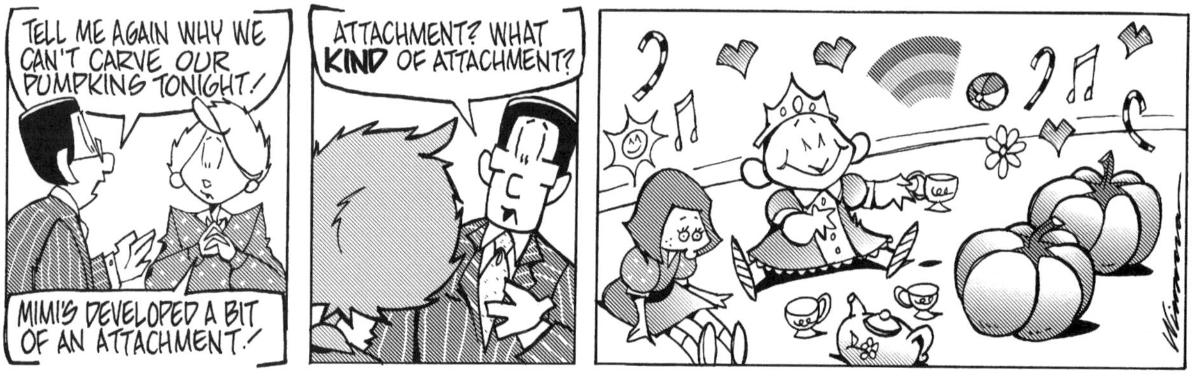
TELL ME AGAIN WHY WE CAN'T CARVE OUR PUMPKINS TONIGHT!
MIMI'S DEVELOPED A BIT OF AN ATTACHMENT!
ATTACHMENT? WHAT **KIND** OF ATTACHMENT?

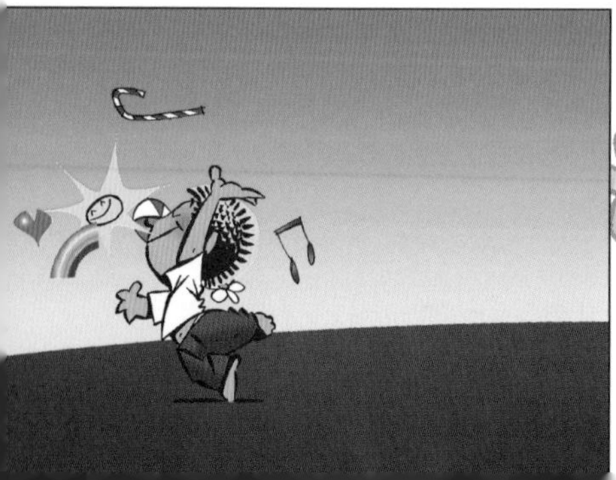

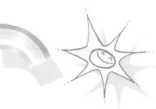

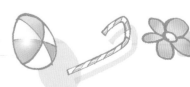

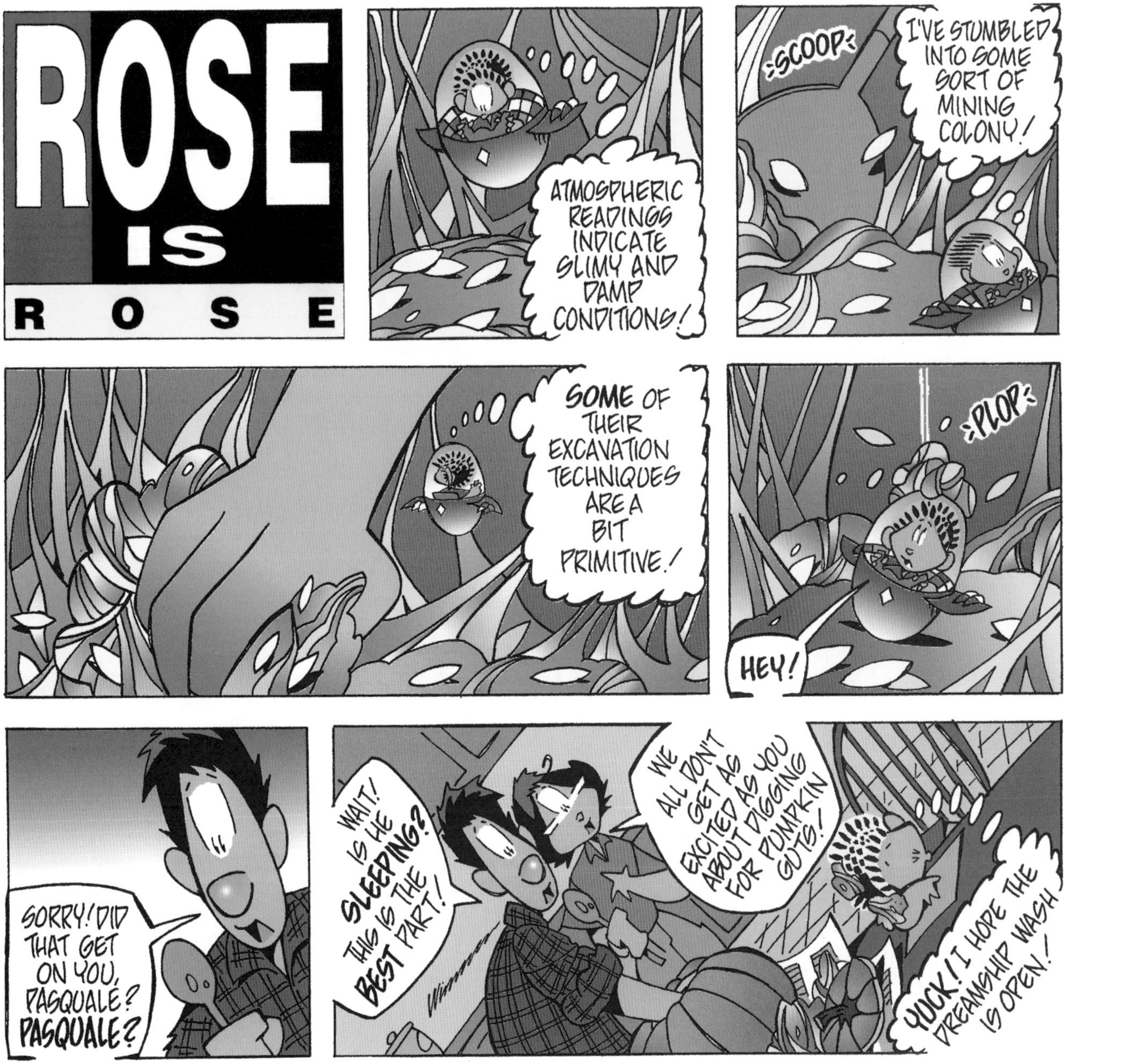
ROSE IS ROSE
ATMOSPHERIC READINGS INDICATE SLIMY AND DAMP CONDITIONS!
SCOOP
I'VE STUMBLED INTO SOME SORT OF MINING COLONY!
SOME OF THEIR EXCAVATION TECHNIQUES ARE A BIT PRIMITIVE!
PLOP
HEY!
SORRY! DID THAT GET ON YOU, PASQUALE? PASQUALE?
WAIT! IS HE SLEEPING? THIS IS THE BEST PART!
WE ALL DON'T GET AS EXCITED AS YOU ABOUT DIGGING FOR PUMPKIN GUTS!
YUCK! I HOPE THE DREAMSHIP WASH IS OPEN!

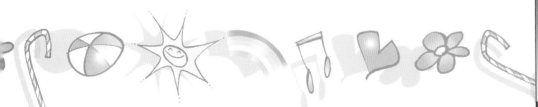

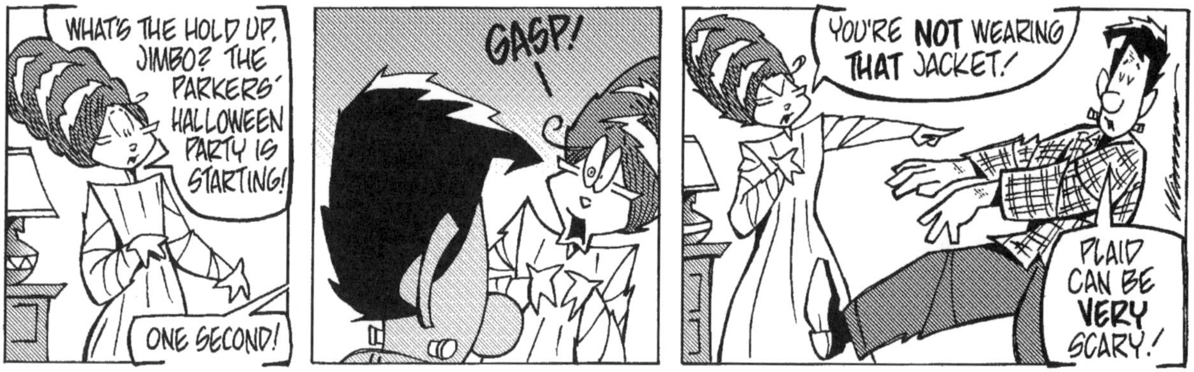
WHAT'S THE HOLD UP, JIMBO? THE PARKERS' HALLOWEEN PARTY IS STARTING!
ONE SECOND!
GASP!
YOU'RE **NOT** WEARING **THAT** JACKET!
PLAID CAN BE **VERY** SCARY!

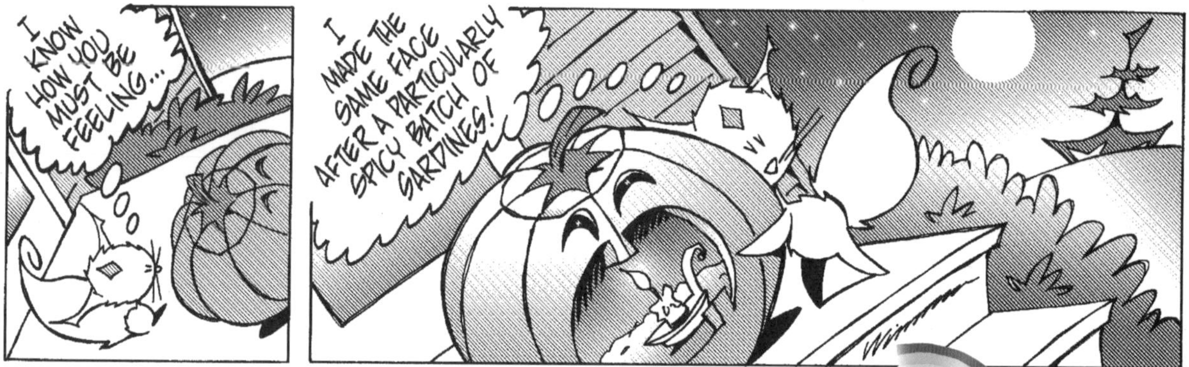
I KNOW HOW YOU MUST BE FEELING...
I MADE THE SAME FACE AFTER A PARTICULARLY SPICY BATCH OF SARDINES!

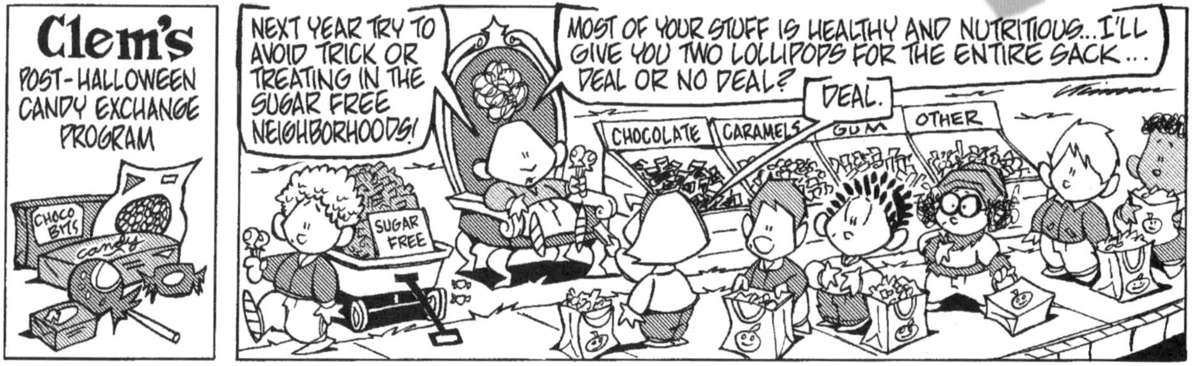
Clem's
POST-HALLOWEEN CANDY EXCHANGE PROGRAM
CHOCO BITS
candy
NEXT YEAR TRY TO AVOID TRICK OR TREATING IN THE SUGAR FREE NEIGHBORHOODS!
SUGAR FREE
MOST OF YOUR STUFF IS HEALTHY AND NUTRITIOUS... I'LL GIVE YOU TWO LOLLIPOPS FOR THE ENTIRE SACK... DEAL OR NO DEAL?
DEAL.
CHOCOLATE
CARAMELS
GUM
OTHER

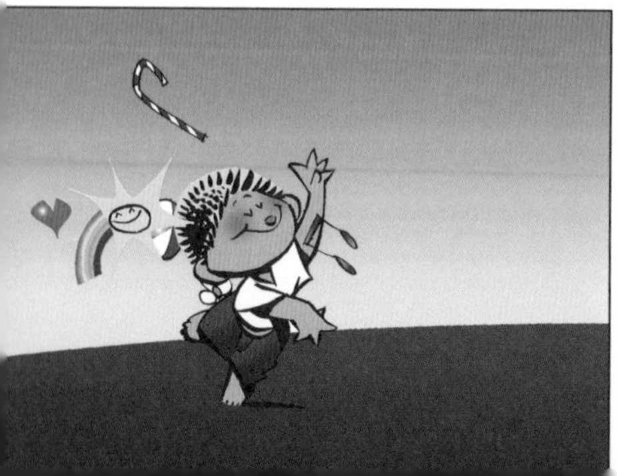

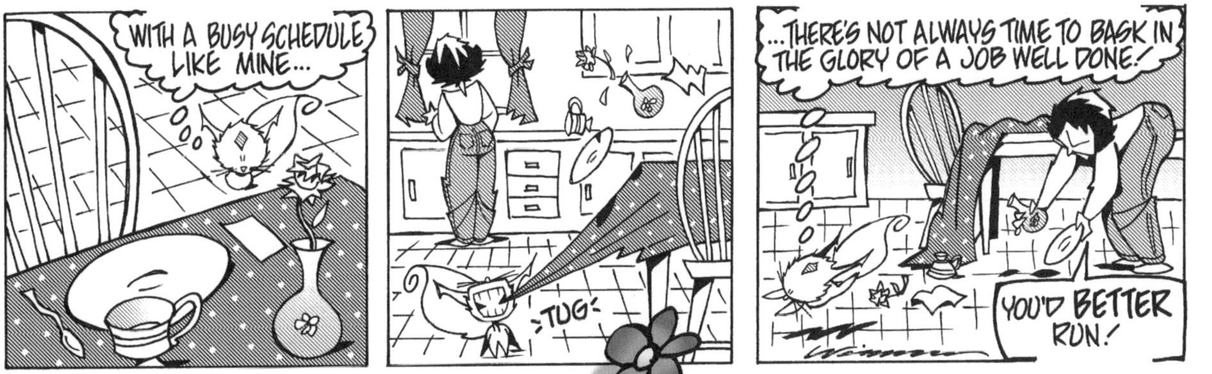
WITH A BUSY SCHEDULE LIKE MINE...
TUG
...THERE'S NOT ALWAYS TIME TO BASK IN THE GLORY OF A JOB WELL DONE!
YOU'D BETTER RUN!

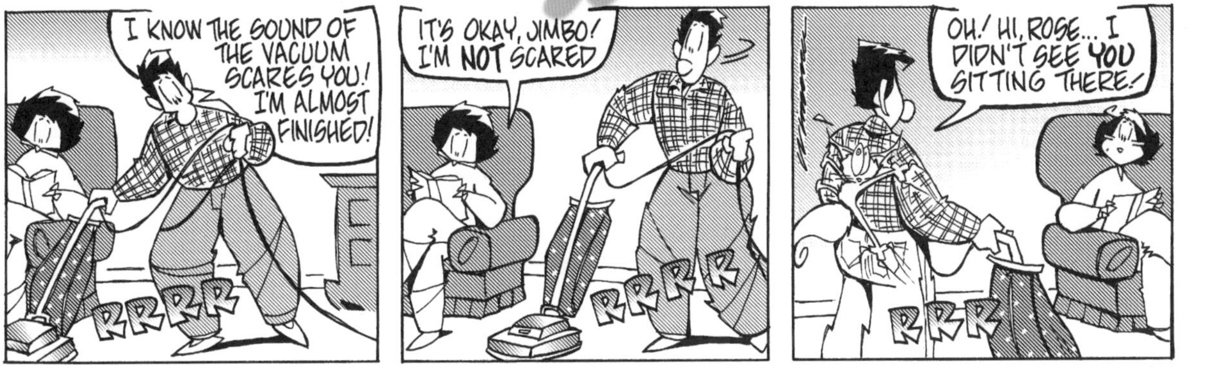
I KNOW THE SOUND OF THE VACUUM SCARES YOU! I'M ALMOST FINISHED!
RRRR
IT'S OKAY, JIMBO! I'M NOT SCARED
RRRR
OH! HI, ROSE... I DIDN'T SEE YOU SITTING THERE!
RRR

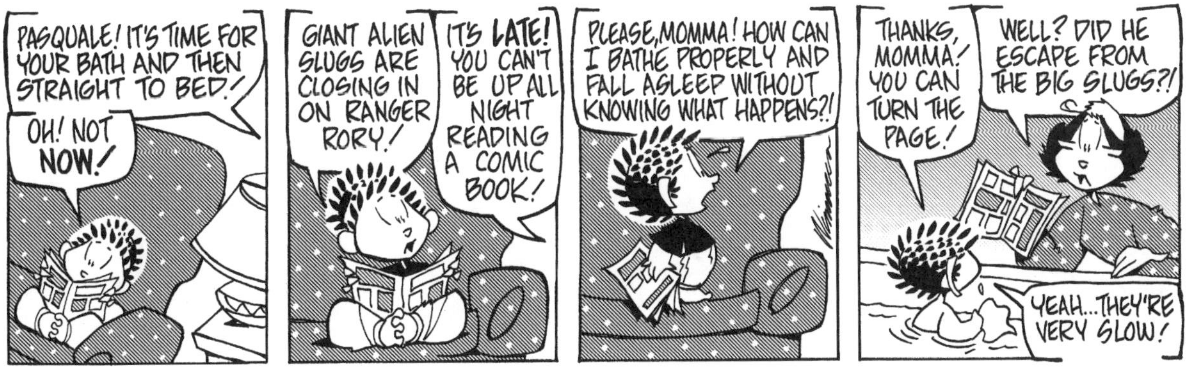
PASQUALE! IT'S TIME FOR YOUR BATH AND THEN STRAIGHT TO BED!
OH! NOT NOW!
GIANT ALIEN SLUGS ARE CLOSING IN ON RANGER RORY!
IT'S LATE! YOU CAN'T BE UP ALL NIGHT READING A COMIC BOOK!
PLEASE, MOMMA! HOW CAN I BATHE PROPERLY AND FALL ASLEEP WITHOUT KNOWING WHAT HAPPENS?!
THANKS, MOMMA! YOU CAN TURN THE PAGE!
WELL? DID HE ESCAPE FROM THE BIG SLUGS?!
YEAH...THEY'RE VERY SLOW!

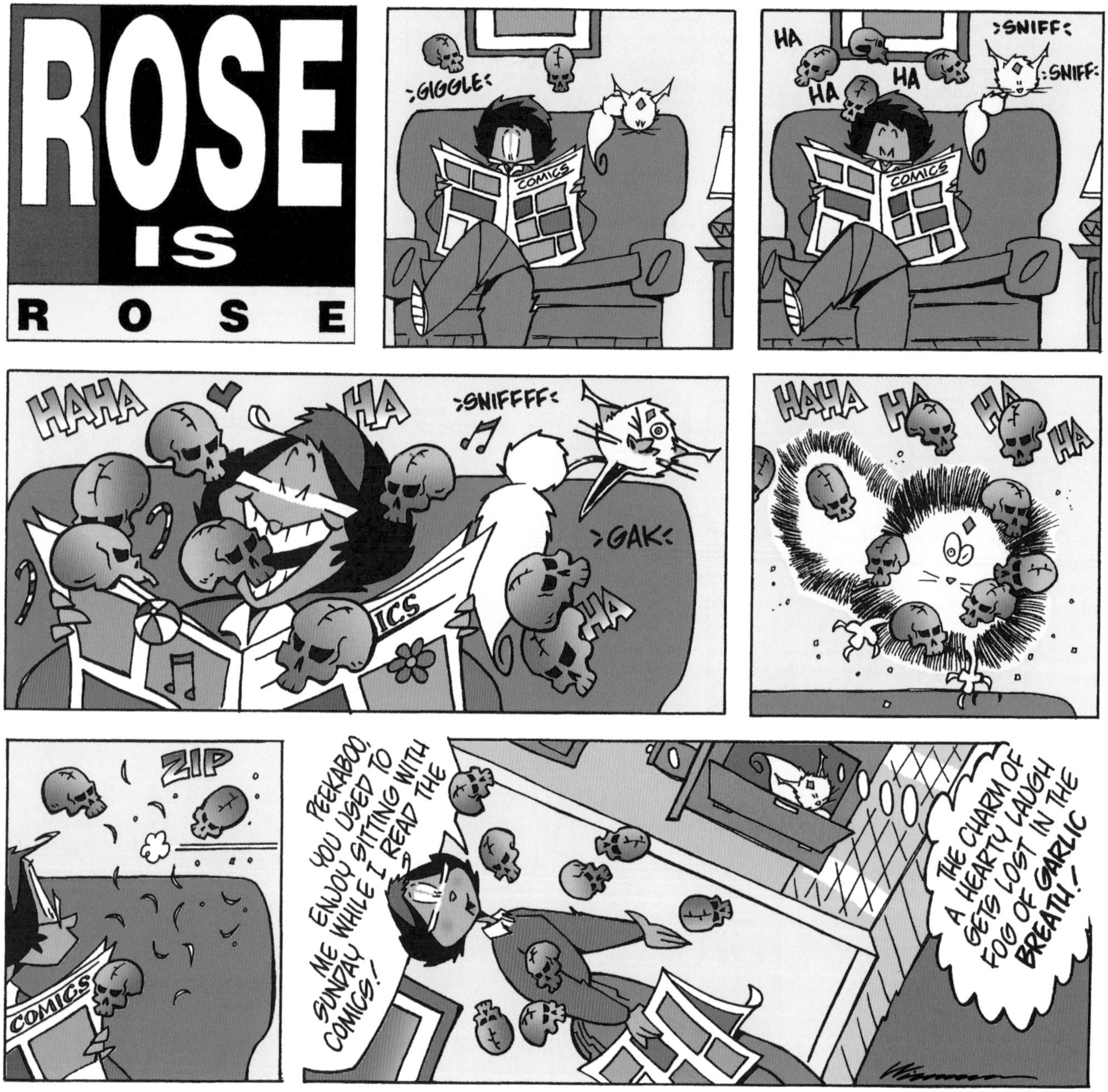
ROSE IS ROSE
>GIGGLE<
COMICS
HA
HA
HA
>SNIFF<
>SNIFF<
COMICS
HAHA
HA
>SNIFFFF<
>GAK<
HA
ICS
HAHA
HA
HA
HA
ZIP
COMICS
PEEKABOO, YOU USED TO ENJOY SITTING WITH ME WHILE I READ THE SUNDAY COMICS!
THE CHARM OF A HEARTY LAUGH GETS LOST IN THE FOG OF GARLIC BREATH!

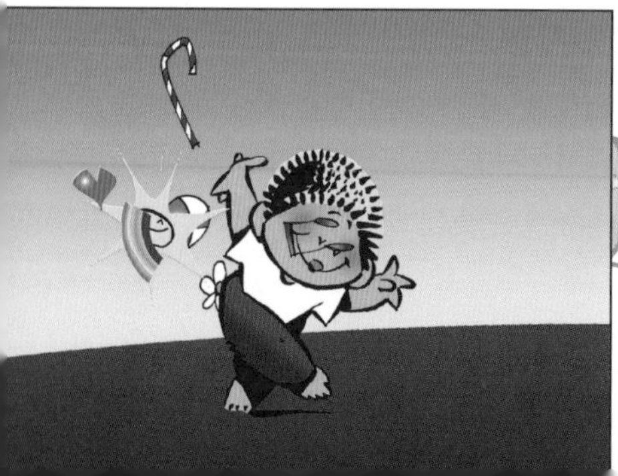

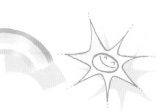

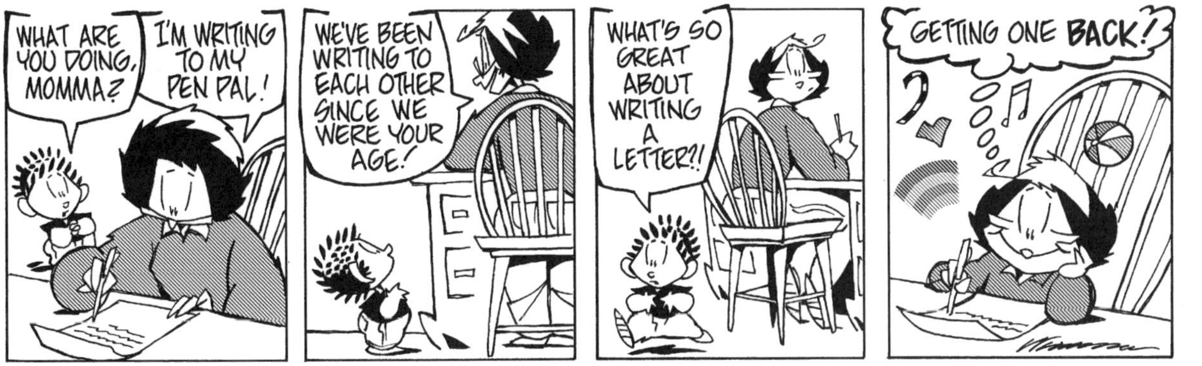
WHAT ARE YOU DOING, MOMMA?
I'M WRITING TO MY PEN PAL!
WE'VE BEEN WRITING TO EACH OTHER SINCE WE WERE YOUR AGE!
WHAT'S SO GREAT ABOUT WRITING A LETTER?!
GETTING ONE BACK!

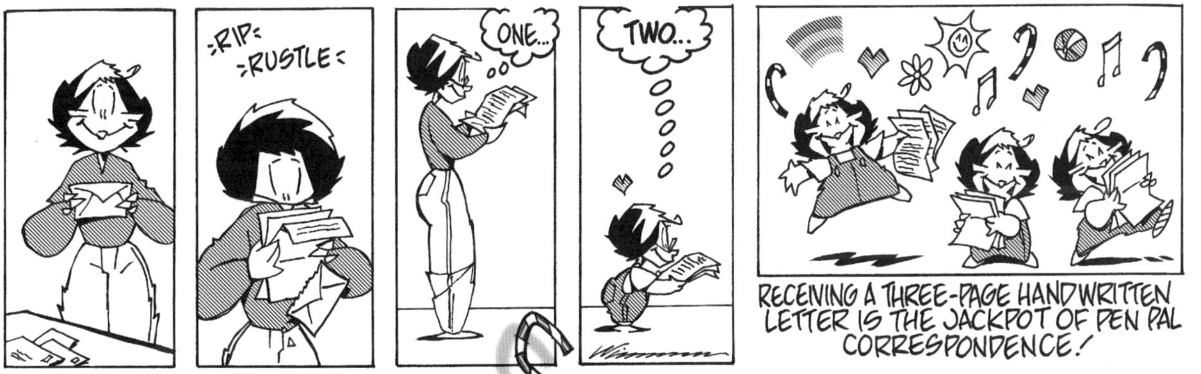
RIP
RUSTLE
ONE...
TWO...
RECEIVING A THREE-PAGE HANDWRITTEN LETTER IS THE JACKPOT OF PEN PAL CORRESPONDENCE!

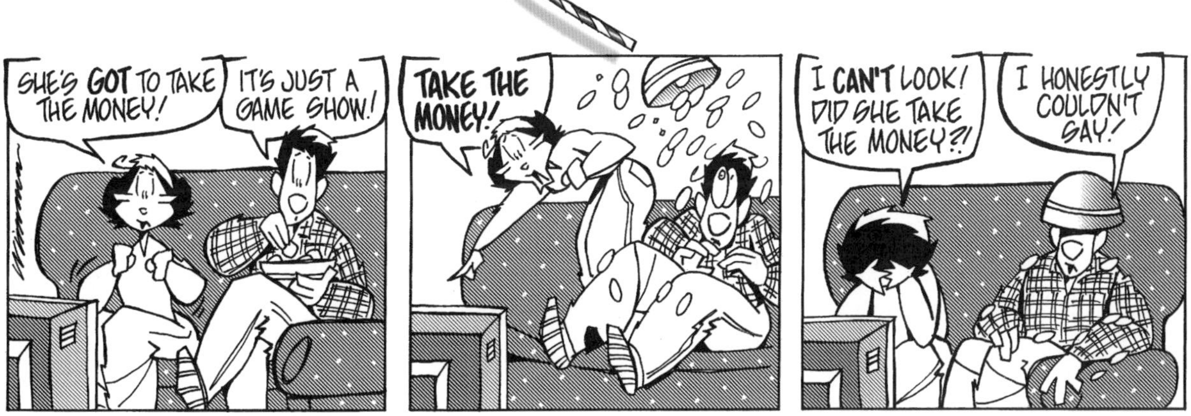
SHE'S GOT TO TAKE THE MONEY!
IT'S JUST A GAME SHOW!
TAKE THE MONEY!
I CAN'T LOOK! DID SHE TAKE THE MONEY?!
I HONESTLY COULDN'T SAY!

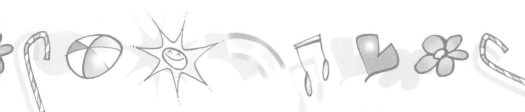

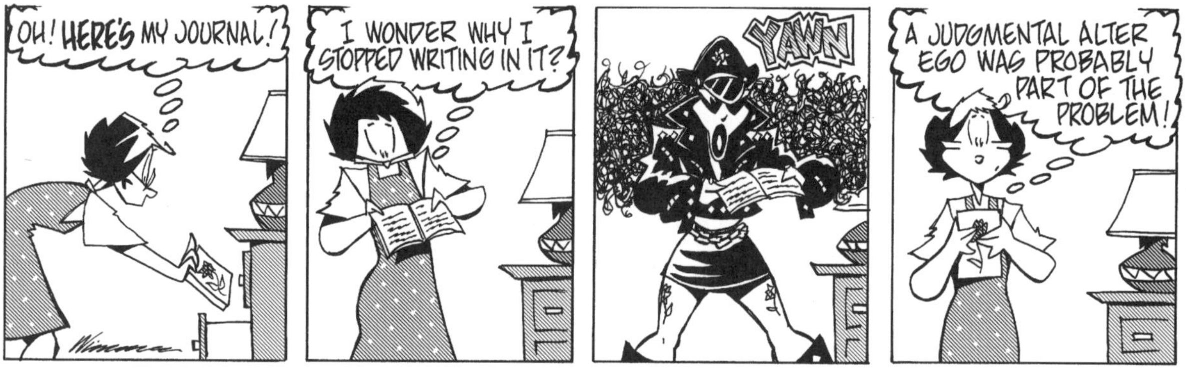
OH! HERE'S MY JOURNAL!
I WONDER WHY I STOPPED WRITING IN IT?
YAWN
A JUDGMENTAL ALTER EGO WAS PROBABLY PART OF THE PROBLEM!

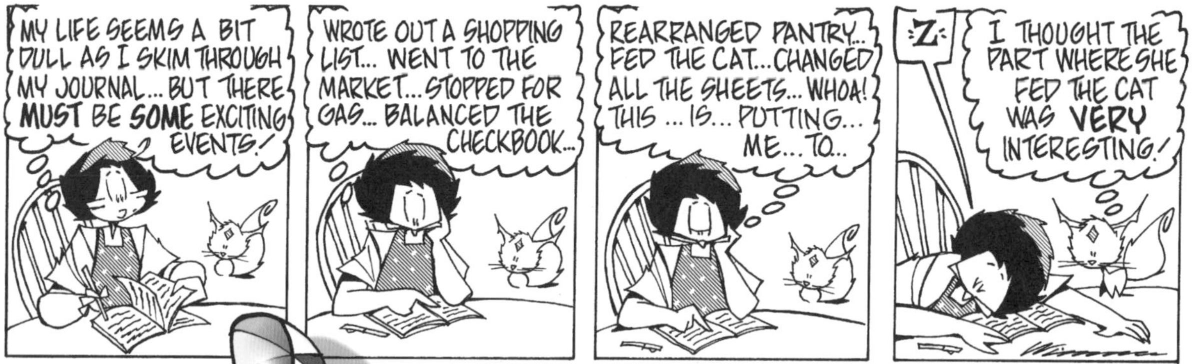
MY LIFE SEEMS A BIT DULL AS I SKIM THROUGH MY JOURNAL... BUT THERE MUST BE SOME EXCITING EVENTS!
WROTE OUT A SHOPPING LIST... WENT TO THE MARKET... STOPPED FOR GAS... BALANCED THE CHECKBOOK...
REARRANGED PANTRY... FED THE CAT... CHANGED ALL THE SHEETS... WHOA! THIS ... IS... PUTTING... ME... TO...
Z
I THOUGHT THE PART WHERE SHE FED THE CAT WAS VERY INTERESTING!

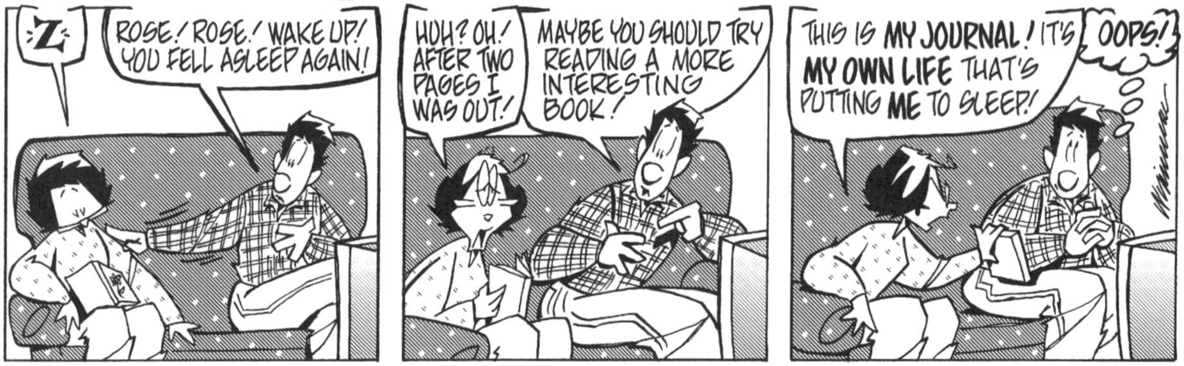
Z
ROSE! ROSE! WAKE UP! YOU FELL ASLEEP AGAIN!
HUH? OH! AFTER TWO PAGES I WAS OUT!
MAYBE YOU SHOULD TRY READING A MORE INTERESTING BOOK!
THIS IS MY JOURNAL! IT'S MY OWN LIFE THAT'S PUTTING ME TO SLEEP!
OOPS!

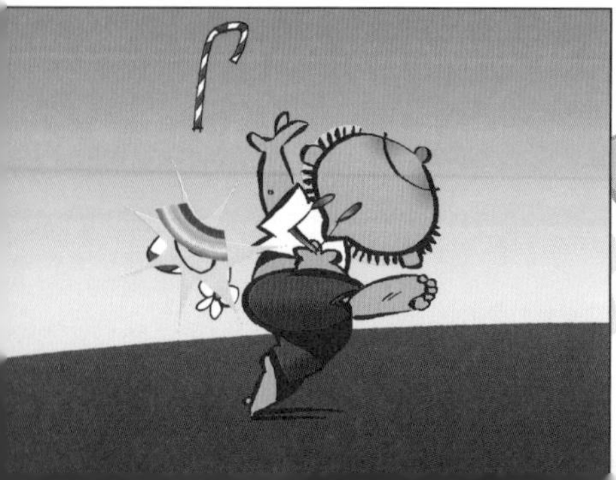

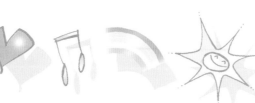

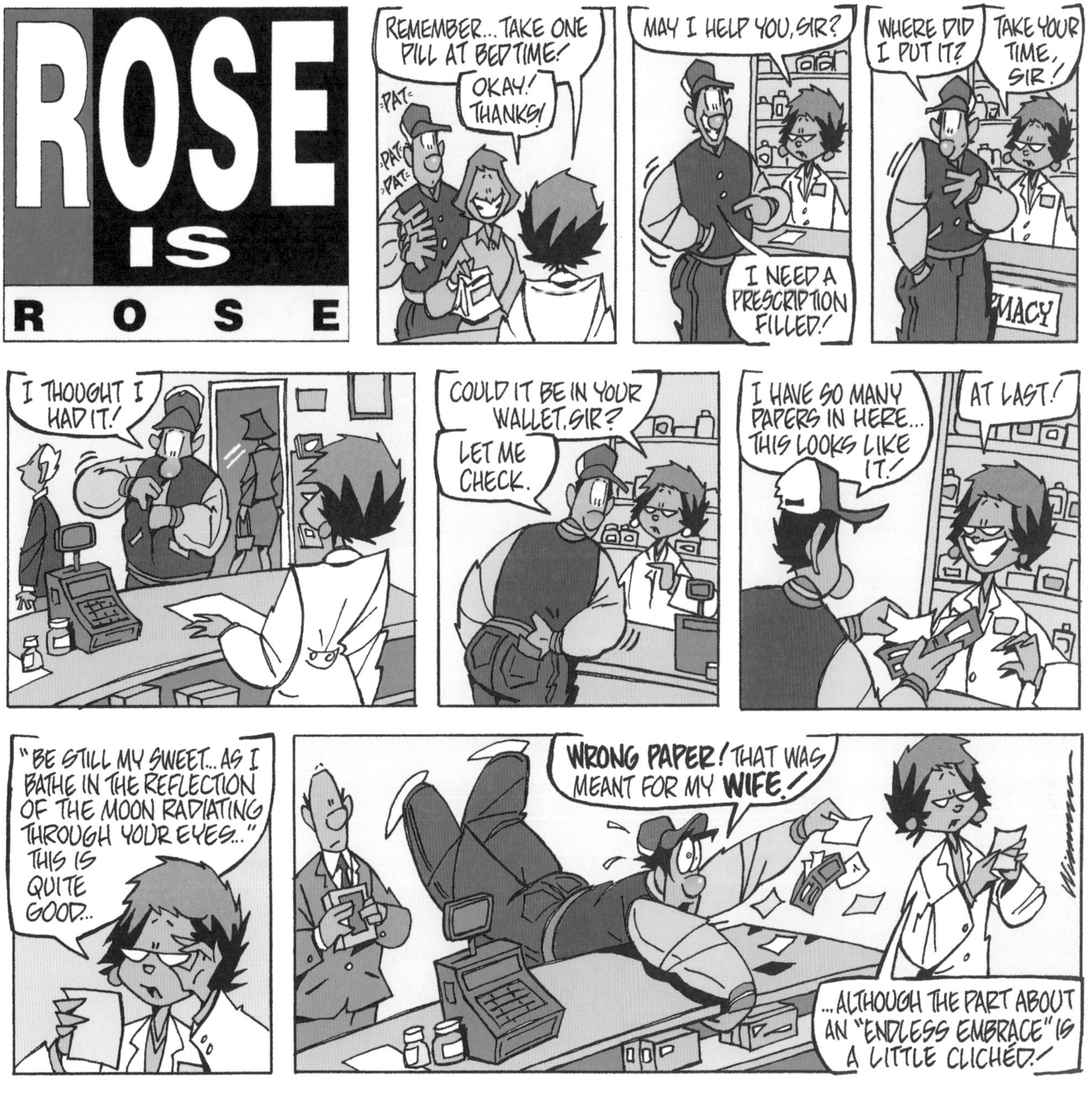
ROSE IS ROSE
REMEMBER... TAKE ONE PILL AT BEDTIME!
OKAY! THANKS!
PAT
PAT
PAT
MAY I HELP YOU, SIR?
I NEED A PRESCRIPTION FILLED!
WHERE DID I PUT IT?
TAKE YOUR TIME, SIR!
MACY
I THOUGHT I HAD IT!
COULD IT BE IN YOUR WALLET, SIR?
LET ME CHECK.
I HAVE SO MANY PAPERS IN HERE... THIS LOOKS LIKE IT!
AT LAST!
"BE STILL MY SWEET... AS I BATHE IN THE REFLECTION OF THE MOON RADIATING THROUGH YOUR EYES..." THIS IS QUITE GOOD...
WRONG PAPER! THAT WAS MEANT FOR MY **WIFE**!
...ALTHOUGH THE PART ABOUT AN "ENDLESS EMBRACE" IS A LITTLE CLICHÉD!

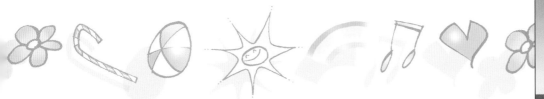

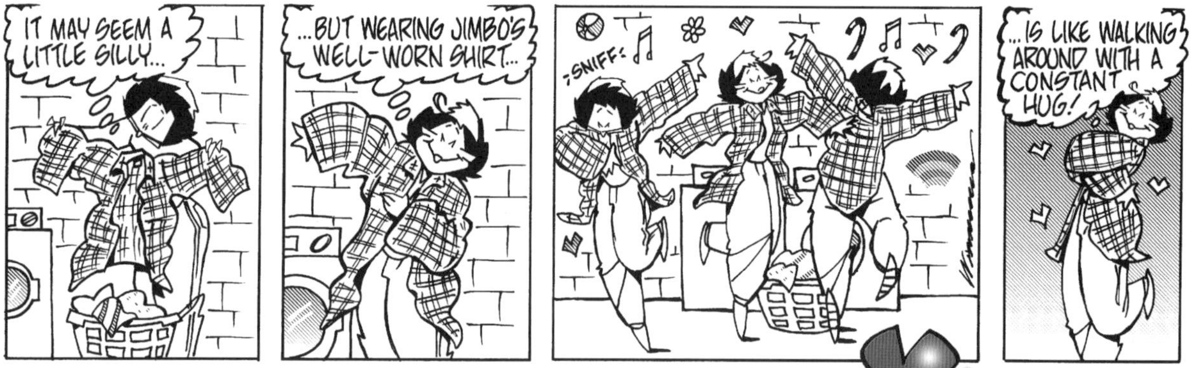
IT MAY SEEM A LITTLE SILLY...
...BUT WEARING JIMBO'S WELL-WORN SHIRT...
SNIFF
...IS LIKE WALKING AROUND WITH A CONSTANT HUG!

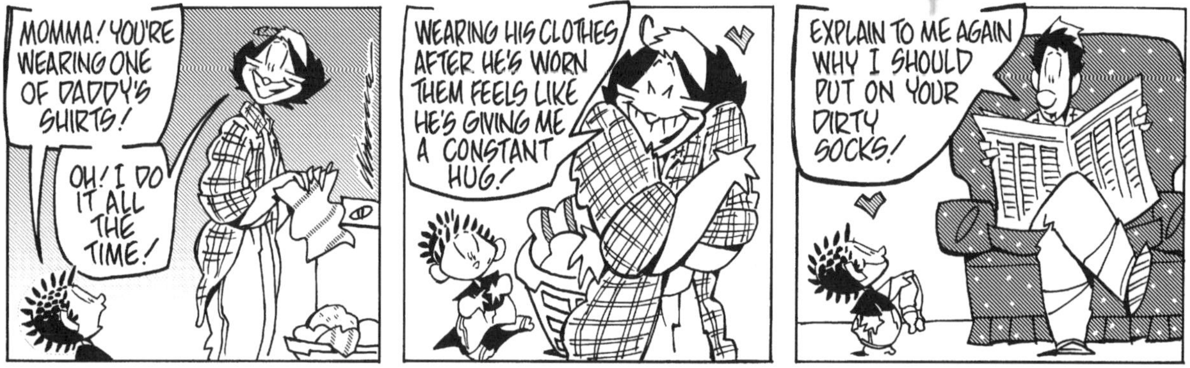
MOMMA! YOU'RE WEARING ONE OF DADDY'S SHIRTS!
OH! I DO IT ALL THE TIME!
WEARING HIS CLOTHES AFTER HE'S WORN THEM FEELS LIKE HE'S GIVING ME A CONSTANT HUG!
EXPLAIN TO ME AGAIN WHY I SHOULD PUT ON YOUR DIRTY SOCKS!

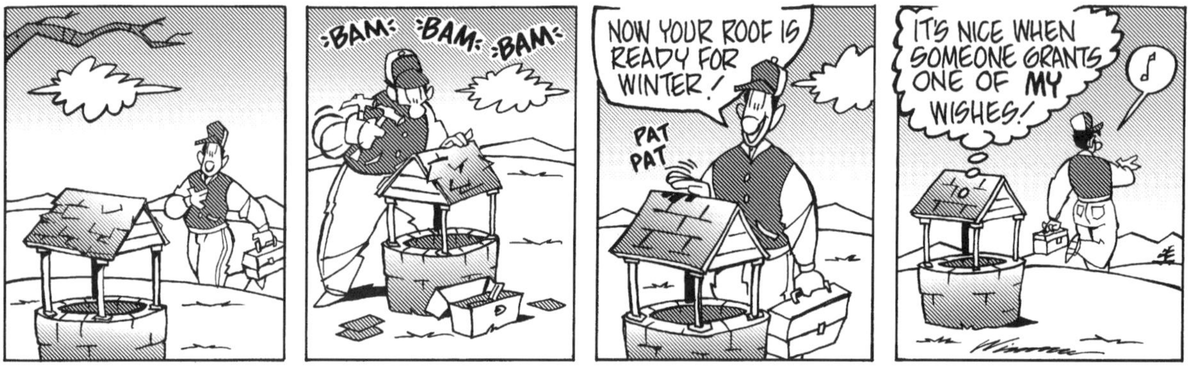
BAM BAM BAM
NOW YOUR ROOF IS READY FOR WINTER!
PAT PAT
IT'S NICE WHEN SOMEONE GRANTS ONE OF MY WISHES!

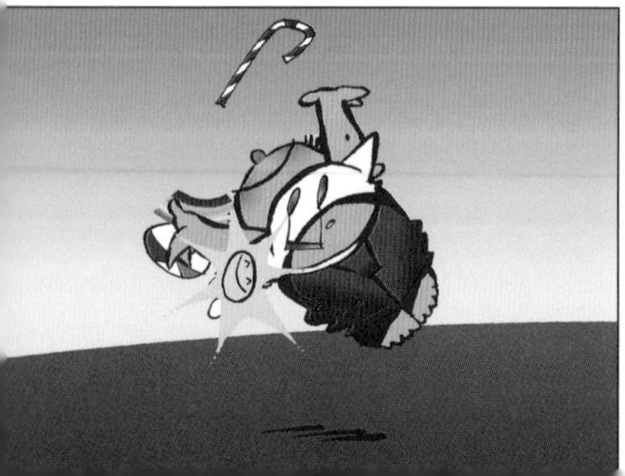

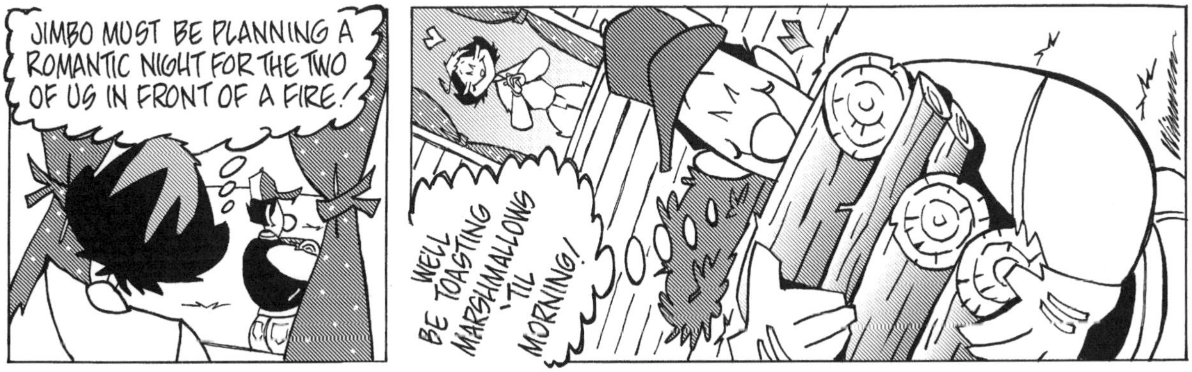
JIMBO MUST BE PLANNING A ROMANTIC NIGHT FOR THE TWO OF US IN FRONT OF A FIRE!
WE'LL BE TOASTING MARSHMALLOWS 'TIL MORNING!

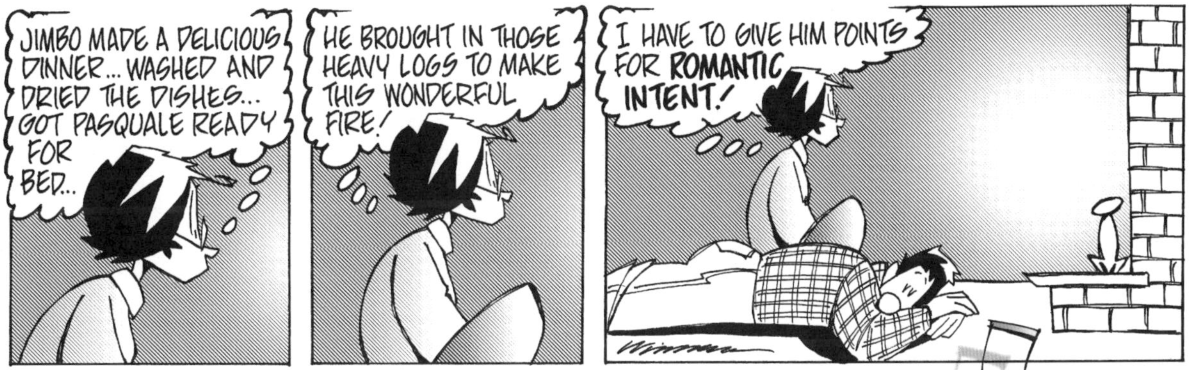
JIMBO MADE A DELICIOUS DINNER... WASHED AND DRIED THE DISHES... GOT PASQUALE READY FOR BED...
HE BROUGHT IN THOSE HEAVY LOGS TO MAKE THIS WONDERFUL FIRE!
I HAVE TO GIVE HIM POINTS FOR **ROMANTIC INTENT**!

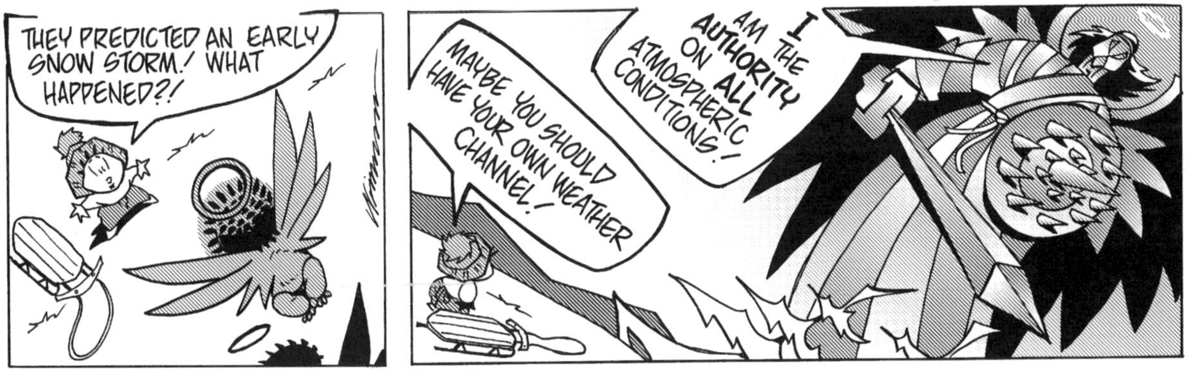
THEY PREDICTED AN EARLY SNOW STORM! WHAT HAPPENED?!
I AM THE **AUTHORITY** ON **ALL** ATMOSPHERIC CONDITIONS!
MAYBE YOU SHOULD HAVE YOUR OWN WEATHER CHANNEL!

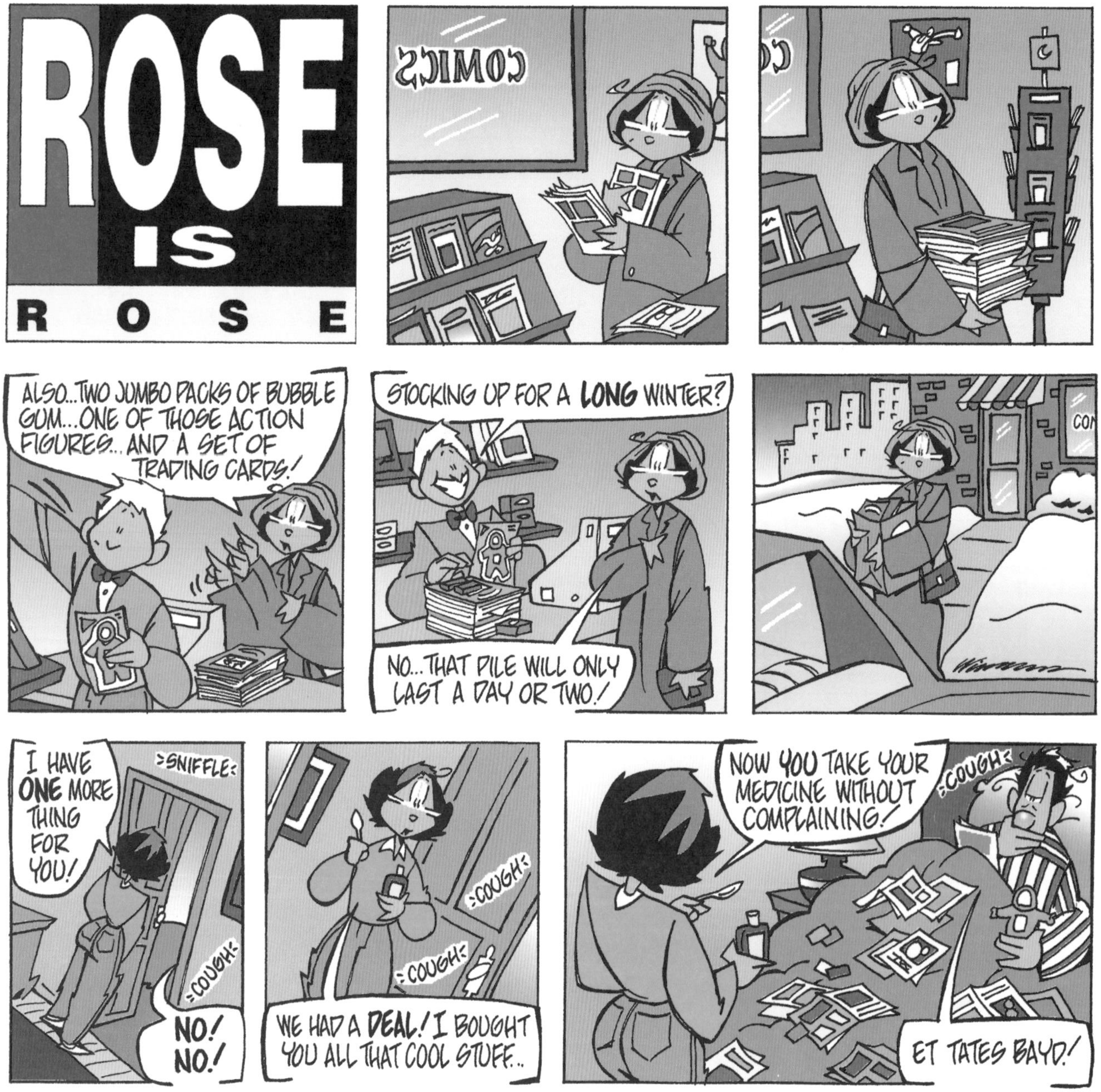
ROSE IS ROSE
COMICS
ALSO...TWO JUMBO PACKS OF BUBBLE GUM...ONE OF THOSE ACTION FIGURES...AND A SET OF TRADING CARDS!
STOCKING UP FOR A **LONG** WINTER?
NO...THAT PILE WILL ONLY LAST A DAY OR TWO!
I HAVE **ONE** MORE THING FOR YOU!
SNIFFLE
COUGH
NO! NO!
COUGH
COUGH
WE HAD A **DEAL!** I BOUGHT YOU ALL THAT COOL STUFF...
NOW **YOU** TAKE YOUR MEDICINE WITHOUT COMPLAINING!
COUGH
ET TATES BAYD!

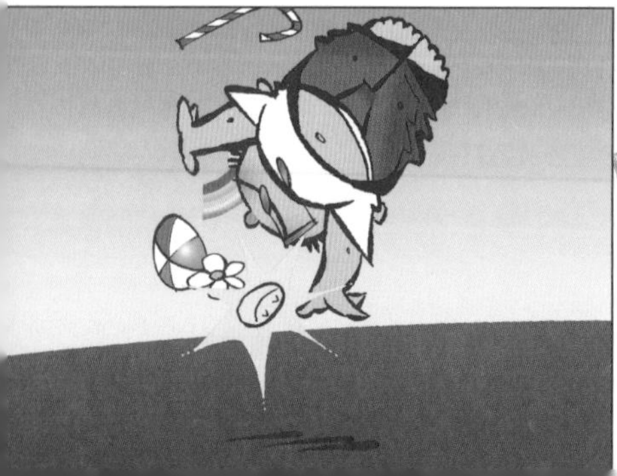

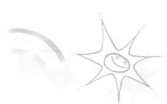

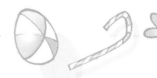

JIMBO! YOU'VE BEEN AT THAT FOR HOURS! GO TO BED!
OKAY, ROSE!
WHAT WERE YOU WORKING ON FOR SO LONG?
WINTER PLANS! G'NIGHT!
WINTER PLANS! OH! I HAVE TO PEEK!
I SHOULD HAVE KNOWN!
SNOWMAN
6 FT

THE JUDGES WILL LOOK FOR A BUFFED SURFACE WITH NO MARKS OR STREAKS!
MOMMA THINKS IT'S A BIG WASTE OF TIME!
SHE SAYS THERE ARE NO SNOW SHOVEL BEAUTY PAGEANTS IN EXISTENCE!
WELL... WHEN THERE ARE... WE'LL BE READY!
WAX
RUB RUB

THAT LOOKS LIKE FUN... ARE YOU SURE IT'S AN EXERCISE?
MOMMA, CAN YOU CHECK MY HOMEWORK?
THE SUCCESS OF ANY FITNESS REGIMEN WILL DEPEND GREATLY ON ONE'S ABILITY TO ELIMINATE DISTRACTIONS!

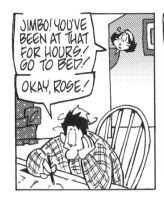

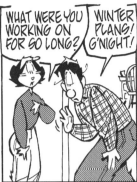

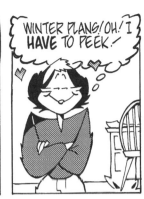

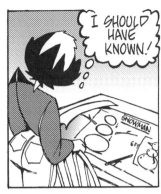

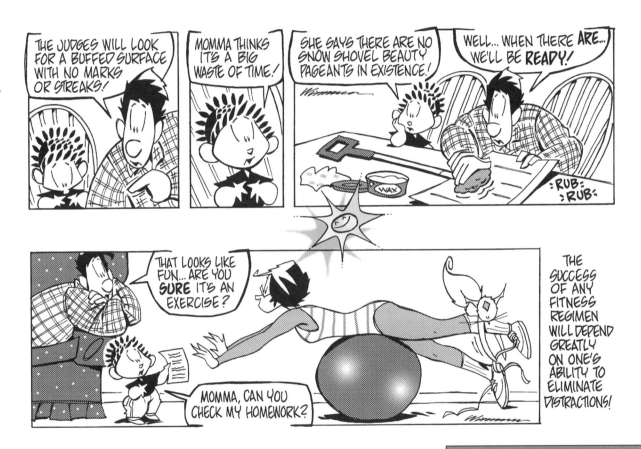

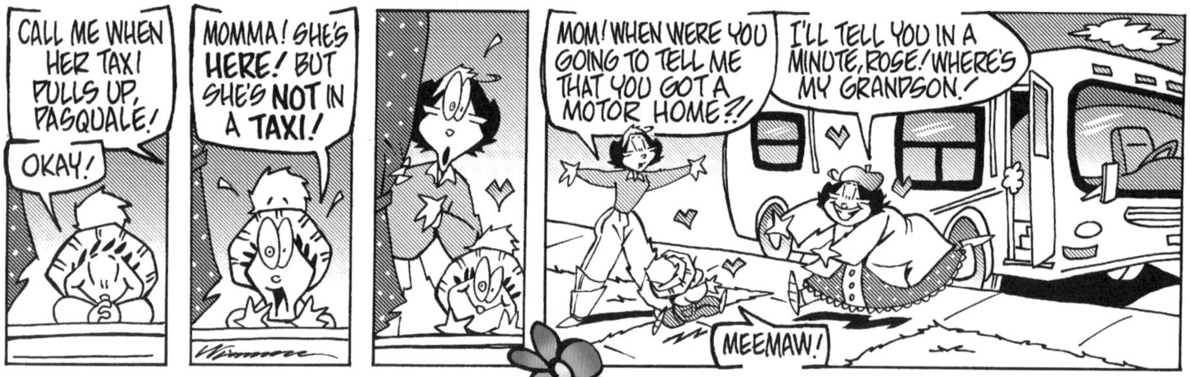
CALL ME WHEN HER TAXI PULLS UP, PASQUALE!
OKAY!
MOMMA! SHE'S HERE! BUT SHE'S NOT IN A TAXI!
MOM! WHEN WERE YOU GOING TO TELL ME THAT YOU GOT A MOTOR HOME?!
I'LL TELL YOU IN A MINUTE, ROSE! WHERE'S MY GRANDSON!
MEEMAW!

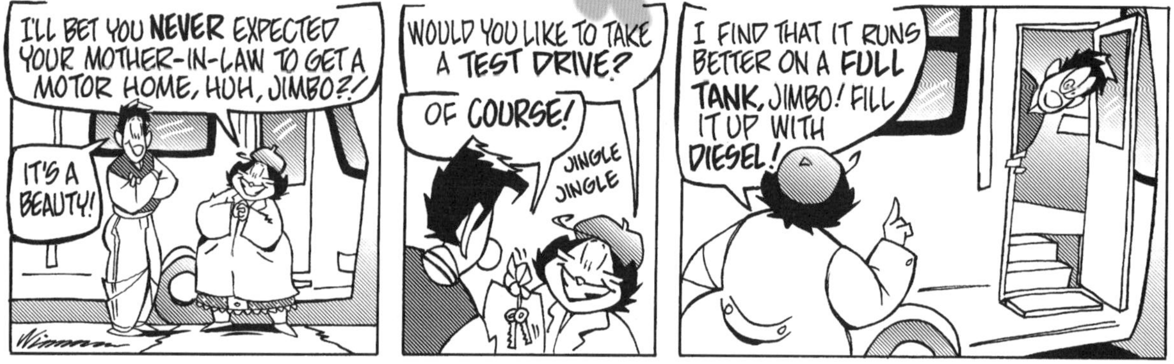
I'LL BET YOU NEVER EXPECTED YOUR MOTHER-IN-LAW TO GET A MOTOR HOME, HUH, JIMBO?!
IT'S A BEAUTY!
WOULD YOU LIKE TO TAKE A TEST DRIVE?
OF COURSE!
JINGLE JINGLE
I FIND THAT IT RUNS BETTER ON A FULL TANK, JIMBO! FILL IT UP WITH DIESEL!

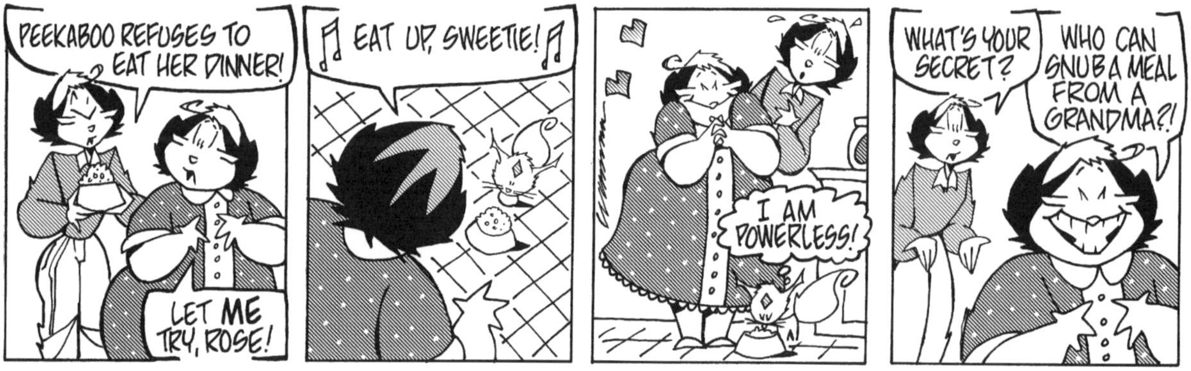
PEEKABOO REFUSES TO EAT HER DINNER!
LET ME TRY, ROSE!
EAT UP, SWEETIE!
I AM POWERLESS!
WHAT'S YOUR SECRET?
WHO CAN SNUB A MEAL FROM A GRANDMA?!

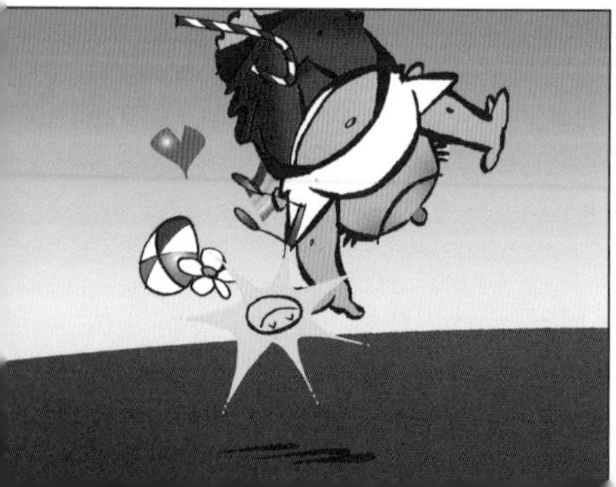

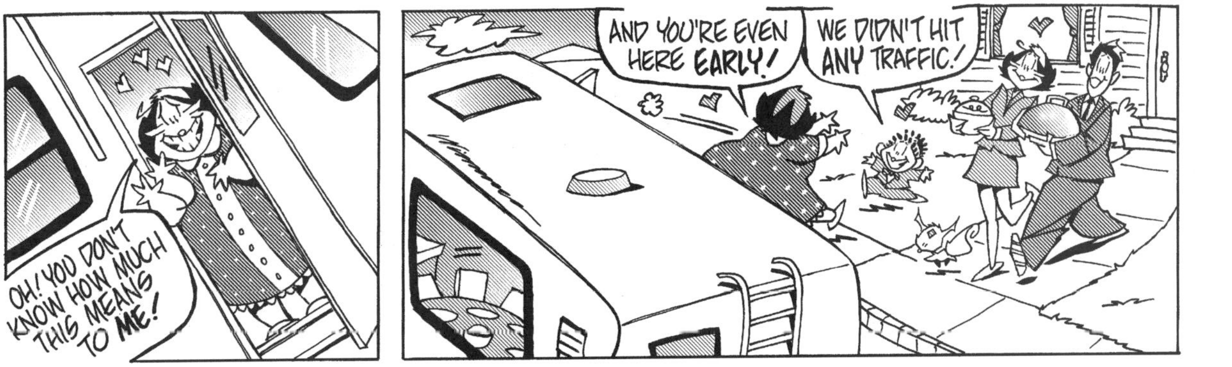
OH! YOU DON'T KNOW HOW MUCH THIS MEANS TO **ME**!
AND YOU'RE EVEN HERE **EARLY**!
WE DIDN'T HIT **ANY** TRAFFIC!

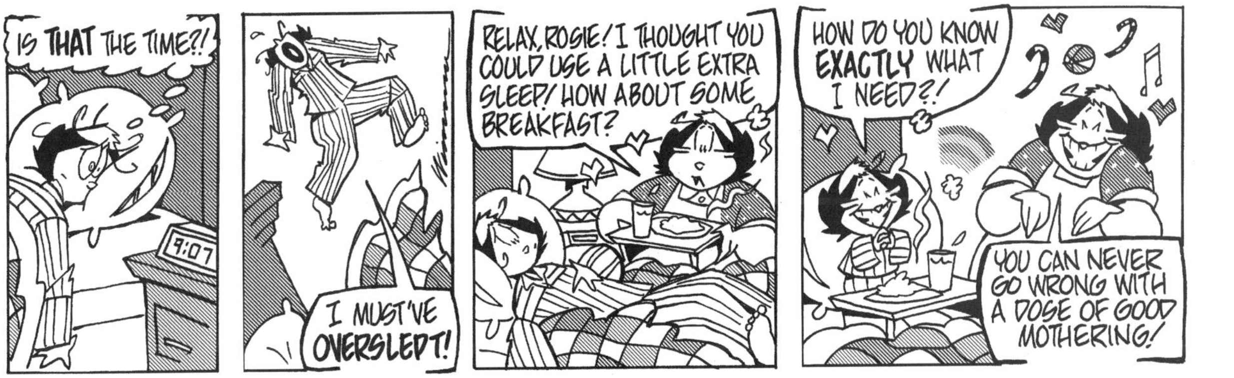
IS **THAT** THE TIME?!
9:07
I MUST'VE **OVERSLEPT**!
RELAX, ROSIE! I THOUGHT YOU COULD USE A LITTLE EXTRA SLEEP! HOW ABOUT SOME BREAKFAST?
HOW DO YOU KNOW **EXACTLY** WHAT I NEED?!
YOU CAN NEVER GO WRONG WITH A DOSE OF GOOD MOTHERING!

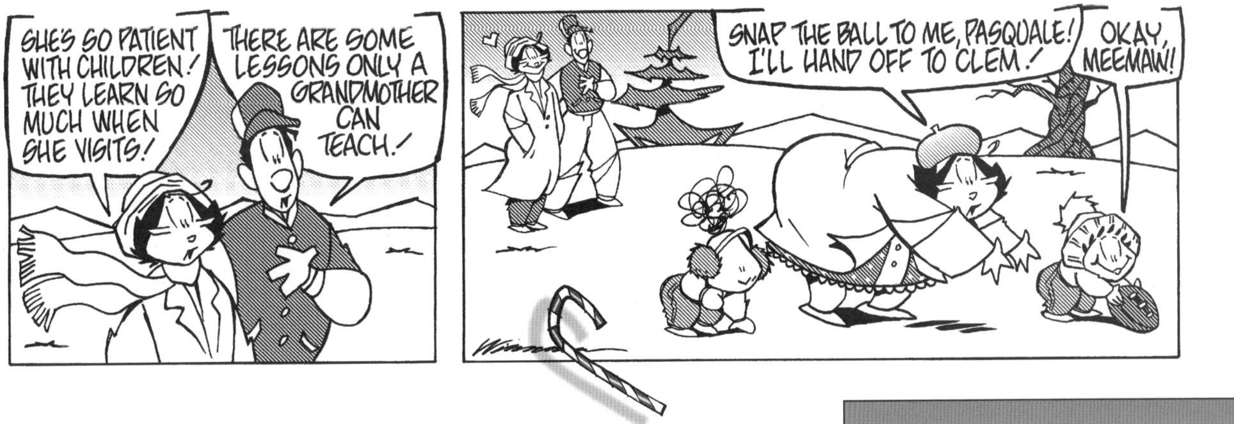
SHE'S SO PATIENT WITH CHILDREN! THEY LEARN SO MUCH WHEN SHE VISITS!
THERE ARE SOME LESSONS ONLY A GRANDMOTHER CAN TEACH!
SNAP THE BALL TO ME, PASQUALE! I'LL HAND OFF TO CLEM!
OKAY, MEEMAW!

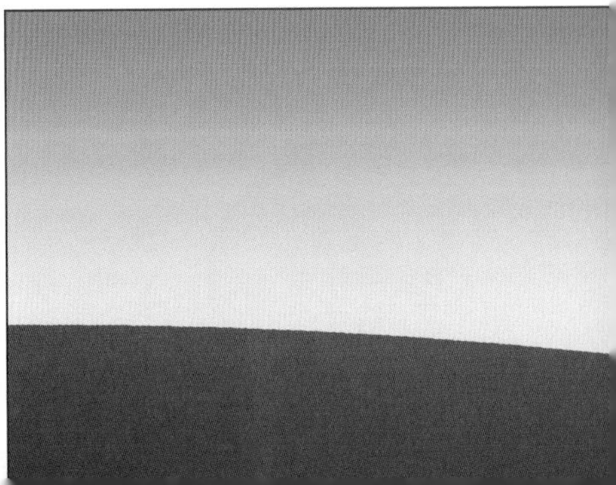

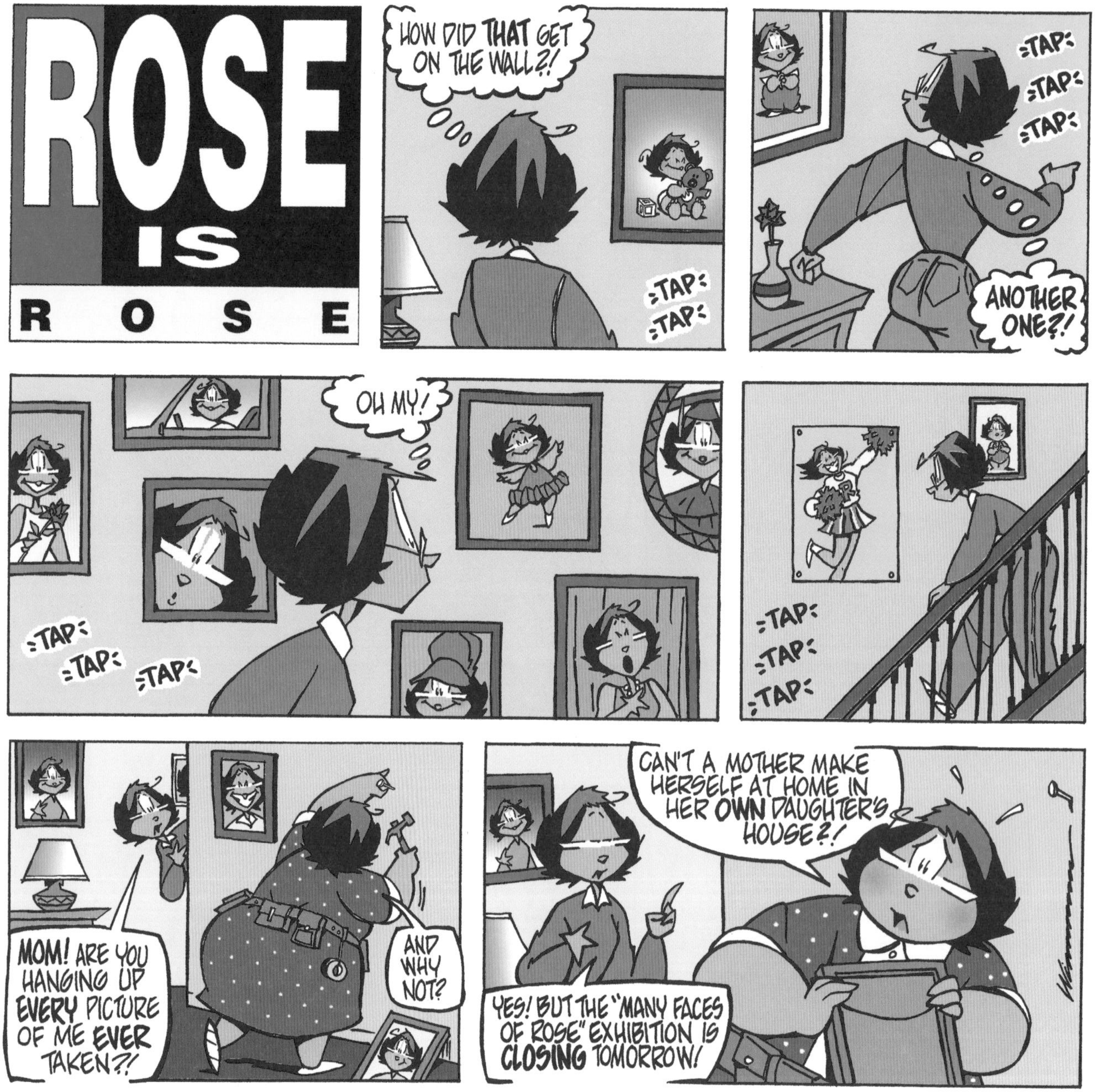
ROSE IS ROSE
HOW DID THAT GET ON THE WALL?!
:TAP:
:TAP:
:TAP:
:TAP:
:TAP:
ANOTHER ONE?!
OH MY!
:TAP:
:TAP:
:TAP:
:TAP:
:TAP:
:TAP:
MOM! ARE YOU HANGING UP EVERY PICTURE OF ME EVER TAKEN?!
AND WHY NOT?
CAN'T A MOTHER MAKE HERSELF AT HOME IN HER OWN DAUGHTER'S HOUSE?!
YES! BUT THE "MANY FACES OF ROSE" EXHIBITION IS CLOSING TOMORROW!

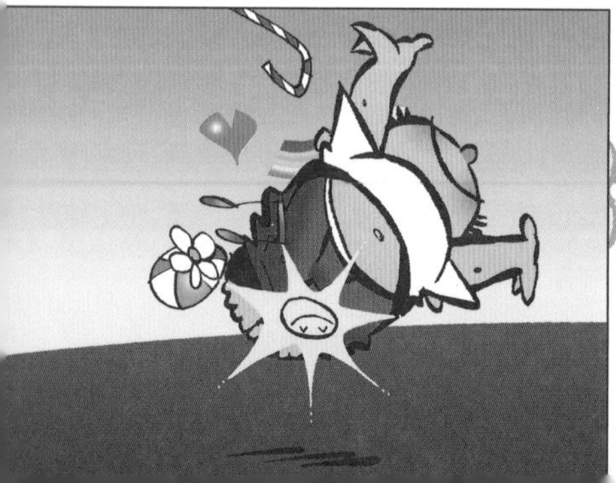

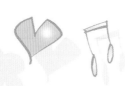

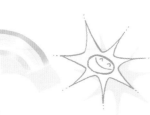

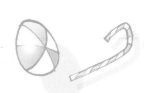

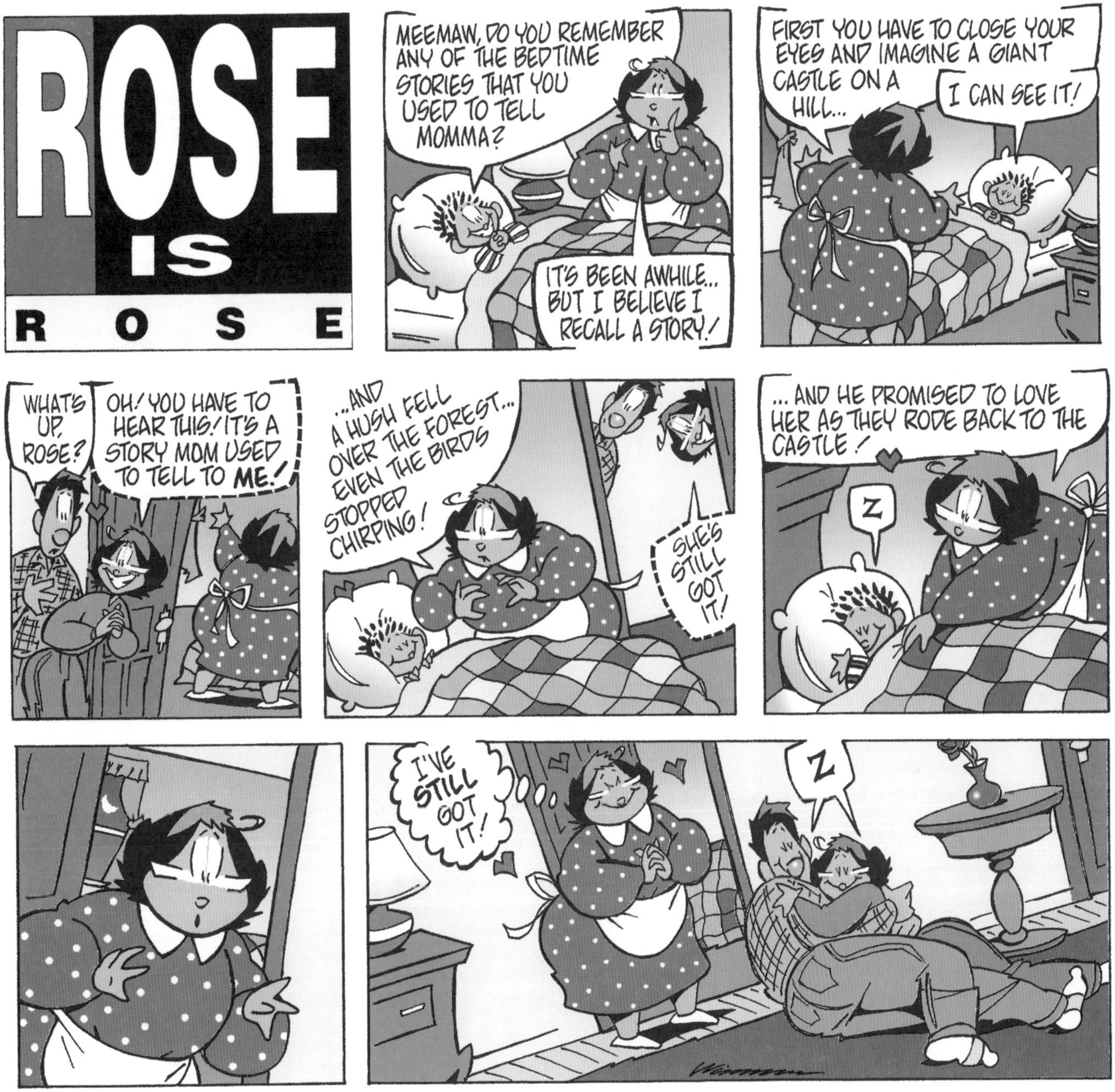
ROSE IS ROSE
MEEMAW, DO YOU REMEMBER ANY OF THE BEDTIME STORIES THAT YOU USED TO TELL MOMMA?
IT'S BEEN AWHILE... BUT I BELIEVE I RECALL A STORY!
FIRST YOU HAVE TO CLOSE YOUR EYES AND IMAGINE A GIANT CASTLE ON A HILL...
I CAN SEE IT!
WHAT'S UP, ROSE?
OH! YOU HAVE TO HEAR THIS! IT'S A STORY MOM USED TO TELL TO **ME**!
...AND A HUSH FELL OVER THE FOREST... EVEN THE BIRDS STOPPED CHIRPING!
SHE'S STILL GOT IT!
... AND HE PROMISED TO LOVE HER AS THEY RODE BACK TO THE CASTLE!
Z
I'VE **STILL** GOT IT!
Z

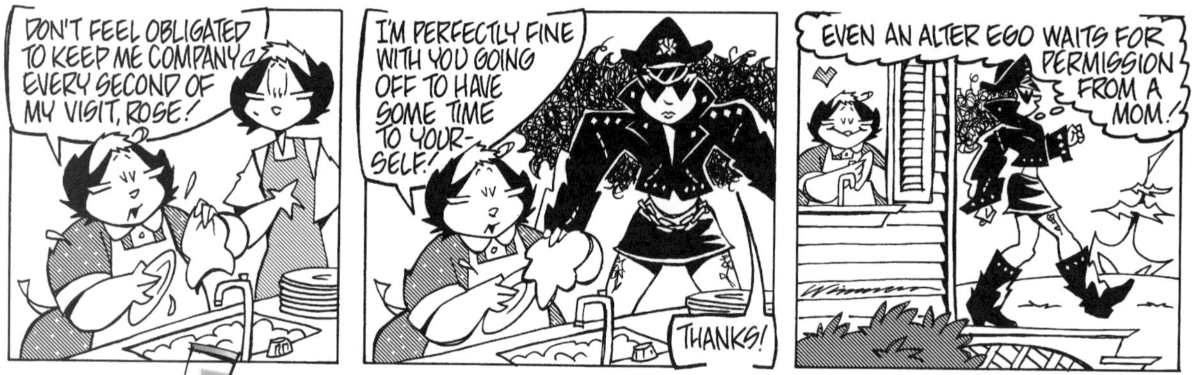
DON'T FEEL OBLIGATED TO KEEP ME COMPANY EVERY SECOND OF MY VISIT, ROSE!
I'M PERFECTLY FINE WITH YOU GOING OFF TO HAVE SOME TIME TO YOUR-SELF!
THANKS!
EVEN AN ALTER EGO WAITS FOR PERMISSION FROM A MOM!

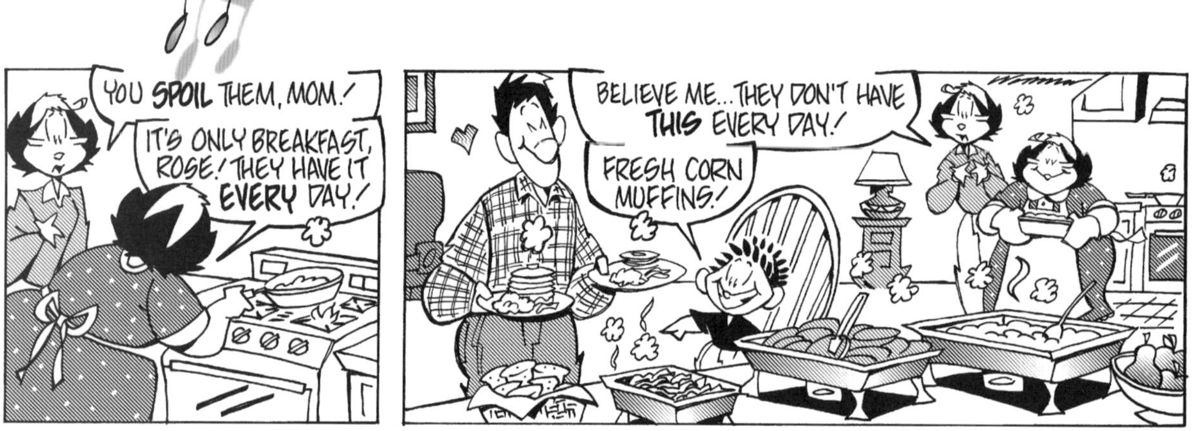
YOU SPOIL THEM, MOM!
IT'S ONLY BREAKFAST, ROSE! THEY HAVE IT EVERY DAY!
BELIEVE ME...THEY DON'T HAVE THIS EVERY DAY!
FRESH CORN MUFFINS!

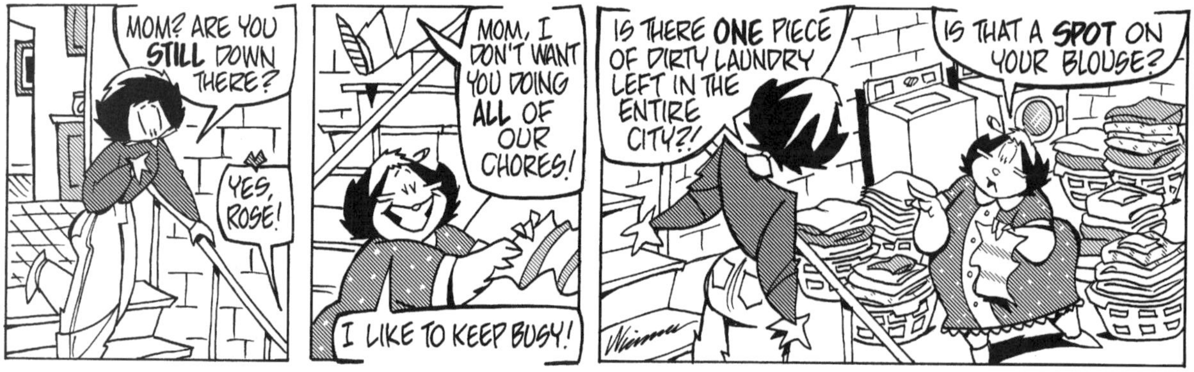
MOM? ARE YOU STILL DOWN THERE?
YES, ROSE!
MOM, I DON'T WANT YOU DOING ALL OF OUR CHORES!
I LIKE TO KEEP BUSY!
IS THERE ONE PIECE OF DIRTY LAUNDRY LEFT IN THE ENTIRE CITY?!
IS THAT A SPOT ON YOUR BLOUSE?

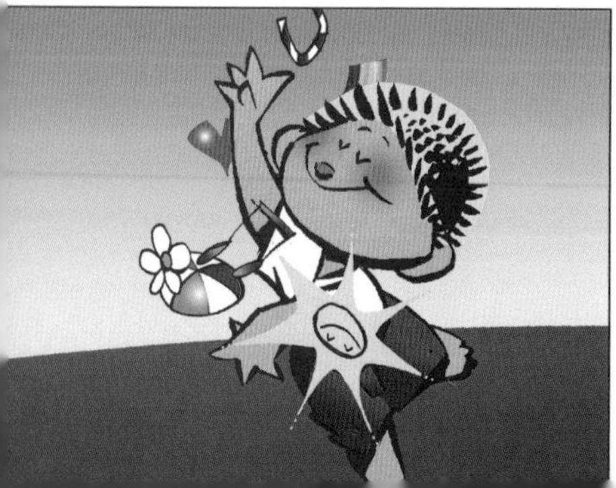

PAT PAT
PAT PAT
I'D LOSE ALL CREDIBILITY IF I DIDN'T CHOOSE THE SUPERIOR LAP!

I WISH YOU DIDN'T HAVE TO LEAVE, MOM!
ME TOO, ROSE!
YOU HAVE A MOBILE HOME! WHY DO YOU NEED TO RUSH OFF?
LET ME CHECK MY ITINERARY... OH! HOT-AIR BALLOONING TOMORROW!
WHEN WERE YOU GOING TO TELL ME ABOUT GOING UP IN A HOT-AIR BALLOON?!
OOPS! THAT'S ON THE ITINERARY LIST OF THINGS NOT TO TELL YOU!

MAYBE ONE OF US SHOULD GO IN THERE!
NO...LET'S GIVE HIM A MOMENT ALONE!
ALTHOUGH JIMBO MAY NOT ALWAYS BE ABLE TO EXPRESS HIS FEELINGS... I WANT YOU TO KNOW...
BEEP
BEEP
...HE'LL MISS YOU TOO!
PAT PAT PAT
SNIFF
BEEP
BEEP

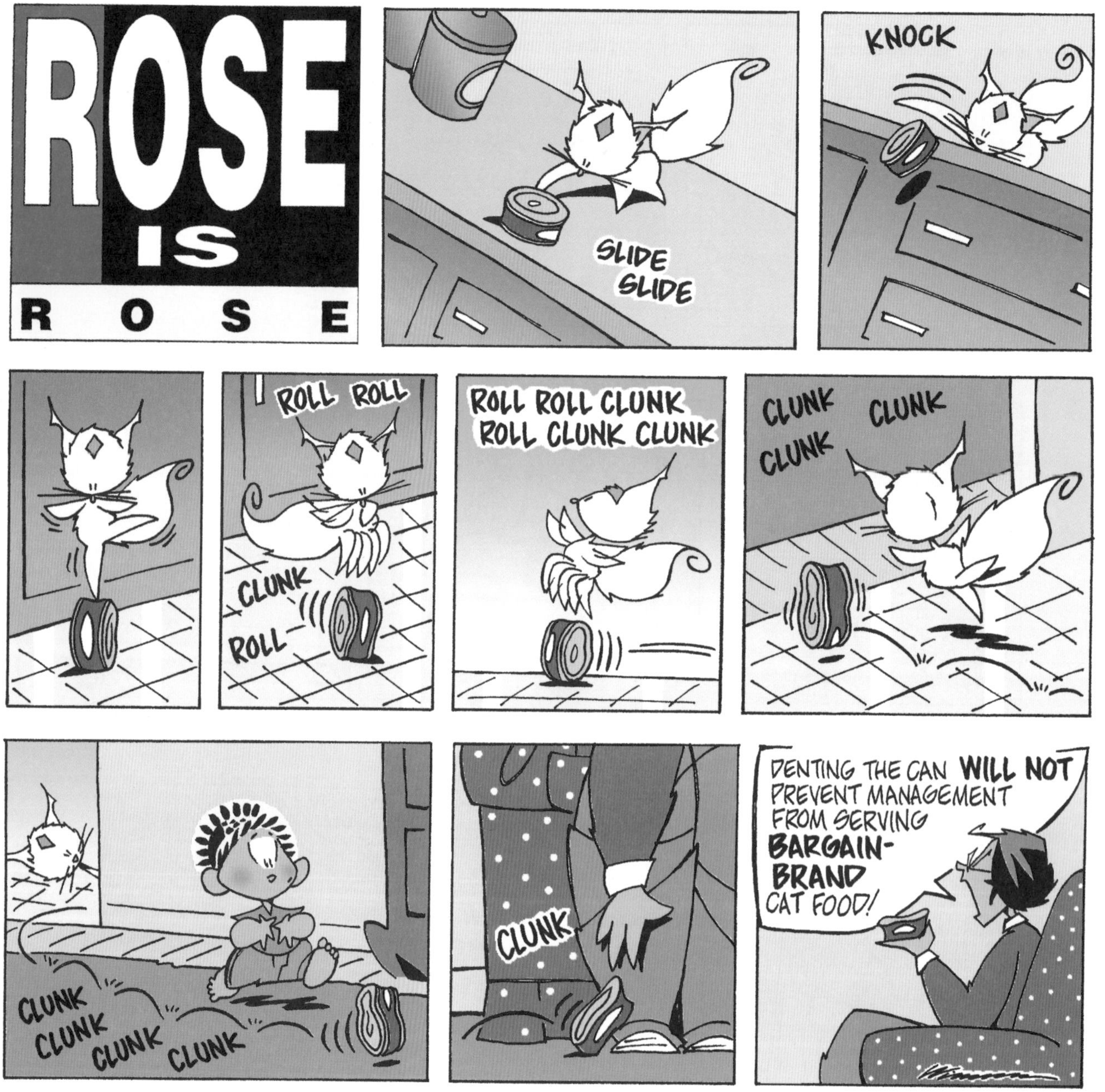
ROSE IS ROSE
SLIDE
SLIDE
KNOCK
ROLL ROLL
CLUNK
ROLL
ROLL ROLL CLUNK
ROLL CLUNK CLUNK
CLUNK
CLUNK
CLUNK
CLUNK
CLUNK
CLUNK
CLUNK
CLUNK
DENTING THE CAN **WILL NOT** PREVENT MANAGEMENT FROM SERVING **BARGAIN-BRAND** CAT FOOD!

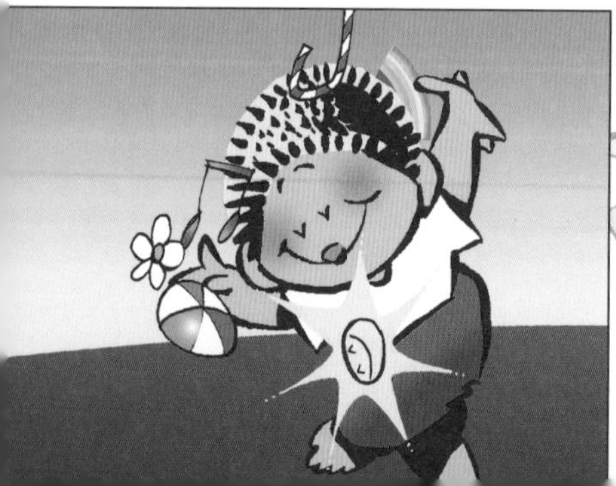

RED...GREEN...BLUE...
RED...GREEN...BLUE...
TWIST
TWIST
PASQUALE, DO YOU MIND A SMALL CHANGE?
WHAT KIND OF CHANGE, MOMMA?
LET'S ADD ORANGE BULBS!
A SKILLED HOLIDAY LIGHTS INSTALLER IS AT THE MERCY OF UNYIELDING DEADLINES AND THE PUBLIC'S CRAVING FOR GARISH ILLUMINATION!

READY FOR A LUNCH BREAK, PASQUALE?
SURE! I'LL JUST PUT IN THESE LAST FEW BULBS!
TWIST
SQUEAK
EXOTIC WALNUTS IN FESTIVE COLORS... GROWING ON A VINE! WHAT WILL THEY THINK OF NEXT!

OOPS! WE MUST HAVE MISSED TWO BULBS, PASQUALE!
DADDY, I KNOW THAT I PUT A BULB IN EACH SOCKET BEFORE WE WENT IN FOR LUNCH!
THESE DON'T LOOK OR FEEL LIKE WALNUTS!
THEY'RE PROBABLY IMPORTED!

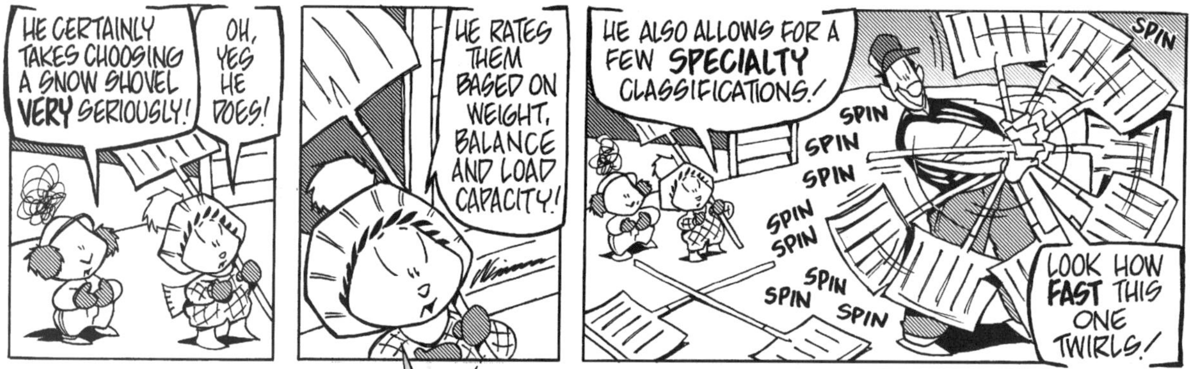
HE CERTAINLY TAKES CHOOSING A SNOW SHOVEL VERY SERIOUSLY!
OH, YES HE DOES!
HE RATES THEM BASED ON WEIGHT, BALANCE AND LOAD CAPACITY!
HE ALSO ALLOWS FOR A FEW SPECIALTY CLASSIFICATIONS!
SPIN
SPIN
SPIN
SPIN
SPIN
SPIN
SPIN
SPIN
SPIN
LOOK HOW FAST THIS ONE TWIRLS!

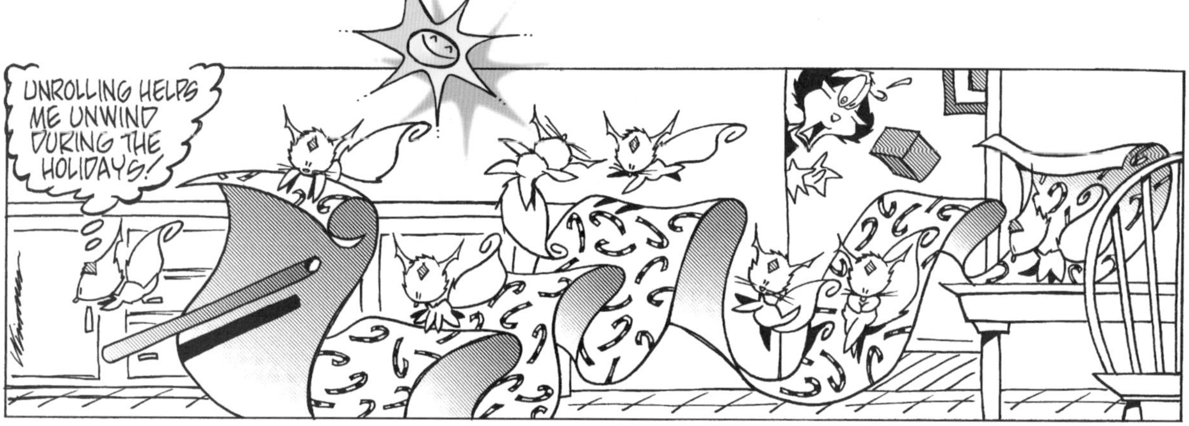
UNROLLING HELPS ME UNWIND DURING THE HOLIDAYS!

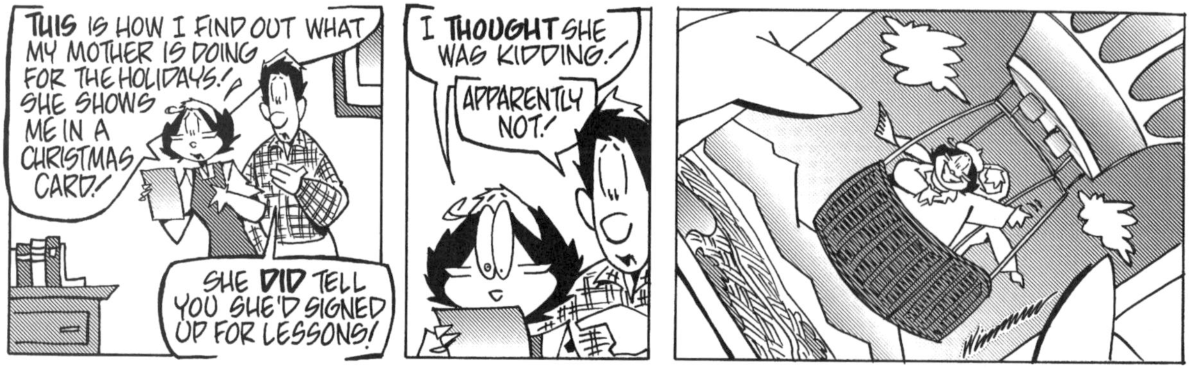
THIS IS HOW I FIND OUT WHAT MY MOTHER IS DOING FOR THE HOLIDAYS! SHE SHOWS ME IN A CHRISTMAS CARD!
SHE DID TELL YOU SHE'D SIGNED UP FOR LESSONS!
I THOUGHT SHE WAS KIDDING!
APPARENTLY NOT!

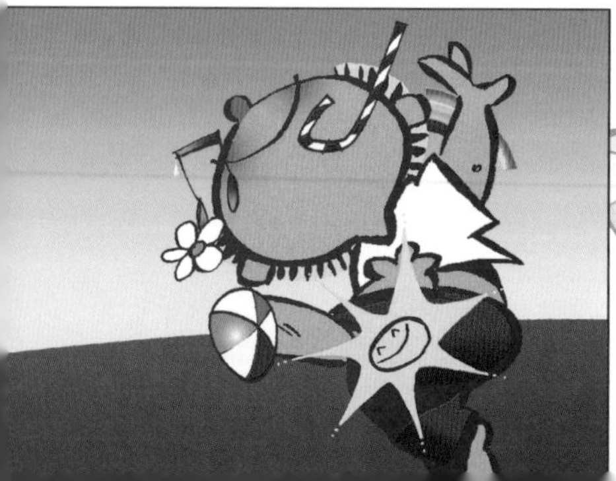

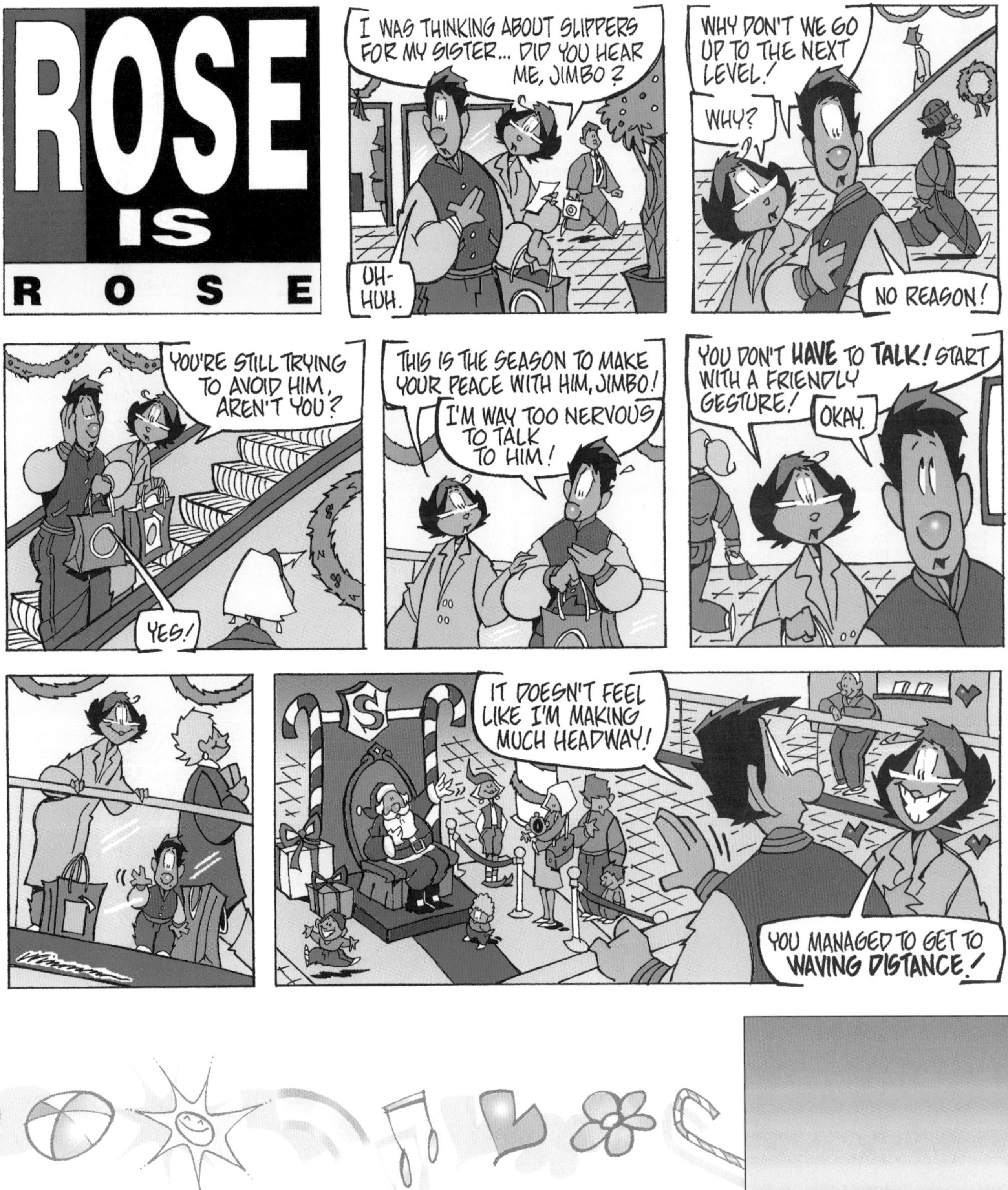
ROSE IS ROSE
I WAS THINKING ABOUT SLIPPERS FOR MY SISTER... DID YOU HEAR ME, JIMBO ?
UH-HUH.
WHY DON'T WE GO UP TO THE NEXT LEVEL!
WHY?
NO REASON!
YOU'RE STILL TRYING TO AVOID HIM, AREN'T YOU?
YES!
THIS IS THE SEASON TO MAKE YOUR PEACE WITH HIM, JIMBO!
I'M WAY TOO NERVOUS TO TALK TO HIM!
YOU DON'T **HAVE** TO **TALK!** START WITH A FRIENDLY GESTURE!
OKAY.
IT DOESN'T FEEL LIKE I'M MAKING MUCH HEADWAY!
YOU MANAGED TO GET TO **WAVING DISTANCE!**

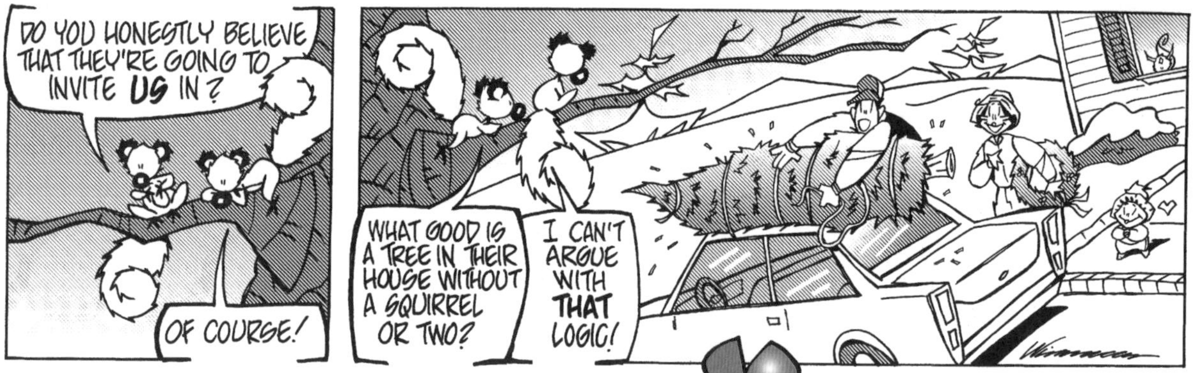
DO YOU HONESTLY BELIEVE THAT THEY'RE GOING TO INVITE **US** IN?
OF COURSE!
WHAT GOOD IS A TREE IN THEIR HOUSE WITHOUT A SQUIRREL OR TWO?
I CAN'T ARGUE WITH **THAT** LOGIC!

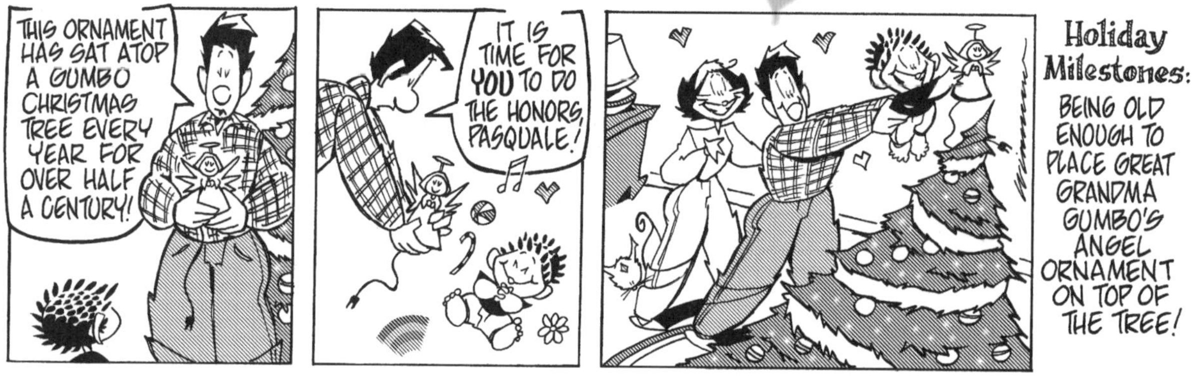
THIS ORNAMENT HAS SAT ATOP A GUMBO CHRISTMAS TREE EVERY YEAR FOR OVER HALF A CENTURY!
IT IS TIME FOR **YOU** TO DO THE HONORS, PASQUALE!
Holiday Milestones:
BEING OLD ENOUGH TO PLACE GREAT GRANDMA GUMBO'S ANGEL ORNAMENT ON TOP OF THE TREE!

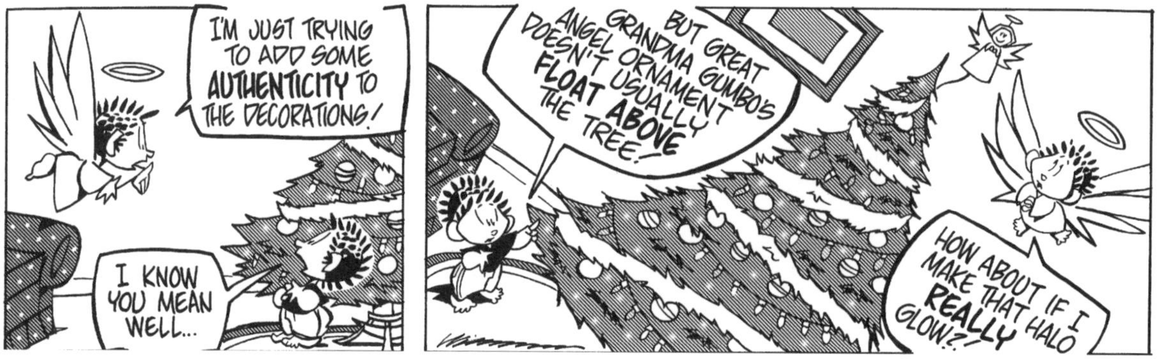
I'M JUST TRYING TO ADD SOME **AUTHENTICITY** TO THE DECORATIONS!
I KNOW YOU MEAN WELL...
BUT GREAT GRANDMA GUMBO'S ANGEL ORNAMENT DOESN'T USUALLY **FLOAT ABOVE** THE TREE!
HOW ABOUT IF I MAKE THAT HALO **REALLY** GLOW?!

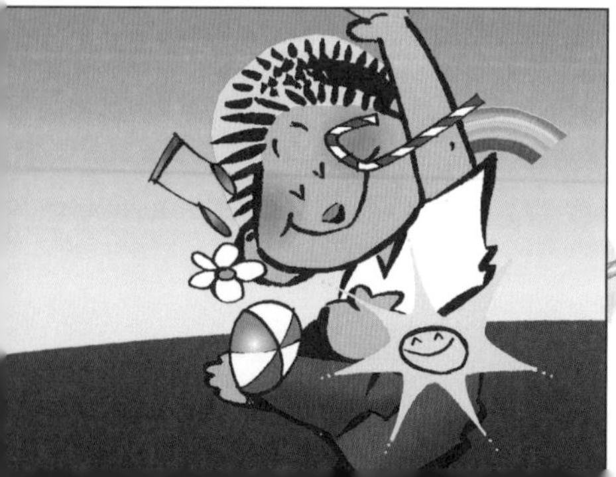

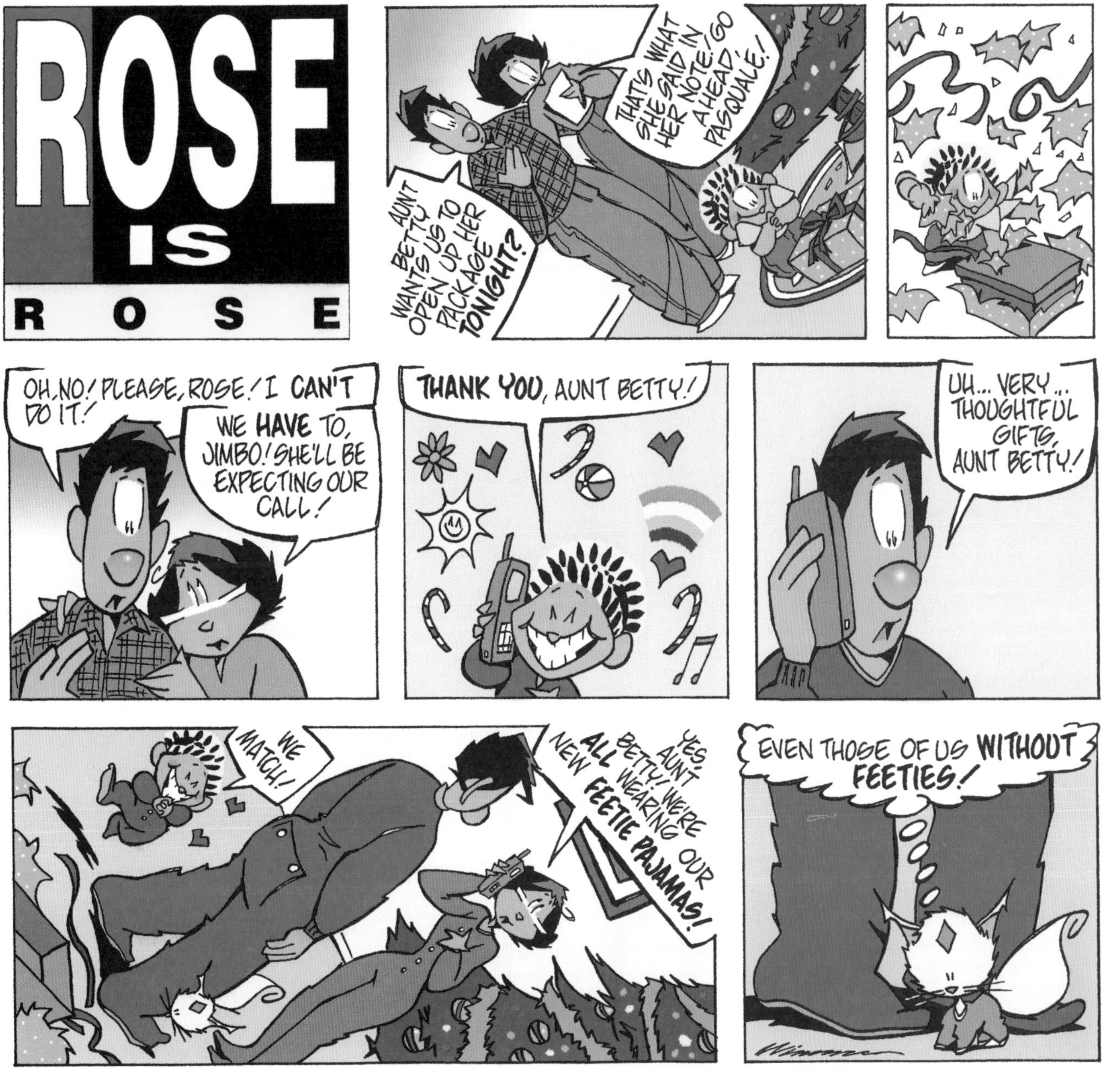
ROSE IS ROSE
AUNT BETTY WANTS US TO OPEN UP HER PACKAGE TONIGHT?
THAT'S WHAT SHE SAID IN HER NOTE! GO AHEAD, PASQUALE!
OH, NO! PLEASE, ROSE! I CAN'T DO IT!
WE HAVE TO, JIMBO! SHE'LL BE EXPECTING OUR CALL!
THANK YOU, AUNT BETTY!
UH... VERY... THOUGHTFUL GIFTS, AUNT BETTY!
WE MATCH!
YES, AUNT BETTY! WE'RE ALL WEARING OUR NEW FEETIE PAJAMAS!
EVEN THOSE OF US WITHOUT FEETIES!

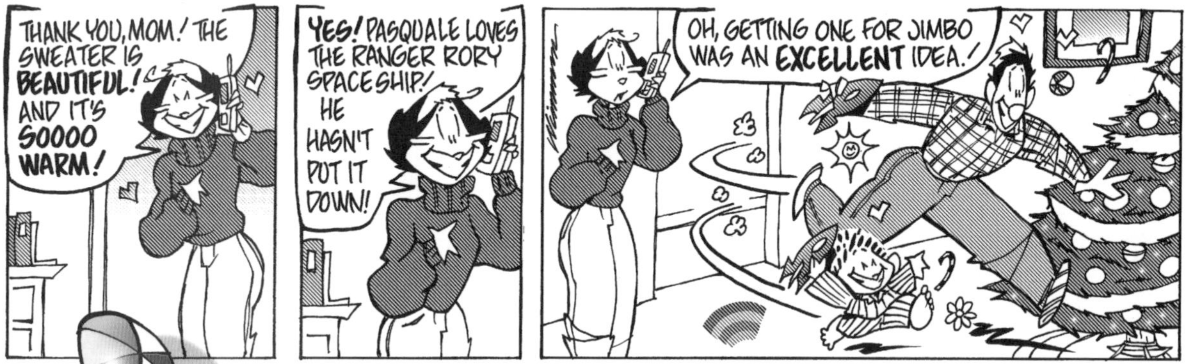
THANK YOU, MOM! THE SWEATER IS BEAUTIFUL! AND IT'S SOOOO WARM!
YES! PASQUALE LOVES THE RANGER RORY SPACESHIP! HE HASN'T PUT IT DOWN!
OH, GETTING ONE FOR JIMBO WAS AN EXCELLENT IDEA!

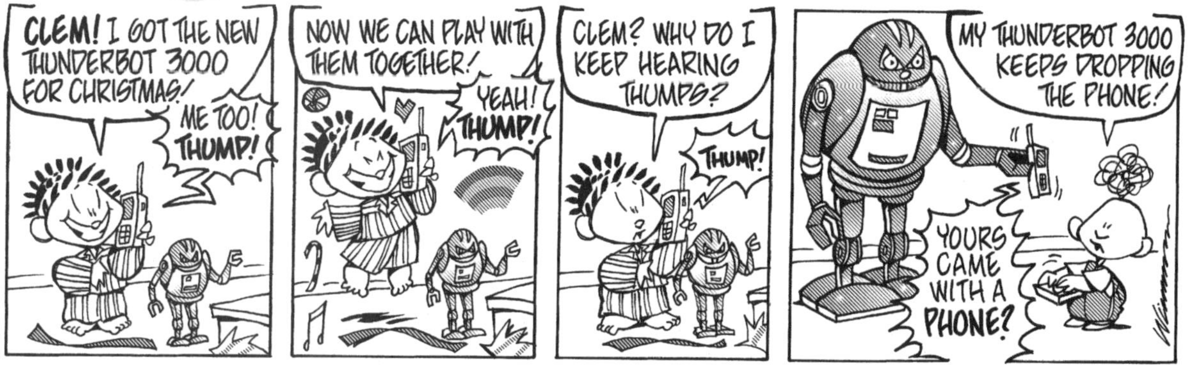
CLEM! I GOT THE NEW THUNDERBOT 3000 FOR CHRISTMAS!
ME TOO! THUMP!
NOW WE CAN PLAY WITH THEM TOGETHER!
YEAH! THUMP!
CLEM? WHY DO I KEEP HEARING THUMPS?
THUMP!
MY THUNDERBOT 3000 KEEPS DROPPING THE PHONE!
YOURS CAME WITH A PHONE?

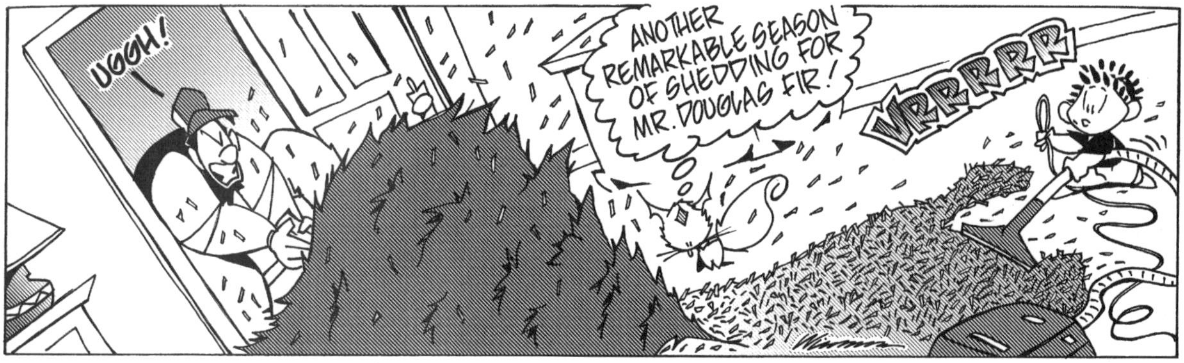
UGGH!
ANOTHER REMARKABLE SEASON OF SHEDDING FOR MR. DOUGLAS FIR!
VRRRRR

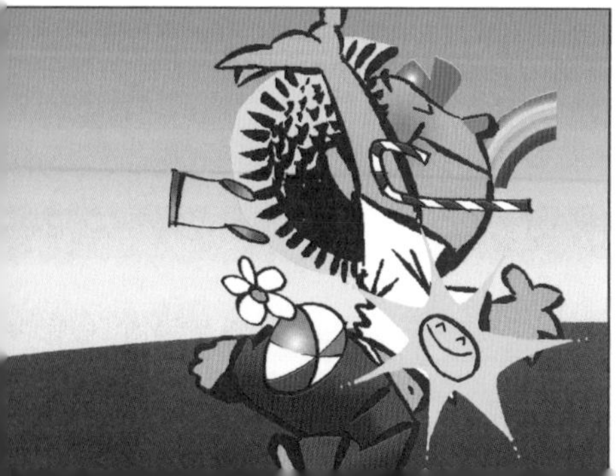

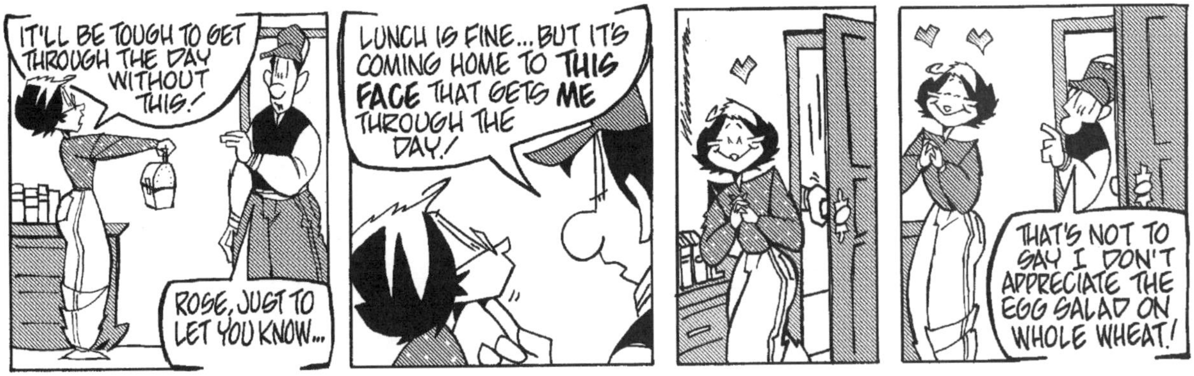
IT'LL BE TOUGH TO GET THROUGH THE DAY WITHOUT THIS!
ROSE, JUST TO LET YOU KNOW...
LUNCH IS FINE... BUT IT'S COMING HOME TO **THIS FACE** THAT GETS **ME** THROUGH THE DAY!
THAT'S NOT TO SAY I DON'T APPRECIATE THE EGG SALAD ON WHOLE WHEAT!

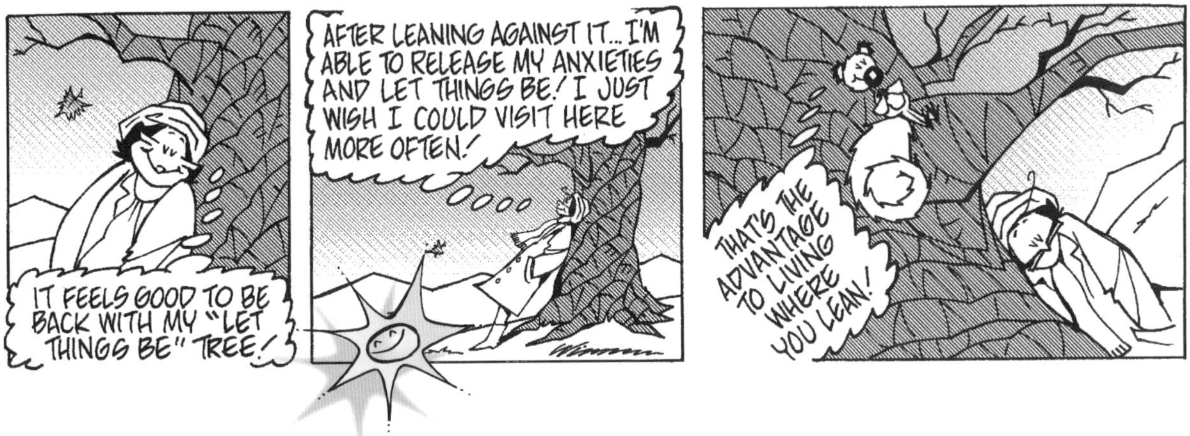
IT FEELS GOOD TO BE BACK WITH MY "LET THINGS BE" TREE!
AFTER LEANING AGAINST IT... I'M ABLE TO RELEASE MY ANXIETIES AND LET THINGS BE! I JUST WISH I COULD VISIT HERE MORE OFTEN!
THAT'S THE ADVANTAGE TO LIVING WHERE YOU LEAN!

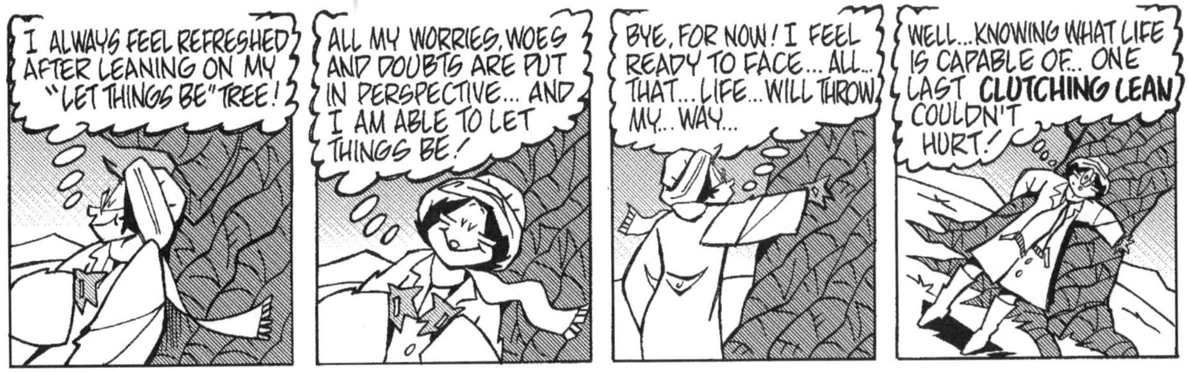
I ALWAYS FEEL REFRESHED AFTER LEANING ON MY "LET THINGS BE" TREE!
ALL MY WORRIES, WOES AND DOUBTS ARE PUT IN PERSPECTIVE... AND I AM ABLE TO LET THINGS BE!
BYE, FOR NOW! I FEEL READY TO FACE... ALL... THAT... LIFE... WILL THROW MY... WAY...
WELL... KNOWING WHAT LIFE IS CAPABLE OF... ONE LAST **CLUTCHING LEAN** COULDN'T HURT!

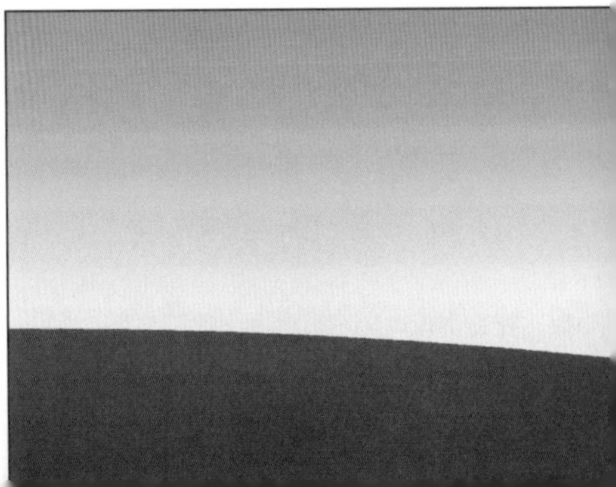

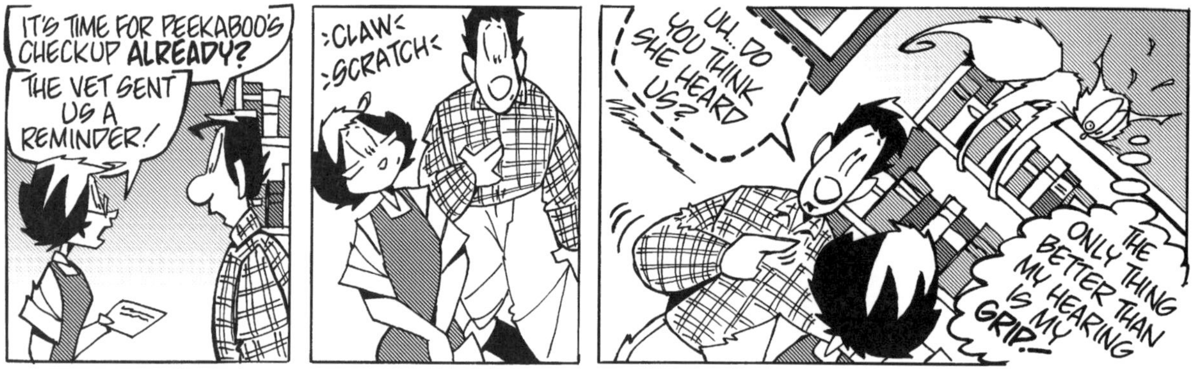
IT'S TIME FOR PEEKABOO'S CHECKUP ALREADY?
THE VET SENT US A REMINDER!
CLAW
SCRATCH
UH... DO YOU THINK SHE HEARD US?
THE ONLY THING BETTER THAN MY HEARING IS MY GRIP!

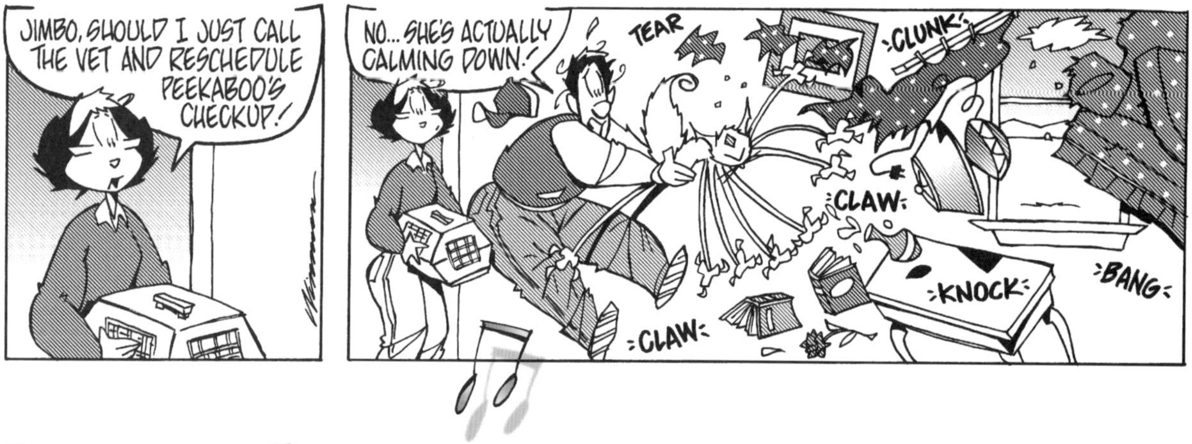
JIMBO, SHOULD I JUST CALL THE VET AND RESCHEDULE PEEKABOO'S CHECKUP!
NO... SHE'S ACTUALLY CALMING DOWN!
TEAR
CLUNK
CLAW
KNOCK
BANG
CLAW

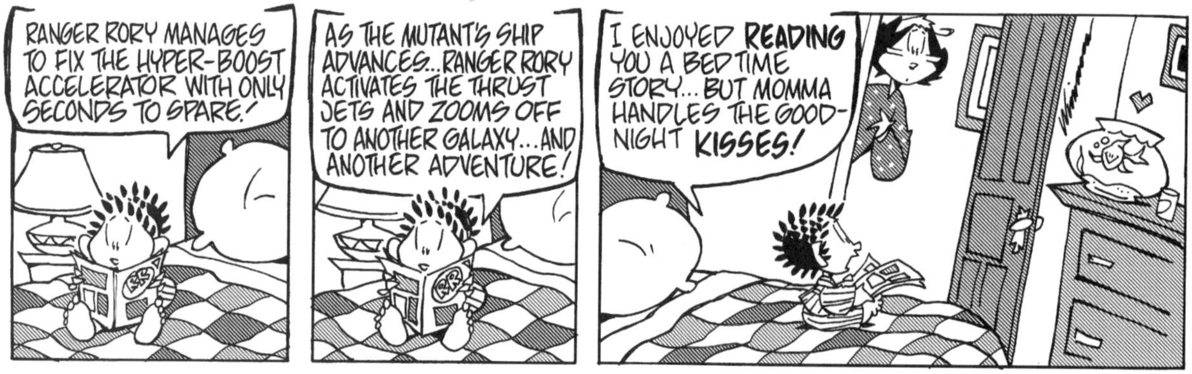
RANGER RORY MANAGES TO FIX THE HYPER-BOOST ACCELERATOR WITH ONLY SECONDS TO SPARE!
AS THE MUTANT'S SHIP ADVANCES...RANGER RORY ACTIVATES THE THRUST JETS AND ZOOMS OFF TO ANOTHER GALAXY... AND ANOTHER ADVENTURE!
I ENJOYED READING YOU A BEDTIME STORY... BUT MOMMA HANDLES THE GOOD-NIGHT KISSES!

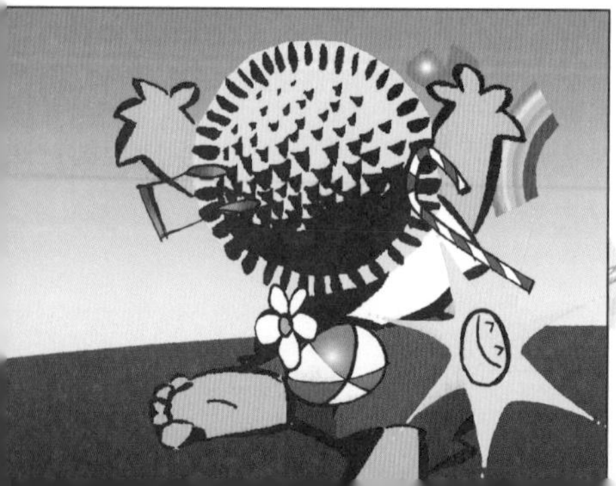

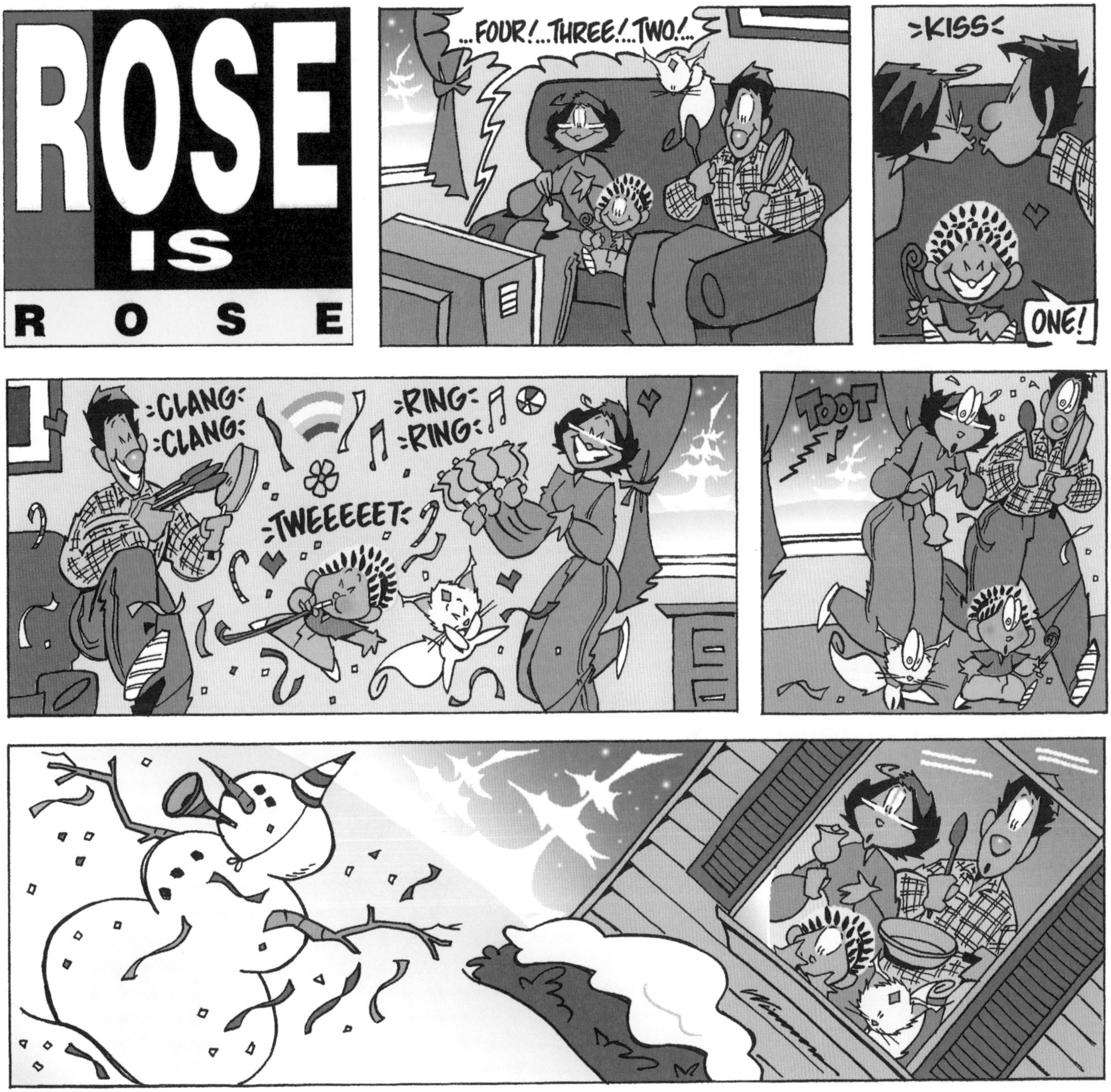
ROSE IS ROSE
...FOUR!...THREE!...TWO!...
KISS
ONE!
CLANG CLANG
RING RING
TWEEEEET
TOOT

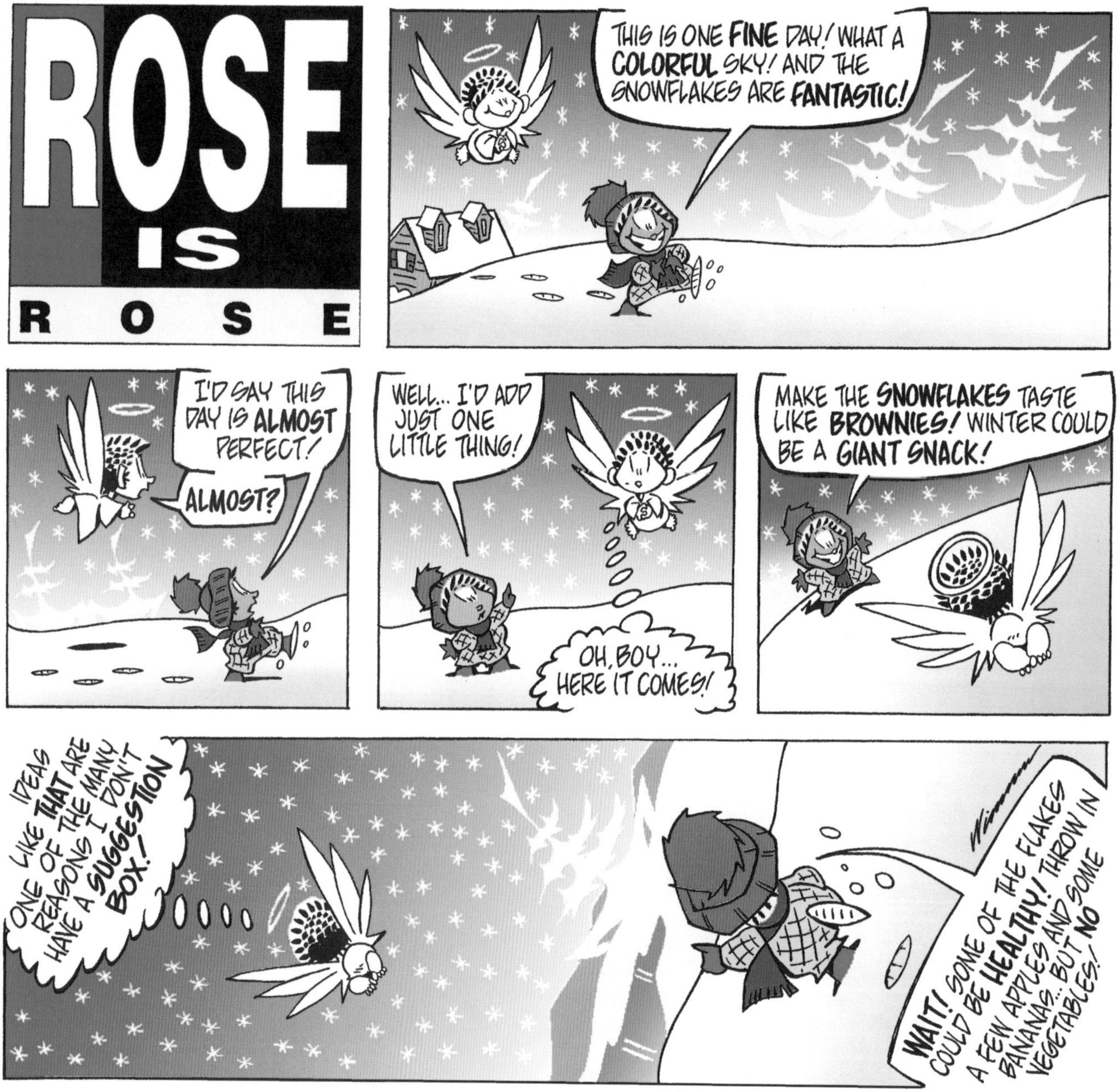

ROSE IS ROSE
THIS IS ONE FINE DAY! WHAT A COLORFUL SKY! AND THE SNOWFLAKES ARE FANTASTIC!
I'D SAY THIS DAY IS ALMOST PERFECT!
ALMOST?
WELL... I'D ADD JUST ONE LITTLE THING!
OH, BOY... HERE IT COMES!
MAKE THE SNOWFLAKES TASTE LIKE BROWNIES! WINTER COULD BE A GIANT SNACK!
WAIT! SOME OF THE FLAKES COULD BE HEALTHY! THROW IN A FEW APPLES AND SOME BANANAS... BUT NO VEGETABLES!
IDEAS LIKE THAT ARE ONE OF THE MANY REASONS I DON'T HAVE A SUGGESTION BOX!

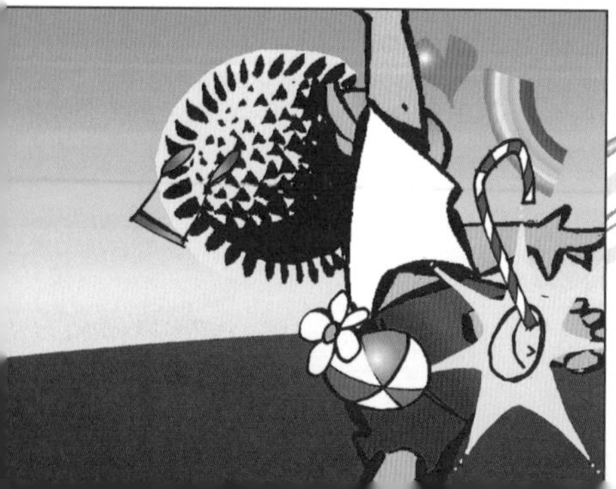

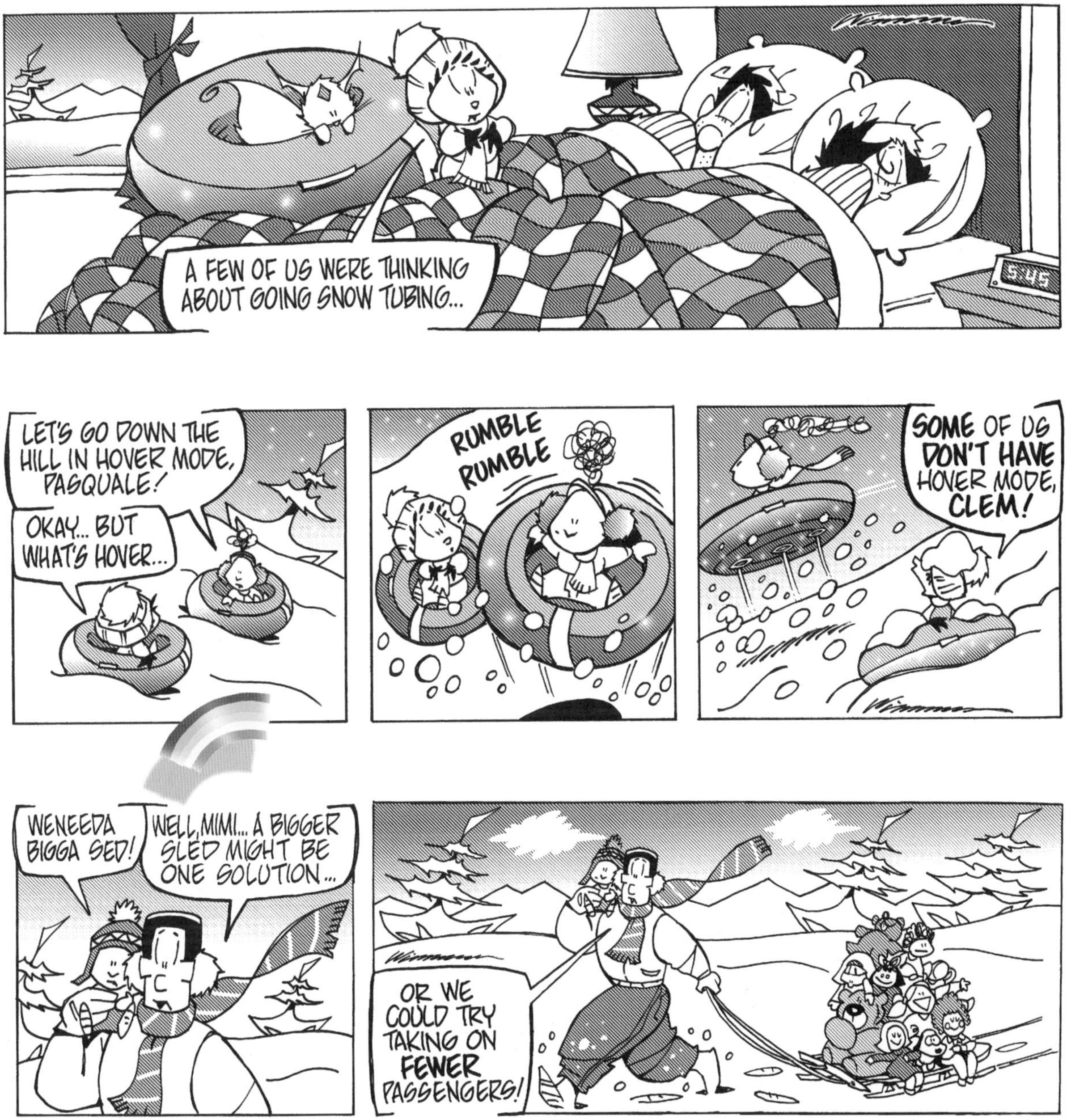
A FEW OF US WERE THINKING ABOUT GOING SNOW TUBING...
LET'S GO DOWN THE HILL IN HOVER MODE, PASQUALE!
OKAY... BUT WHAT'S HOVER...
RUMBLE RUMBLE
SOME OF US DON'T HAVE HOVER MODE, CLEM!
WENEEDA BIGGA SED!
WELL, MIMI... A BIGGER SLED MIGHT BE ONE SOLUTION...
OR WE COULD TRY TAKING ON FEWER PASSENGERS!

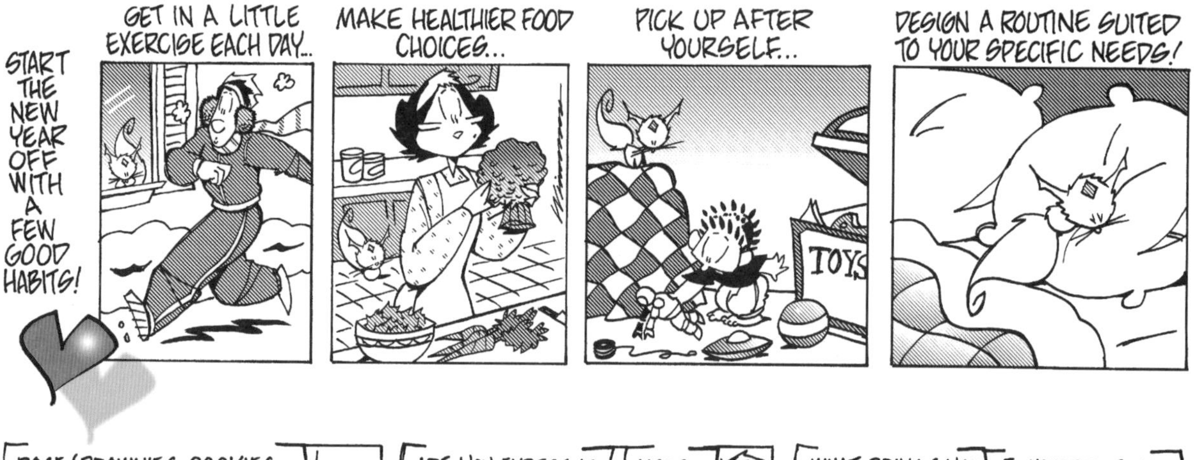
START THE NEW YEAR OFF WITH A FEW GOOD HABITS!
GET IN A LITTLE EXERCISE EACH DAY...
MAKE HEALTHIER FOOD CHOICES...
PICK UP AFTER YOURSELF...
TOYS
DESIGN A ROUTINE SUITED TO YOUR SPECIFIC NEEDS!

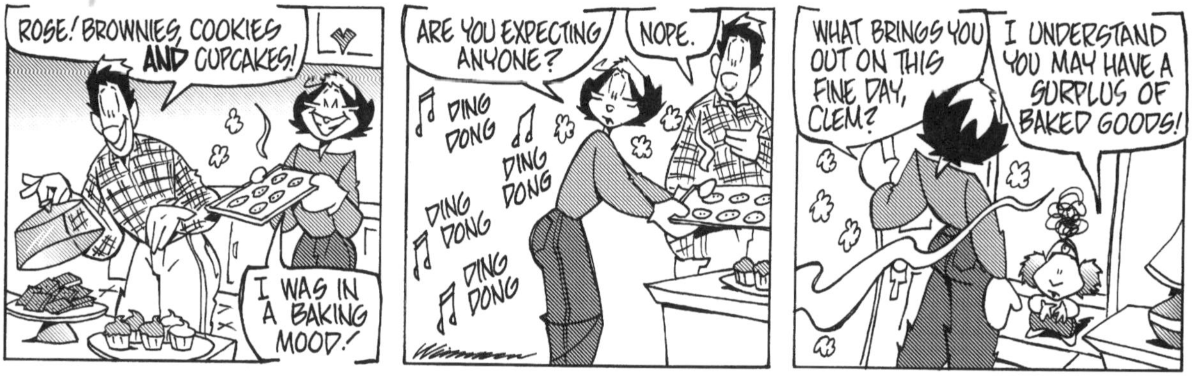
ROSE! BROWNIES, COOKIES AND CUPCAKES!
I WAS IN A BAKING MOOD!
ARE YOU EXPECTING ANYONE?
NOPE.
DING DONG
DING DONG
DING DONG
DING DONG
WHAT BRINGS YOU OUT ON THIS FINE DAY, CLEM?
I UNDERSTAND YOU MAY HAVE A SURPLUS OF BAKED GOODS!

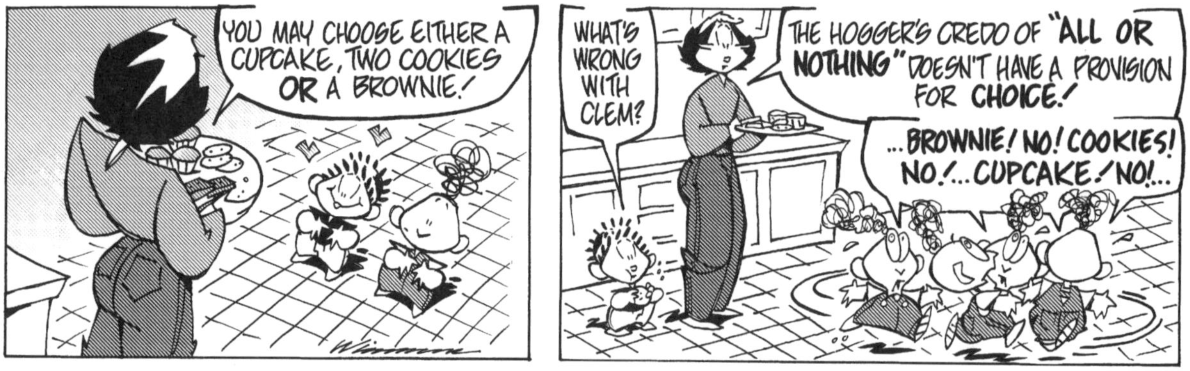
YOU MAY CHOOSE EITHER A CUPCAKE, TWO COOKIES OR A BROWNIE!
WHAT'S WRONG WITH CLEM?
THE HOGGER'S CREDO OF "ALL OR NOTHING" DOESN'T HAVE A PROVISION FOR CHOICE!
...BROWNIE! NO! COOKIES! NO!...CUPCAKE! NO!...

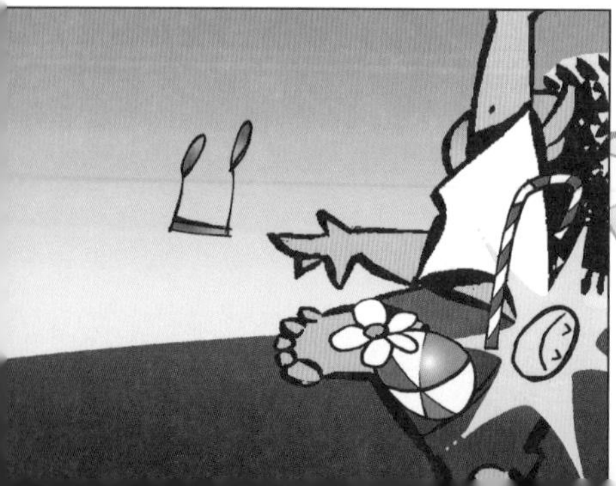

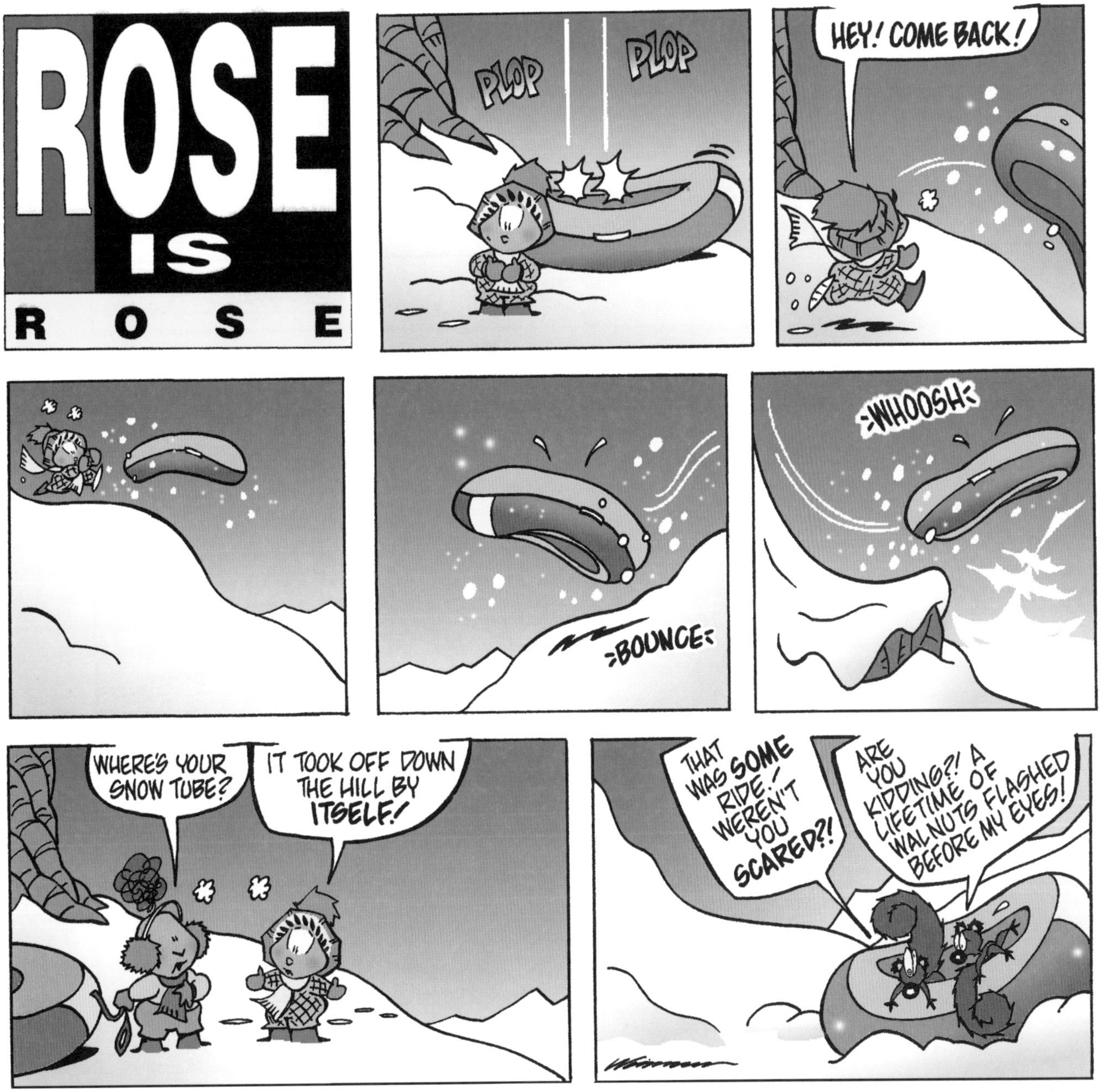
ROSE IS ROSE
PLOP PLOP
HEY! COME BACK!
WHOOSH
BOUNCE
WHERE'S YOUR SNOW TUBE?
IT TOOK OFF DOWN THE HILL BY ITSELF!
THAT WAS SOME RIDE! WEREN'T YOU SCARED?!
ARE YOU KIDDING?! A LIFETIME OF WALNUTS FLASHED BEFORE MY EYES!

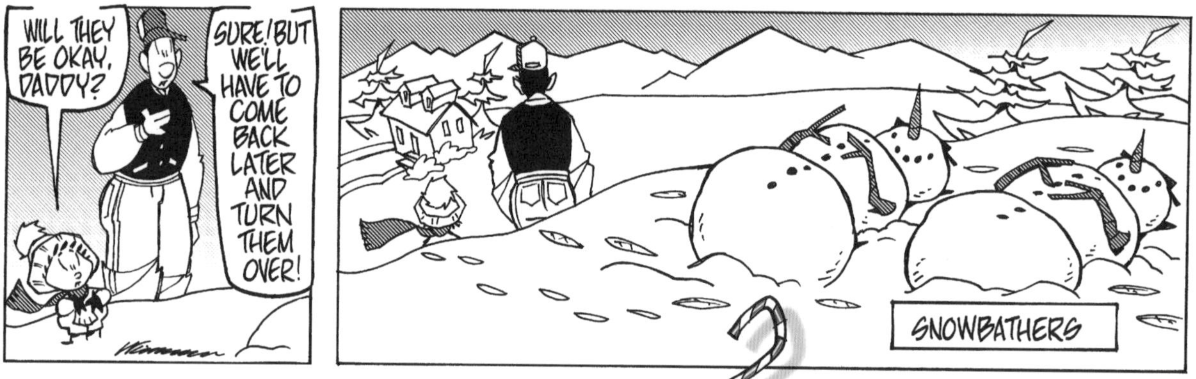
WILL THEY BE OKAY, DADDY?
SURE! BUT WE'LL HAVE TO COME BACK LATER AND TURN THEM OVER!
SNOWBATHERS

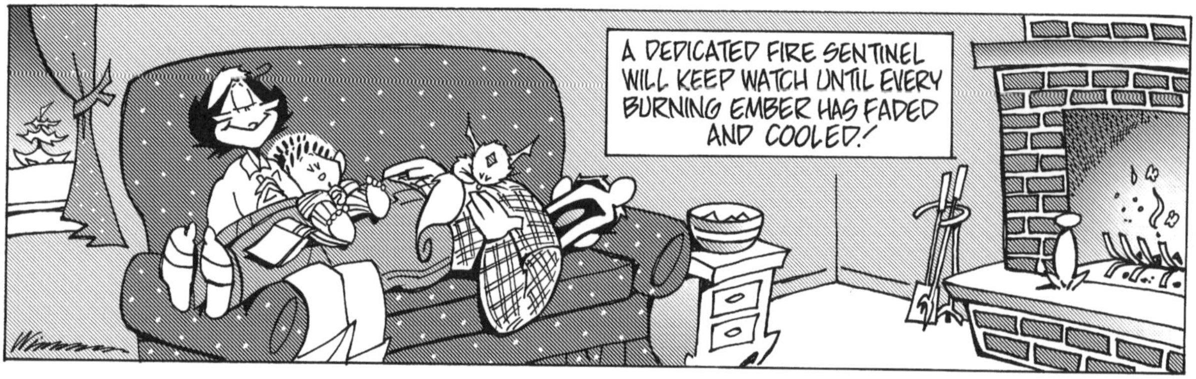
A DEDICATED FIRE SENTINEL WILL KEEP WATCH UNTIL EVERY BURNING EMBER HAS FADED AND COOLED!

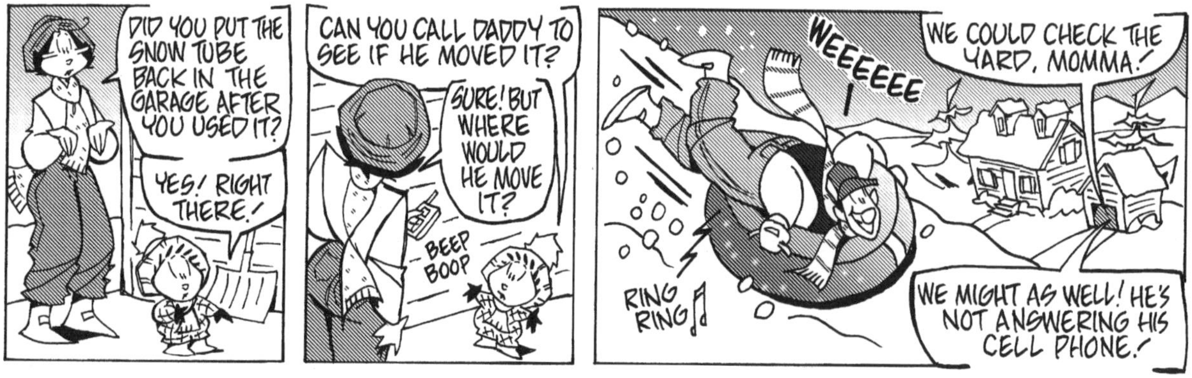
DID YOU PUT THE SNOW TUBE BACK IN THE GARAGE AFTER YOU USED IT?
YES! RIGHT THERE!
CAN YOU CALL DADDY TO SEE IF HE MOVED IT?
SURE! BUT WHERE WOULD HE MOVE IT?
BEEP BOOP
WEEEEEE
RING RING
WE COULD CHECK THE YARD, MOMMA!
WE MIGHT AS WELL! HE'S NOT ANSWERING HIS CELL PHONE!

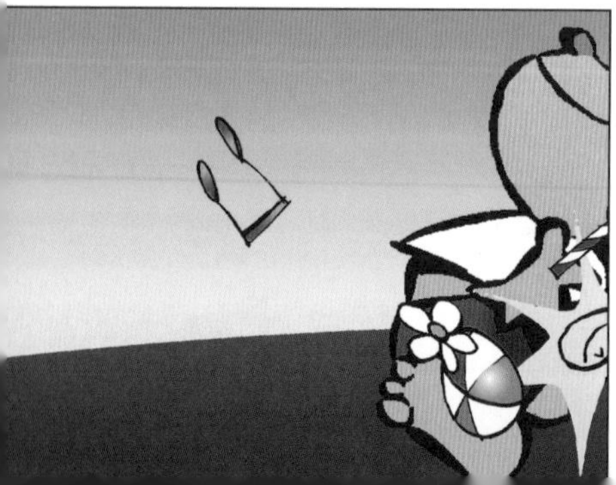

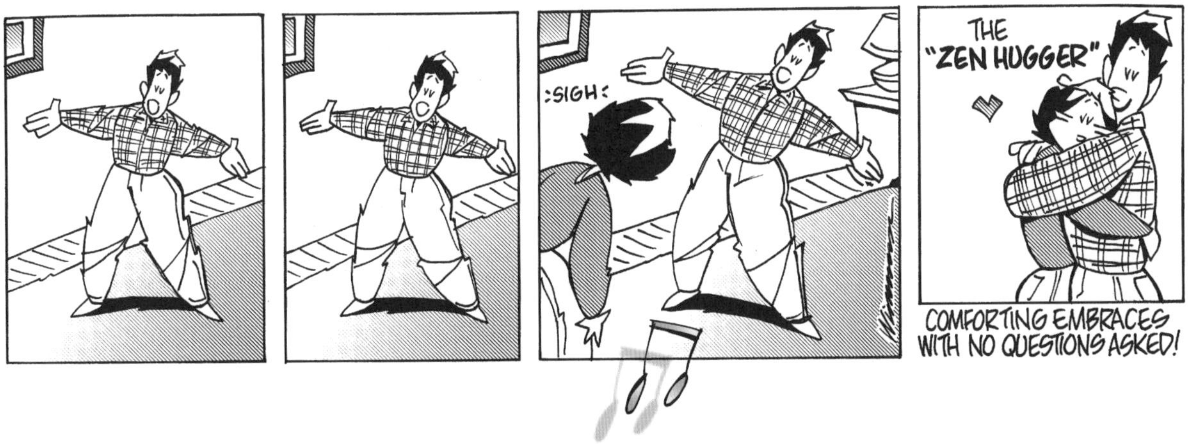
:SIGH:
THE "ZEN HUGGER"
COMFORTING EMBRACES WITH NO QUESTIONS ASKED!

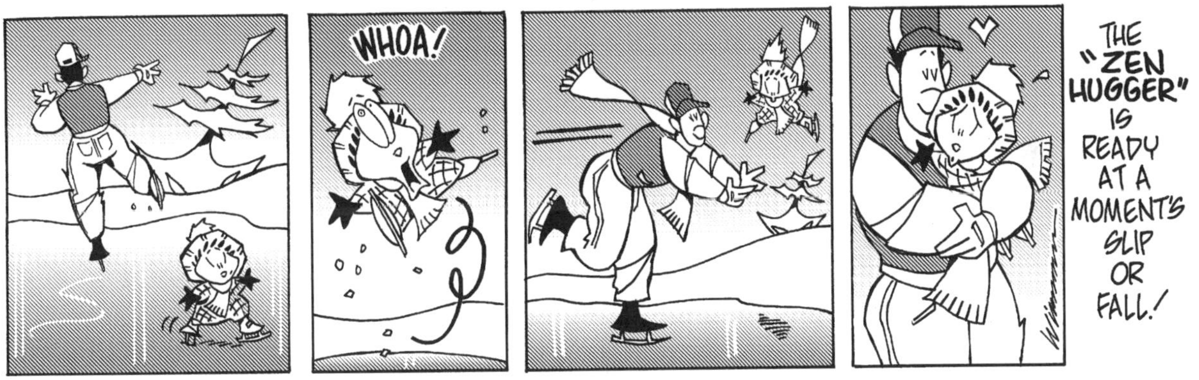
WHOA!
THE "ZEN HUGGER" IS READY AT A MOMENT'S SLIP OR FALL!

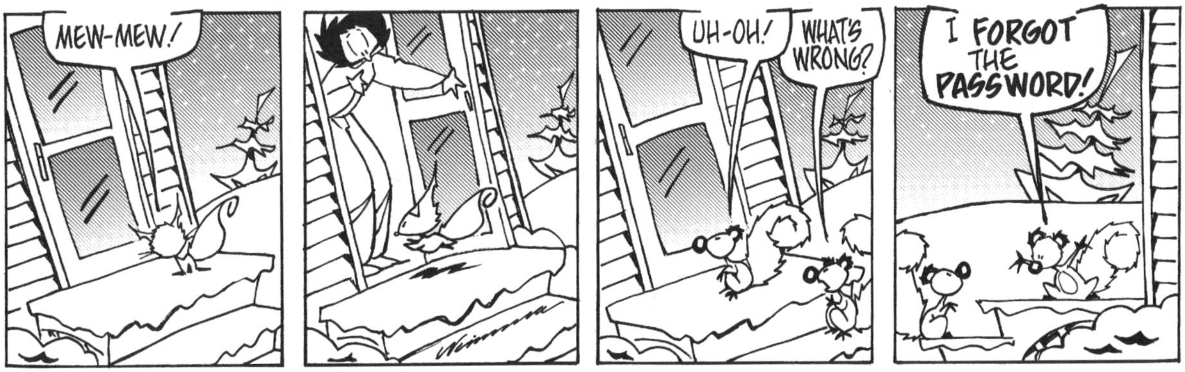
MEW-MEW!
UH-OH!
WHAT'S WRONG?
I FORGOT THE PASSWORD!

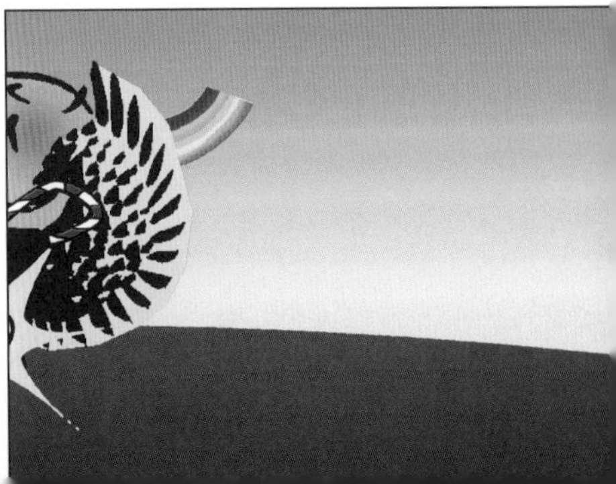

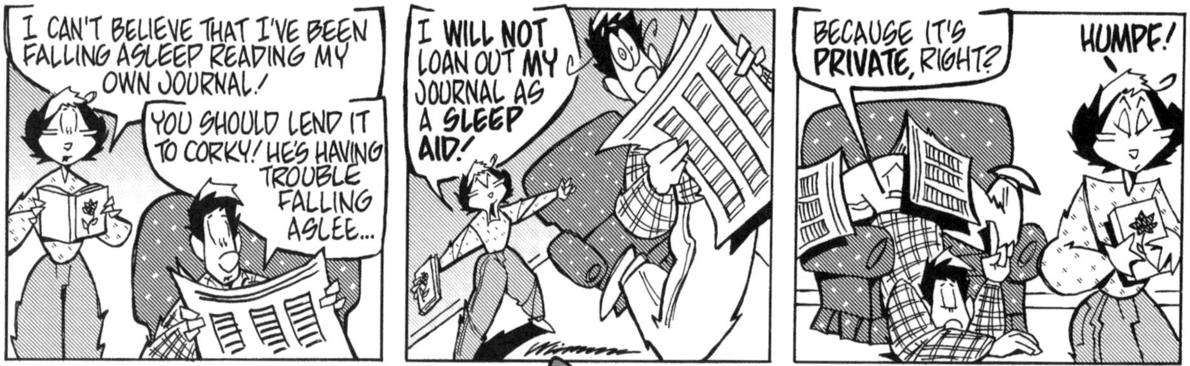
I CAN'T BELIEVE THAT I'VE BEEN FALLING ASLEEP READING MY OWN JOURNAL!
YOU SHOULD LEND IT TO CORKY! HE'S HAVING TROUBLE FALLING ASLEE...
I **WILL NOT** LOAN OUT **MY** JOURNAL AS A **SLEEP AID**!
BECAUSE IT'S **PRIVATE**, RIGHT?
HUMPF!

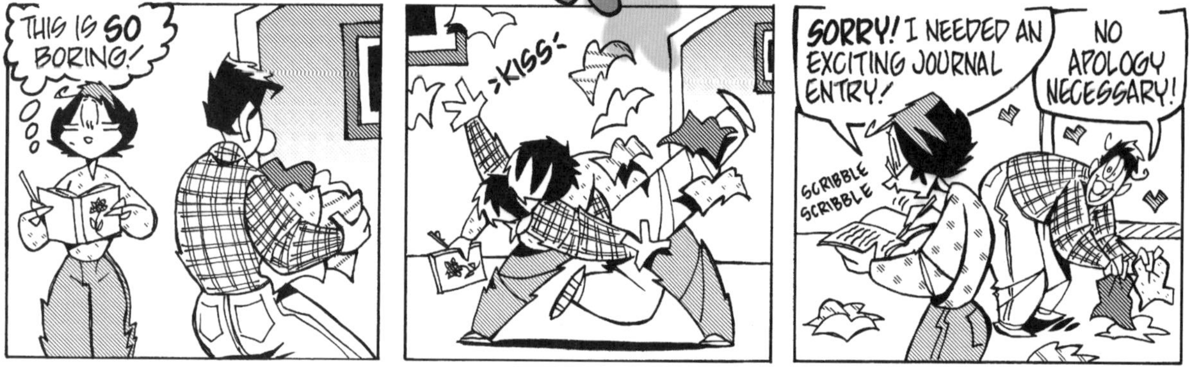
THIS IS **SO** BORING!
KISS
SORRY! I NEEDED AN EXCITING JOURNAL ENTRY!
NO APOLOGY NECESSARY!
SCRIBBLE SCRIBBLE

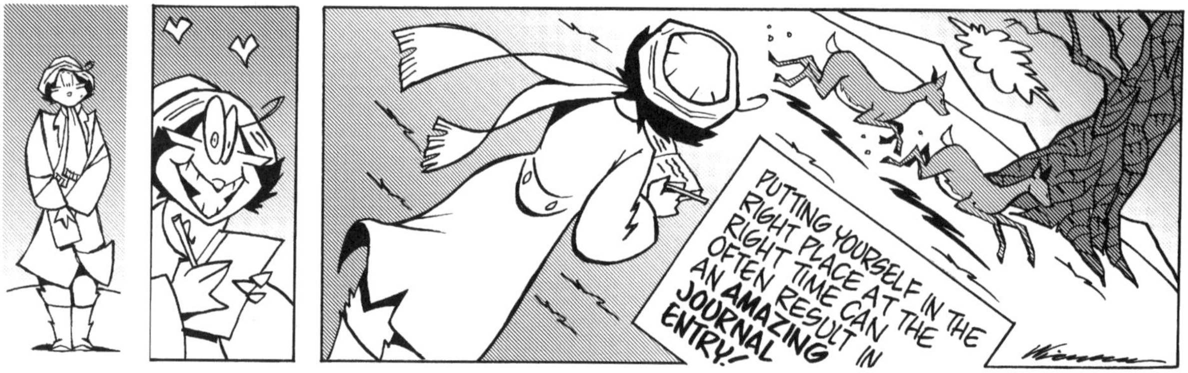
PUTTING YOURSELF IN THE RIGHT PLACE AT THE RIGHT TIME CAN OFTEN RESULT IN AN **AMAZING JOURNAL ENTRY!**

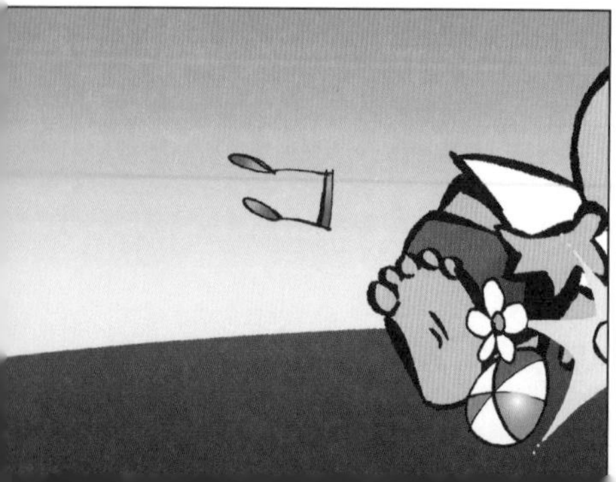

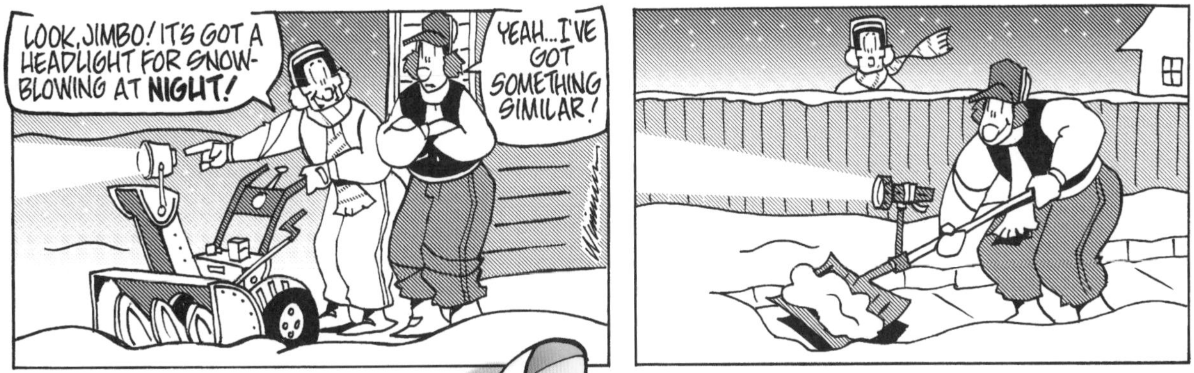
LOOK, JIMBO! IT'S GOT A HEADLIGHT FOR SNOW-BLOWING AT **NIGHT**!
YEAH...I'VE GOT SOMETHING SIMILAR!

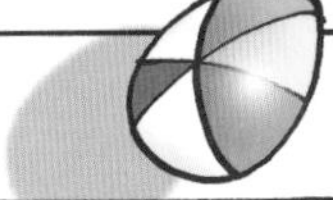

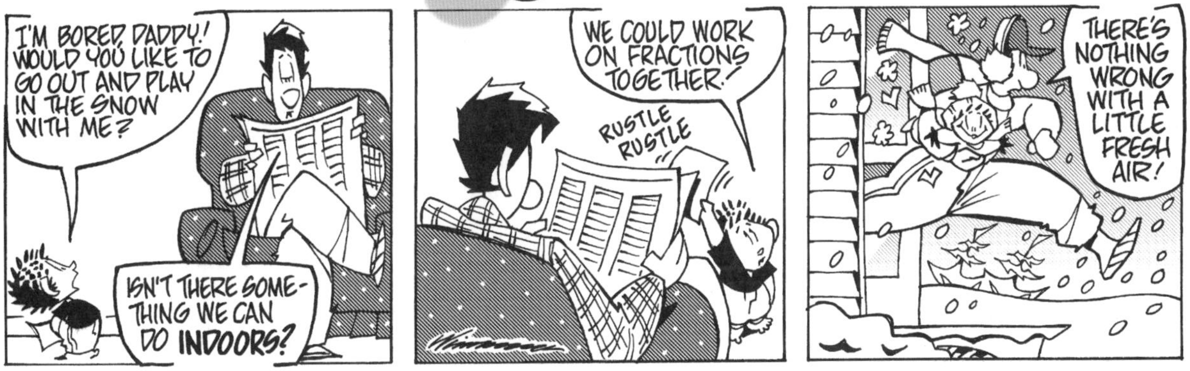
I'M BORED, DADDY! WOULD YOU LIKE TO GO OUT AND PLAY IN THE SNOW WITH ME?
ISN'T THERE SOME-THING WE CAN DO **INDOORS?**
WE COULD WORK ON FRACTIONS TOGETHER!
RUSTLE RUSTLE
THERE'S NOTHING WRONG WITH A LITTLE FRESH AIR!

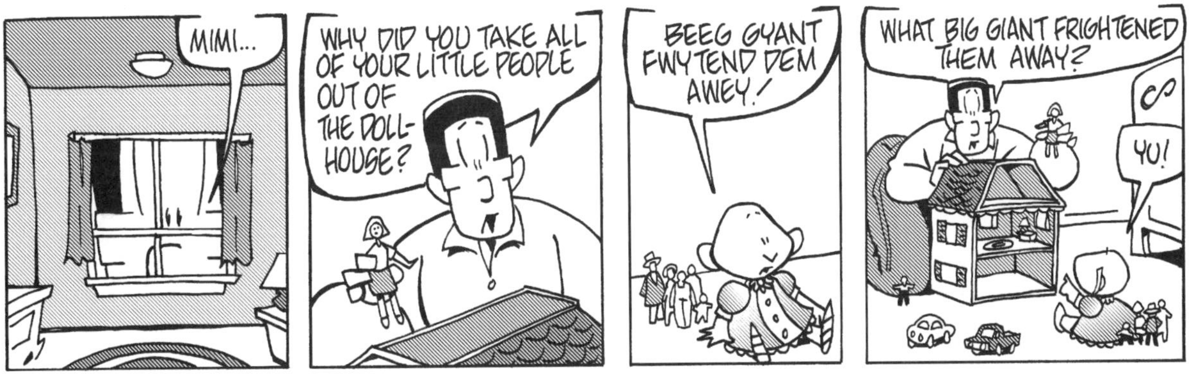
MIMI...
WHY DID YOU TAKE ALL OF YOUR LITTLE PEOPLE OUT OF THE DOLL-HOUSE?
BEEG GYANT FWYTEND DEM AWEY!
WHAT BIG GIANT FRIGHTENED THEM AWAY?
YU!

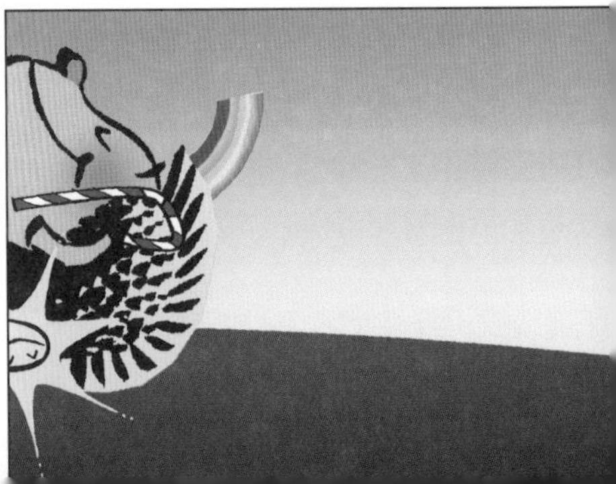

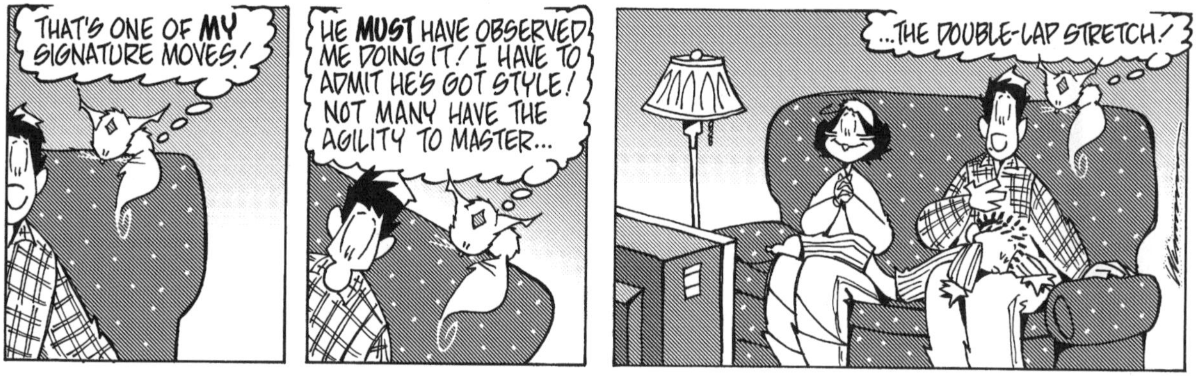
THAT'S ONE OF **MY** SIGNATURE MOVES!
HE **MUST** HAVE OBSERVED ME DOING IT! I HAVE TO ADMIT HE'S GOT STYLE! NOT MANY HAVE THE AGILITY TO MASTER...
...THE DOUBLE-LAP STRETCH!

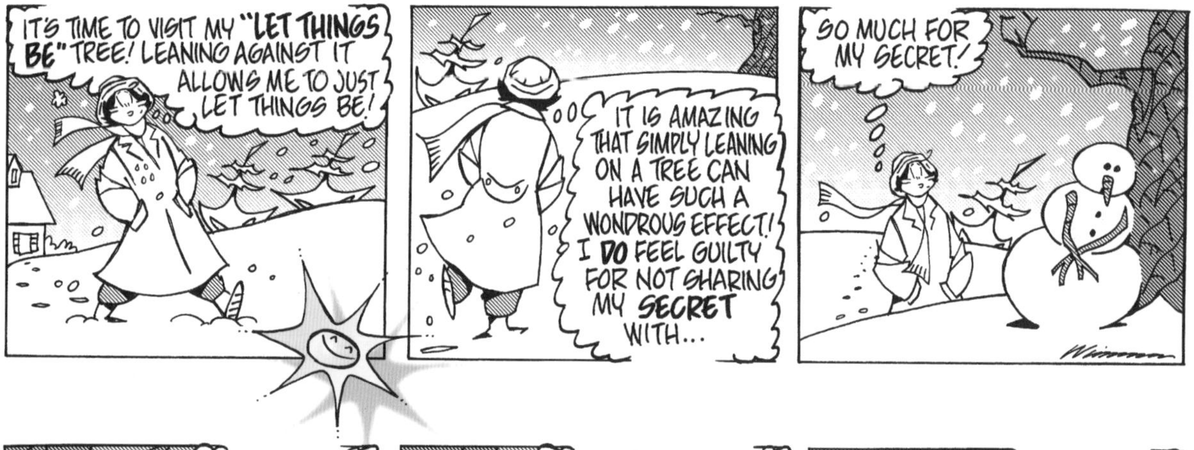
IT'S TIME TO VISIT MY **"LET THINGS BE"** TREE! LEANING AGAINST IT ALLOWS ME TO JUST LET THINGS BE!
IT IS AMAZING THAT SIMPLY LEANING ON A TREE CAN HAVE SUCH A WONDROUS EFFECT! I **DO** FEEL GUILTY FOR NOT SHARING MY **SECRET** WITH...
SO MUCH FOR MY SECRET!

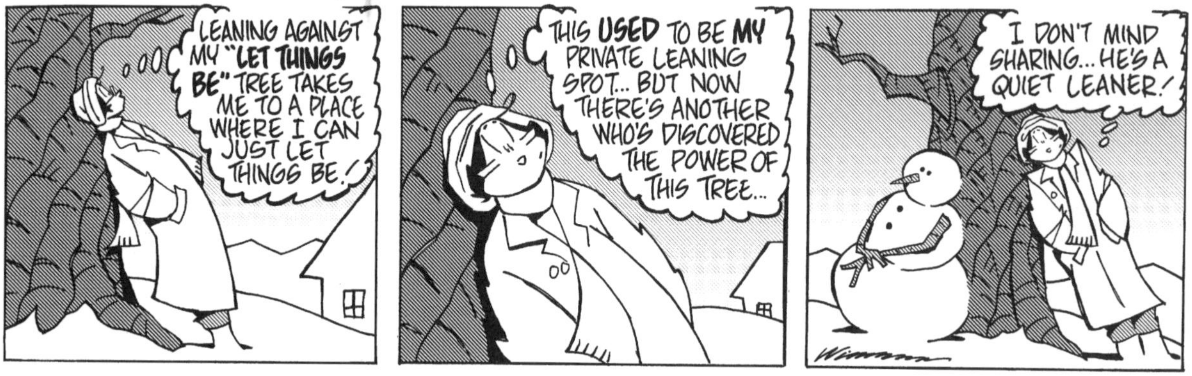
LEANING AGAINST MY **"LET THINGS BE"** TREE TAKES ME TO A PLACE WHERE I CAN JUST LET THINGS BE!
THIS **USED** TO BE **MY** PRIVATE LEANING SPOT... BUT NOW THERE'S ANOTHER WHO'S DISCOVERED THE POWER OF THIS TREE...
I DON'T MIND SHARING... HE'S A QUIET LEANER!

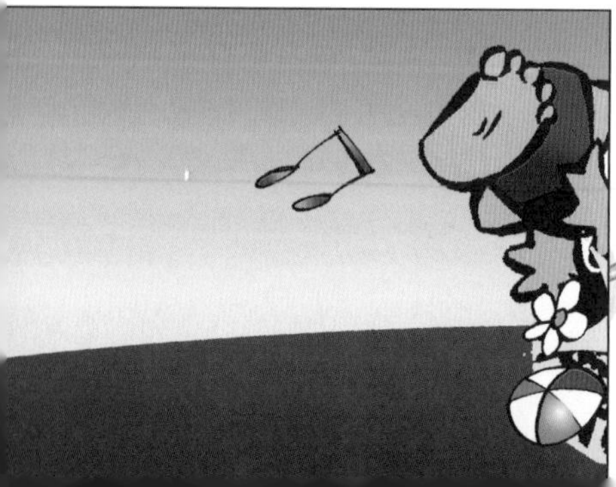

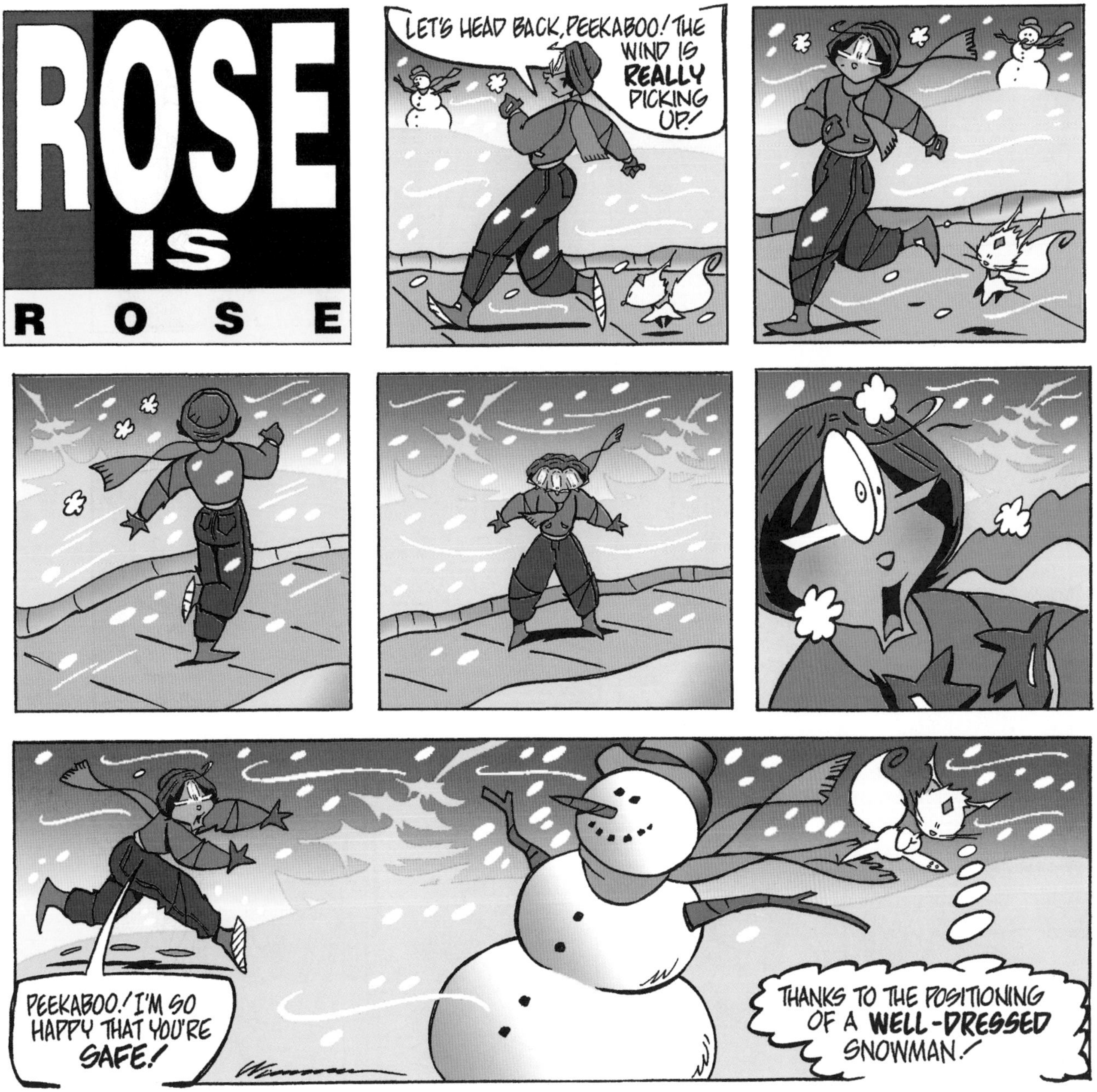
ROSE IS ROSE
LET'S HEAD BACK, PEEKABOO! THE WIND IS **REALLY** PICKING UP!
PEEKABOO! I'M SO HAPPY THAT YOU'RE **SAFE!**
THANKS TO THE POSITIONING OF A **WELL-DRESSED** SNOWMAN!

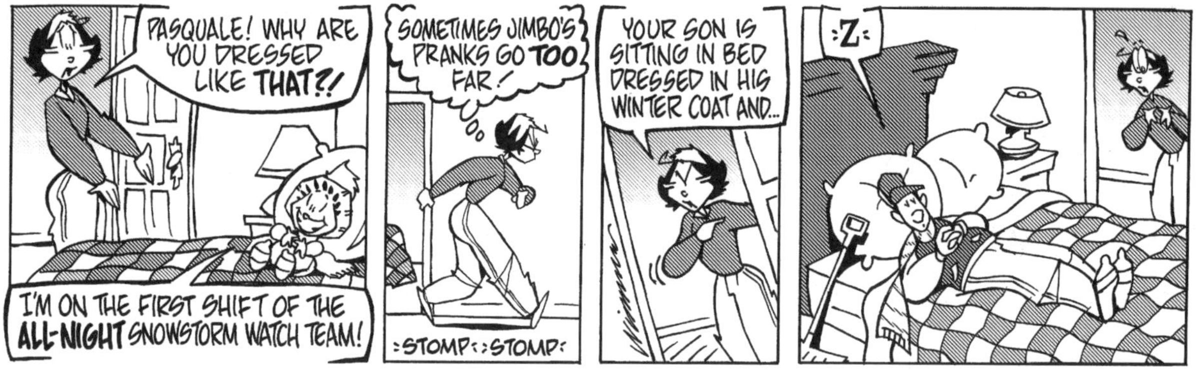
PASQUALE! WHY ARE YOU DRESSED LIKE THAT?!
I'M ON THE FIRST SHIFT OF THE ALL-NIGHT SNOWSTORM WATCH TEAM!
SOMETIMES JIMBO'S PRANKS GO TOO FAR!
STOMP STOMP
YOUR SON IS SITTING IN BED DRESSED IN HIS WINTER COAT AND...
Z

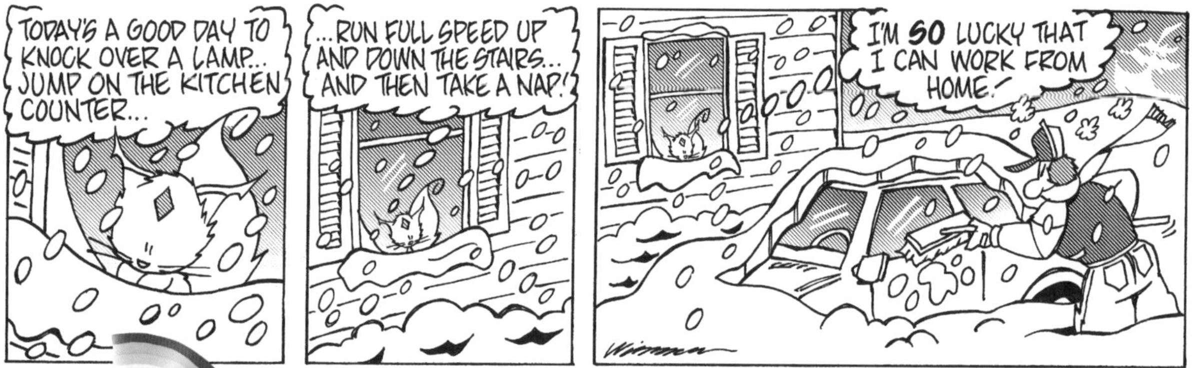
TODAY'S A GOOD DAY TO KNOCK OVER A LAMP... JUMP ON THE KITCHEN COUNTER...
...RUN FULL SPEED UP AND DOWN THE STAIRS... AND THEN TAKE A NAP!
I'M SO LUCKY THAT I CAN WORK FROM HOME!

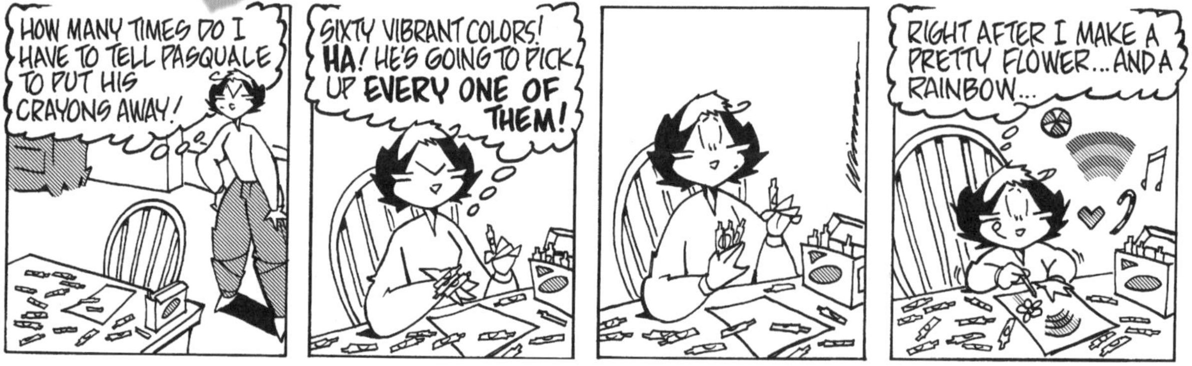
HOW MANY TIMES DO I HAVE TO TELL PASQUALE TO PUT HIS CRAYONS AWAY!
SIXTY VIBRANT COLORS! HA! HE'S GOING TO PICK UP EVERY ONE OF THEM!
RIGHT AFTER I MAKE A PRETTY FLOWER... AND A RAINBOW...

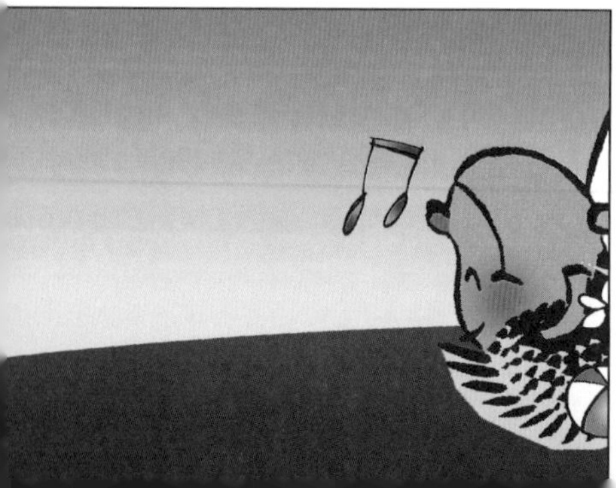

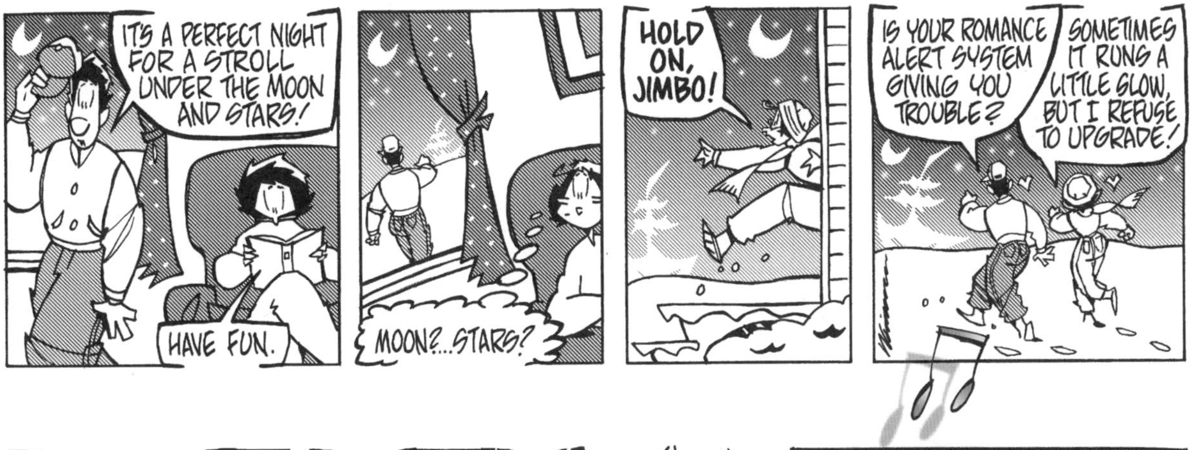
IT'S A PERFECT NIGHT FOR A STROLL UNDER THE MOON AND STARS!
HAVE FUN.
MOON?...STARS?
HOLD ON, JIMBO!
IS YOUR ROMANCE ALERT SYSTEM GIVING YOU TROUBLE?
SOMETIMES IT RUNS A LITTLE SLOW, BUT I REFUSE TO UPGRADE!

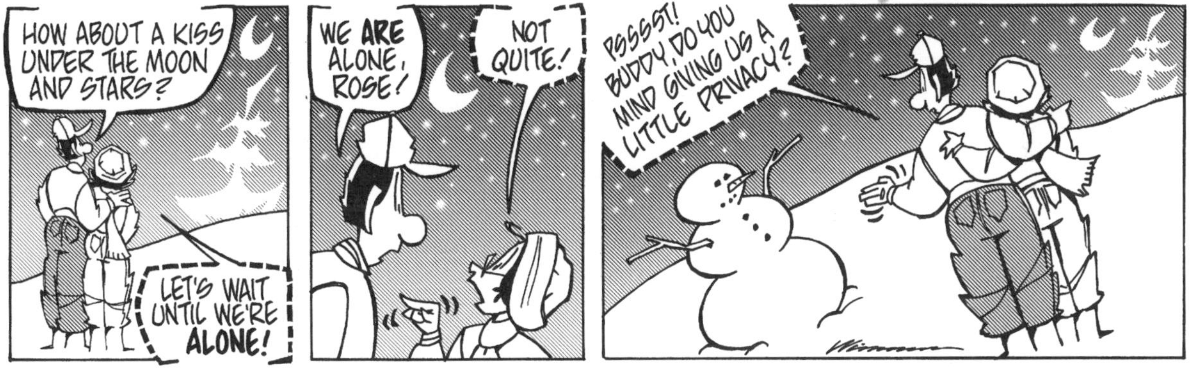
HOW ABOUT A KISS UNDER THE MOON AND STARS?
LET'S WAIT UNTIL WE'RE **ALONE!**
WE **ARE** ALONE, ROSE!
NOT QUITE!
PSSSST! BUDDY, DO YOU MIND GIVING US A LITTLE PRIVACY?

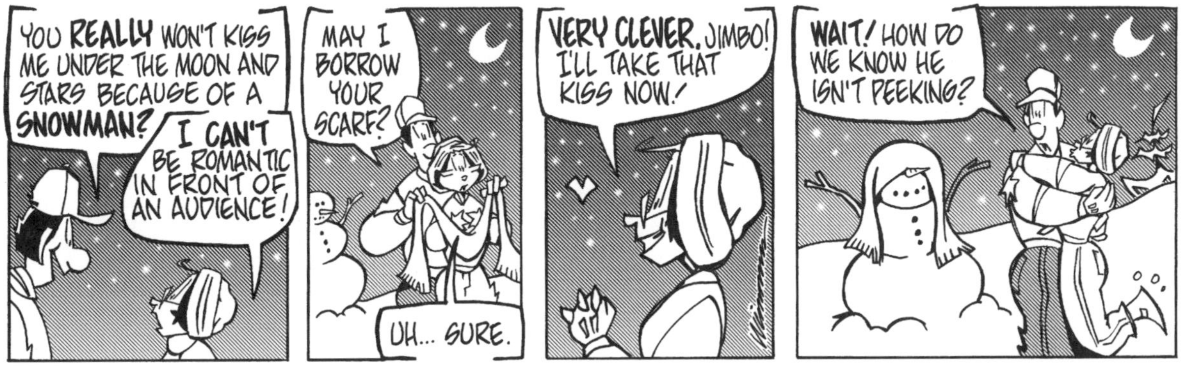
YOU **REALLY** WON'T KISS ME UNDER THE MOON AND STARS BECAUSE OF A **SNOWMAN?**
I CAN'T BE ROMANTIC IN FRONT OF AN AUDIENCE!
MAY I BORROW YOUR SCARF?
UH... SURE.
VERY CLEVER, JIMBO! I'LL TAKE THAT KISS NOW!
WAIT! HOW DO WE KNOW HE ISN'T PEEKING?

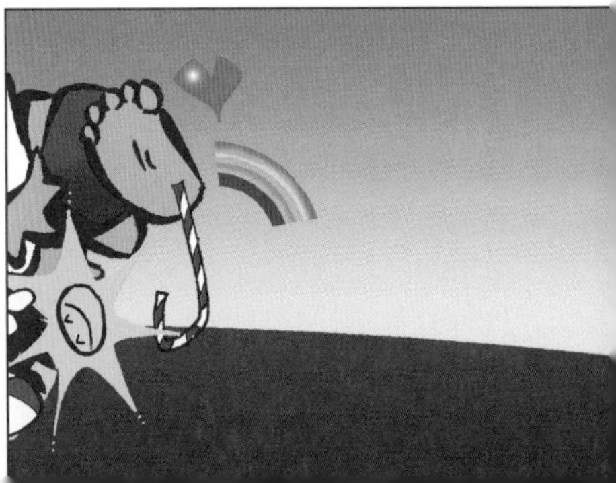

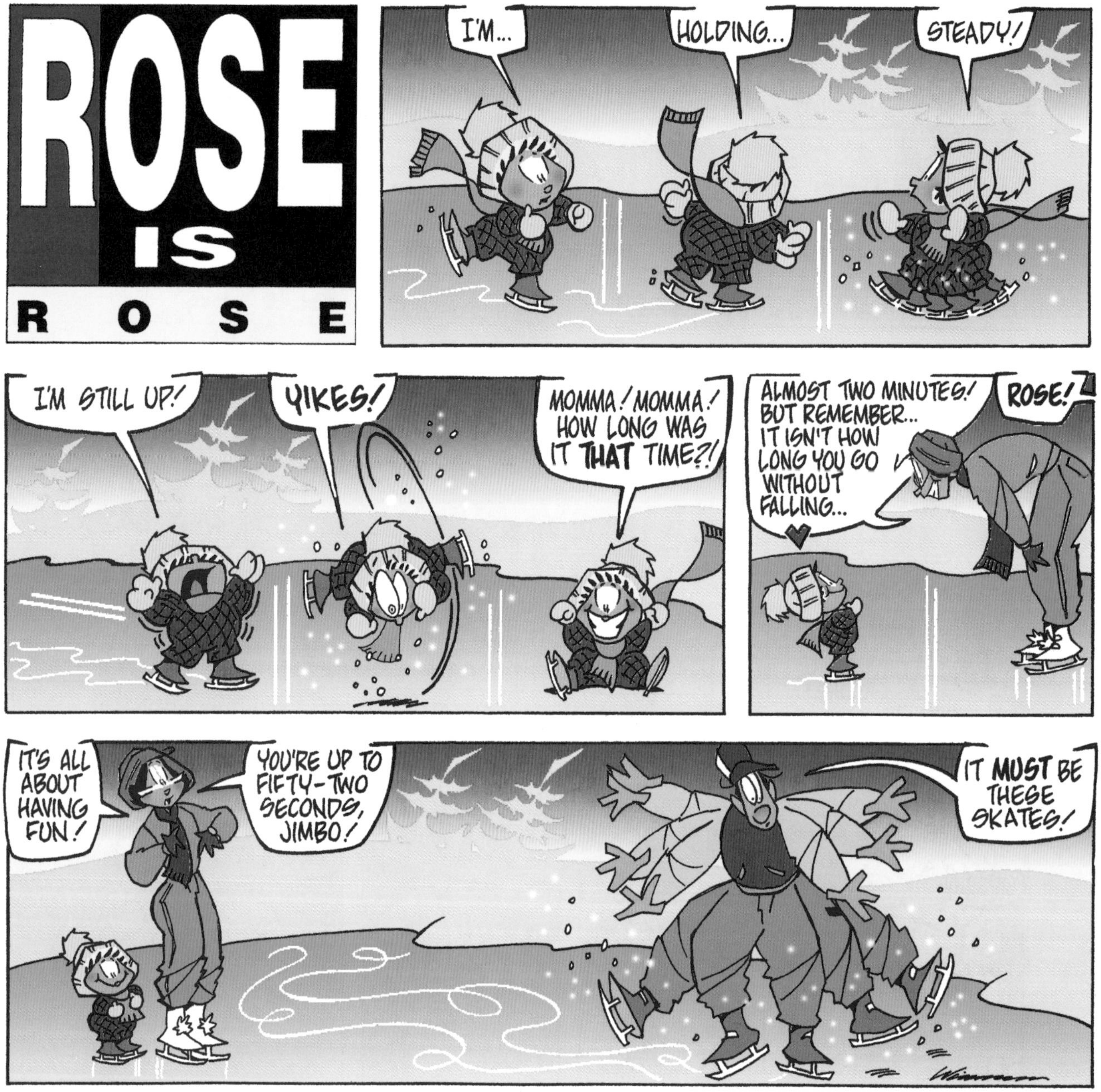
ROSE IS ROSE
I'M...
HOLDING...
STEADY!
I'M STILL UP!
YIKES!
MOMMA! MOMMA! HOW LONG WAS IT THAT TIME?!
ALMOST TWO MINUTES! BUT REMEMBER... IT ISN'T HOW LONG YOU GO WITHOUT FALLING...
ROSE!
IT'S ALL ABOUT HAVING FUN!
YOU'RE UP TO FIFTY-TWO SECONDS, JIMBO!
IT MUST BE THESE SKATES!

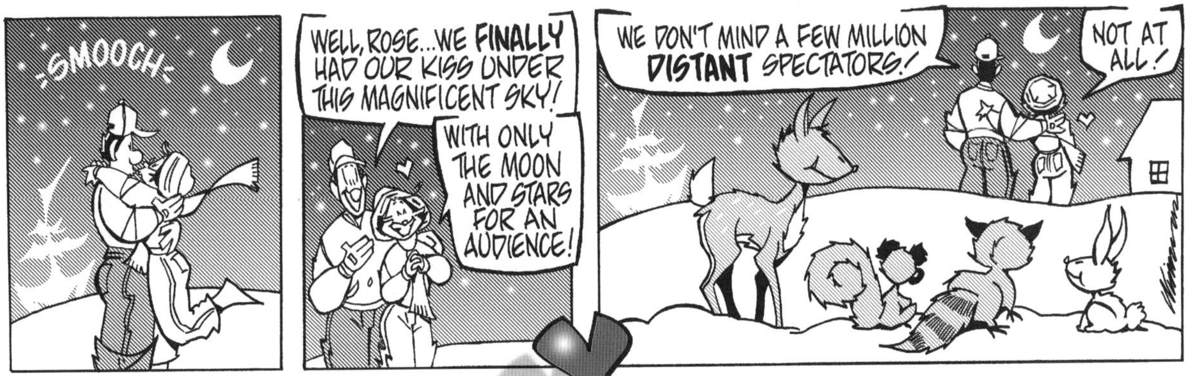
SMOOCH
WELL, ROSE... WE FINALLY HAD OUR KISS UNDER THIS MAGNIFICENT SKY!
WITH ONLY THE MOON AND STARS FOR AN AUDIENCE!
WE DON'T MIND A FEW MILLION DISTANT SPECTATORS!
NOT AT ALL!

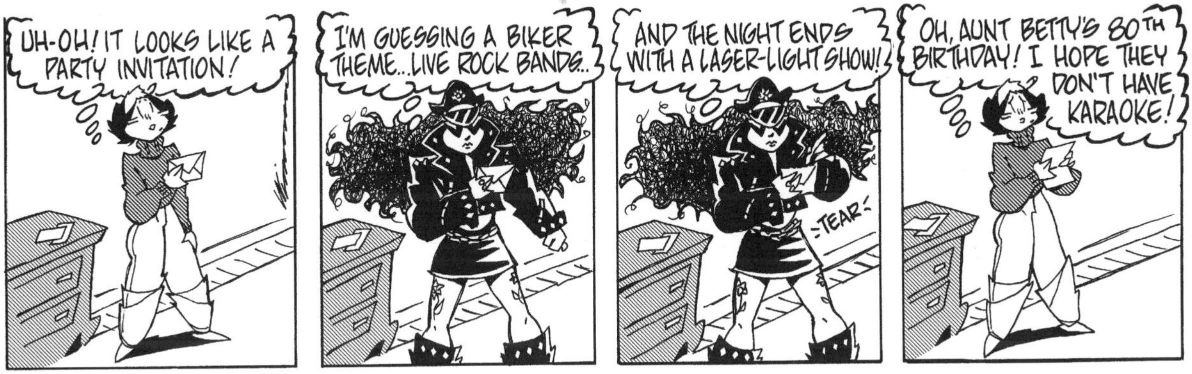
UH-OH! IT LOOKS LIKE A PARTY INVITATION!
I'M GUESSING A BIKER THEME... LIVE ROCK BANDS...
AND THE NIGHT ENDS WITH A LASER-LIGHT SHOW!
TEAR
OH, AUNT BETTY'S 80TH BIRTHDAY! I HOPE THEY DON'T HAVE KARAOKE!

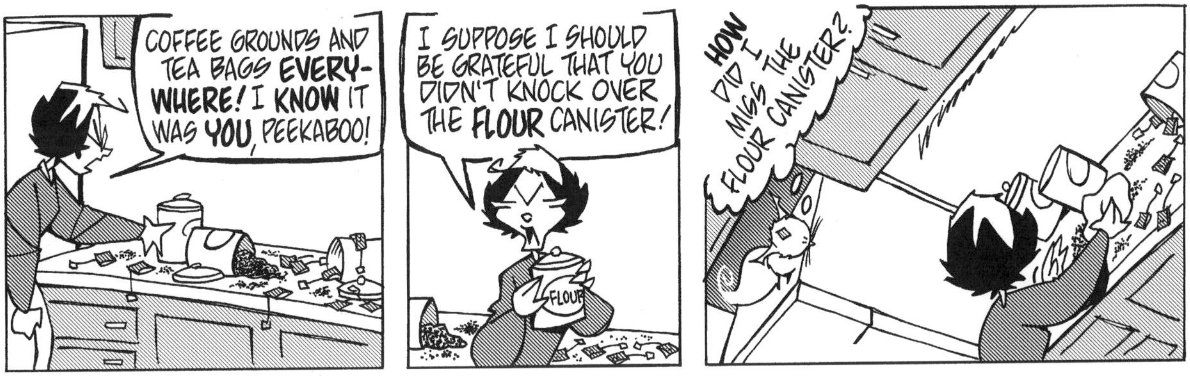
COFFEE GROUNDS AND TEA BAGS EVERY-WHERE! I KNOW IT WAS YOU, PEEKABOO!
I SUPPOSE I SHOULD BE GRATEFUL THAT YOU DIDN'T KNOCK OVER THE FLOUR CANISTER!
FLOUR
HOW DID I MISS THE FLOUR CANISTER?

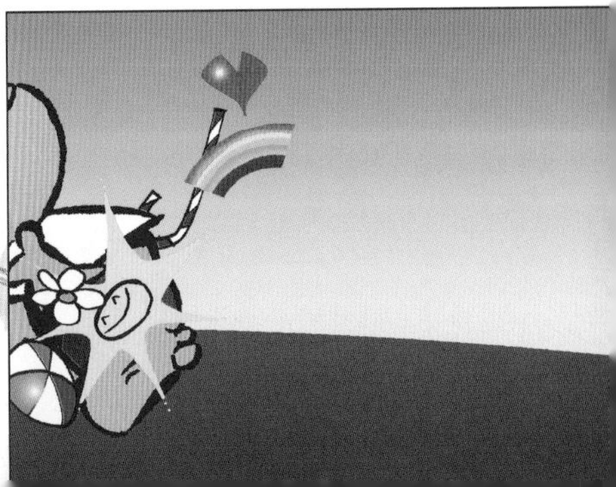

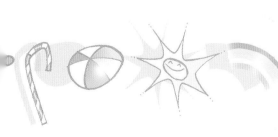

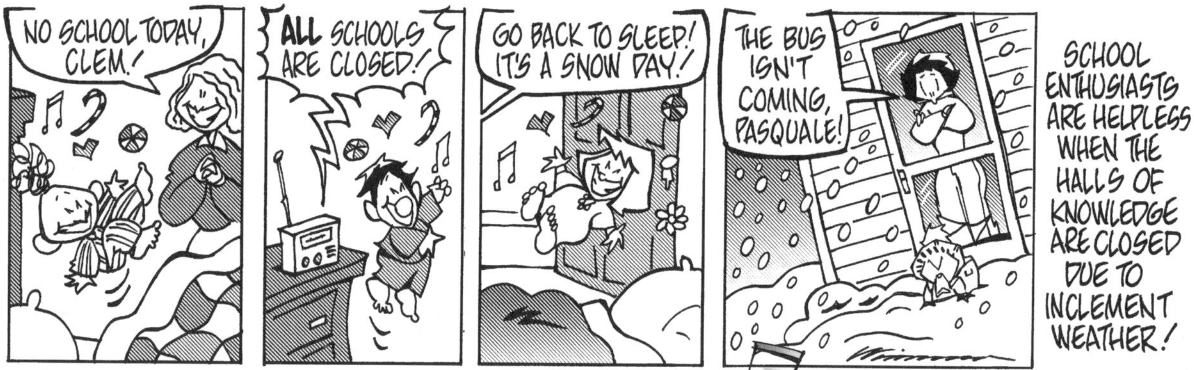
NO SCHOOL TODAY, CLEM!
ALL SCHOOLS ARE CLOSED!
GO BACK TO SLEEP! IT'S A SNOW DAY!
THE BUS ISN'T COMING, PASQUALE!
SCHOOL ENTHUSIASTS ARE HELPLESS WHEN THE HALLS OF KNOWLEDGE ARE CLOSED DUE TO INCLEMENT WEATHER!

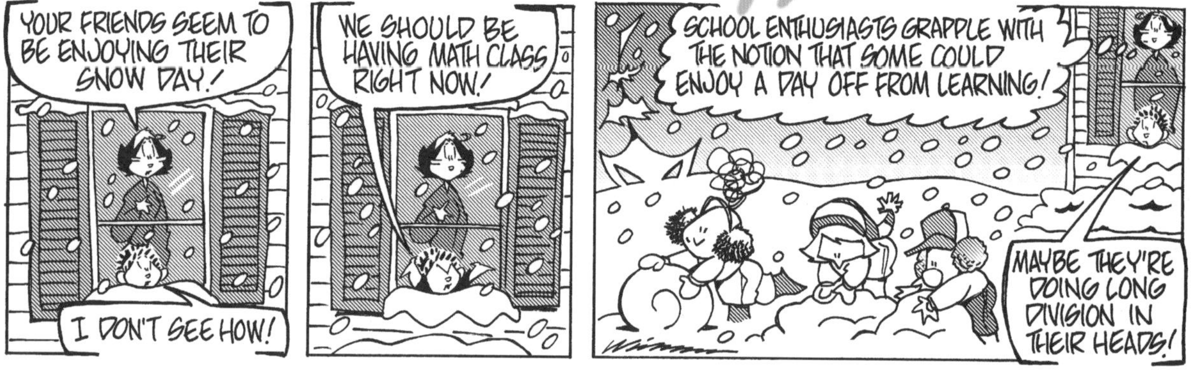
YOUR FRIENDS SEEM TO BE ENJOYING THEIR SNOW DAY!
I DON'T SEE HOW!
WE SHOULD BE HAVING MATH CLASS RIGHT NOW!
SCHOOL ENTHUSIASTS GRAPPLE WITH THE NOTION THAT SOME COULD ENJOY A DAY OFF FROM LEARNING!
MAYBE THEY'RE DOING LONG DIVISION IN THEIR HEADS!

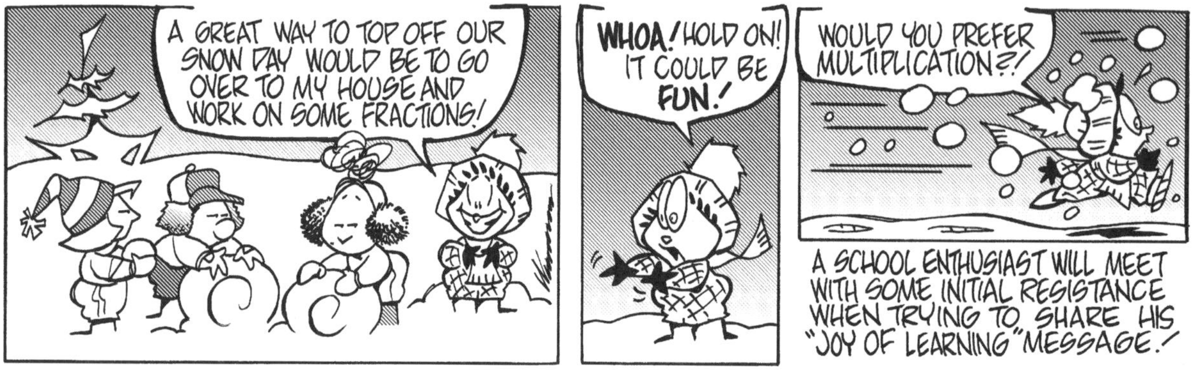
A GREAT WAY TO TOP OFF OUR SNOW DAY WOULD BE TO GO OVER TO MY HOUSE AND WORK ON SOME FRACTIONS!
WHOA! HOLD ON! IT COULD BE FUN!
WOULD YOU PREFER MULTIPLICATION?!
A SCHOOL ENTHUSIAST WILL MEET WITH SOME INITIAL RESISTANCE WHEN TRYING TO SHARE HIS "JOY OF LEARNING" MESSAGE!

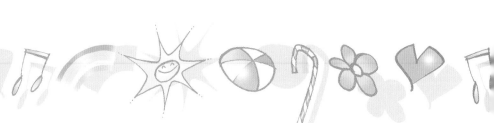

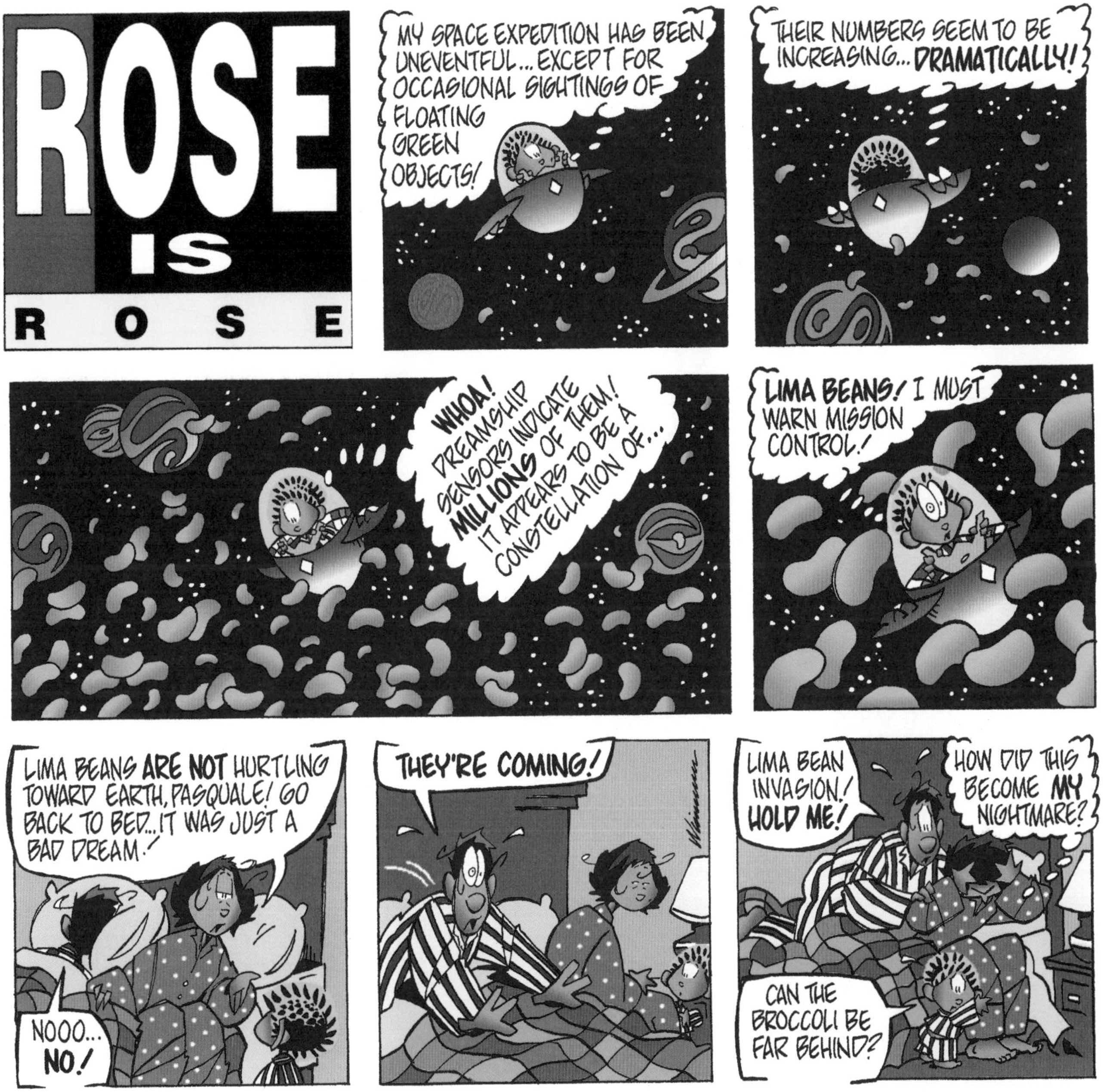
ROSE IS ROSE
MY SPACE EXPEDITION HAS BEEN UNEVENTFUL... EXCEPT FOR OCCASIONAL SIGHTINGS OF FLOATING GREEN OBJECTS!
THEIR NUMBERS SEEM TO BE INCREASING... DRAMATICALLY!
WHOA! DREAMSHIP SENSORS INDICATE MILLIONS OF THEM! IT APPEARS TO BE A CONSTELLATION OF...
LIMA BEANS! I MUST WARN MISSION CONTROL!
LIMA BEANS ARE NOT HURTLING TOWARD EARTH, PASQUALE! GO BACK TO BED... IT WAS JUST A BAD DREAM!
NOOO... NO!
THEY'RE COMING!
LIMA BEAN INVASION! HOLD ME!
HOW DID THIS BECOME MY NIGHTMARE?
CAN THE BROCCOLI BE FAR BEHIND?

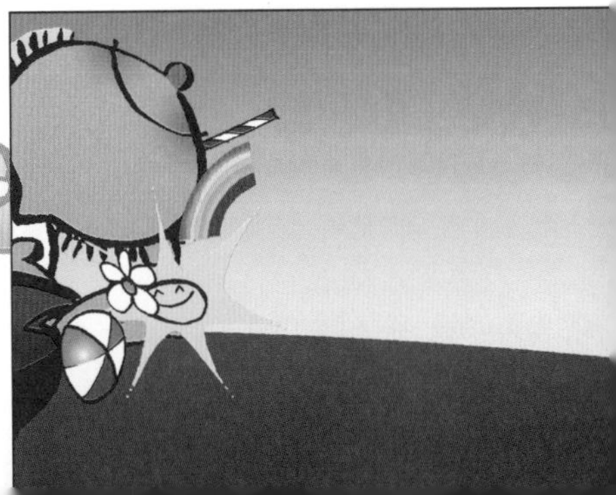

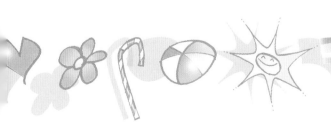

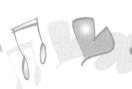

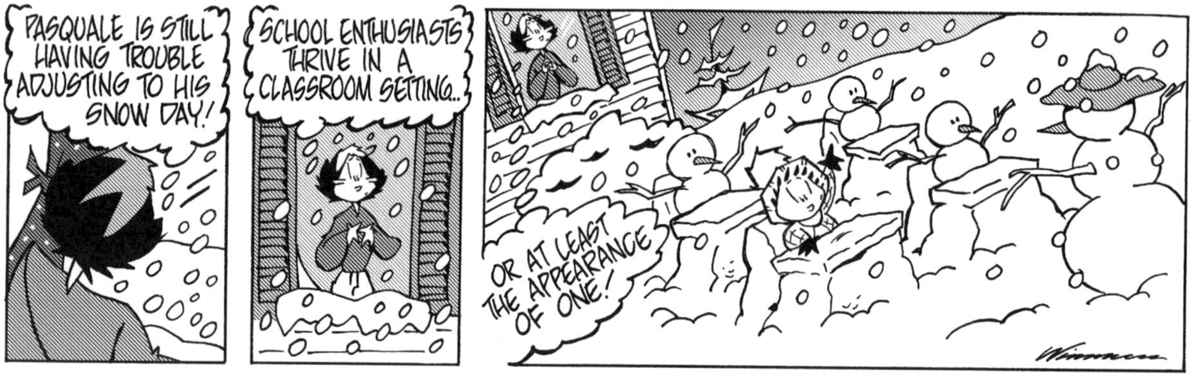
PASQUALE IS STILL HAVING TROUBLE ADJUSTING TO HIS SNOW DAY!
SCHOOL ENTHUSIASTS THRIVE IN A CLASSROOM SETTING...
OR AT LEAST THE APPEARANCE OF ONE!

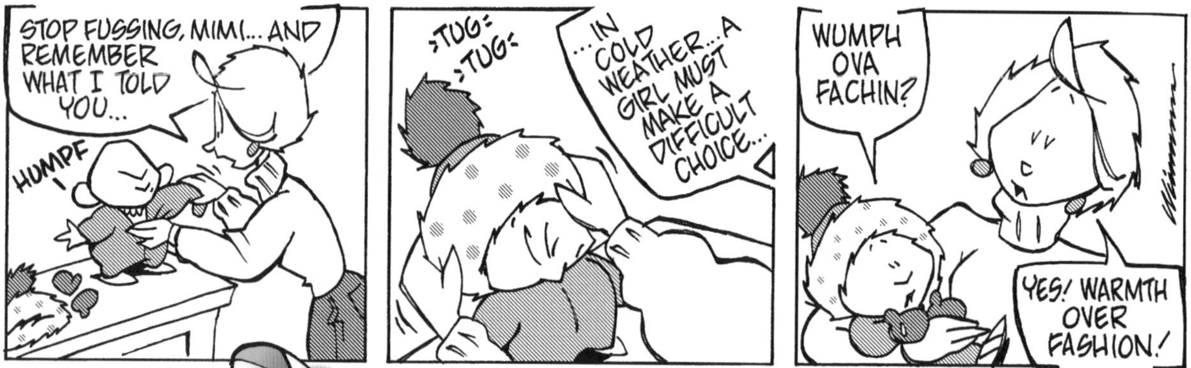
STOP FUSSING, MIMI... AND REMEMBER WHAT I TOLD YOU...
HUMPF
TUG
TUG
...IN COLD WEATHER...A GIRL MUST MAKE A DIFFICULT CHOICE...
WUMPH OVA FACHIN?
YES! WARMTH OVER FASHION!

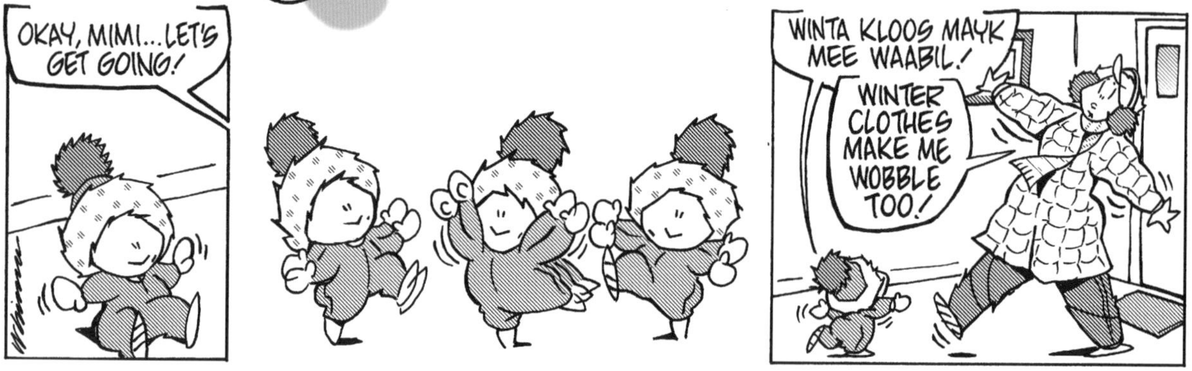
OKAY, MIMI...LET'S GET GOING!
WINTA KLOOS MAYK MEE WAABIL!
WINTER CLOTHES MAKE ME WOBBLE TOO!

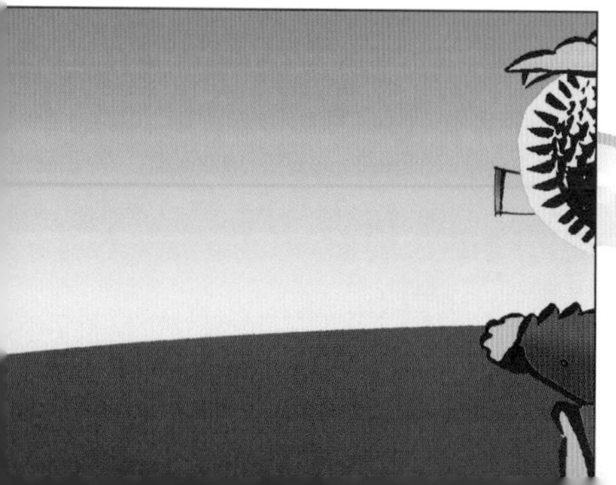

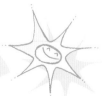

A SKILLED WINTER BARBECUER IS ABLE TO IGNITE A GRILL **IN BLIZZARD CONDITIONS** USING ONLY TWENTY-SEVEN BOOKS OF MATCHES!

WHY DOESN'T DADDY COME INSIDE INSTEAD OF FREEZING?

HIS SENSE OF HONOR WON'T LET HIM LEAVE AN IGNITED GRILL!

AND THE FUNNY DANCE?

WINTER BARBECUERS REFER TO IT AS THE "CIRCULATION TWO-STEP"!

CHATTER CHATTER

PAT PAT

STOMP STOMP

JIMBO! YOU MUST BE **FREEZING!** ABBY MADE YOU A CUP OF COFFEE!

OH, THANK YOU, CORKY!

CHATTER

WE COULDN'T BELIEVE YOU WERE BARBECUING IN THIS WEATHER!

UMMM!

-SIP-

SO WE FIGURED YOU WOULDN'T MIND COOKING US A FEW VEGGIE BURGERS!

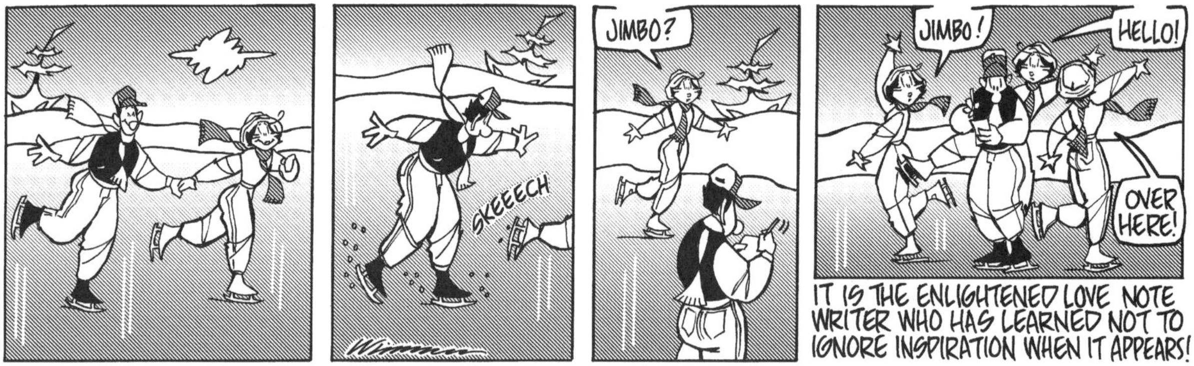
SKEEECH
JIMBO?
JIMBO!
HELLO!
OVER HERE!
IT IS THE ENLIGHTENED LOVE NOTE WRITER WHO HAS LEARNED NOT TO IGNORE INSPIRATION WHEN IT APPEARS!

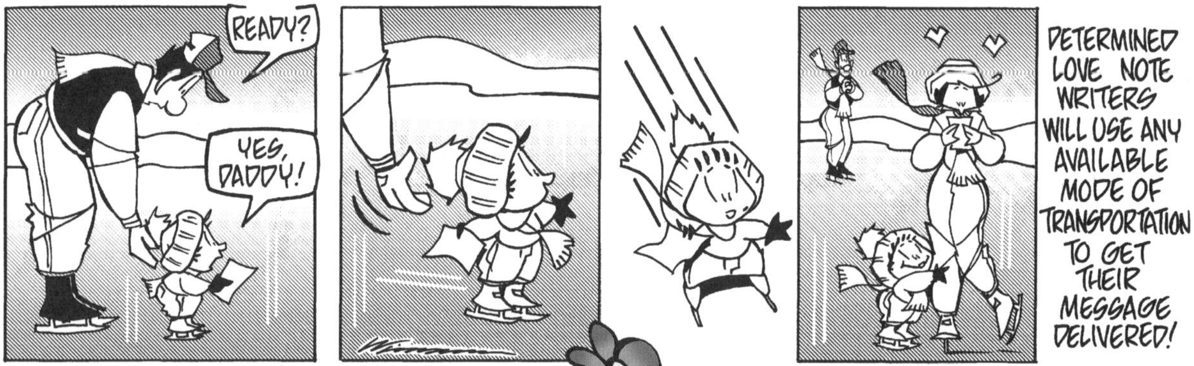
READY?
YES, DADDY!
DETERMINED LOVE NOTE WRITERS WILL USE ANY AVAILABLE MODE OF TRANSPORTATION TO GET THEIR MESSAGE DELIVERED!

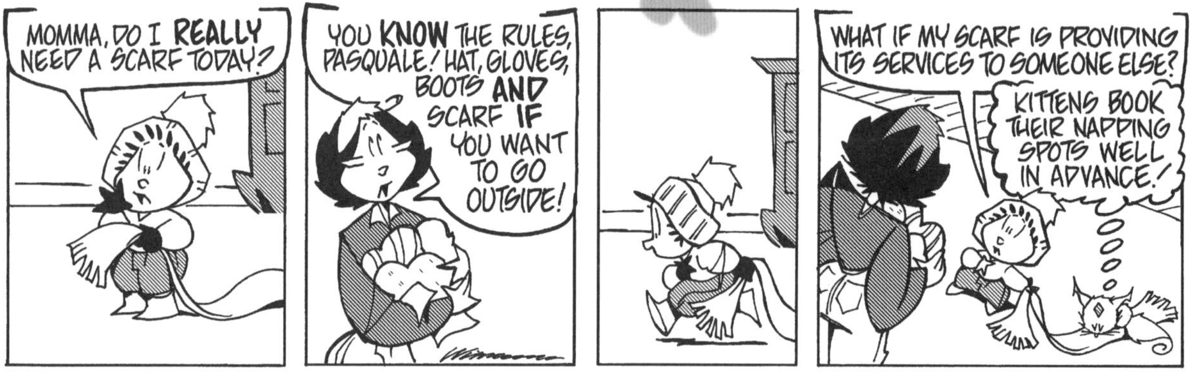
MOMMA, DO I **REALLY** NEED A SCARF TODAY?
YOU **KNOW** THE RULES, PASQUALE! HAT, GLOVES, BOOTS **AND** SCARF **IF** YOU WANT TO GO OUTSIDE!
WHAT IF MY SCARF IS PROVIDING ITS SERVICES TO SOMEONE ELSE?
KITTENS BOOK THEIR NAPPING SPOTS WELL IN ADVANCE!

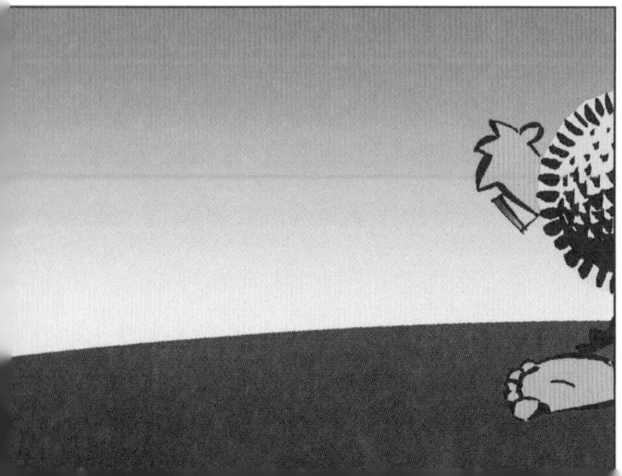

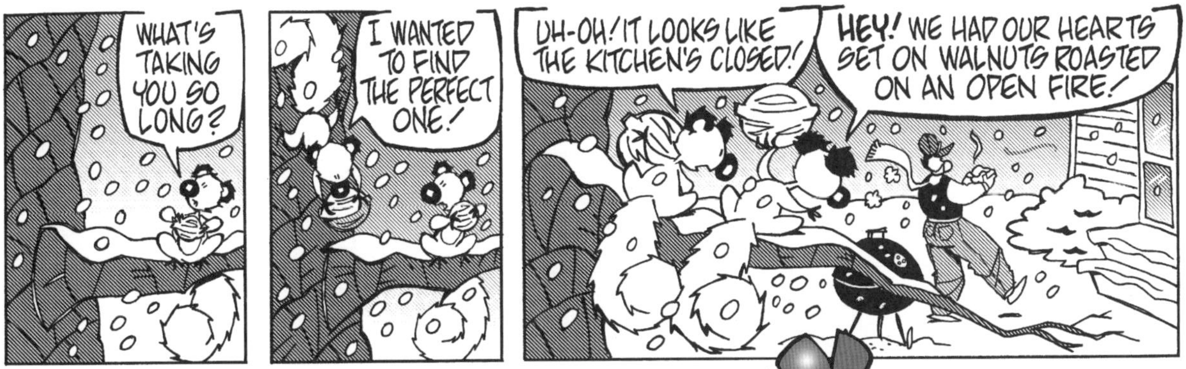
WHAT'S TAKING YOU SO LONG?
I WANTED TO FIND THE PERFECT ONE!
UH-OH! IT LOOKS LIKE THE KITCHEN'S CLOSED!
HEY! WE HAD OUR HEARTS SET ON WALNUTS ROASTED ON AN OPEN FIRE!

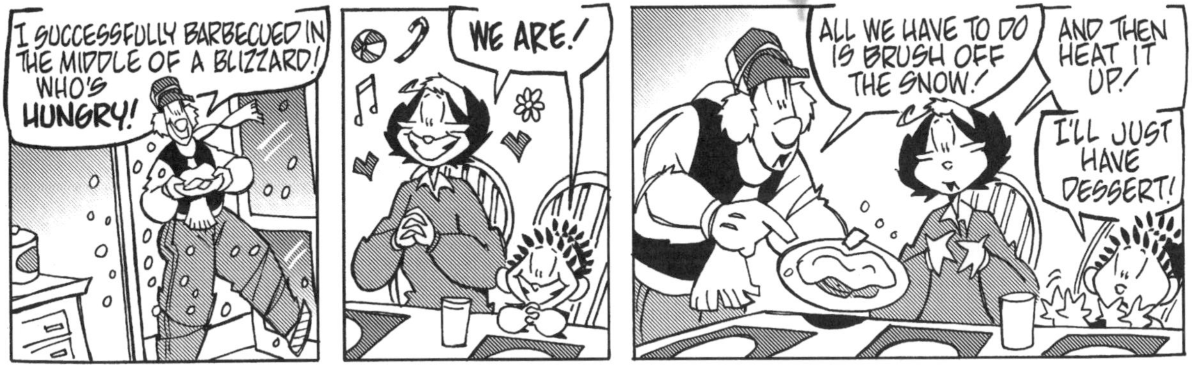
I SUCCESSFULLY BARBECUED IN THE MIDDLE OF A BLIZZARD! WHO'S HUNGRY!
WE ARE!
ALL WE HAVE TO DO IS BRUSH OFF THE SNOW!
AND THEN HEAT IT UP!
I'LL JUST HAVE DESSERT!

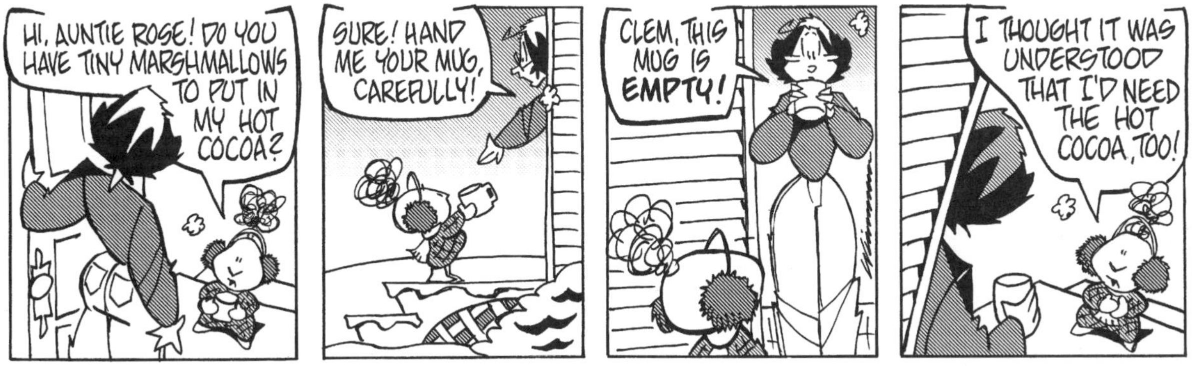
HI, AUNTIE ROSE! DO YOU HAVE TINY MARSHMALLOWS TO PUT IN MY HOT COCOA?
SURE! HAND ME YOUR MUG, CAREFULLY!
CLEM, THIS MUG IS EMPTY!
I THOUGHT IT WAS UNDERSTOOD THAT I'D NEED THE HOT COCOA, TOO!

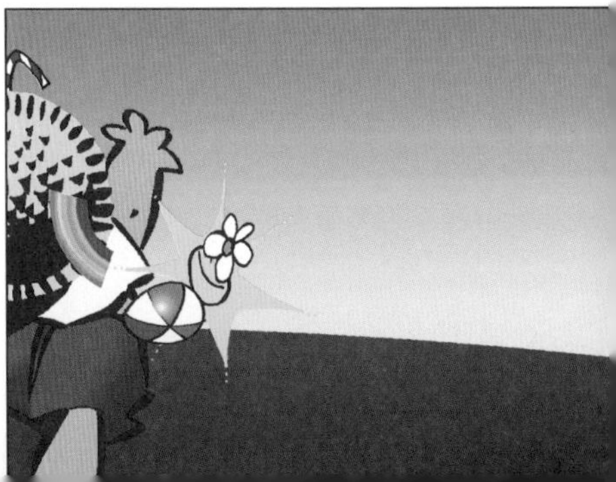

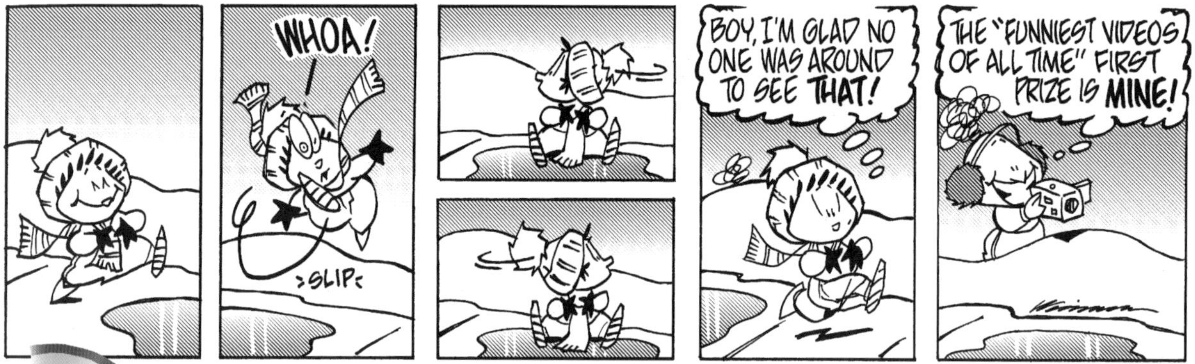
WHOA!
SLIP
BOY, I'M GLAD NO ONE WAS AROUND TO SEE **THAT**!
THE "FUNNIEST VIDEOS OF ALL TIME" FIRST PRIZE IS **MINE**!

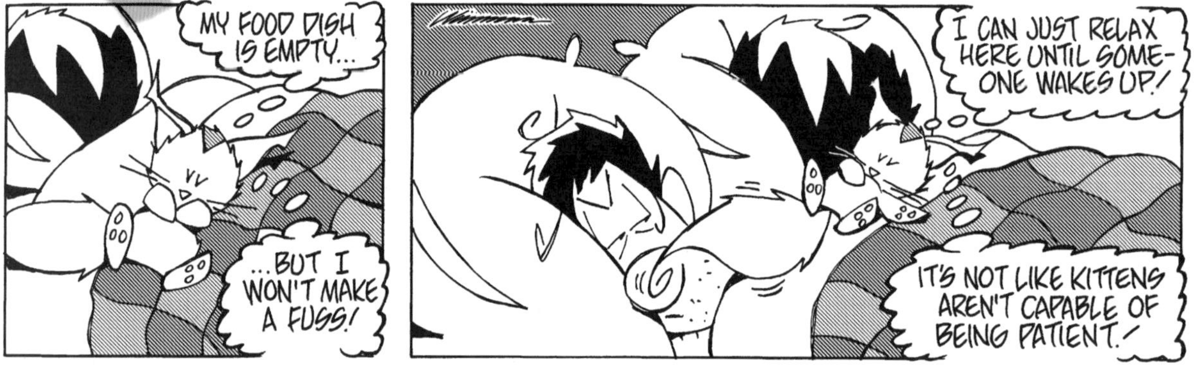
MY FOOD DISH IS EMPTY...
...BUT I WON'T MAKE A FUSS!
I CAN JUST RELAX HERE UNTIL SOME-ONE WAKES UP!
IT'S NOT LIKE KITTENS AREN'T CAPABLE OF BEING PATIENT!

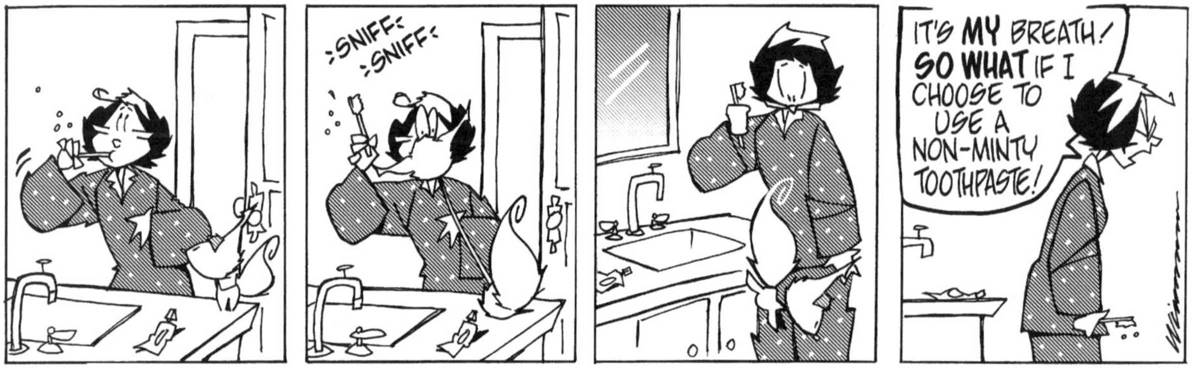
SNIFF
SNIFF
IT'S **MY** BREATH! **SO WHAT** IF I CHOOSE TO USE A NON-MINTY TOOTHPASTE!

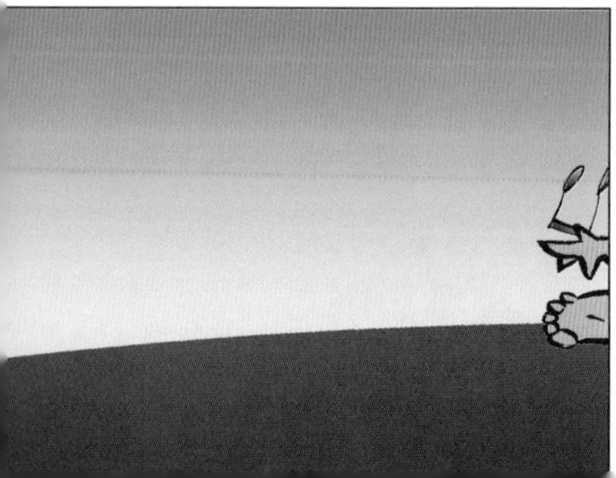

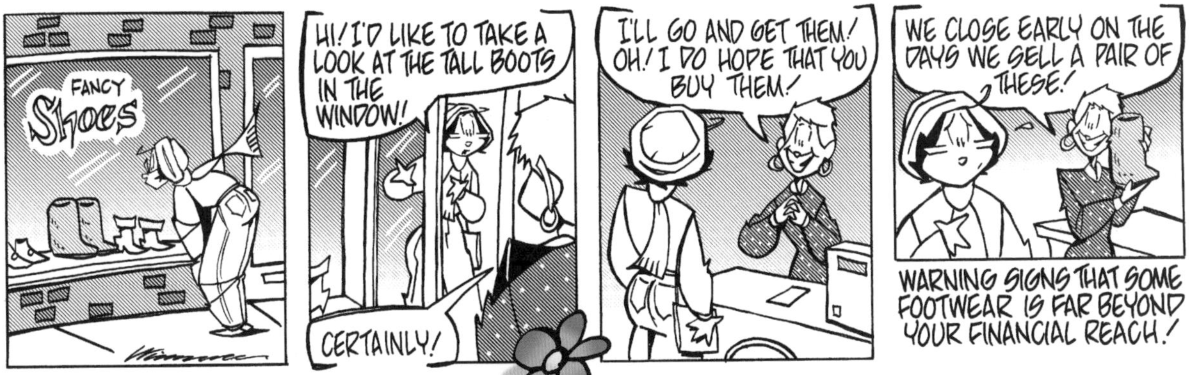
FANCY Shoes
HI! I'D LIKE TO TAKE A LOOK AT THE TALL BOOTS IN THE WINDOW!
CERTAINLY!
I'LL GO AND GET THEM! OH! I DO HOPE THAT YOU BUY THEM!
WE CLOSE EARLY ON THE DAYS WE SELL A PAIR OF THESE!
WARNING SIGNS THAT SOME FOOTWEAR IS FAR BEYOND YOUR FINANCIAL REACH!

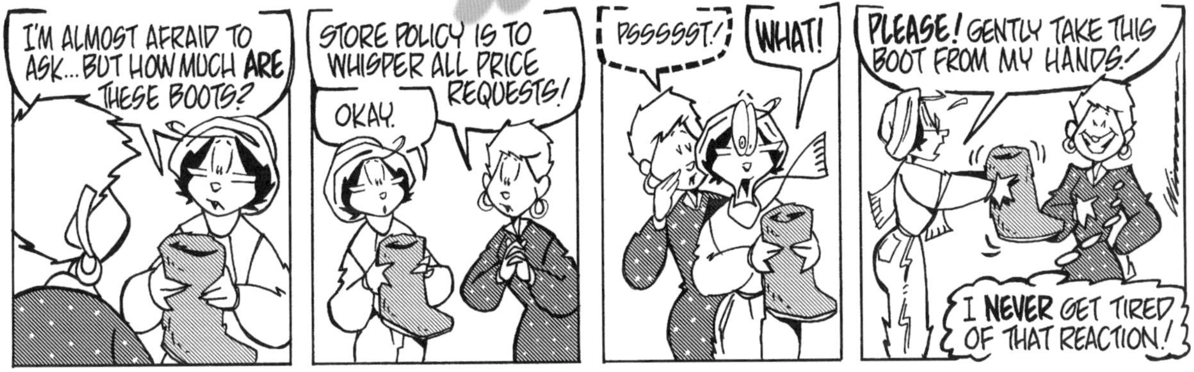
I'M ALMOST AFRAID TO ASK... BUT HOW MUCH **ARE** THESE BOOTS?
STORE POLICY IS TO WHISPER ALL PRICE REQUESTS!
OKAY.
PSSSSST!
WHAT!
PLEASE! GENTLY TAKE THIS BOOT FROM MY HANDS!
I **NEVER** GET TIRED OF THAT REACTION!

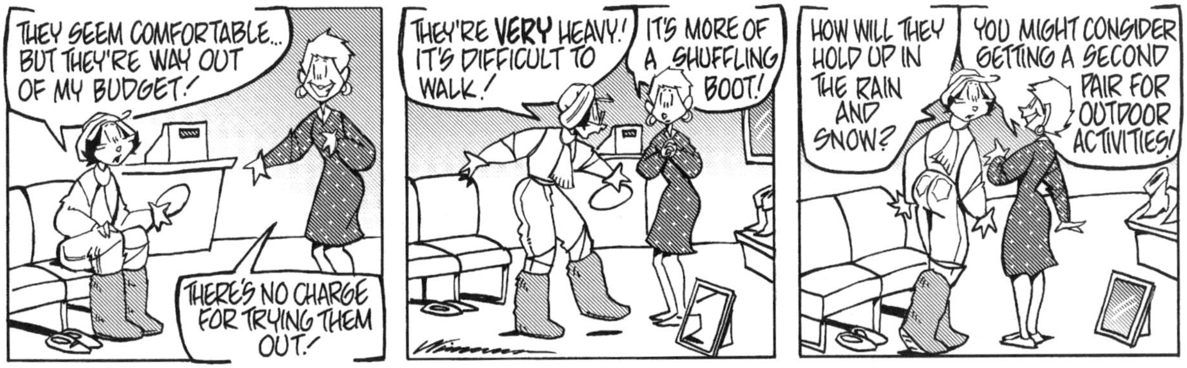
THEY SEEM COMFORTABLE... BUT THEY'RE WAY OUT OF MY BUDGET!
THERE'S NO CHARGE FOR TRYING THEM OUT!
THEY'RE **VERY** HEAVY! IT'S DIFFICULT TO WALK!
IT'S MORE OF A SHUFFLING BOOT!
HOW WILL THEY HOLD UP IN THE RAIN AND SNOW?
YOU MIGHT CONSIDER GETTING A SECOND PAIR FOR OUTDOOR ACTIVITIES!

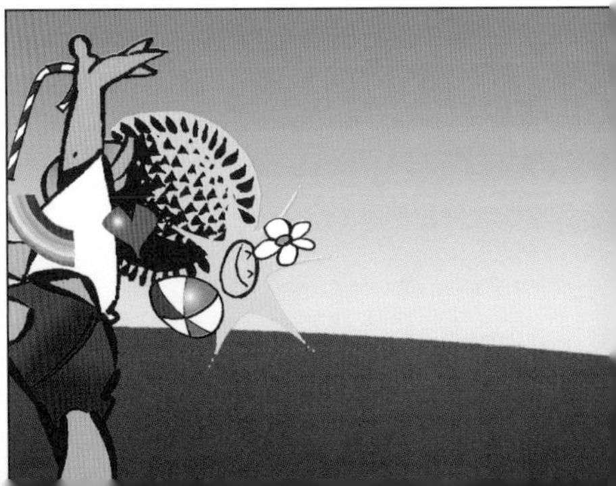

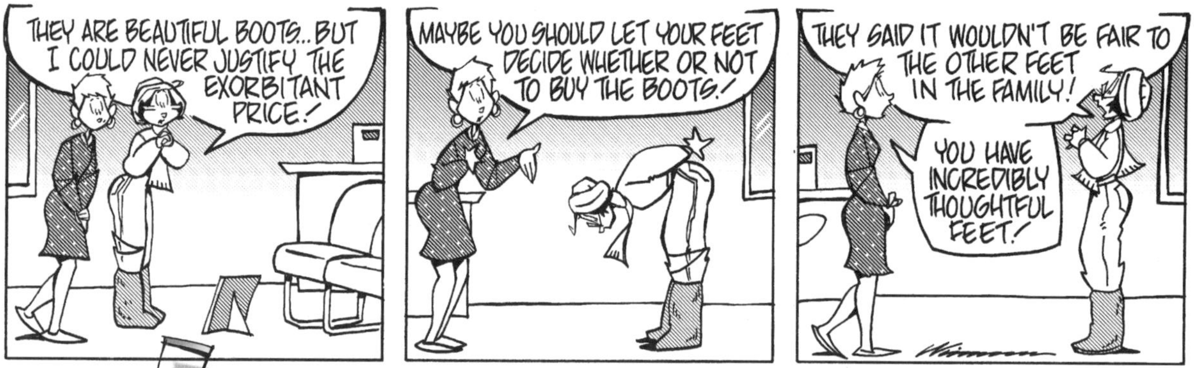
THEY ARE BEAUTIFUL BOOTS...BUT I COULD NEVER JUSTIFY THE EXORBITANT PRICE!
MAYBE YOU SHOULD LET YOUR FEET DECIDE WHETHER OR NOT TO BUY THE BOOTS!
THEY SAID IT WOULDN'T BE FAIR TO THE OTHER FEET IN THE FAMILY!
YOU HAVE INCREDIBLY THOUGHTFUL FEET!

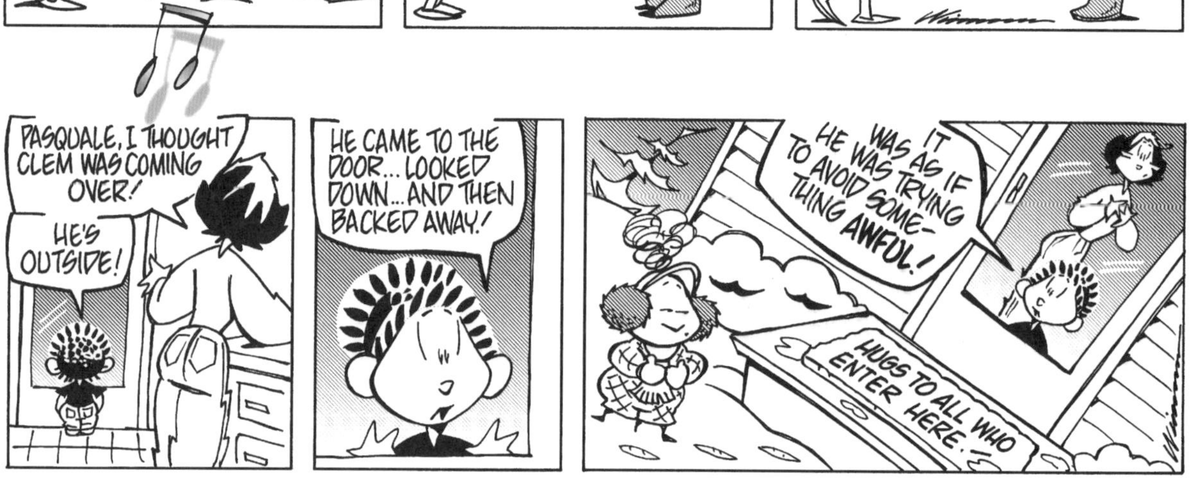
PASQUALE, I THOUGHT CLEM WAS COMING OVER!
HE'S OUTSIDE!
HE CAME TO THE DOOR... LOOKED DOWN... AND THEN BACKED AWAY!
IT WAS AS IF HE WAS TRYING TO AVOID SOME-THING AWFUL!
HUGS TO ALL WHO ENTER HERE.

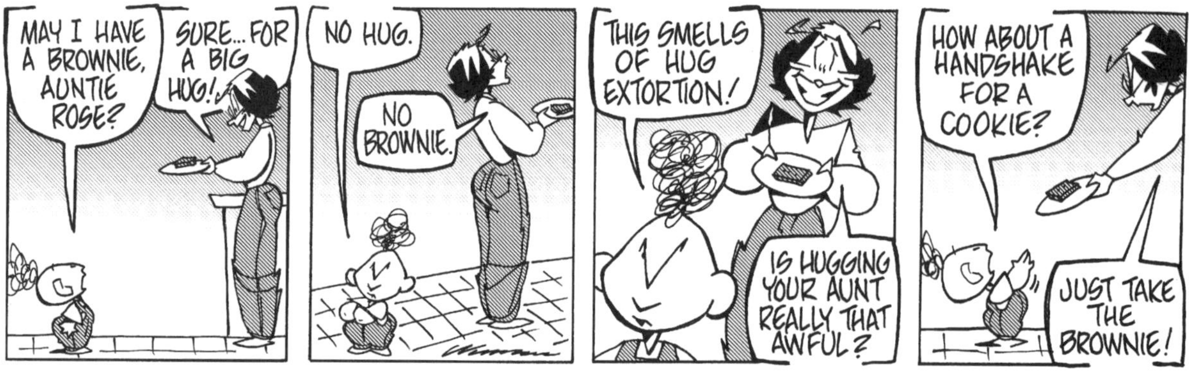
MAY I HAVE A BROWNIE, AUNTIE ROSE?
SURE... FOR A BIG HUG!
NO HUG.
NO BROWNIE.
THIS SMELLS OF HUG EXTORTION!
IS HUGGING YOUR AUNT REALLY THAT AWFUL?
HOW ABOUT A HANDSHAKE FOR A COOKIE?
JUST TAKE THE BROWNIE!

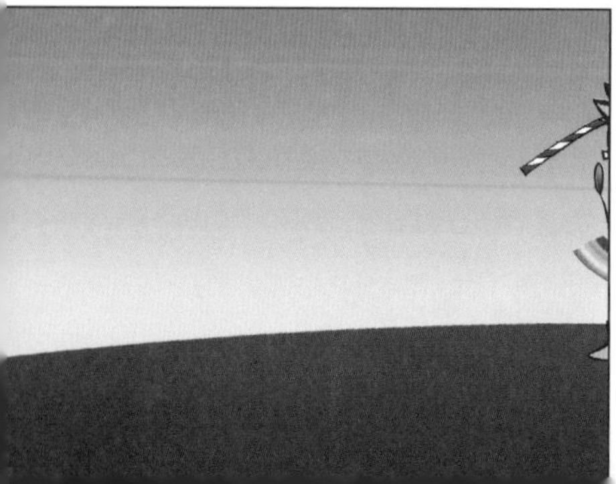

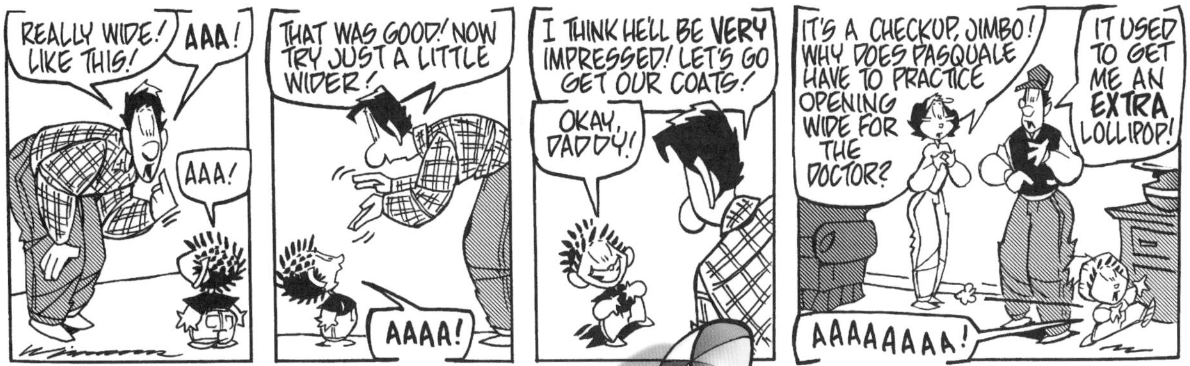
REALLY WIDE! LIKE THIS!
AAA!
AAA!
THAT WAS GOOD! NOW TRY JUST A LITTLE WIDER!
AAAA!
I THINK HE'LL BE **VERY** IMPRESSED! LET'S GO GET OUR COATS!
OKAY, DADDY!
IT'S A CHECKUP, JIMBO! WHY DOES PASQUALE HAVE TO PRACTICE OPENING WIDE FOR THE DOCTOR?
IT USED TO GET ME AN **EXTRA** LOLLIPOP!
AAAAAAAA!

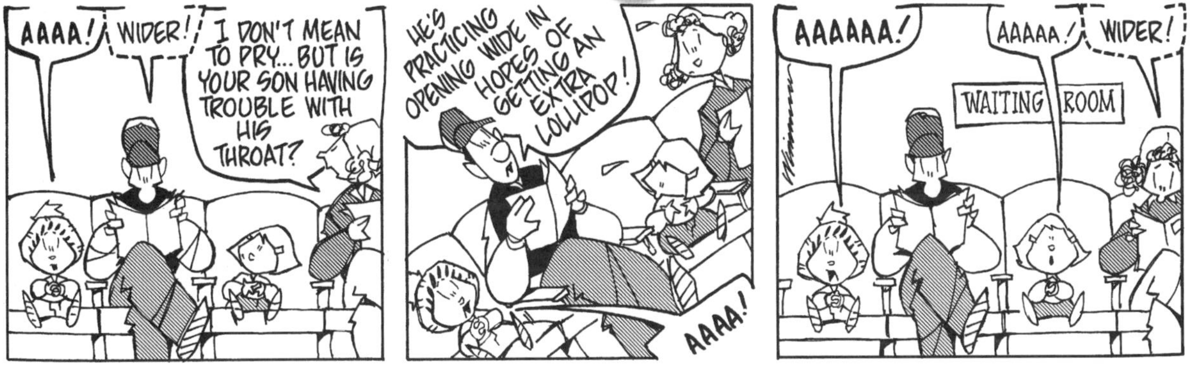
AAAA!
WIDER!
I DON'T MEAN TO PRY... BUT IS YOUR SON HAVING TROUBLE WITH HIS THROAT?
HE'S PRACTICING OPENING WIDE IN HOPES OF GETTING AN EXTRA LOLLIPOP!
AAAA!
AAAAAA!
WAITING ROOM
AAAAA!
WIDER!

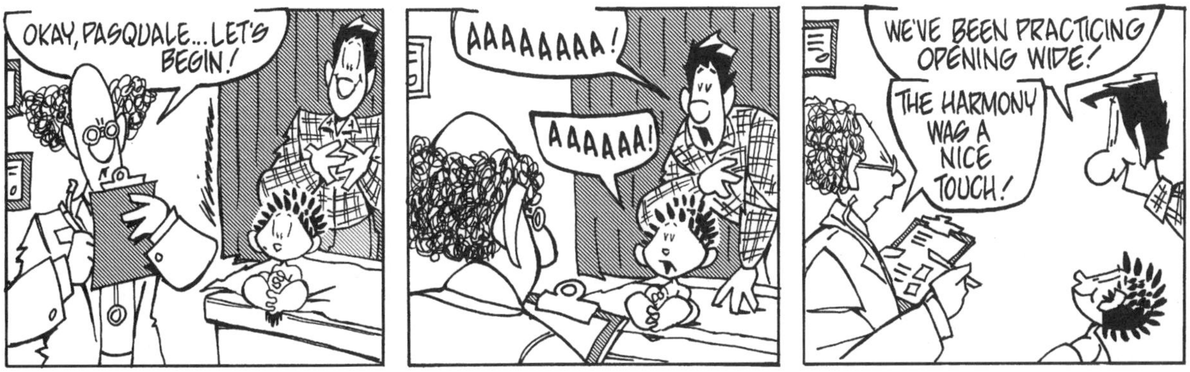
OKAY, PASQUALE... LET'S BEGIN!
AAAAAAAA!
AAAAAA!
WE'VE BEEN PRACTICING OPENING WIDE!
THE HARMONY WAS A NICE TOUCH!

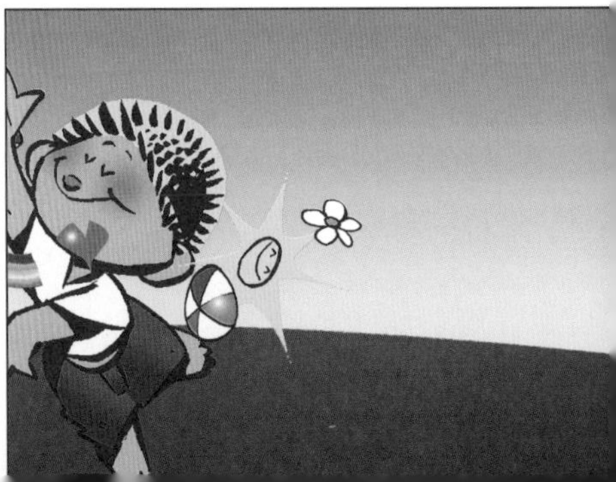

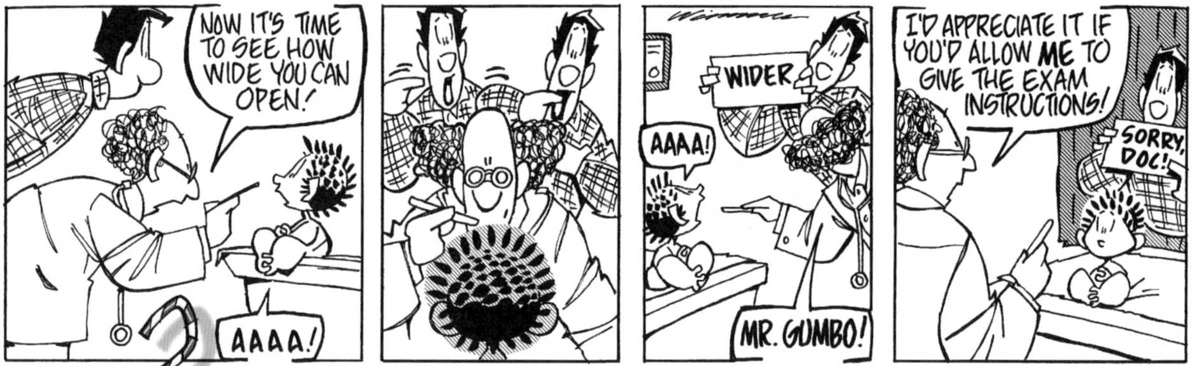
NOW IT'S TIME TO SEE HOW WIDE YOU CAN OPEN!
AAAA!
WIDER
AAAA!
MR. GUMBO!
I'D APPRECIATE IT IF YOU'D ALLOW **ME** TO GIVE THE EXAM INSTRUCTIONS!
SORRY, DOC!

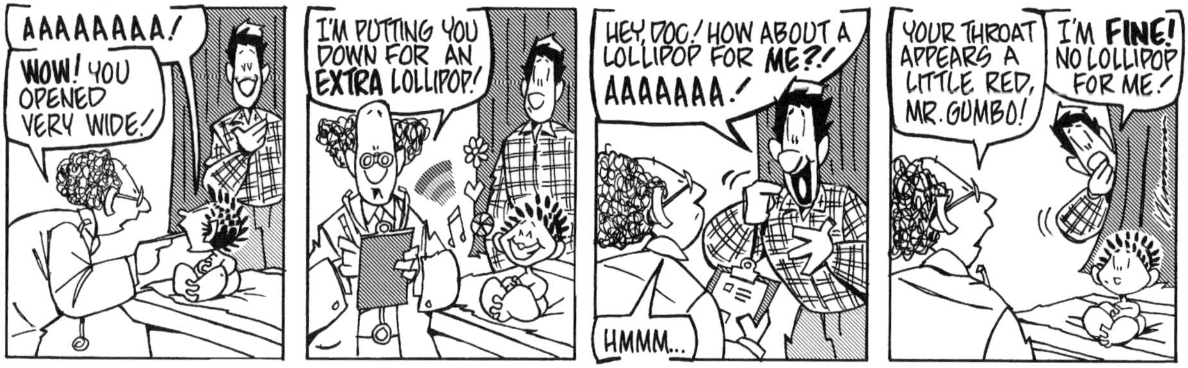
AAAAAAAA!
WOW! YOU OPENED VERY WIDE!
I'M PUTTING YOU DOWN FOR AN **EXTRA** LOLLIPOP!
HEY, DOC! HOW ABOUT A LOLLIPOP FOR **ME?!** AAAAAAA!
HMMM...
YOUR THROAT APPEARS A LITTLE RED, MR. GUMBO!
I'M **FINE!** NO LOLLIPOP FOR ME!

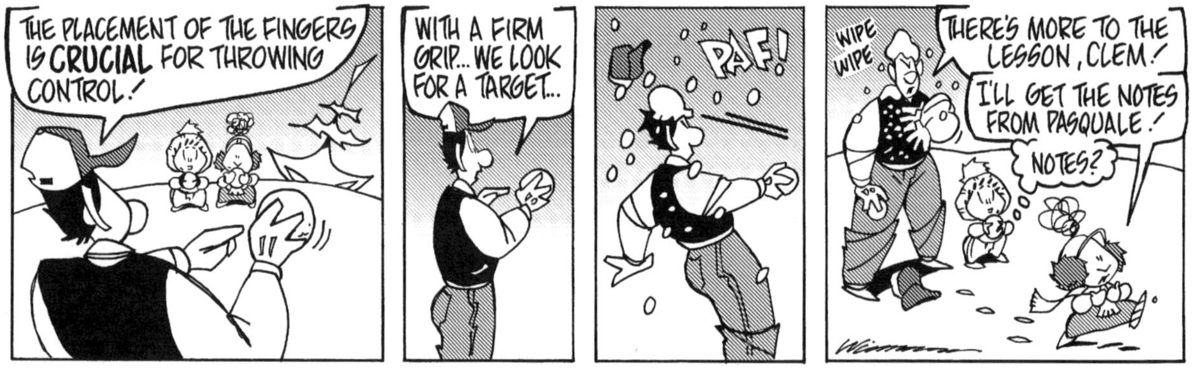
THE PLACEMENT OF THE FINGERS IS **CRUCIAL** FOR THROWING CONTROL!
WITH A FIRM GRIP... WE LOOK FOR A TARGET...
PAF!
WIPE WIPE
THERE'S MORE TO THE LESSON, CLEM!
I'LL GET THE NOTES FROM PASQUALE!
NOTES?

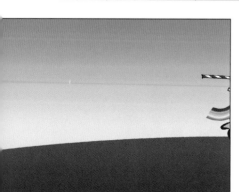

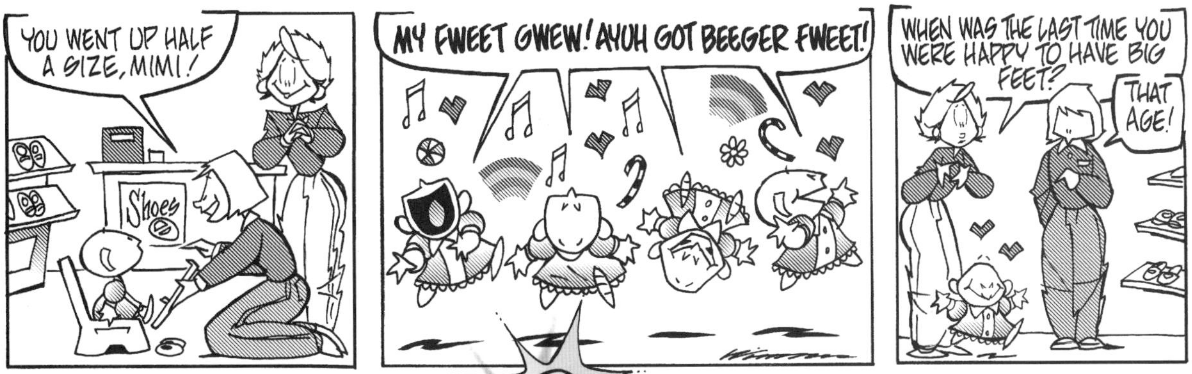
YOU WENT UP HALF A SIZE, MIMI!
MY FWEET GWEW! AYUH GOT BEEGER FWEET!
WHEN WAS THE LAST TIME YOU WERE HAPPY TO HAVE BIG FEET?
THAT AGE!

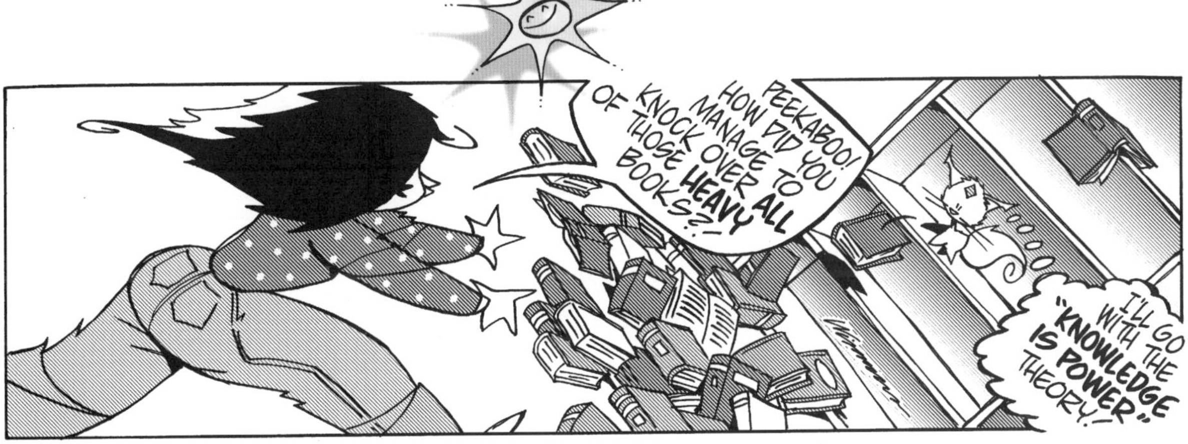
PEEKABOO! HOW DID YOU MANAGE TO KNOCK OVER ALL OF THOSE HEAVY BOOKS?!
I'LL GO WITH THE "KNOWLEDGE IS POWLEDGE" THEORY!

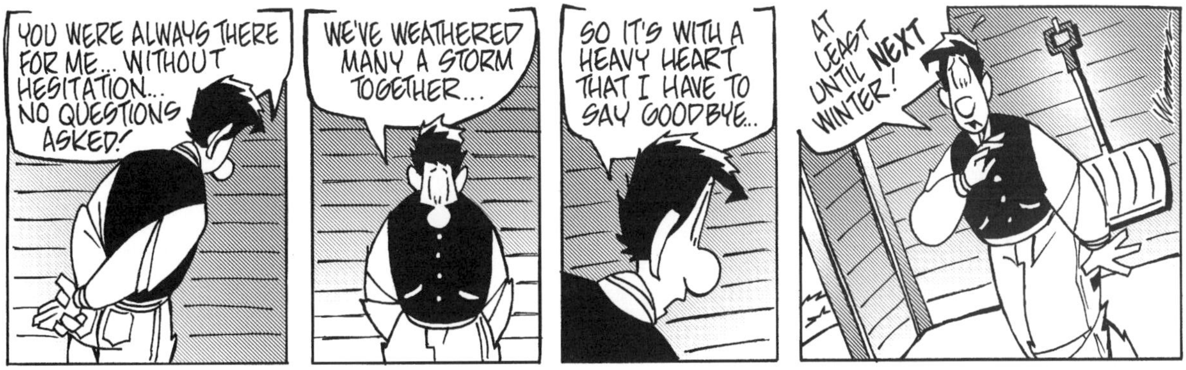
YOU WERE ALWAYS THERE FOR ME... WITHOUT HESITATION... NO QUESTIONS ASKED!
WE'VE WEATHERED MANY A STORM TOGETHER...
SO IT'S WITH A HEAVY HEART THAT I HAVE TO SAY GOODBYE...
AT LEAST UNTIL NEXT WINTER!

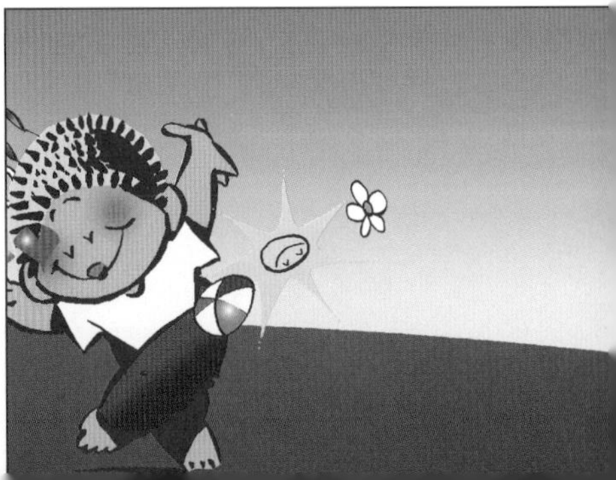

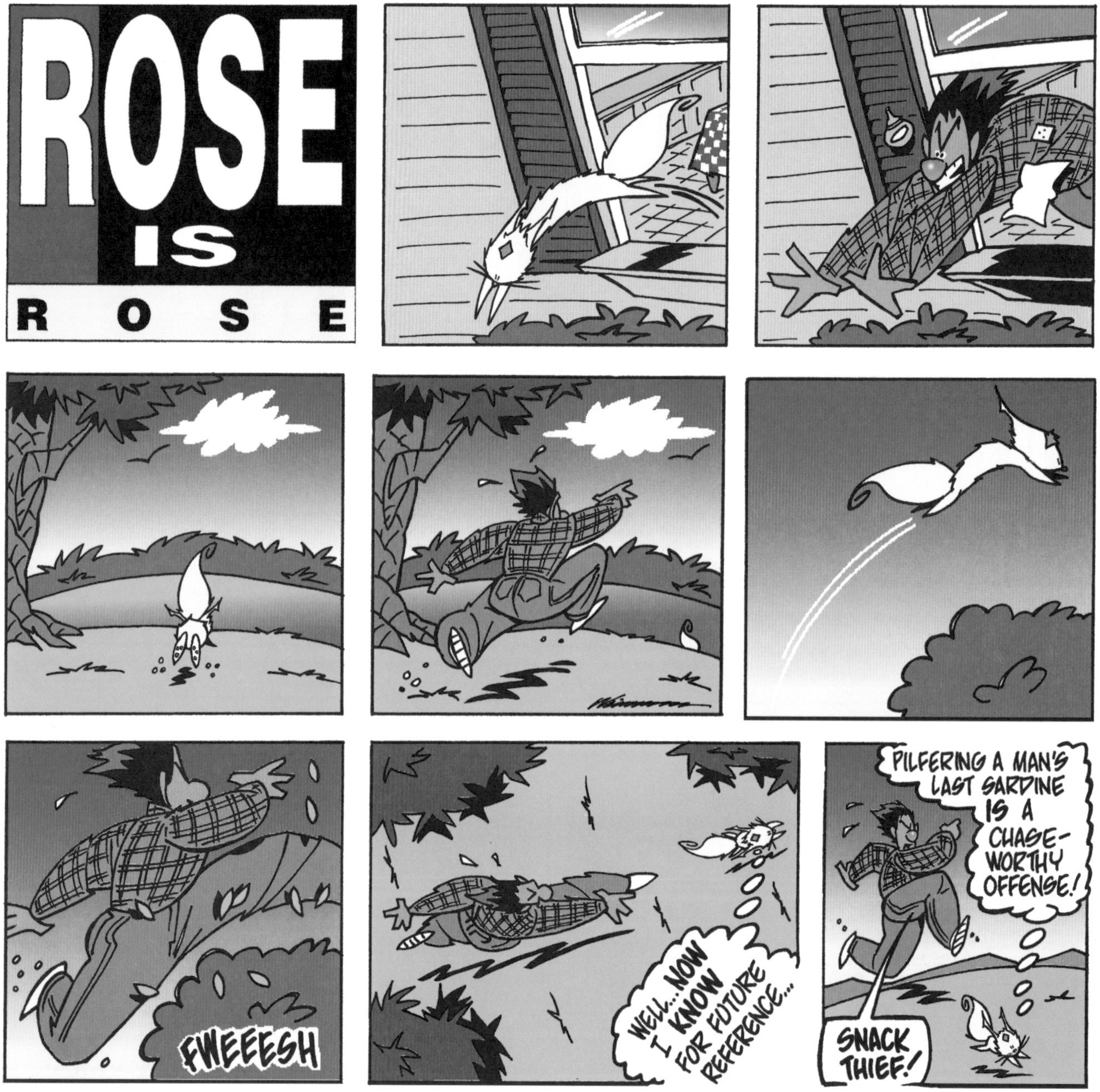
ROSE IS ROSE
FWEEESH
WELL... NOW I KNOW FOR FUTURE REFERENCE...
PILFERING A MAN'S LAST SARDINE IS A CHASE-WORTHY OFFENSE!
SNACK THIEF!

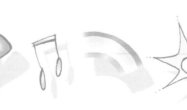

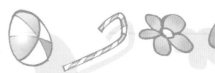

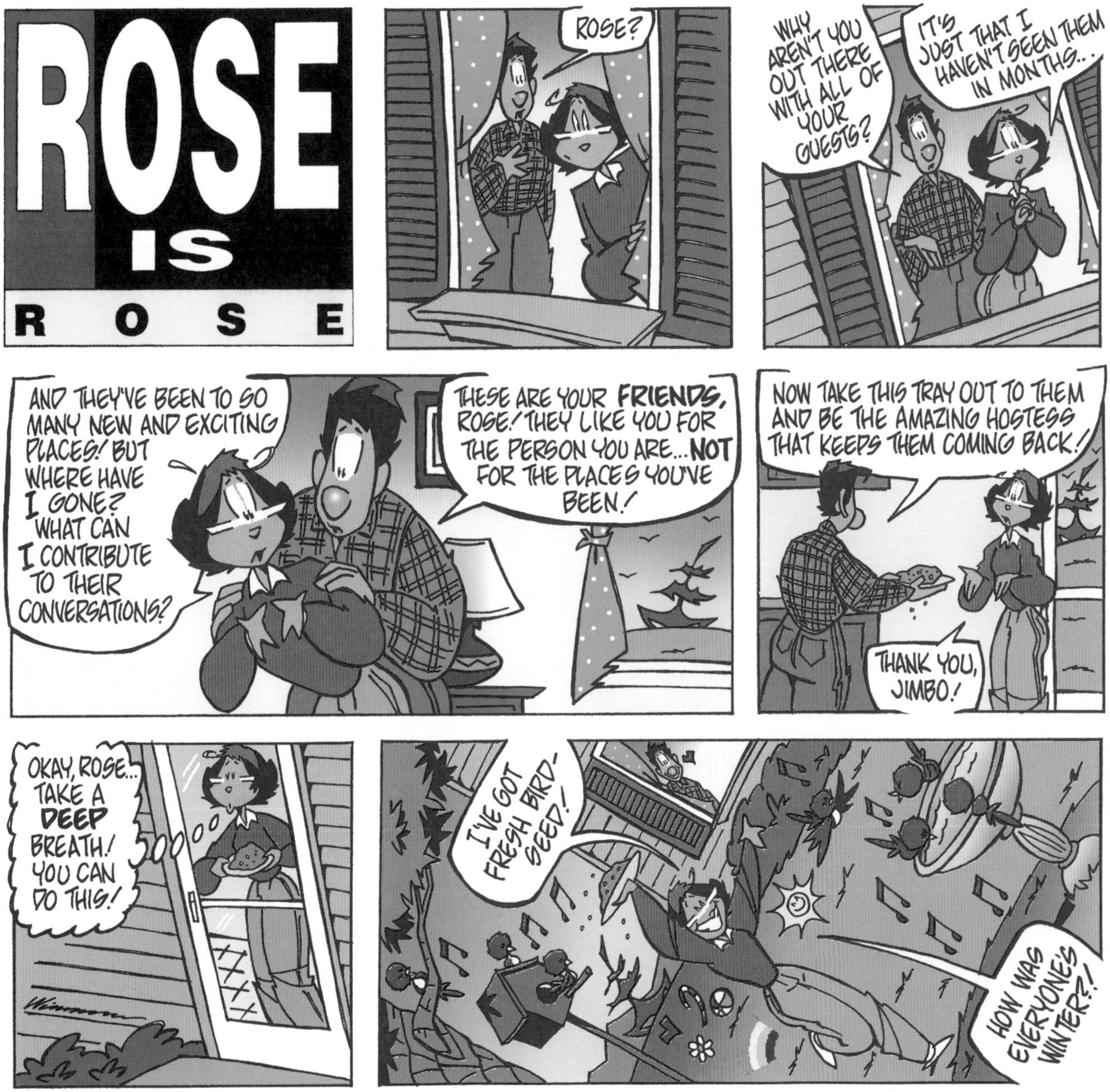
ROSE IS ROSE
ROSE?
WHY AREN'T YOU OUT THERE WITH ALL OF YOUR GUESTS?
IT'S JUST THAT I HAVEN'T SEEN THEM IN MONTHS...
AND THEY'VE BEEN TO SO MANY NEW AND EXCITING PLACES! BUT WHERE HAVE I GONE? WHAT CAN I CONTRIBUTE TO THEIR CONVERSATIONS?
THESE ARE YOUR FRIENDS, ROSE! THEY LIKE YOU FOR THE PERSON YOU ARE... NOT FOR THE PLACES YOU'VE BEEN!
NOW TAKE THIS TRAY OUT TO THEM AND BE THE AMAZING HOSTESS THAT KEEPS THEM COMING BACK!
THANK YOU, JIMBO!
OKAY, ROSE... TAKE A DEEP BREATH! YOU CAN DO THIS!
I'VE GOT FRESH BIRD-SEED!
HOW WAS EVERYONE'S WINTER?!

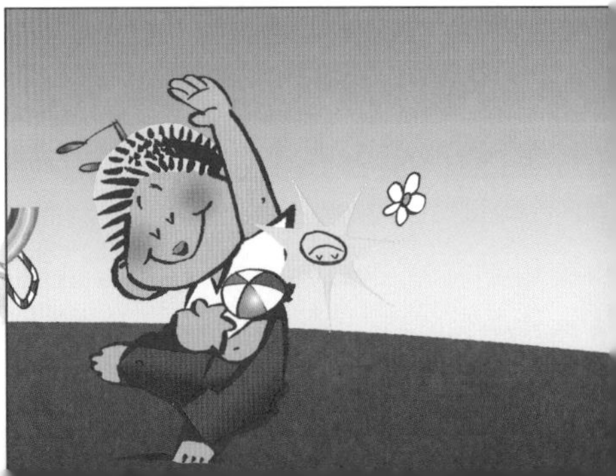

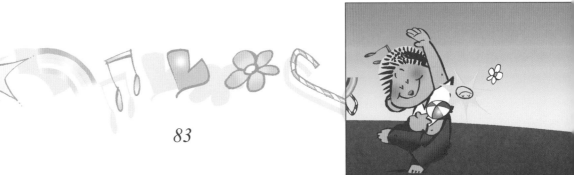

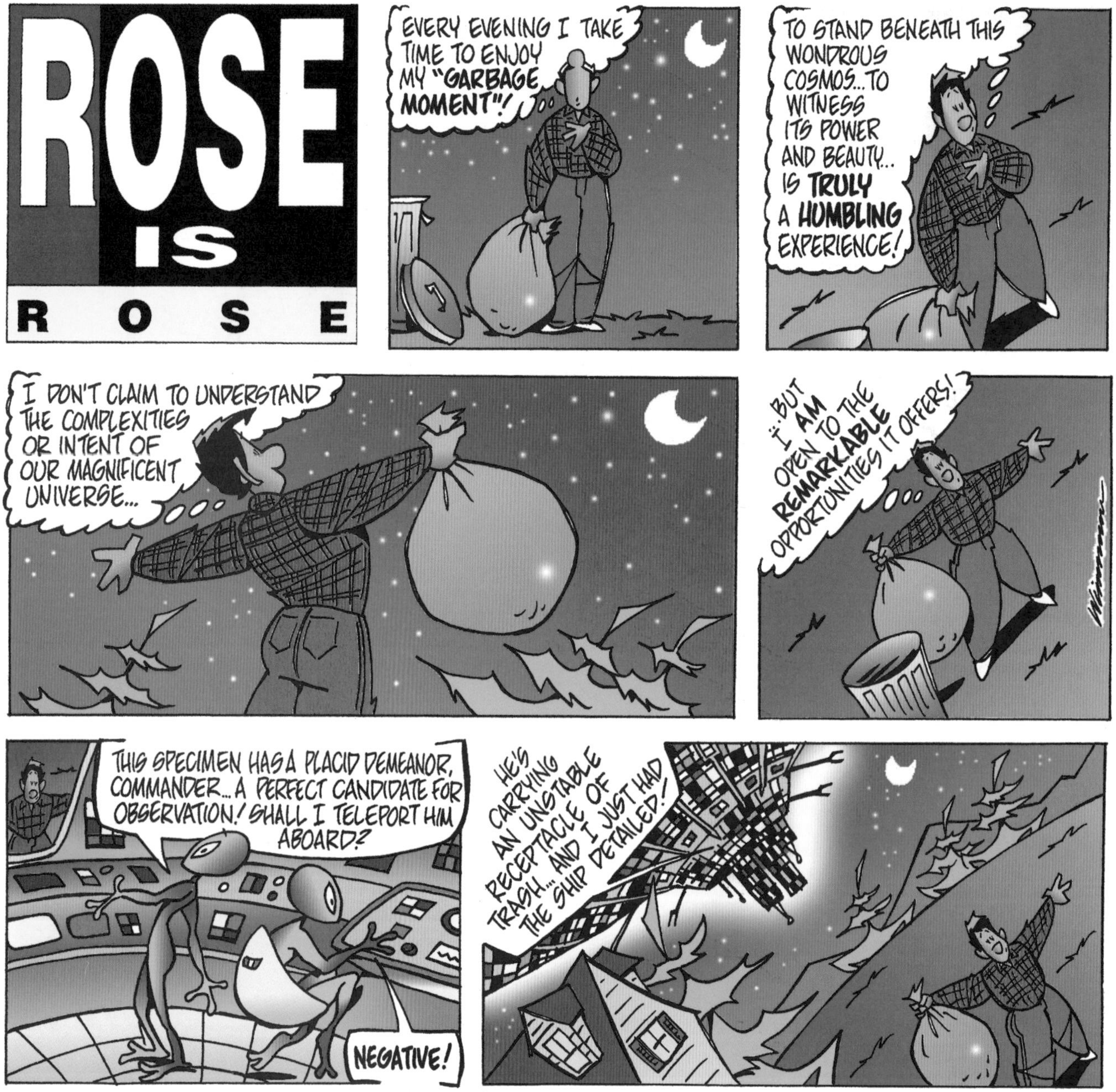
ROSE IS ROSE
EVERY EVENING I TAKE TIME TO ENJOY MY "GARBAGE MOMENT"!
TO STAND BENEATH THIS WONDROUS COSMOS... TO WITNESS ITS POWER AND BEAUTY... IS TRULY A HUMBLING EXPERIENCE!
I DON'T CLAIM TO UNDERSTAND THE COMPLEXITIES OR INTENT OF OUR MAGNIFICENT UNIVERSE...
...BUT I AM OPEN TO THE REMARKABLE OPPORTUNITIES IT OFFERS!
THIS SPECIMEN HAS A PLACID DEMEANOR, COMMANDER... A PERFECT CANDIDATE FOR OBSERVATION! SHALL I TELEPORT HIM ABOARD?
NEGATIVE!
HE'S CARRYING AN UNSTABLE RECEPTACLE OF TRASH... AND I JUST HAD THE SHIP DETAILED!

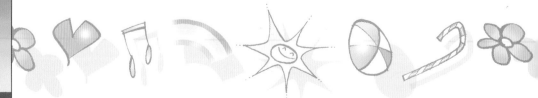

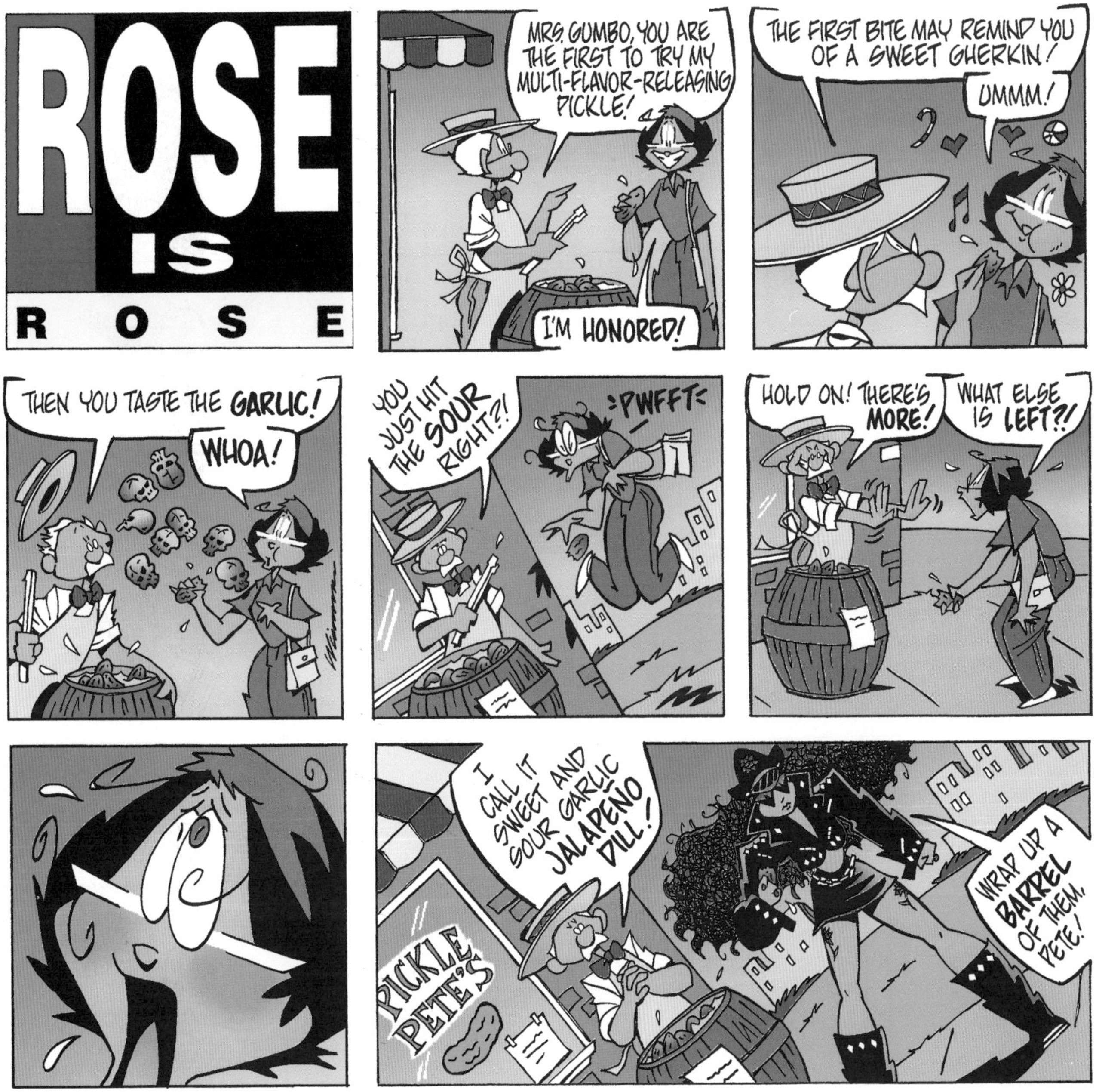
ROSE IS ROSE
MRS. GUMBO, YOU ARE THE FIRST TO TRY MY MULTI-FLAVOR-RELEASING PICKLE!
I'M HONORED!
THE FIRST BITE MAY REMIND YOU OF A SWEET GHERKIN!
UMMM!
THEN YOU TASTE THE GARLIC!
WHOA!
YOU JUST HIT THE SOUR RIGHT?!
=PWFFT=
HOLD ON! THERE'S MORE!
WHAT ELSE IS LEFT?!
I CALL IT SWEET AND SOUR GARLIC JALAPEÑO DILL!
WRAP UP A BARREL OF THEM, PETE!
PICKLE PETE'S

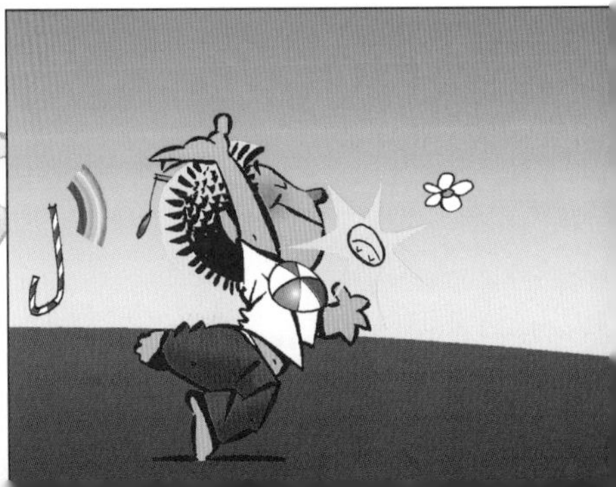

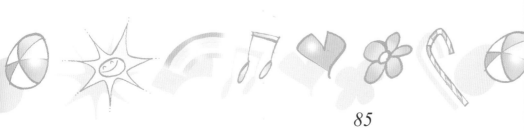

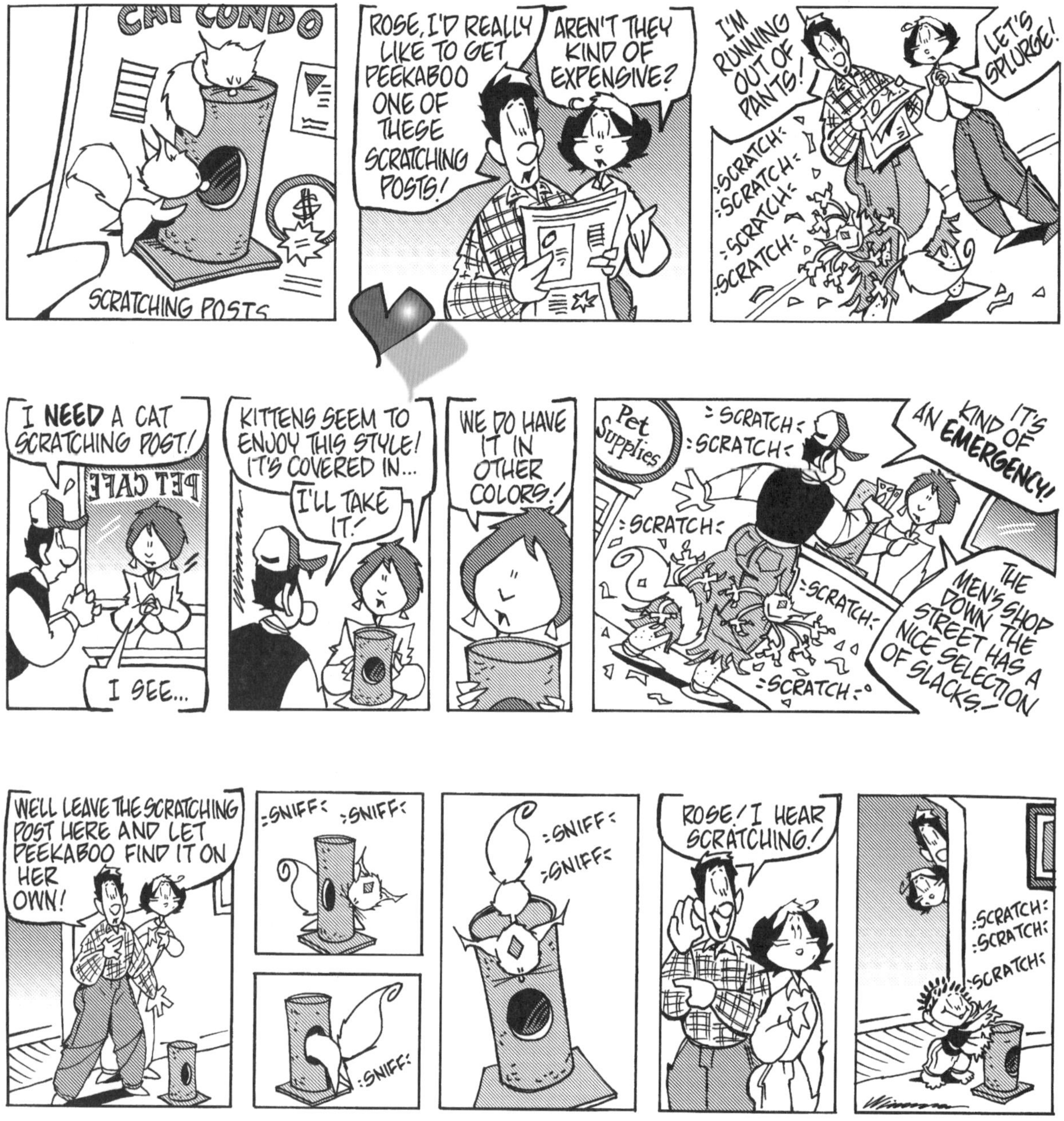
CAT CONDO
SCRATCHING POSTS
ROSE, I'D REALLY LIKE TO GET PEEKABOO ONE OF THESE SCRATCHING POSTS!
AREN'T THEY KIND OF EXPENSIVE?
I'M RUNNING OUT OF PANTS!
LET'S SPLURGE!
SCRATCH
SCRATCH
SCRATCH
SCRATCH
I NEED A CAT SCRATCHING POST!
I SEE...
KITTENS SEEM TO ENJOY THIS STYLE! IT'S COVERED IN...
I'LL TAKE IT!
WE DO HAVE IT IN OTHER COLORS!
Pet Supplies
SCRATCH
SCRATCH
IT'S KIND OF AN EMERGENCY!
SCRATCH
SCRATCH
THE MEN'S SHOP DOWN THE STREET HAS A NICE SELECTION OF SLACKS!
SCRATCH
WE'LL LEAVE THE SCRATCHING POST HERE AND LET PEEKABOO FIND IT ON HER OWN!
SNIFF
SNIFF
SNIFF
SNIFF
SNIFF
ROSE! I HEAR SCRATCHING!
SCRATCH
SCRATCH
SCRATCH

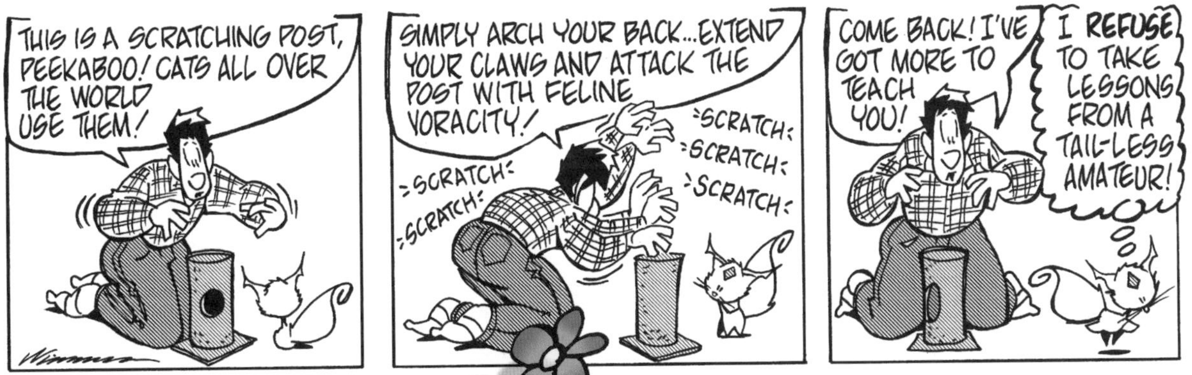
THIS IS A SCRATCHING POST, PEEKABOO! CATS ALL OVER THE WORLD USE THEM!
SIMPLY ARCH YOUR BACK...EXTEND YOUR CLAWS AND ATTACK THE POST WITH FELINE VORACITY!
SCRATCH
SCRATCH
SCRATCH
SCRATCH
SCRATCH
SCRATCH
COME BACK! I'VE GOT MORE TO TEACH YOU!
I **REFUSE** TO TAKE LESSONS FROM A TAIL-LESS AMATEUR!

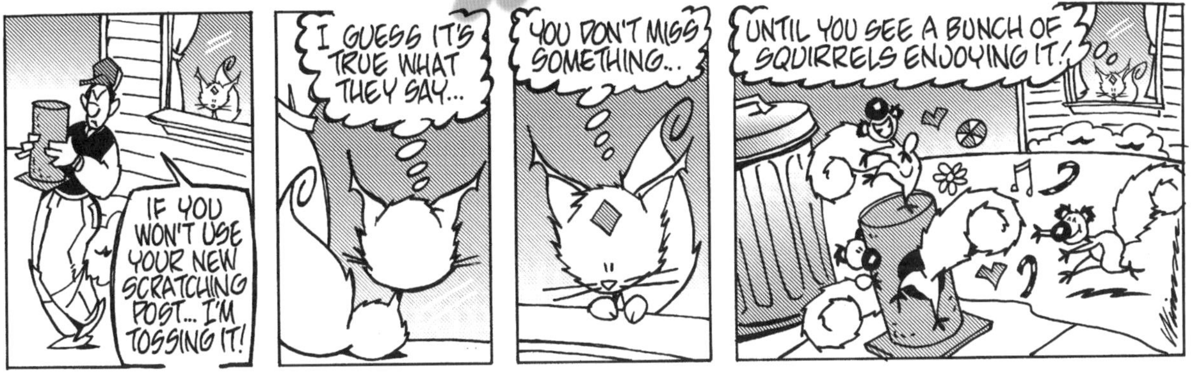
IF YOU WON'T USE YOUR NEW SCRATCHING POST... I'M TOSSING IT!
I GUESS IT'S TRUE WHAT THEY SAY...
YOU DON'T MISS SOMETHING..
UNTIL YOU SEE A BUNCH OF SQUIRRELS ENJOYING IT!

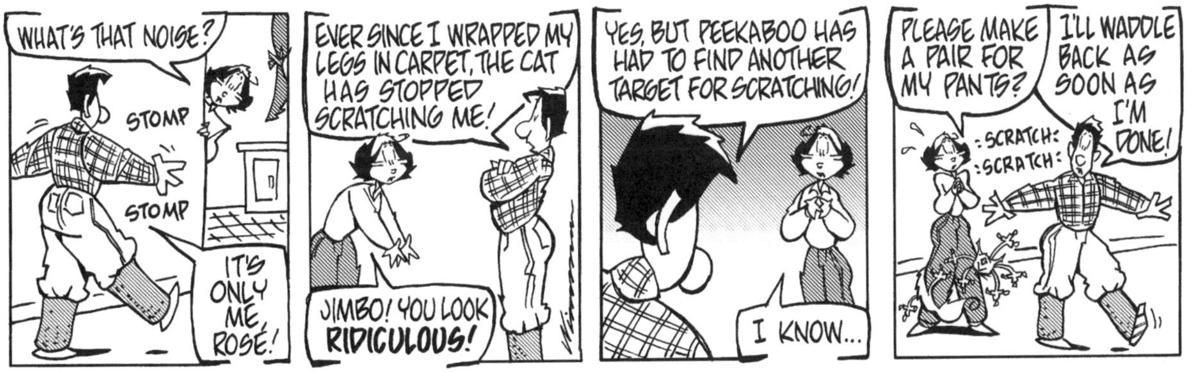
WHAT'S THAT NOISE?
STOMP
STOMP
IT'S ONLY ME ROSÉ!
EVER SINCE I WRAPPED MY LEGS IN CARPET, THE CAT HAS STOPPED SCRATCHING ME!
JIMBO! YOU LOOK **RIDICULOUS**!
YES, BUT PEEKABOO HAS HAD TO FIND ANOTHER TARGET FOR SCRATCHING!
I KNOW...
PLEASE MAKE A PAIR FOR MY PANTS?
SCRATCH
SCRATCH
I'LL WADDLE BACK AS SOON AS I'M DONE!

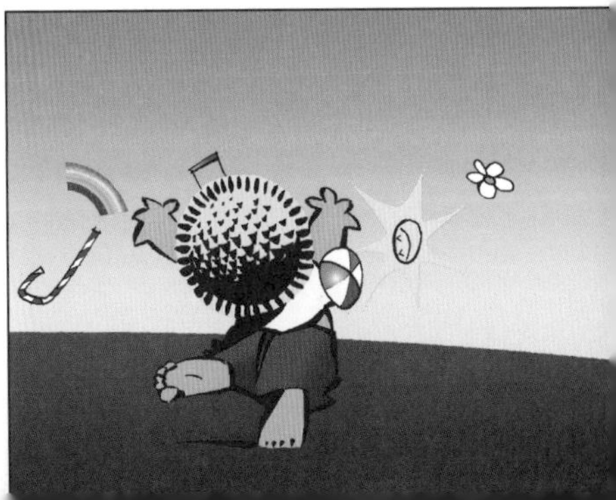

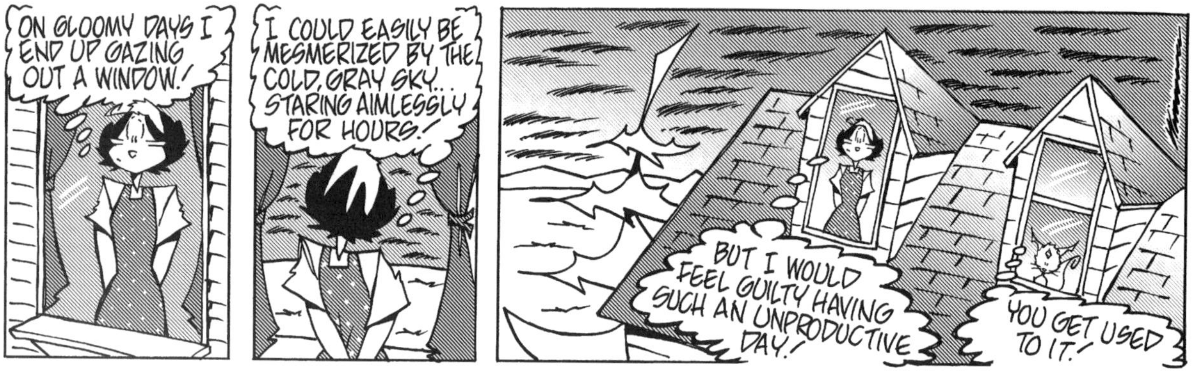
ON GLOOMY DAYS I END UP GAZING OUT A WINDOW!
I COULD EASILY BE MESMERIZED BY THE COLD, GRAY SKY... STARING AIMLESSLY FOR HOURS!
BUT I WOULD FEEL GUILTY HAVING SUCH AN UNPRODUCTIVE DAY!
YOU GET USED TO IT!

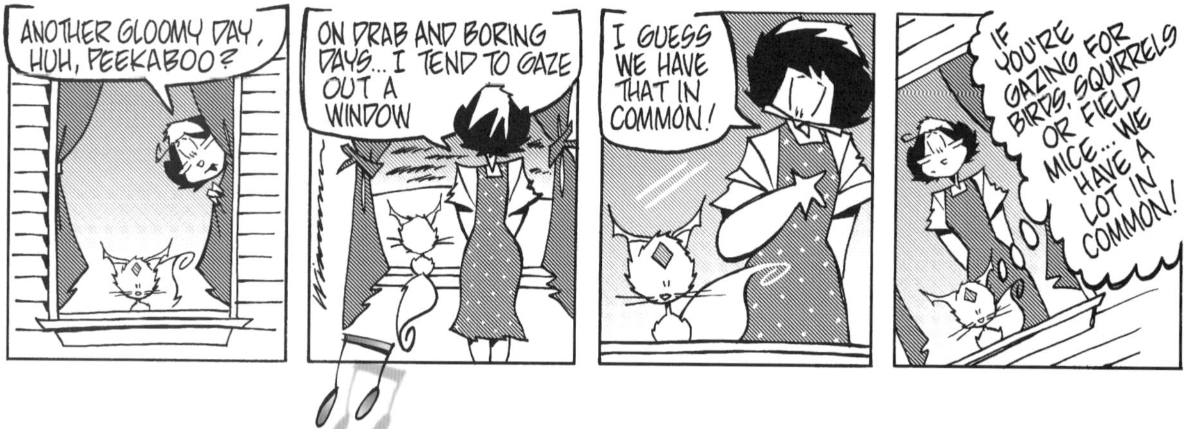
ANOTHER GLOOMY DAY, HUH, PEEKABOO?
ON DRAB AND BORING DAYS... I TEND TO GAZE OUT A WINDOW
I GUESS WE HAVE THAT IN COMMON!
IF YOU'RE GAZING FOR BIRDS, SQUIRRELS OR FIELD MICE... WE HAVE A LOT IN COMMON!

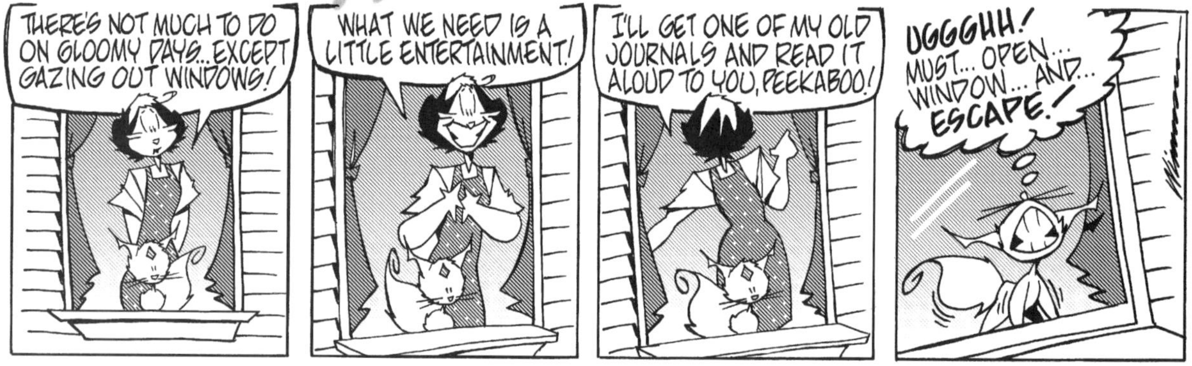
THERE'S NOT MUCH TO DO ON GLOOMY DAYS...EXCEPT GAZING OUT WINDOWS!
WHAT WE NEED IS A LITTLE ENTERTAINMENT!
I'LL GET ONE OF MY OLD JOURNALS AND READ IT ALOUD TO YOU, PEEKABOO!
UGGGHH! MUST... OPEN... WINDOW... AND... ESCAPE!

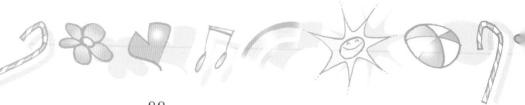

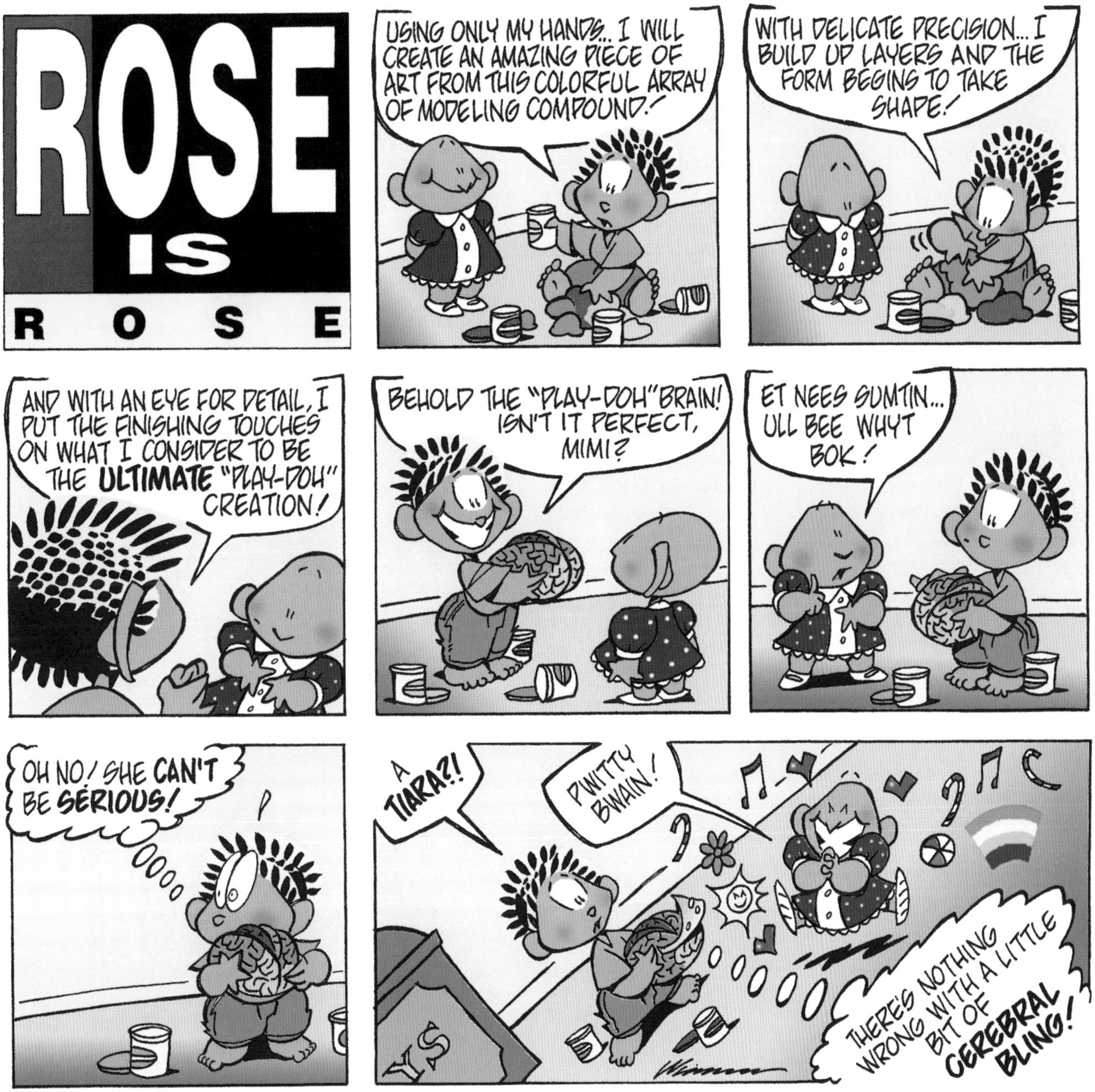
ROSE IS ROSE
USING ONLY MY HANDS.. I WILL CREATE AN AMAZING PIECE OF ART FROM THIS COLORFUL ARRAY OF MODELING COMPOUND!
WITH DELICATE PRECISION... I BUILD UP LAYERS AND THE FORM BEGINS TO TAKE SHAPE!
AND WITH AN EYE FOR DETAIL, I PUT THE FINISHING TOUCHES ON WHAT I CONSIDER TO BE THE **ULTIMATE** "PLAY-DOH" CREATION!
BEHOLD THE "PLAY-DOH" BRAIN! ISN'T IT PERFECT, MIMI?
ET NEES SUMTIN... ULL BEE WHYT BOK!
OH NO! SHE **CAN'T** BE **SERIOUS!**
A **TIARA?!**
P'WITTY B'WAIN!
THERE'S NOTHING WRONG WITH A LITTLE BIT OF **CEREBRAL BLING!**

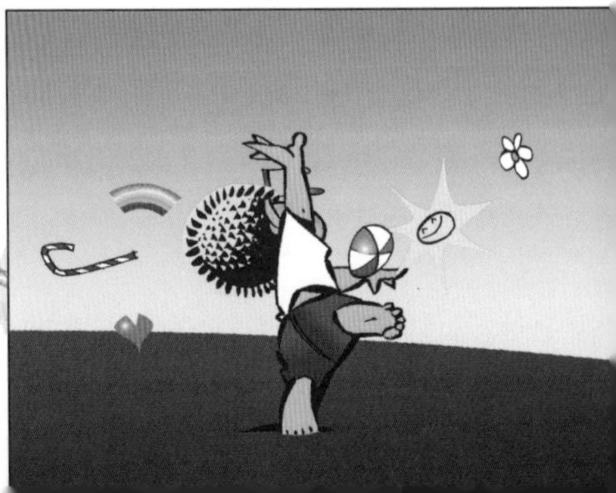

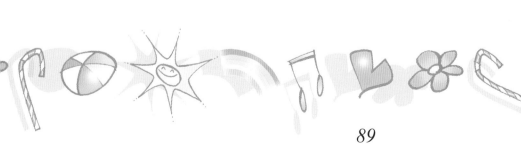

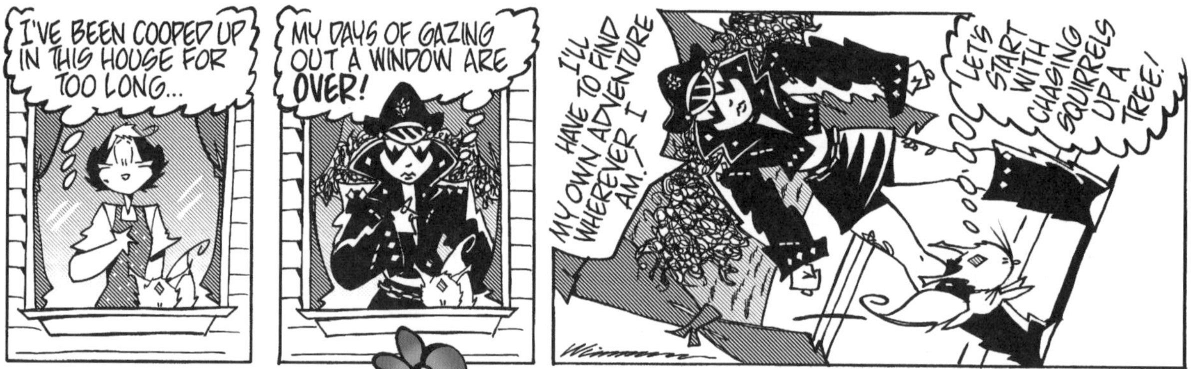
I'VE BEEN COOPED UP IN THIS HOUSE FOR TOO LONG...
MY DAYS OF GAZING OUT A WINDOW ARE OVER!
I'LL HAVE TO FIND MY OWN ADVENTURE WHEREVER I AM!
LET'S START WITH CHASING SQUIRRELS UP A TREE!

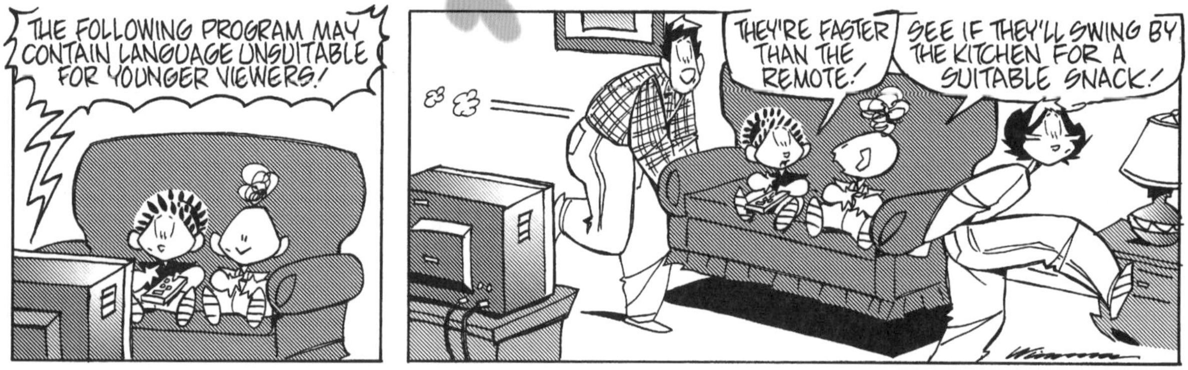
THE FOLLOWING PROGRAM MAY CONTAIN LANGUAGE UNSUITABLE FOR YOUNGER VIEWERS!
THEY'RE FASTER THAN THE REMOTE!
SEE IF THEY'LL SWING BY THE KITCHEN FOR A SUITABLE SNACK!

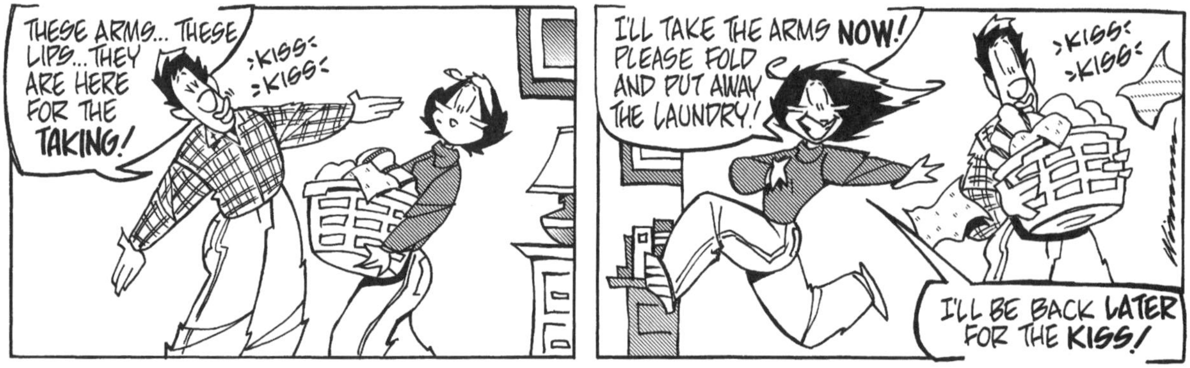
THESE ARMS... THESE LIPS... THEY ARE HERE FOR THE TAKING!
›KISS‹ ›KISS‹
I'LL TAKE THE ARMS NOW! PLEASE FOLD AND PUT AWAY THE LAUNDRY!
›KISS‹ ›KISS‹
I'LL BE BACK LATER FOR THE KISS!

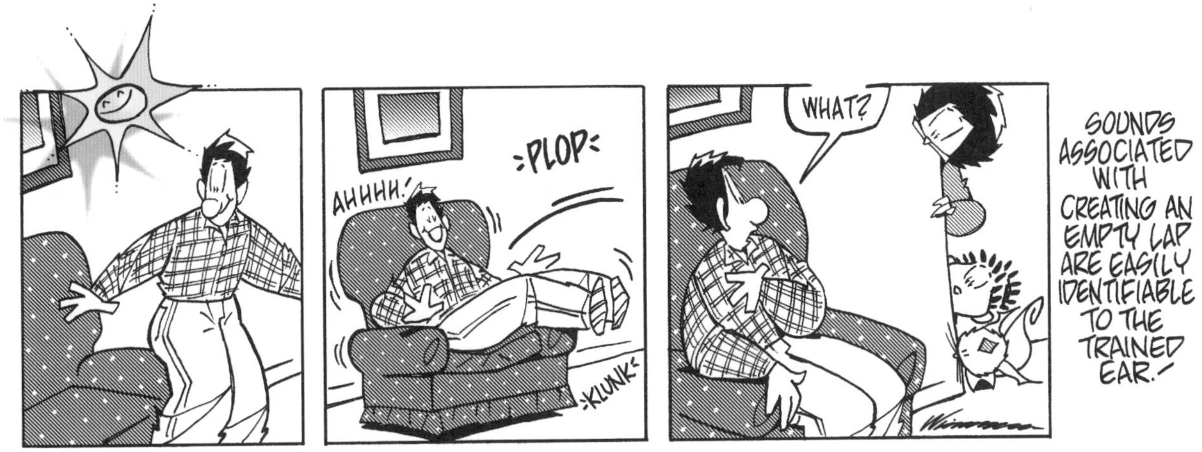

=PLOP=
AHHHH!
KLUNK
WHAT?
SOUNDS ASSOCIATED WITH CREATING AN EMPTY LAP ARE EASILY IDENTIFIABLE TO THE TRAINED EAR.

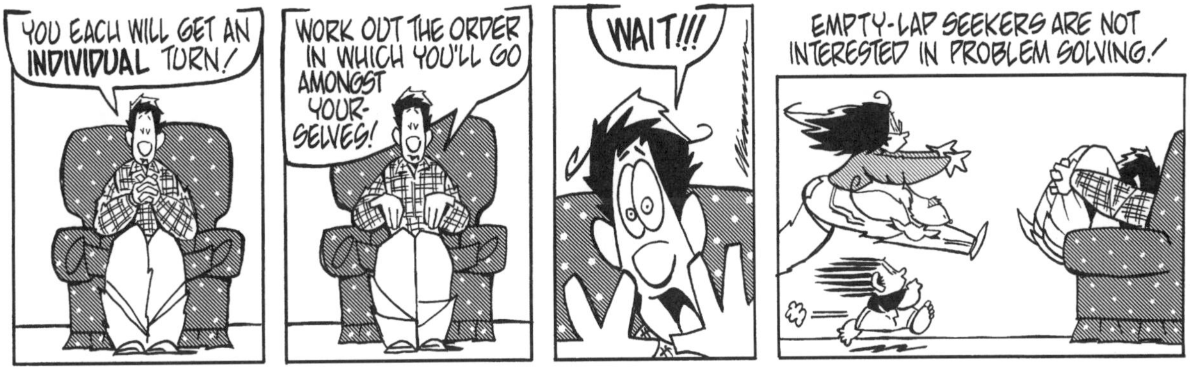

YOU EACH WILL GET AN INDIVIDUAL TURN!
WORK OUT THE ORDER IN WHICH YOU'LL GO AMONGST YOURSELVES!
WAIT!!!
EMPTY-LAP SEEKERS ARE NOT INTERESTED IN PROBLEM SOLVING.

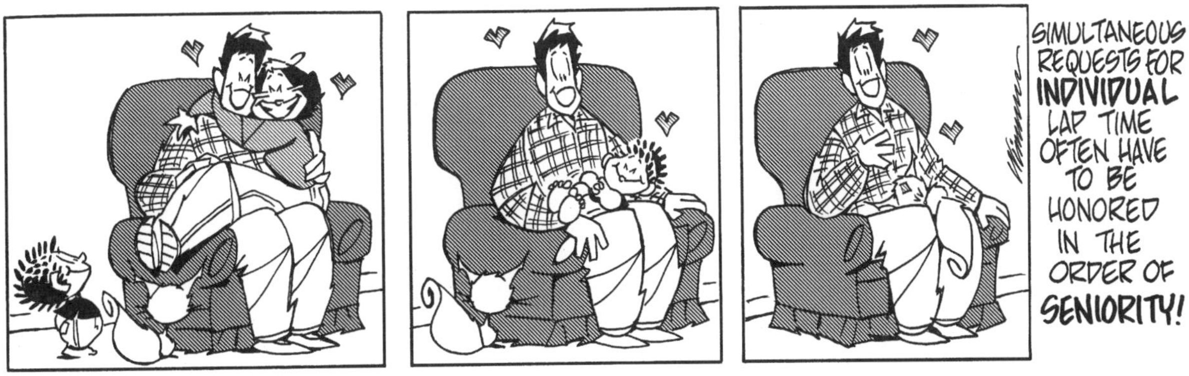

SIMULTANEOUS REQUESTS FOR INDIVIDUAL LAP TIME OFTEN HAVE TO BE HONORED IN THE ORDER OF SENIORITY!

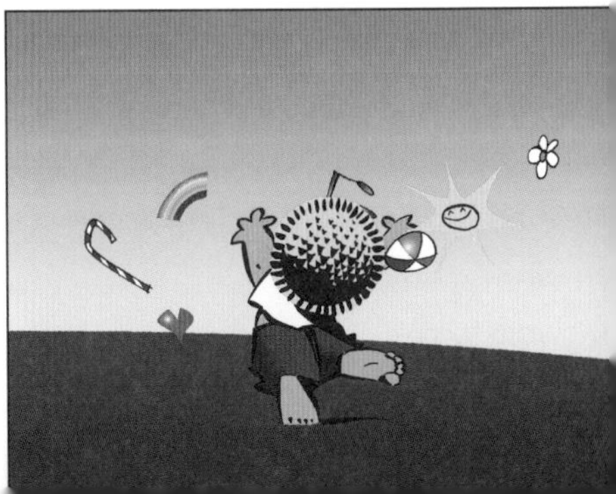

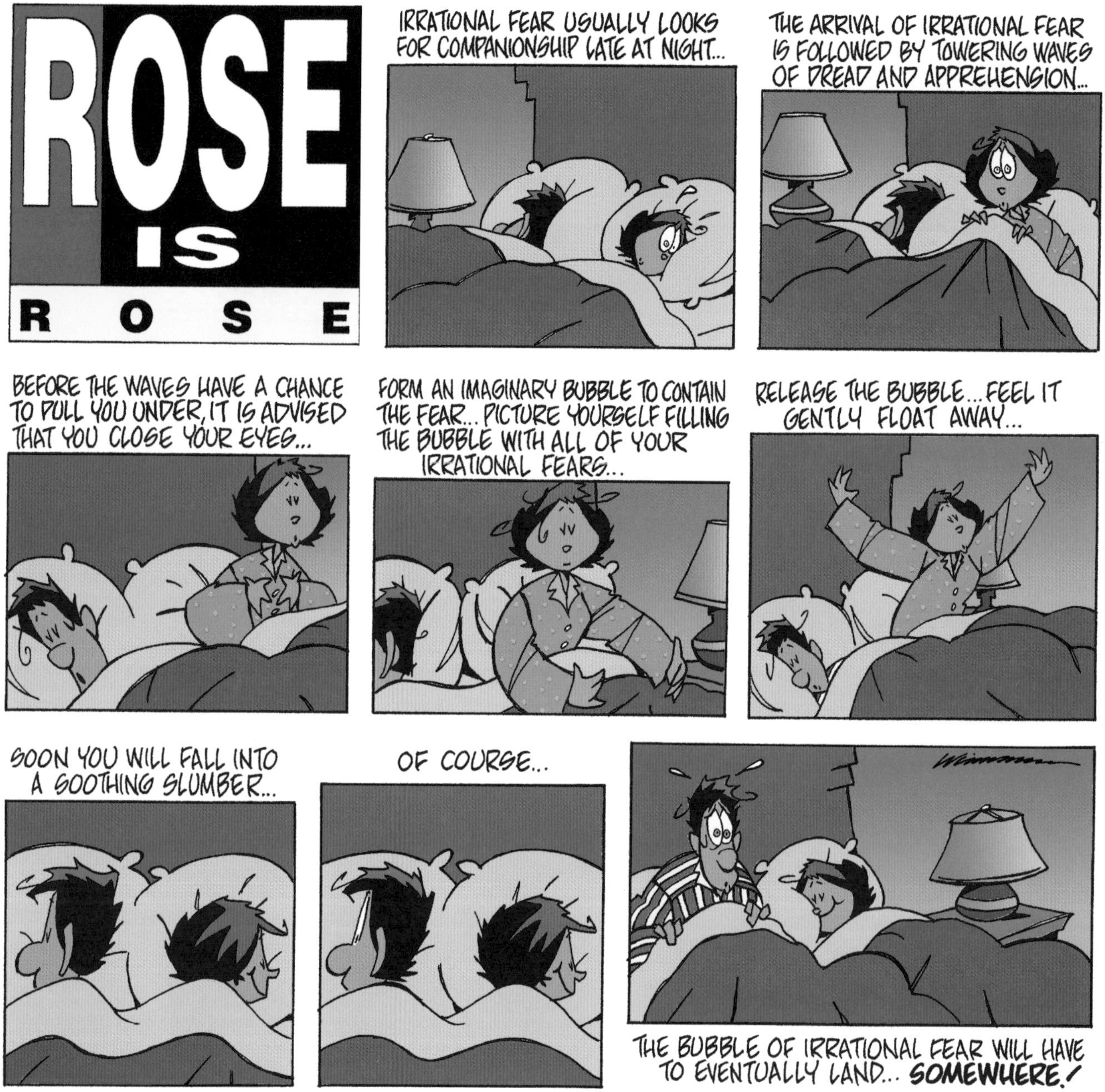
ROSE IS ROSE
IRRATIONAL FEAR USUALLY LOOKS FOR COMPANIONSHIP LATE AT NIGHT...
THE ARRIVAL OF IRRATIONAL FEAR IS FOLLOWED BY TOWERING WAVES OF DREAD AND APPREHENSION...
BEFORE THE WAVES HAVE A CHANCE TO PULL YOU UNDER, IT IS ADVISED THAT YOU CLOSE YOUR EYES...
FORM AN IMAGINARY BUBBLE TO CONTAIN THE FEAR... PICTURE YOURSELF FILLING THE BUBBLE WITH ALL OF YOUR IRRATIONAL FEARS...
RELEASE THE BUBBLE... FEEL IT GENTLY FLOAT AWAY...
SOON YOU WILL FALL INTO A SOOTHING SLUMBER...
OF COURSE...
THE BUBBLE OF IRRATIONAL FEAR WILL HAVE TO EVENTUALLY LAND... **SOMEWHERE!**

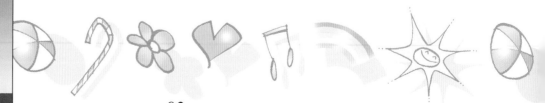

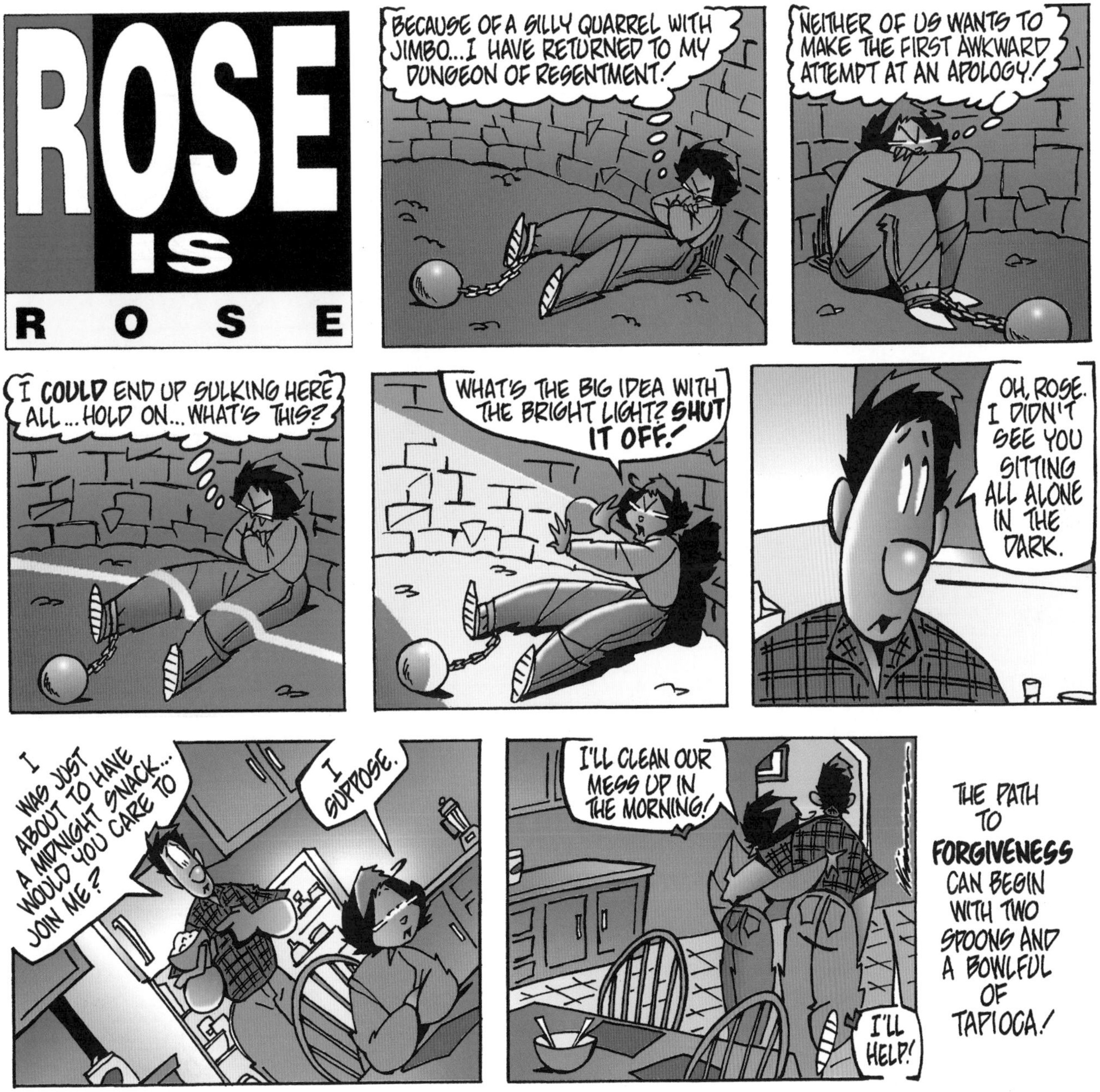
ROSE IS ROSE
BECAUSE OF A SILLY QUARREL WITH JIMBO...I HAVE RETURNED TO MY DUNGEON OF RESENTMENT!
NEITHER OF US WANTS TO MAKE THE FIRST AWKWARD ATTEMPT AT AN APOLOGY!
I **COULD** END UP SULKING HERE ALL... HOLD ON... WHAT'S THIS?
WHAT'S THE BIG IDEA WITH THE BRIGHT LIGHT? **SHUT IT OFF!**
OH, ROSE. I DIDN'T SEE YOU SITTING ALL ALONE IN THE DARK.
I WAS JUST ABOUT TO HAVE A MIDNIGHT SNACK... WOULD YOU CARE TO JOIN ME?
I SUPPOSE.
I'LL CLEAN OUR MESS UP IN THE MORNING!
I'LL HELP!
THE PATH TO **FORGIVENESS** CAN BEGIN WITH TWO SPOONS AND A BOWLFUL OF TAPIOCA!

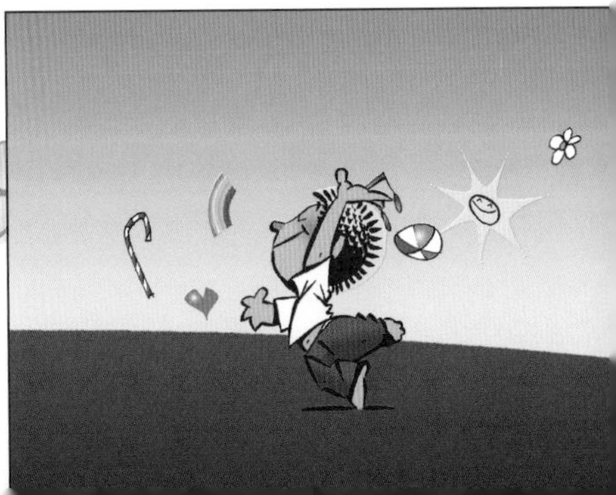

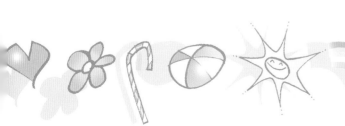

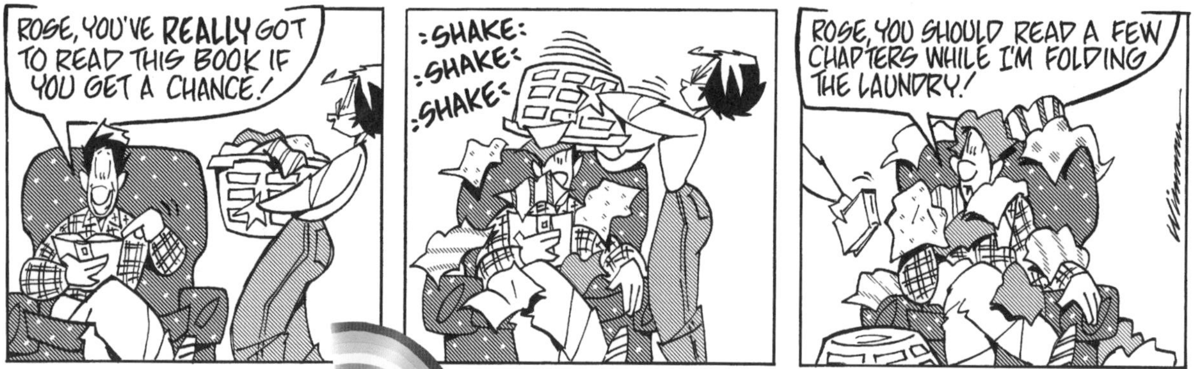
ROSE, YOU'VE REALLY GOT TO READ THIS BOOK IF YOU GET A CHANCE!
:SHAKE: :SHAKE: :SHAKE:
ROSE, YOU SHOULD READ A FEW CHAPTERS WHILE I'M FOLDING THE LAUNDRY!

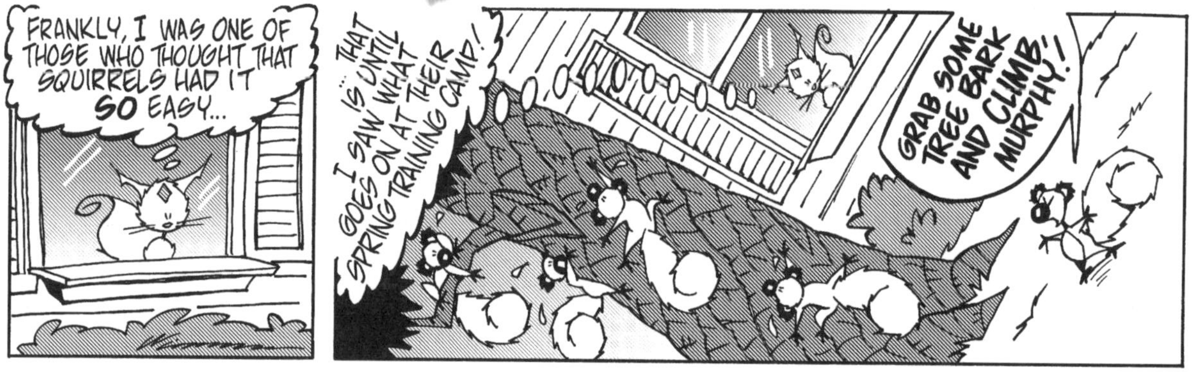
FRANKLY, I WAS ONE OF THOSE WHO THOUGHT THAT SQUIRRELS HAD IT SO EASY...
THAT IS... UNTIL I SAW WHAT GOES ON AT THEIR SPRING TRAINING CAMP!
GRAB SOME TREE BARK AND CLIMB, MURPHY!

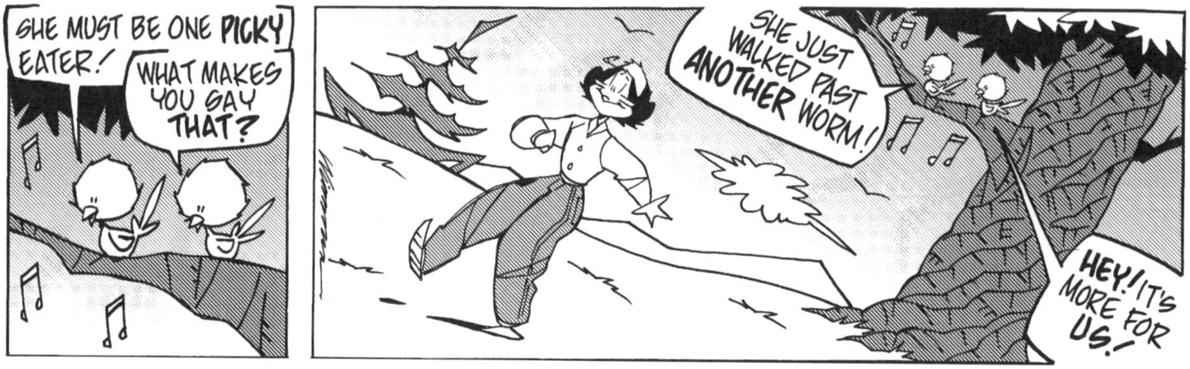
SHE MUST BE ONE PICKY EATER!
WHAT MAKES YOU SAY THAT?
SHE JUST WALKED PAST ANOTHER WORM!
HEY! IT'S MORE FOR US!

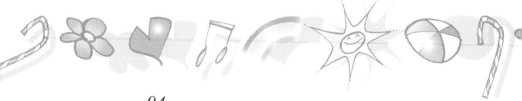

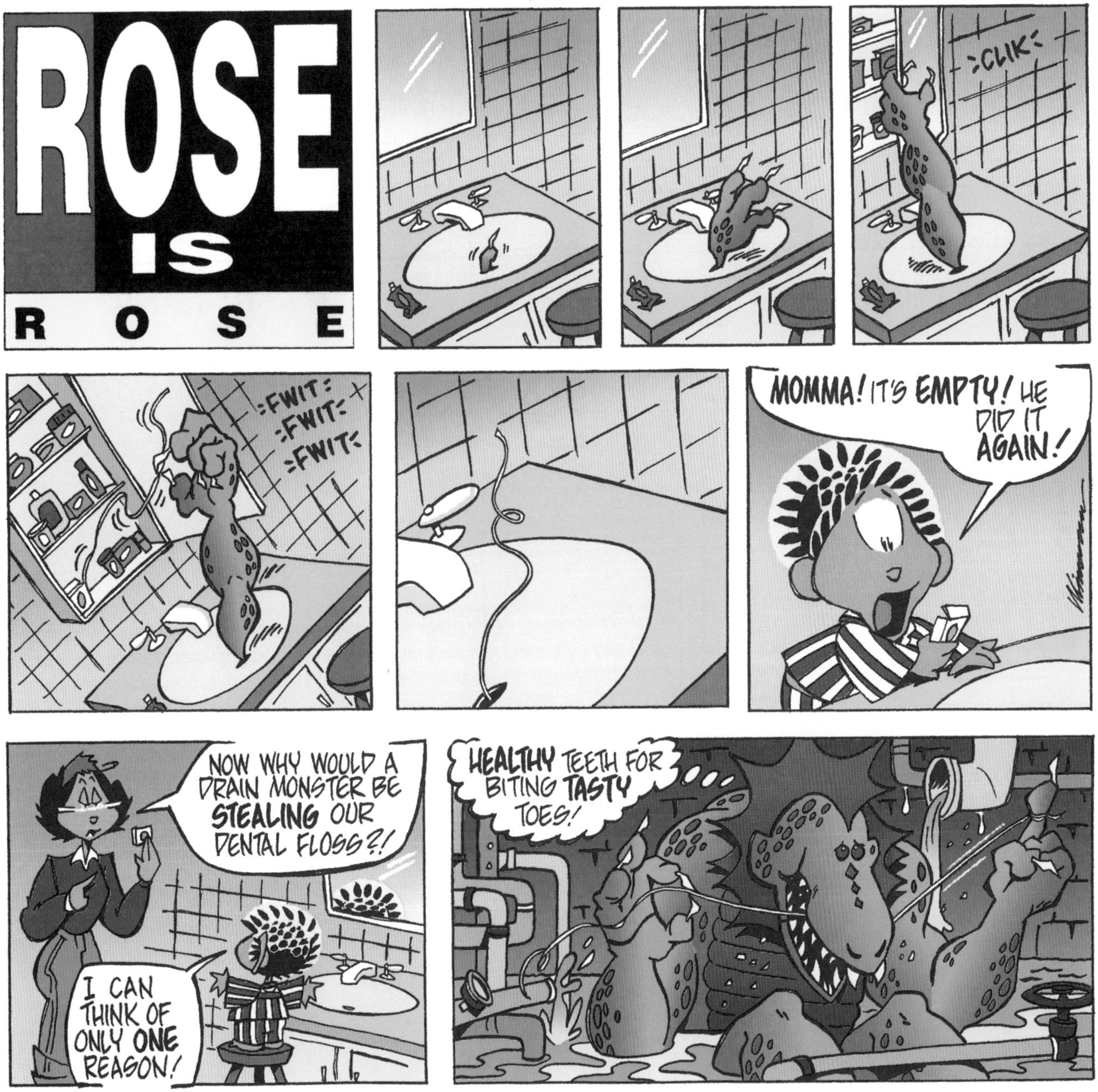
ROSE IS ROSE
CLIK
FWIT FWIT FWIT
MOMMA! IT'S EMPTY! HE DID IT AGAIN!
NOW WHY WOULD A DRAIN MONSTER BE STEALING OUR DENTAL FLOSS?!
I CAN THINK OF ONLY ONE REASON!
HEALTHY TEETH FOR BITING TASTY TOES!

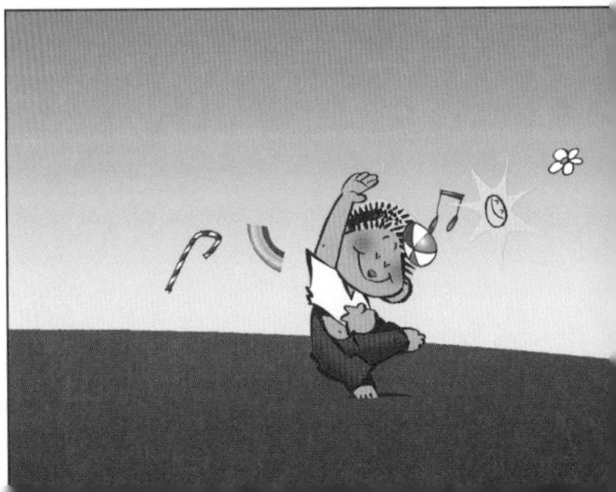

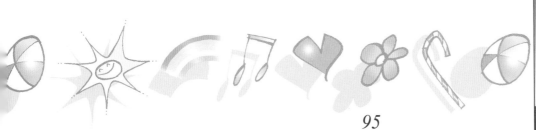

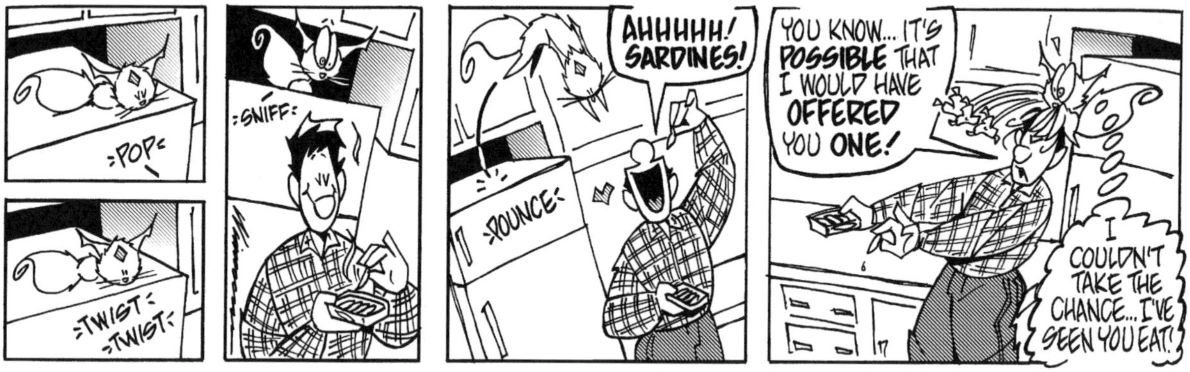

POP
SNIFF
TWIST TWIST
POUNCE
AHHHHH! SARDINES!
YOU KNOW... IT'S **POSSIBLE** THAT I WOULD HAVE **OFFERED** YOU **ONE**!
I COULDN'T TAKE THE CHANCE... I'VE SEEN YOU EAT!

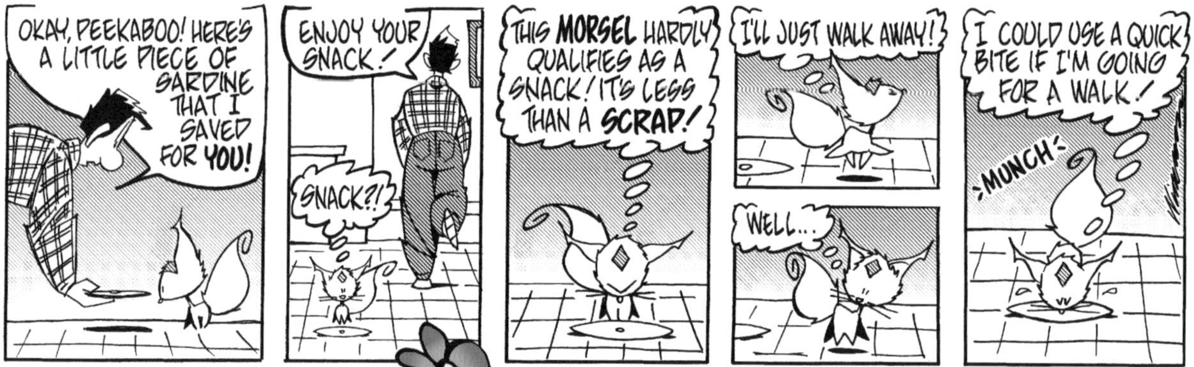

OKAY, PEEKABOO! HERE'S A LITTLE PIECE OF SARDINE THAT I SAVED FOR **YOU**!
ENJOY YOUR SNACK!
SNACK?!
THIS **MORSEL** HARDLY QUALIFIES AS A SNACK! IT'S LESS THAN A **SCRAP**!
I'LL JUST WALK AWAY!
WELL...
I COULD USE A QUICK BITE IF I'M GOING FOR A WALK!
MUNCH

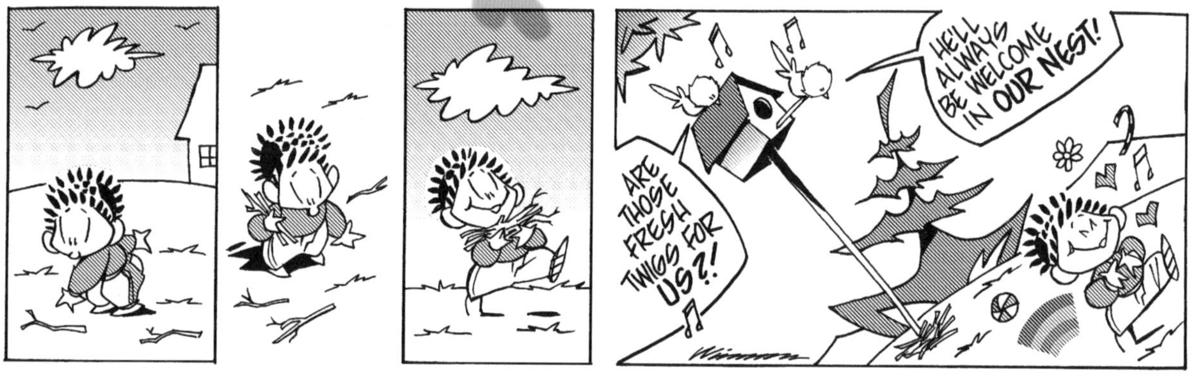

ARE THOSE FRESH TWIGS FOR **US**?!
HE'LL ALWAYS BE WELCOME IN **OUR NEST**!

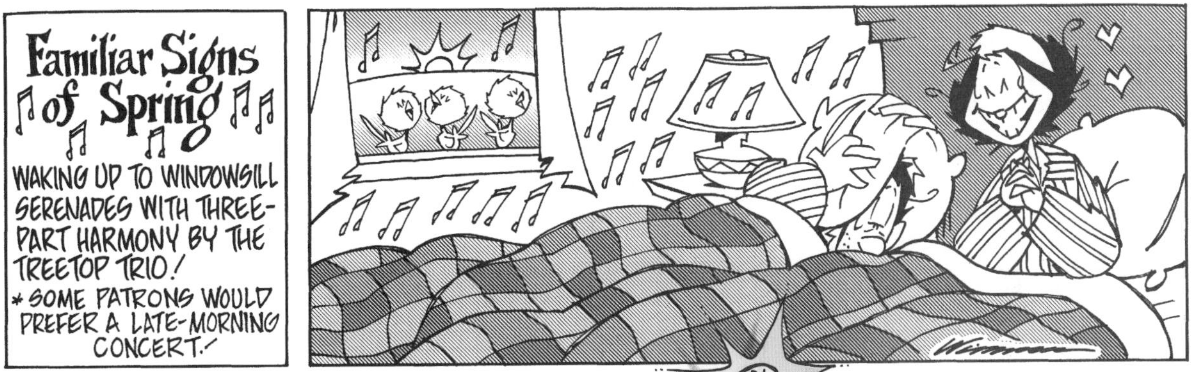
Familiar Signs of Spring
WAKING UP TO WINDOWSILL SERENADES WITH THREE-PART HARMONY BY THE TREETOP TRIO!
* SOME PATRONS WOULD PREFER A LATE-MORNING CONCERT.!

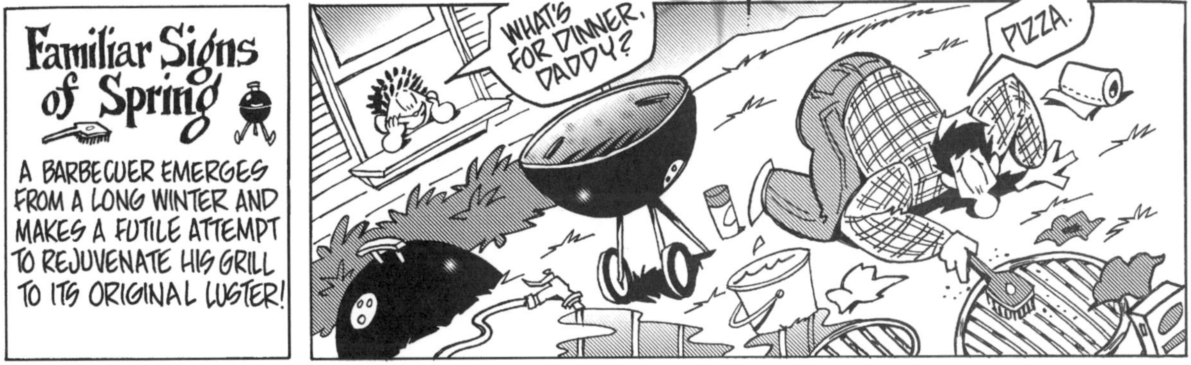
Familiar Signs of Spring
A BARBECUER EMERGES FROM A LONG WINTER AND MAKES A FUTILE ATTEMPT TO REJUVENATE HIS GRILL TO ITS ORIGINAL LUSTER!
WHAT'S FOR DINNER, DADDY?
PIZZA.

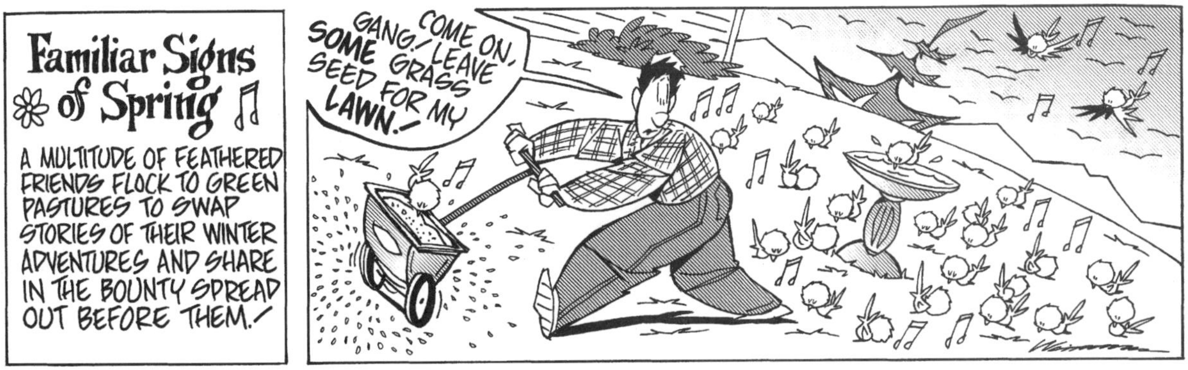
Familiar Signs of Spring
A MULTITUDE OF FEATHERED FRIENDS FLOCK TO GREEN PASTURES TO SWAP STORIES OF THEIR WINTER ADVENTURES AND SHARE IN THE BOUNTY SPREAD OUT BEFORE THEM.!
COME ON, GANG! LEAVE SOME GRASS SEED FOR MY LAWN.!

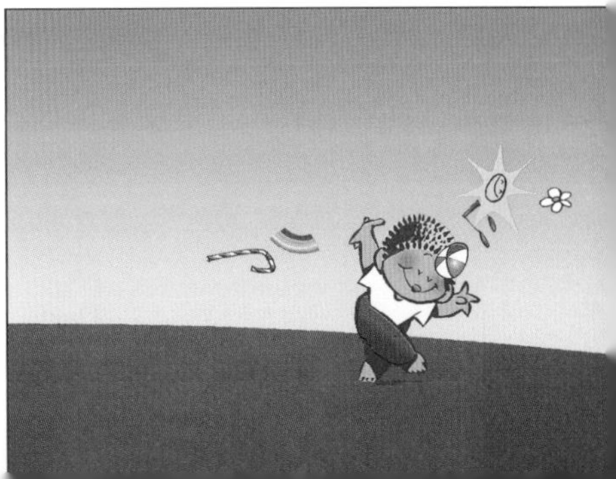

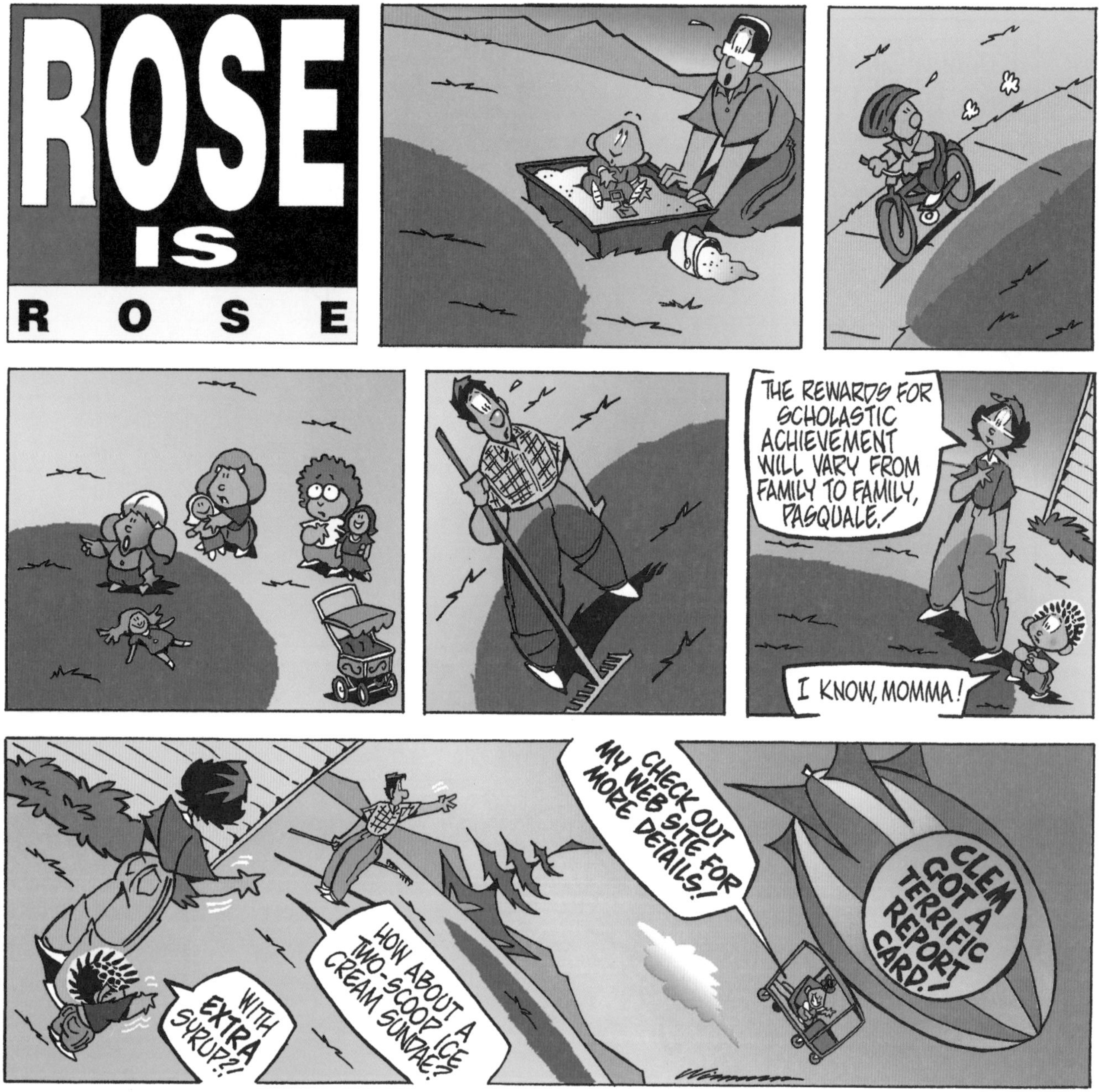
ROSE IS ROSE
THE REWARDS FOR SCHOLASTIC ACHIEVEMENT WILL VARY FROM FAMILY TO FAMILY, PASQUALE!
I KNOW, MOMMA!
CHECK OUT MY WEB SITE FOR MORE DETAILS!
CLEM GOT A TERRIFIC REPORT CARD!
HOW ABOUT A TWO-SCOOP ICE CREAM SUNDAE?
WITH EXTRA SYRUP?!

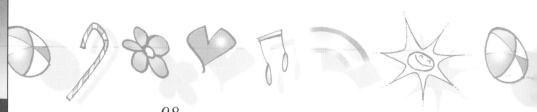

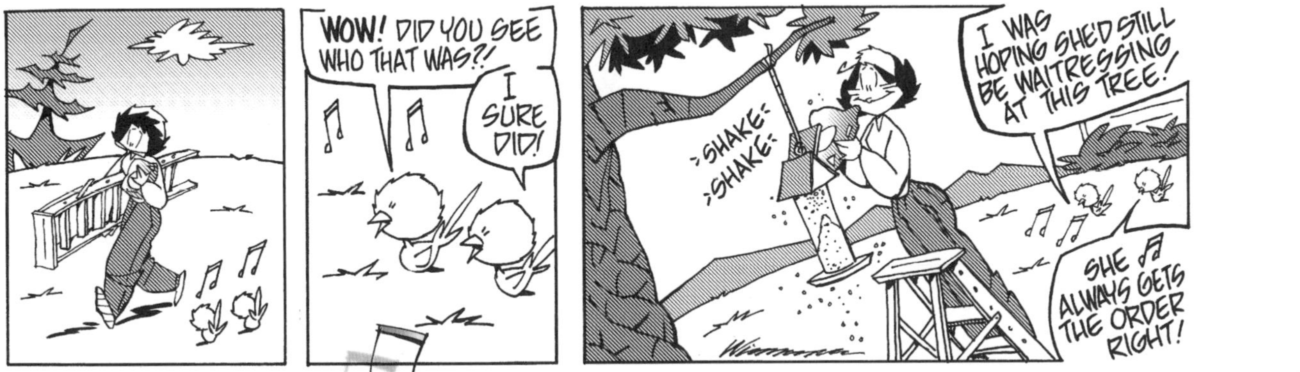
WOW! DID YOU SEE WHO THAT WAS?!
I SURE DID!
I WAS HOPING SHE'D STILL BE WAITRESSING AT THIS TREE!
SHAKE
SHAKE
SHE ALWAYS GETS THE ORDER RIGHT!

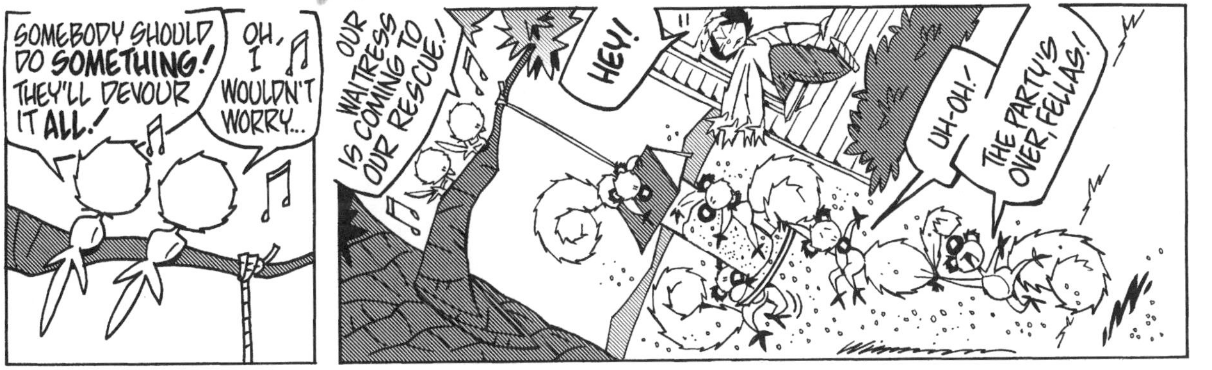
SOMEBODY SHOULD DO SOMETHING! THEY'LL DEVOUR IT ALL!
OH, I WOULDN'T WORRY...
OUR WAITRESS IS COMING TO OUR RESCUE!
HEY!
UH-OH!
THE PARTY'S OVER, FELLAS!

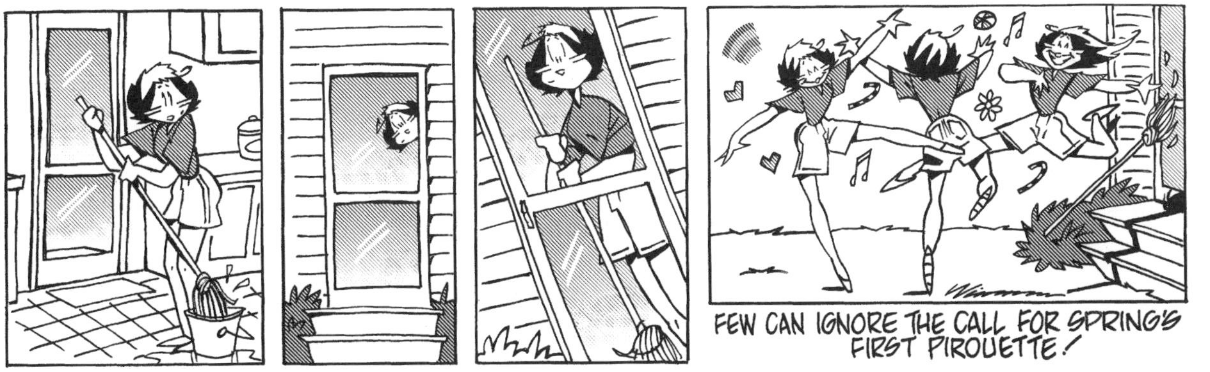
FEW CAN IGNORE THE CALL FOR SPRING'S FIRST PIROUETTE!

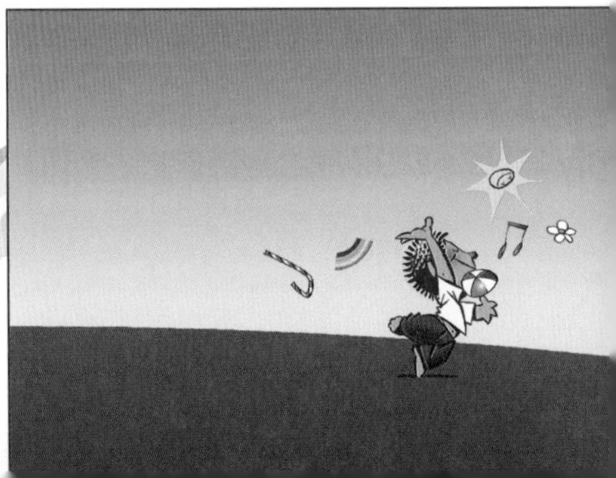

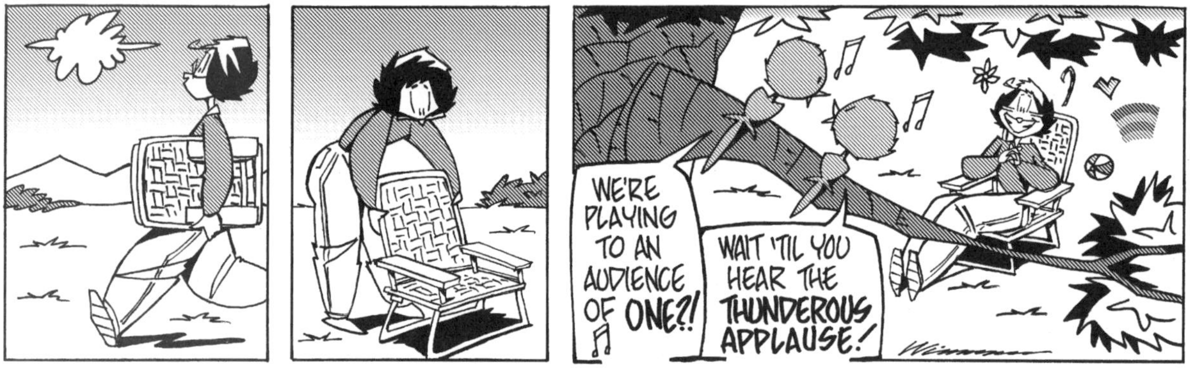
WE'RE PLAYING TO AN AUDIENCE OF ONE?!
WAIT 'TIL YOU HEAR THE THUNDEROUS APPLAUSE!

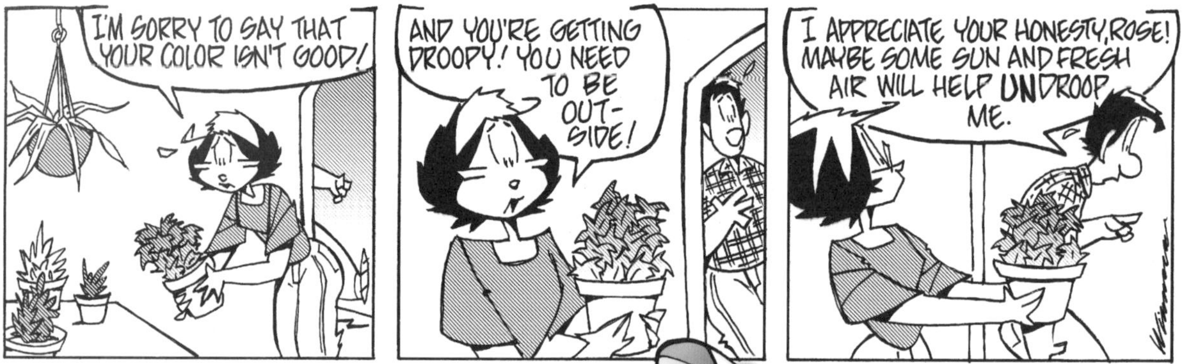
I'M SORRY TO SAY THAT YOUR COLOR ISN'T GOOD!
AND YOU'RE GETTING DROOPY! YOU NEED TO BE OUT-SIDE!
I APPRECIATE YOUR HONESTY, ROSE! MAYBE SOME SUN AND FRESH AIR WILL HELP UNDROOP ME.

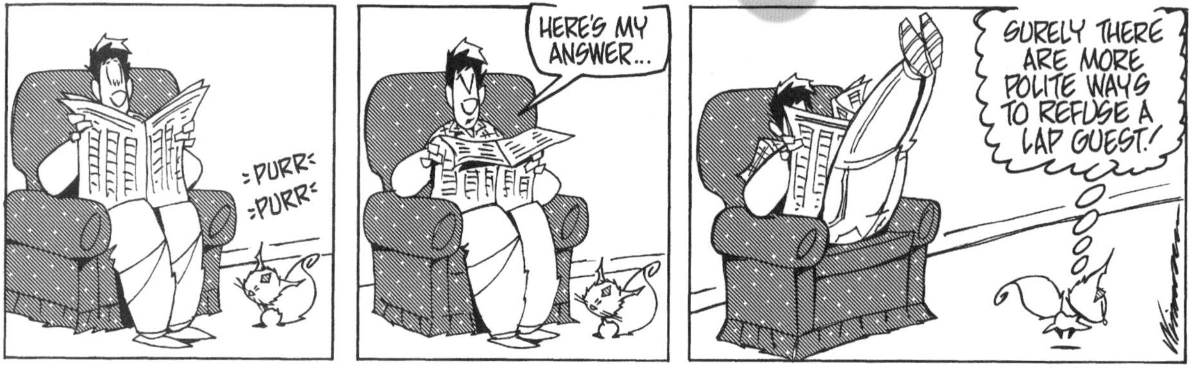
=PURR=
=PURR=
HERE'S MY ANSWER...
SURELY THERE ARE MORE POLITE WAYS TO REFUSE A LAP GUEST!

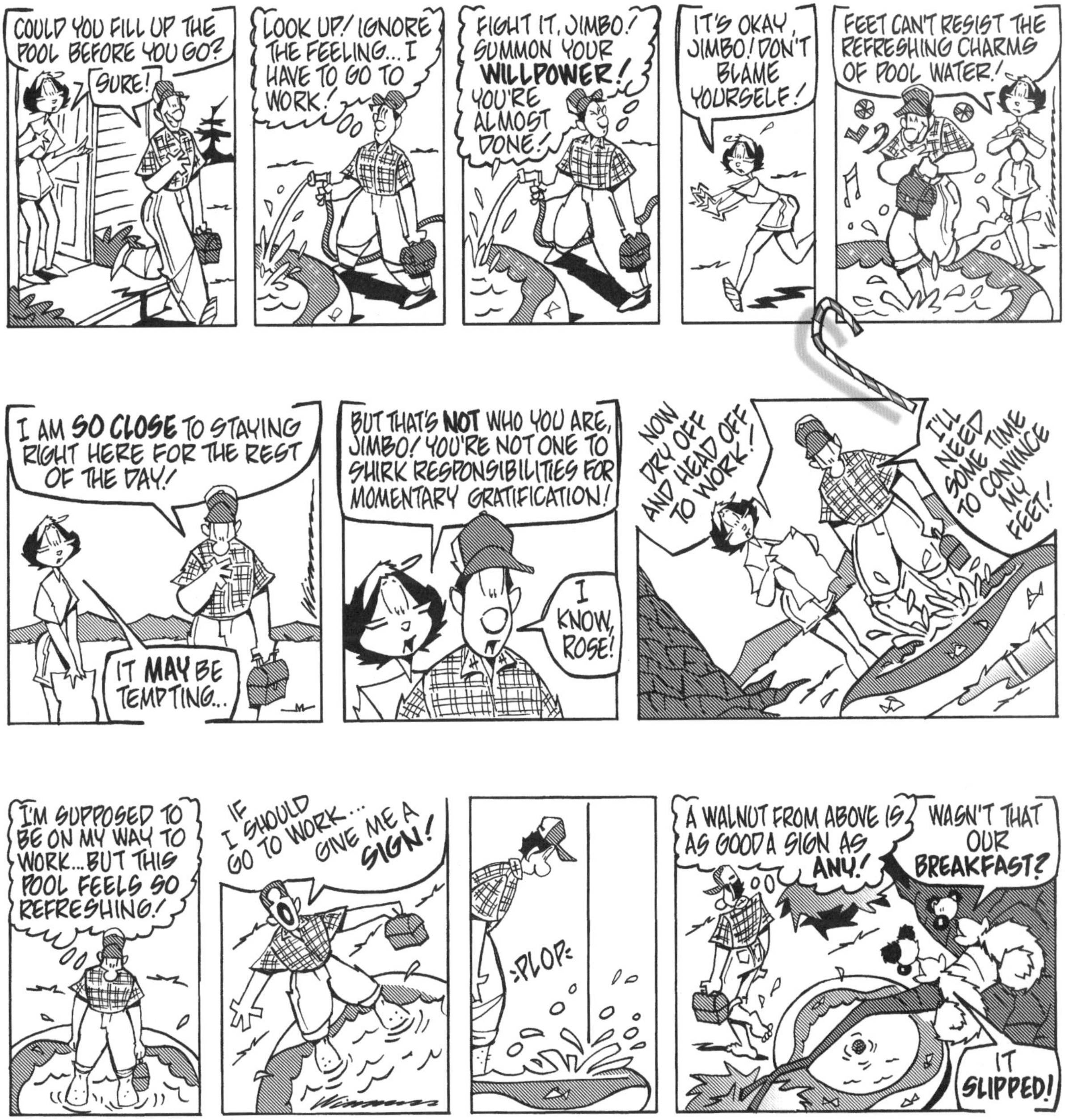
COULD YOU FILL UP THE POOL BEFORE YOU GO?
SURE!
LOOK UP! IGNORE THE FEELING... I HAVE TO GO TO WORK!
FIGHT IT, JIMBO! SUMMON YOUR WILLPOWER! YOU'RE ALMOST DONE!
IT'S OKAY, JIMBO! DON'T BLAME YOURSELF!
FEET CAN'T RESIST THE REFRESHING CHARMS OF POOL WATER!
I AM SO CLOSE TO STAYING RIGHT HERE FOR THE REST OF THE DAY!
IT MAY BE TEMPTING...
BUT THAT'S NOT WHO YOU ARE, JIMBO! YOU'RE NOT ONE TO SHIRK RESPONSIBILITIES FOR MOMENTARY GRATIFICATION!
I KNOW, ROSE!
NOW DRY OFF AND HEAD OFF TO WORK!
I'LL NEED SOME TIME TO CONVINCE MY FEET!
I'M SUPPOSED TO BE ON MY WAY TO WORK... BUT THIS POOL FEELS SO REFRESHING!
IF I SHOULD GO TO WORK... GIVE ME A SIGN!
PLOP
A WALNUT FROM ABOVE IS AS GOOD A SIGN AS ANY!
WASN'T THAT OUR BREAKFAST?
IT SLIPPED!

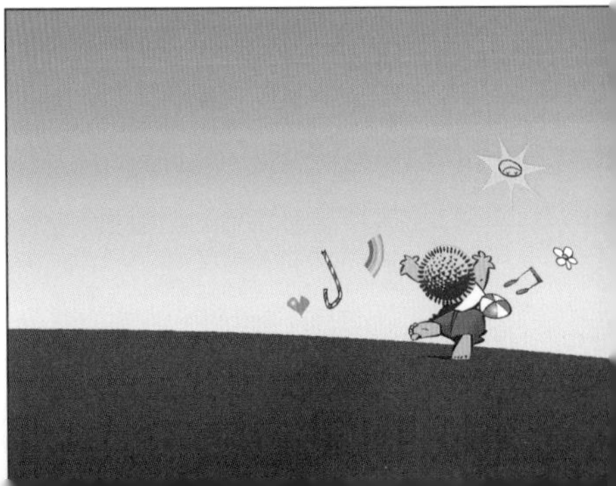

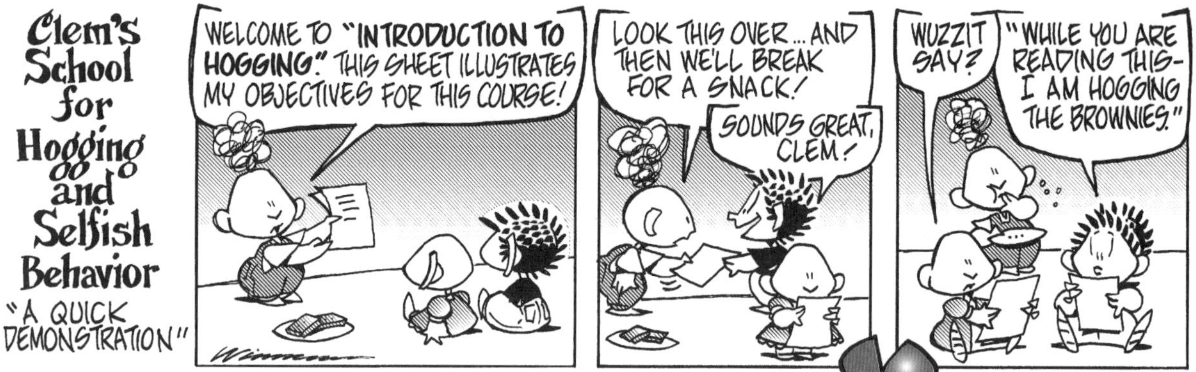
Clem's School for Hogging and Selfish Behavior
"A QUICK DEMONSTRATION"
WELCOME TO "INTRODUCTION TO HOGGING." THIS SHEET ILLUSTRATES MY OBJECTIVES FOR THIS COURSE!
LOOK THIS OVER... AND THEN WE'LL BREAK FOR A SNACK!
SOUNDS GREAT, CLEM!
WUZZIT SAY?
"WHILE YOU ARE READING THIS- I AM HOGGING THE BROWNIES."

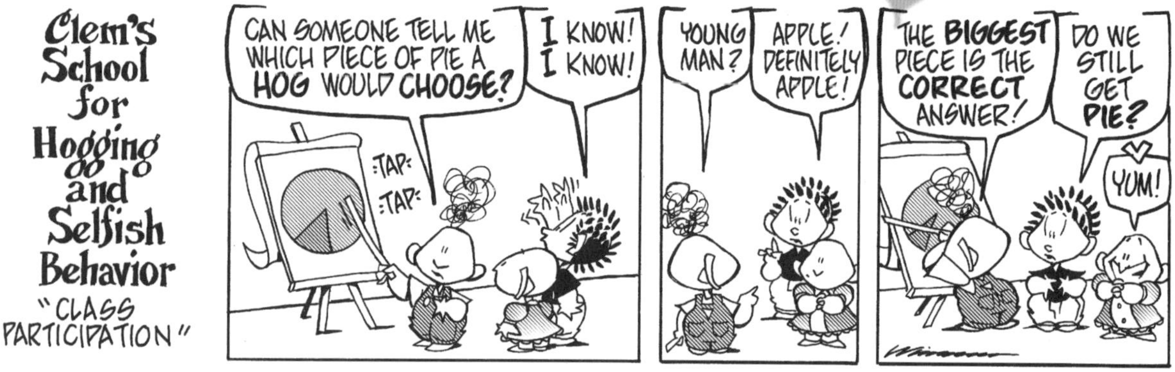
Clem's School for Hogging and Selfish Behavior
"CLASS PARTICIPATION"
CAN SOMEONE TELL ME WHICH PIECE OF PIE A HOG WOULD CHOOSE?
I KNOW! I KNOW!
TAP
TAP
YOUNG MAN?
APPLE! DEFINITELY APPLE!
THE BIGGEST PIECE IS THE CORRECT ANSWER!
DO WE STILL GET PIE?
YUM!

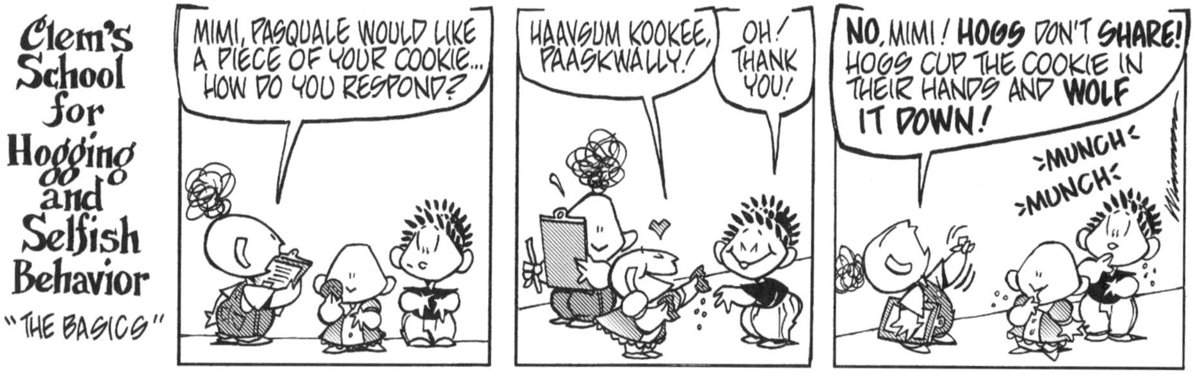
Clem's School for Hogging and Selfish Behavior
"THE BASICS"
MIMI, PASQUALE WOULD LIKE A PIECE OF YOUR COOKIE... HOW DO YOU RESPOND?
HAAVSUM KOOKEE, PAASKWALLY!
OH! THANK YOU!
NO, MIMI! HOGS DON'T SHARE! HOGS CUP THE COOKIE IN THEIR HANDS AND WOLF IT DOWN!
MUNCH
MUNCH

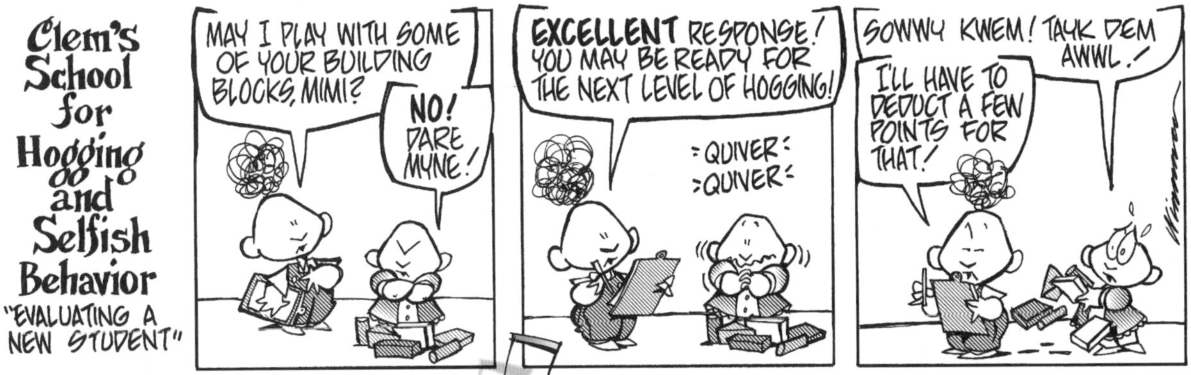

Clem's School for Hogging and Selfish Behavior
"EVALUATING A NEW STUDENT"
MAY I PLAY WITH SOME OF YOUR BUILDING BLOCKS, MIMI?
NO! DARE MYNE!
EXCELLENT RESPONSE! YOU MAY BE READY FOR THE NEXT LEVEL OF HOGGING!
:QUIVER: :QUIVER:
SOWWY KWEM! TAYK DEM AWWL!
I'LL HAVE TO DEDUCT A FEW POINTS FOR THAT!

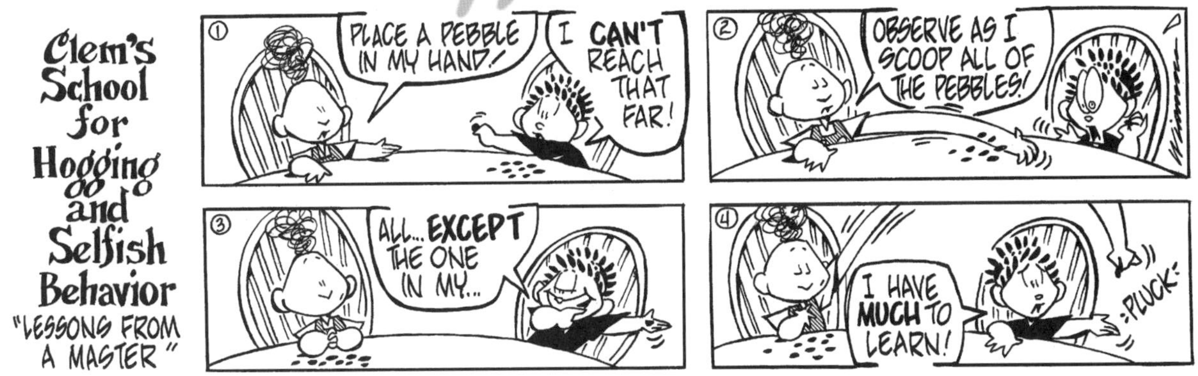

Clem's School for Hogging and Selfish Behavior
"LESSONS FROM A MASTER"
1
PLACE A PEBBLE IN MY HAND!
I CAN'T REACH THAT FAR!
2
OBSERVE AS I SCOOP ALL OF THE PEBBLES!
3
ALL... EXCEPT THE ONE IN MY...
4
I HAVE MUCH TO LEARN!
:PLUCK:

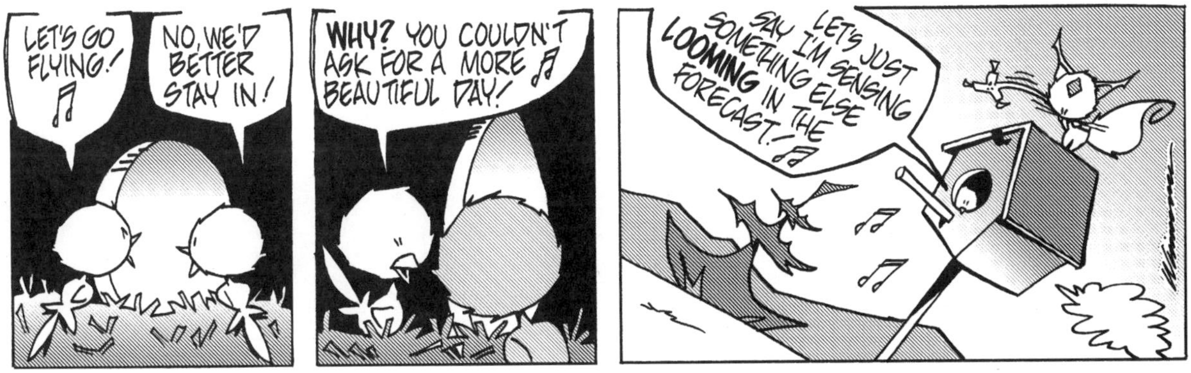

LET'S GO FLYING!
NO, WE'D BETTER STAY IN!
WHY? YOU COULDN'T ASK FOR A MORE BEAUTIFUL DAY!
LET'S JUST SAY I'M SENSING SOMETHING ELSE LOOMING IN THE FORECAST!

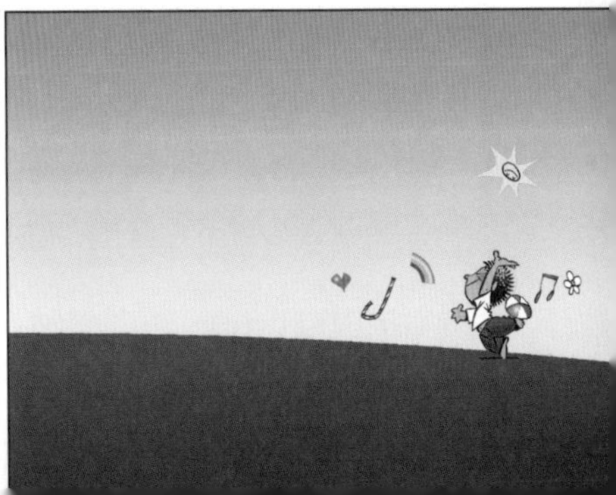

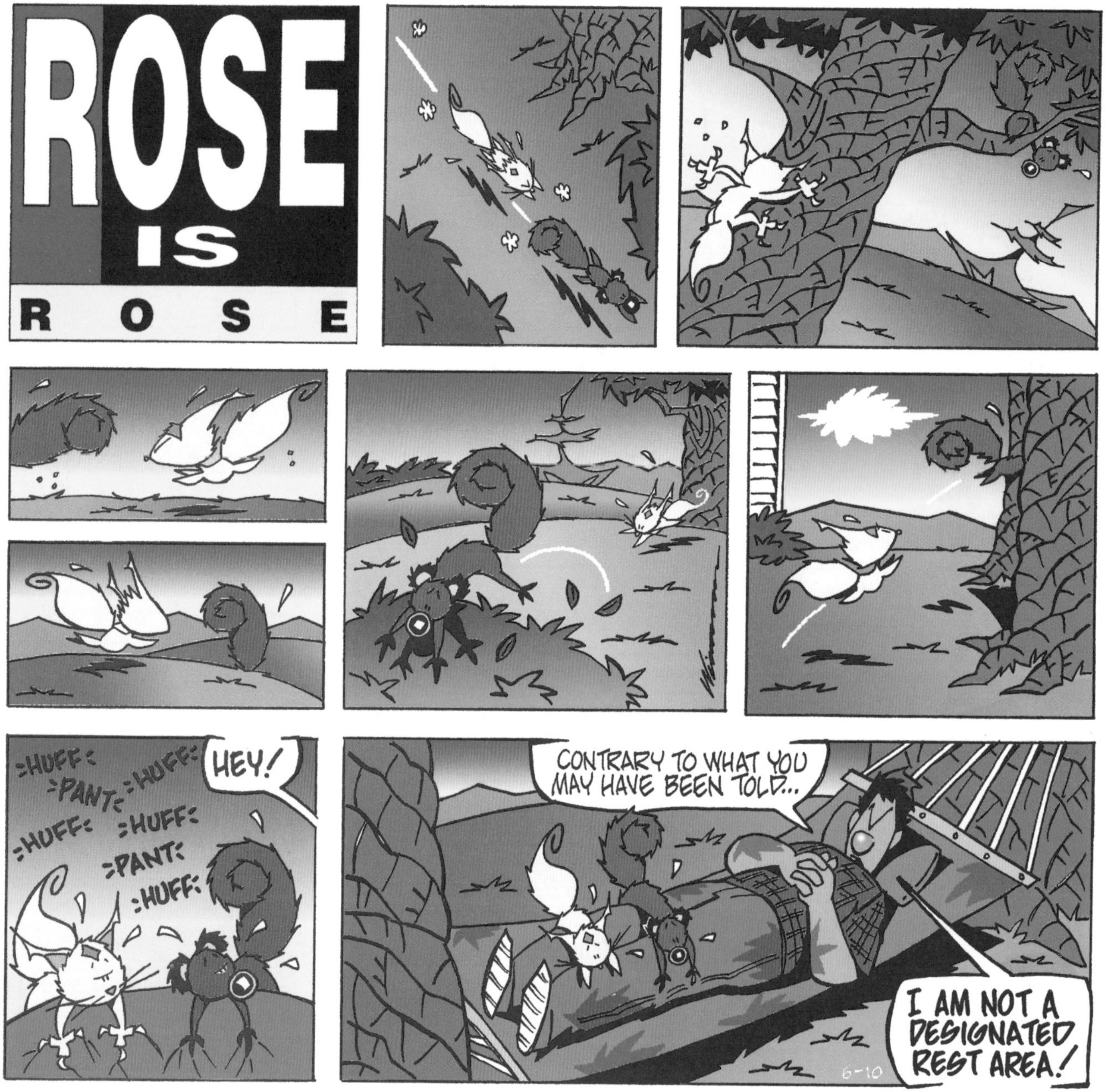
ROSE IS ROSE
HUFF
PANT
HUFF
HUFF
HUFF
PANT
HUFF
HEY!
CONTRARY TO WHAT YOU MAY HAVE BEEN TOLD...
I AM NOT A DESIGNATED REST AREA!
6-10

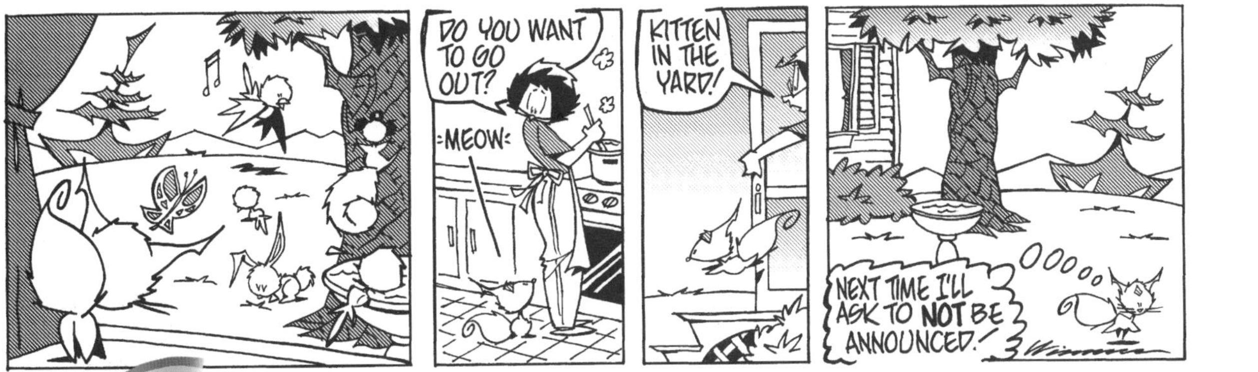
DO YOU WANT TO GO OUT?
=MEOW=
KITTEN IN THE YARD!
NEXT TIME I'LL ASK TO **NOT** BE ANNOUNCED!

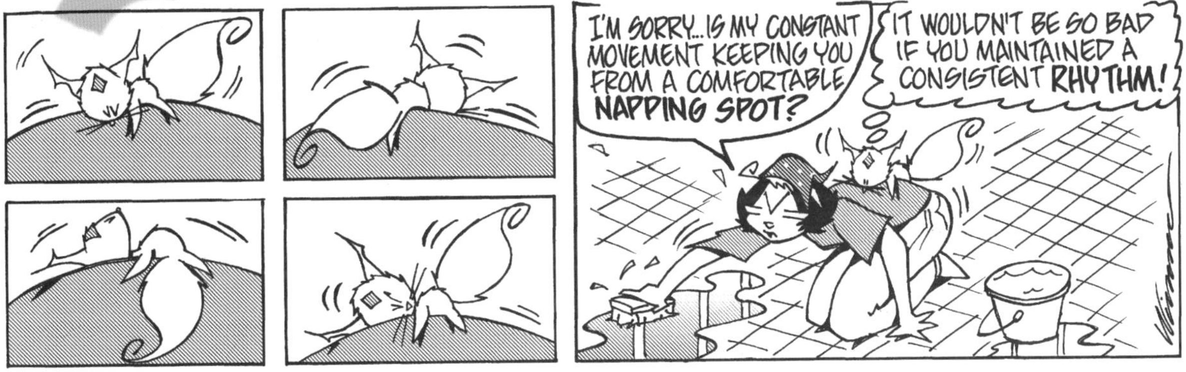
I'M SORRY...IS MY CONSTANT MOVEMENT KEEPING YOU FROM A COMFORTABLE **NAPPING SPOT?**
IT WOULDN'T BE SO BAD IF YOU MAINTAINED A CONSISTENT **RHYTHM!**

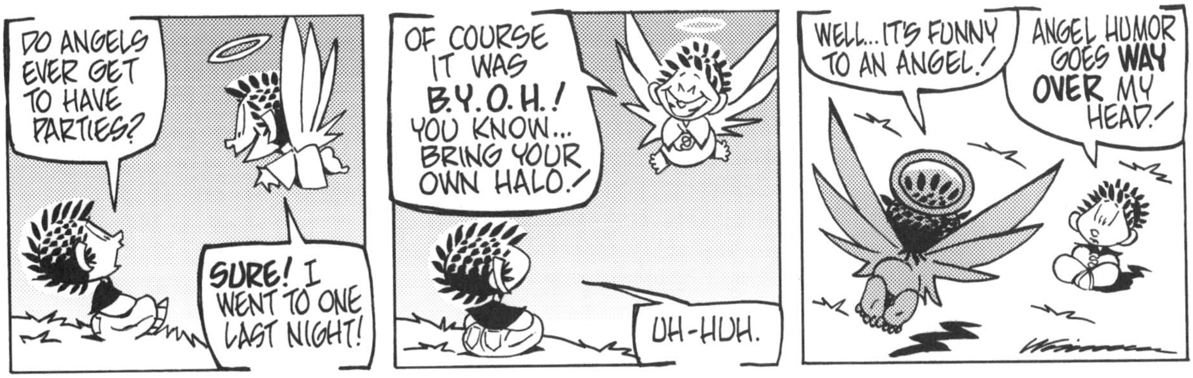
DO ANGELS EVER GET TO HAVE PARTIES?
SURE! I WENT TO ONE LAST NIGHT!
OF COURSE IT WAS **B.Y.O.H.!** YOU KNOW... BRING YOUR OWN HALO!
UH-HUH.
WELL... IT'S FUNNY TO AN ANGEL!
ANGEL HUMOR GOES **WAY OVER** MY HEAD!

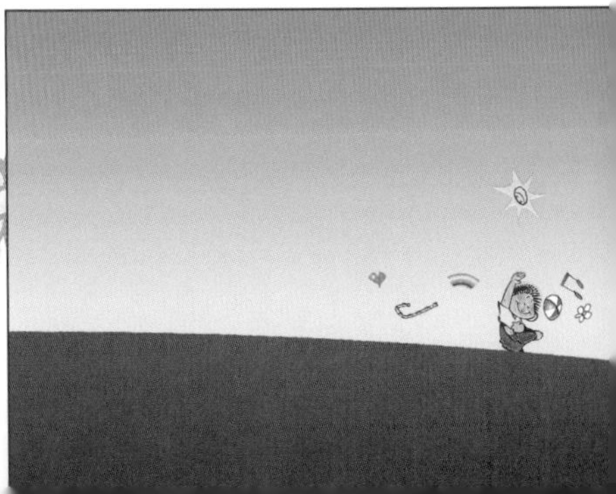

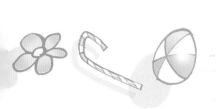

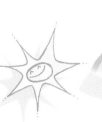

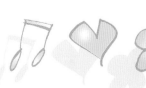

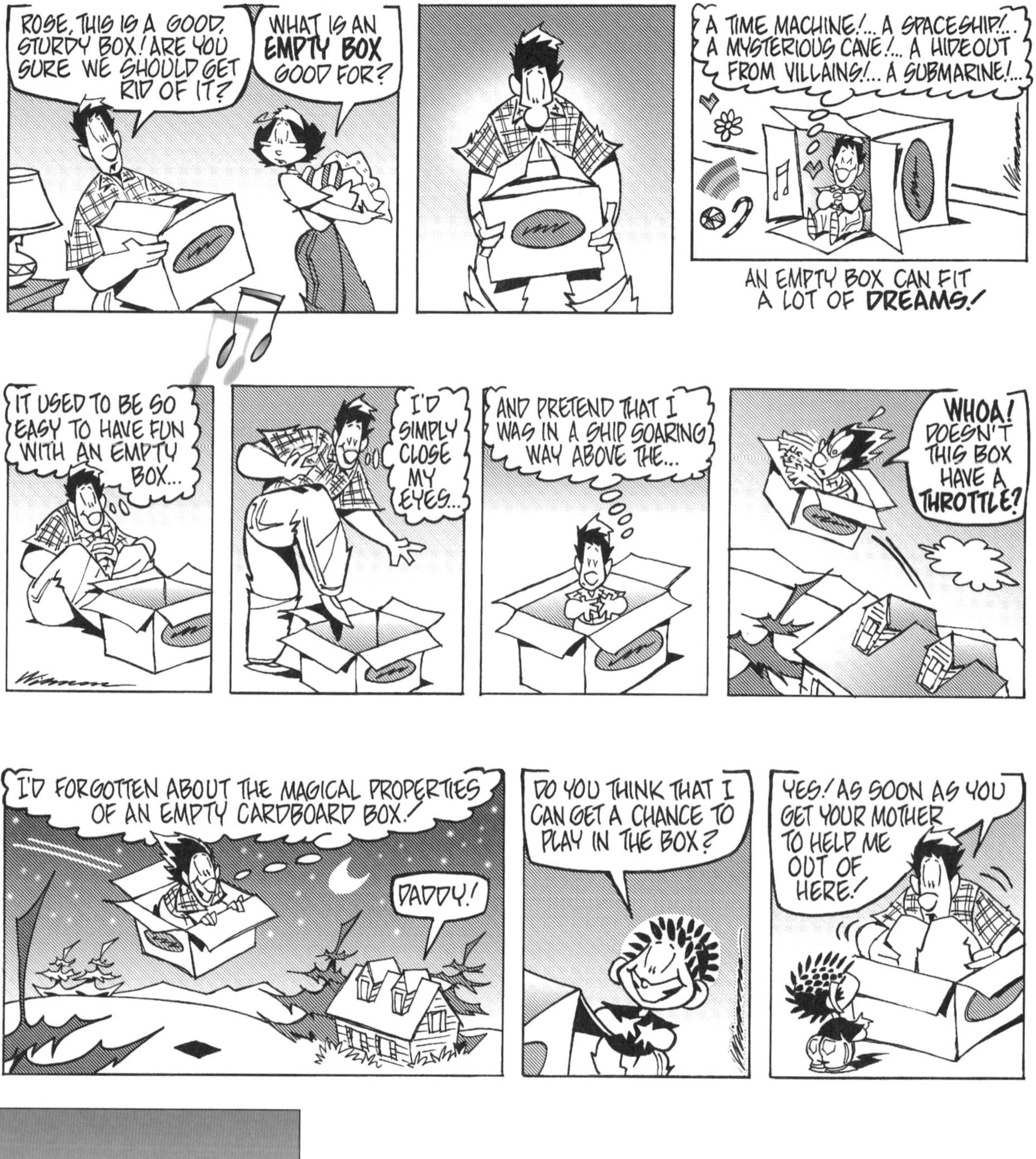
ROSE, THIS IS A GOOD, STURDY BOX! ARE YOU SURE WE SHOULD GET RID OF IT?
WHAT IS AN **EMPTY BOX** GOOD FOR?
A TIME MACHINE!... A SPACESHIP!... A MYSTERIOUS CAVE!... A HIDEOUT FROM VILLAINS!... A SUBMARINE!...
AN EMPTY BOX CAN FIT A LOT OF **DREAMS!**
IT USED TO BE SO EASY TO HAVE FUN WITH AN EMPTY BOX...
I'D SIMPLY CLOSE MY EYES...
AND PRETEND THAT I WAS IN A SHIP SOARING WAY ABOVE THE...
WHOA! DOESN'T THIS BOX HAVE A **THROTTLE?**
I'D FORGOTTEN ABOUT THE MAGICAL PROPERTIES OF AN EMPTY CARDBOARD BOX!
DADDY!
DO YOU THINK THAT I CAN GET A CHANCE TO PLAY IN THE BOX?
YES! AS SOON AS YOU GET YOUR MOTHER TO HELP ME OUT OF HERE!

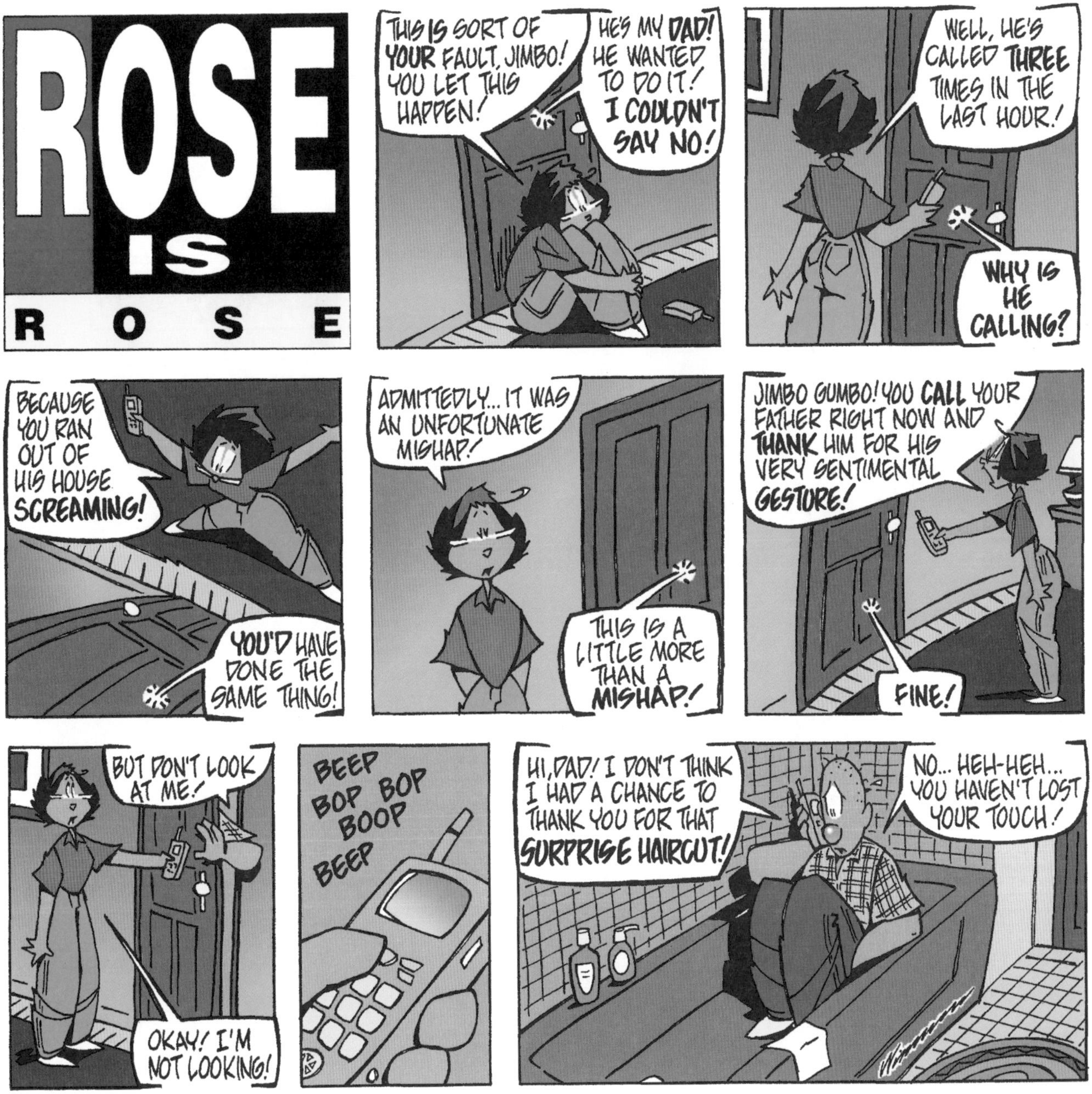
ROSE IS ROSE
THIS IS SORT OF YOUR FAULT, JIMBO! YOU LET THIS HAPPEN!
HE'S MY DAD! HE WANTED TO DO IT! I COULDN'T SAY NO!
WELL, HE'S CALLED THREE TIMES IN THE LAST HOUR!
WHY IS HE CALLING?
BECAUSE YOU RAN OUT OF HIS HOUSE SCREAMING!
YOU'D HAVE DONE THE SAME THING!
ADMITTEDLY... IT WAS AN UNFORTUNATE MISHAP!
THIS IS A LITTLE MORE THAN A MISHAP!
JIMBO GUMBO! YOU CALL YOUR FATHER RIGHT NOW AND THANK HIM FOR HIS VERY SENTIMENTAL GESTURE!
FINE!
BUT DON'T LOOK AT ME!
OKAY! I'M NOT LOOKING!
BEEP BOP BOP BOOP BEEP
HI, DAD! I DON'T THINK I HAD A CHANCE TO THANK YOU FOR THAT SURPRISE HAIRCUT!
NO... HEH-HEH... YOU HAVEN'T LOST YOUR TOUCH!

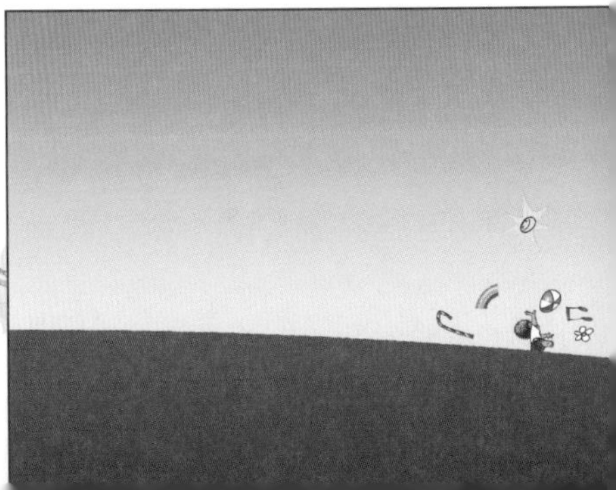

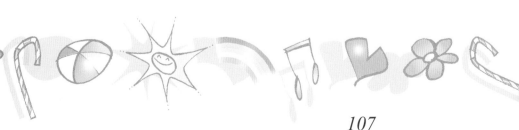

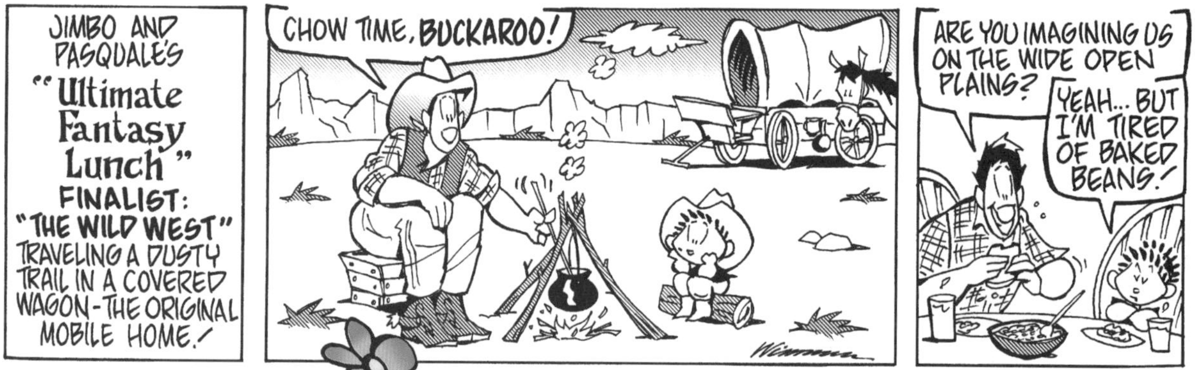
JIMBO AND PASQUALE'S "Ultimate Fantasy Lunch" FINALIST: "THE WILD WEST" TRAVELING A DUSTY TRAIL IN A COVERED WAGON-THE ORIGINAL MOBILE HOME!
CHOW TIME, BUCKAROO!
ARE YOU IMAGINING US ON THE WIDE OPEN PLAINS?
YEAH... BUT I'M TIRED OF BAKED BEANS!

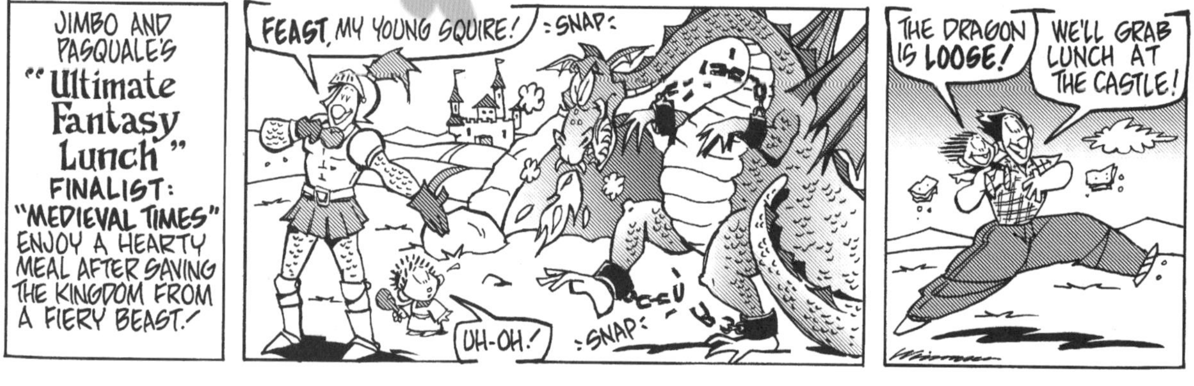
JIMBO AND PASQUALE'S "Ultimate Fantasy Lunch" FINALIST: "MEDIEVAL TIMES" ENJOY A HEARTY MEAL AFTER SAVING THE KINGDOM FROM A FIERY BEAST!
FEAST, MY YOUNG SQUIRE!
SNAP
UH-OH!
SNAP
THE DRAGON IS LOOSE!
WE'LL GRAB LUNCH AT THE CASTLE!

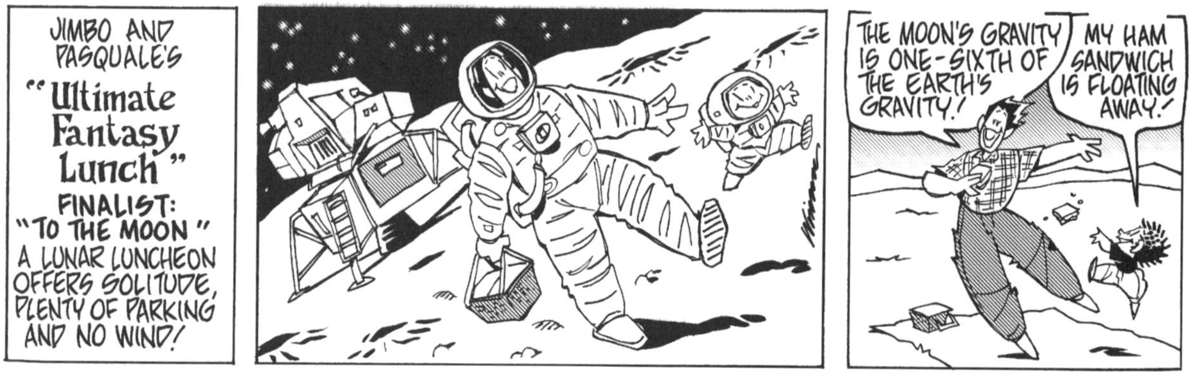
JIMBO AND PASQUALE'S "Ultimate Fantasy Lunch" FINALIST: "TO THE MOON" A LUNAR LUNCHEON OFFERS SOLITUDE, PLENTY OF PARKING AND NO WIND!
THE MOON'S GRAVITY IS ONE-SIXTH OF THE EARTH'S GRAVITY!
MY HAM SANDWICH IS FLOATING AWAY!

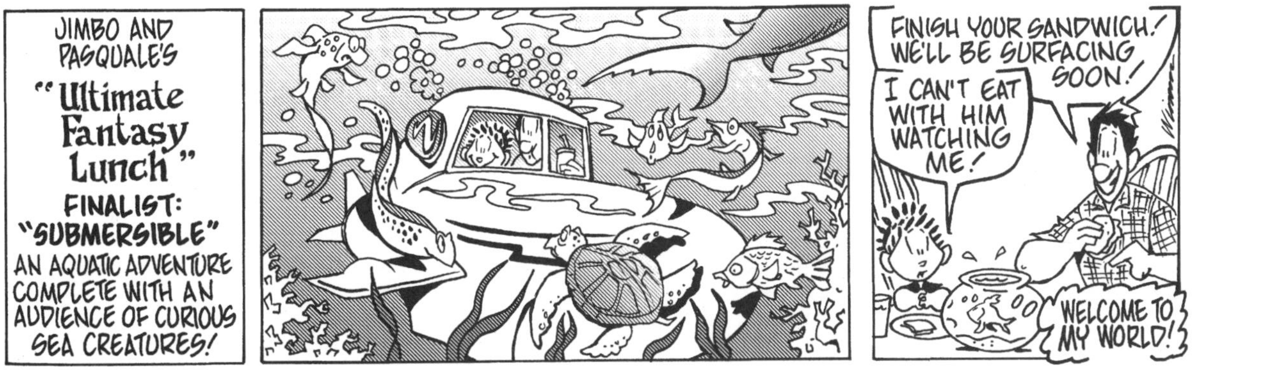
JIMBO AND PASQUALE'S "Ultimate Fantasy Lunch" FINALIST: "SUBMERSIBLE" AN AQUATIC ADVENTURE COMPLETE WITH AN AUDIENCE OF CURIOUS SEA CREATURES!
FINISH YOUR SANDWICH! WE'LL BE SURFACING SOON!
I CAN'T EAT WITH HIM WATCHING ME!
WELCOME TO MY WORLD!

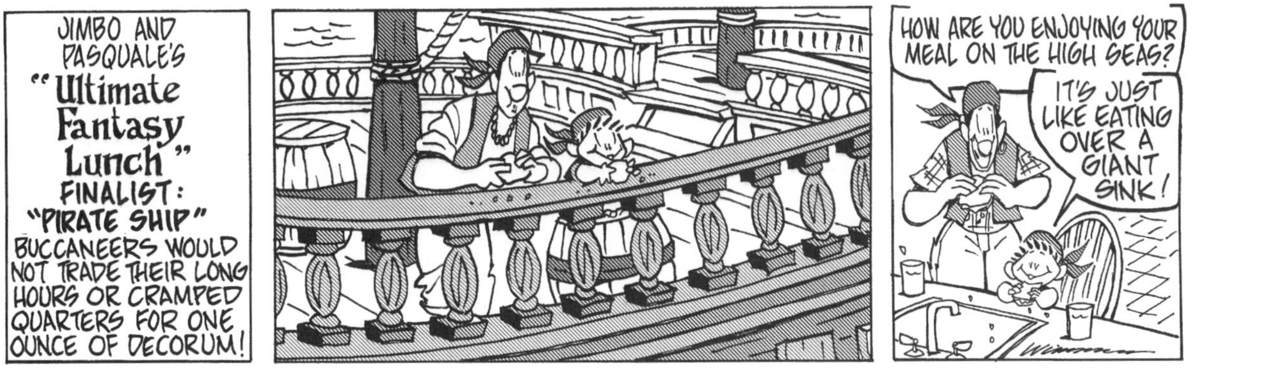
JIMBO AND PASQUALE'S "Ultimate Fantasy Lunch" FINALIST: "PIRATE SHIP" BUCCANEERS WOULD NOT TRADE THEIR LONG HOURS OR CRAMPED QUARTERS FOR ONE OUNCE OF DECORUM!
HOW ARE YOU ENJOYING YOUR MEAL ON THE HIGH SEAS?
IT'S JUST LIKE EATING OVER A GIANT SINK!

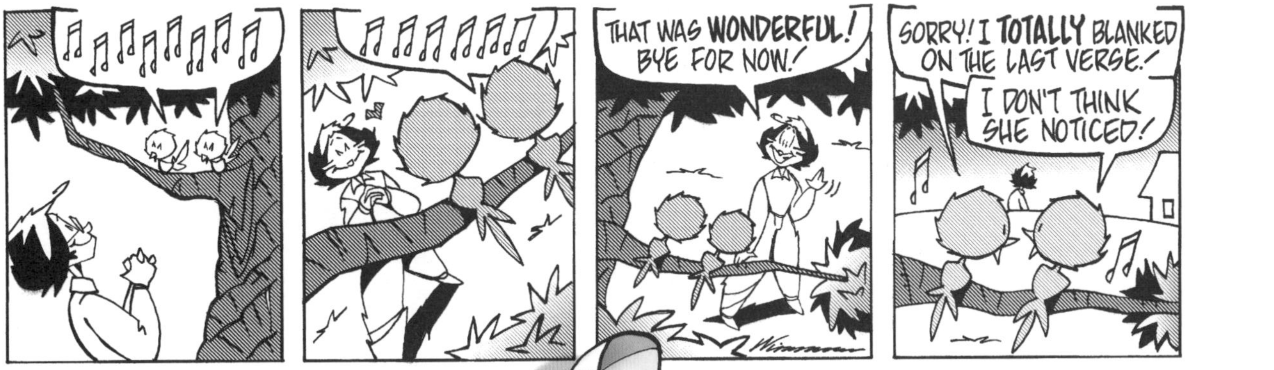
THAT WAS WONDERFUL! BYE FOR NOW!
SORRY! I TOTALLY BLANKED ON THE LAST VERSE!
I DON'T THINK SHE NOTICED!

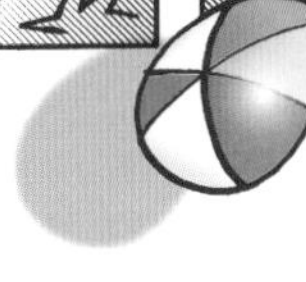

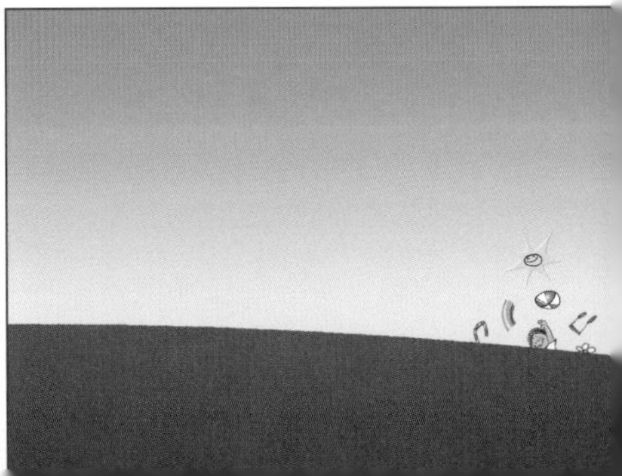

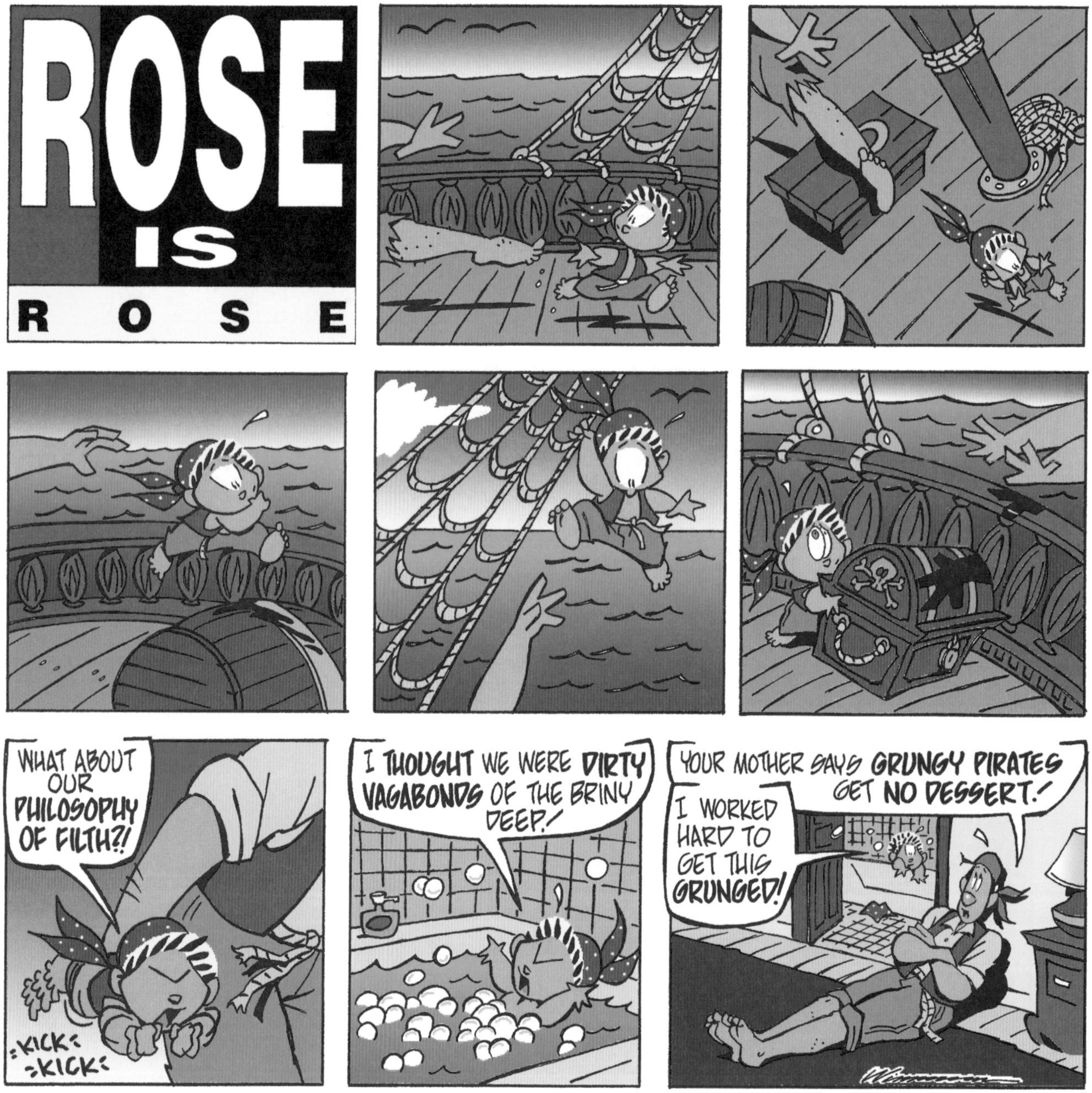
ROSE IS ROSE
WHAT ABOUT OUR PHILOSOPHY OF FILTH?!
KICK KICK
I THOUGHT WE WERE DIRTY VAGABONDS OF THE BRINY DEEP!
YOUR MOTHER SAYS GRUNGY PIRATES GET NO DESSERT!
I WORKED HARD TO GET THIS GRUNGED!

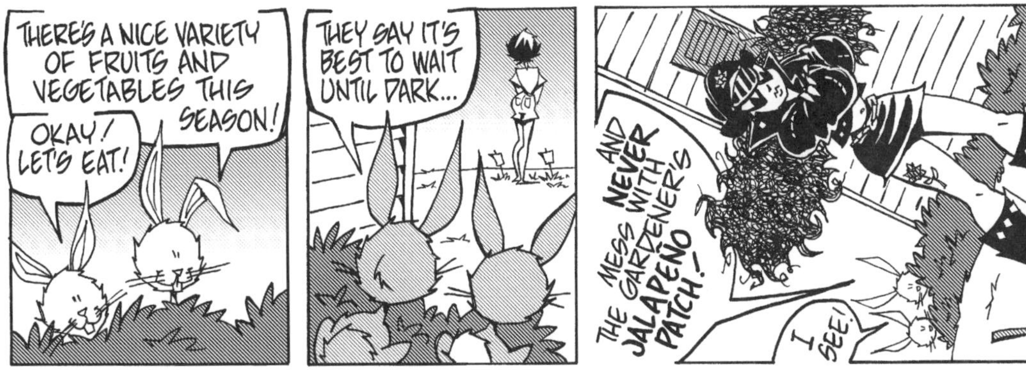
THERE'S A NICE VARIETY OF FRUITS AND VEGETABLES THIS SEASON!
OKAY! LET'S EAT!
THEY SAY IT'S BEST TO WAIT UNTIL DARK...
AND NEVER MESS WITH THE GARDENER'S JALAPEÑO PATCH!
I SEE!

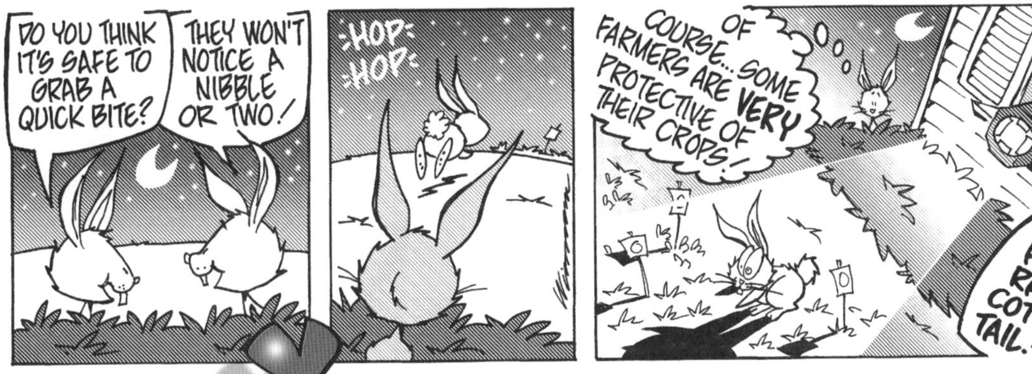
DO YOU THINK IT'S SAFE TO GRAB A QUICK BITE?
THEY WON'T NOTICE A NIBBLE OR TWO!
HOP
HOP
OF COURSE... SOME FARMERS ARE VERY PROTECTIVE OF THEIR CROPS!
HOP AWAY FROM THE RADISHES, COTTON-TAIL!

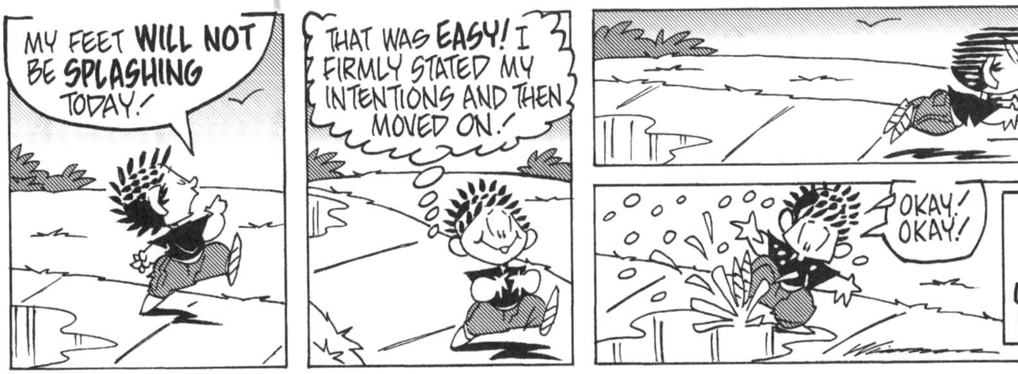
MY FEET WILL NOT BE SPLASHING TODAY!
THAT WAS EASY! I FIRMLY STATED MY INTENTIONS AND THEN MOVED ON!
OKAY! OKAY!
PUDDLES HAVE A KNACK FOR UNSPOKEN PERSUASION!

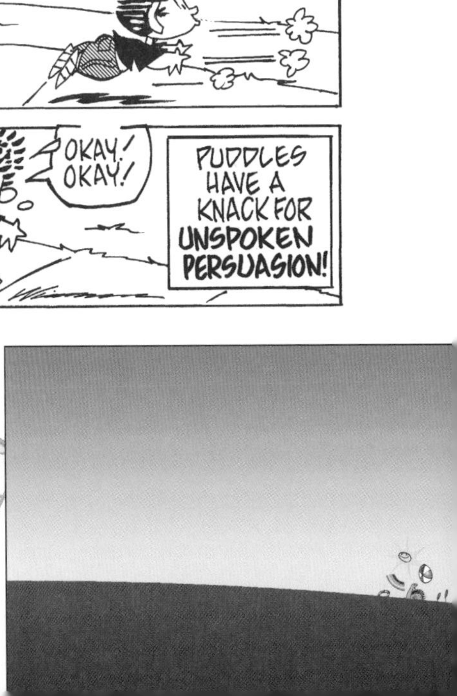

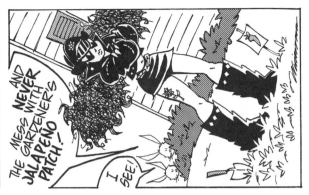

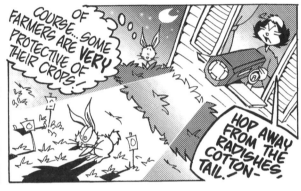

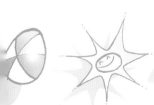

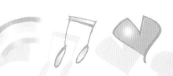

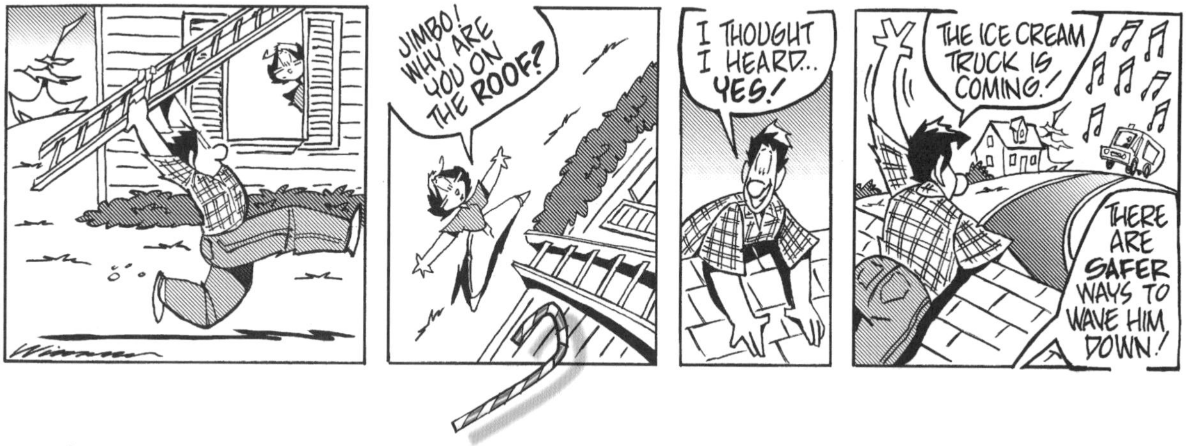
JIMBO! WHY ARE YOU ON THE ROOF?
I THOUGHT I HEARD... YES!
THE ICE CREAM TRUCK IS COMING!
THERE ARE SAFER WAYS TO WAVE HIM DOWN!

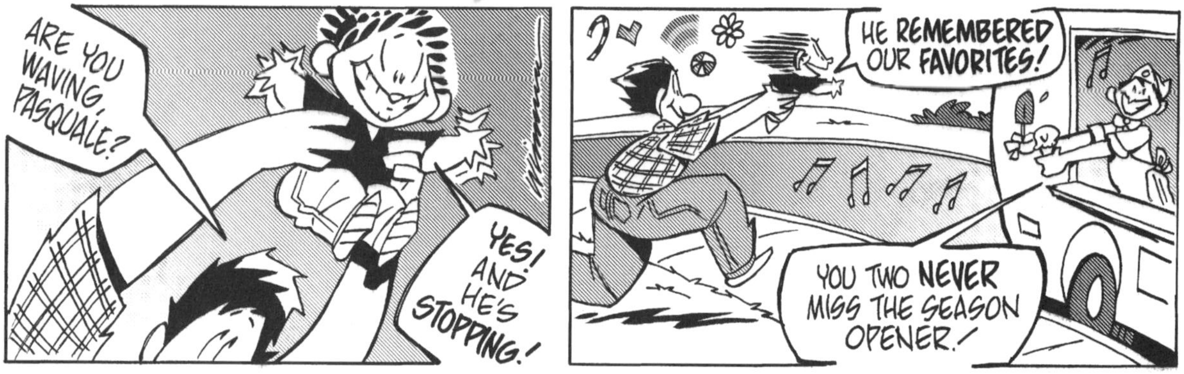
ARE YOU WAVING, PASQUALE?
YES! AND HE'S STOPPING!
HE REMEMBERED OUR FAVORITES!
YOU TWO NEVER MISS THE SEASON OPENER!

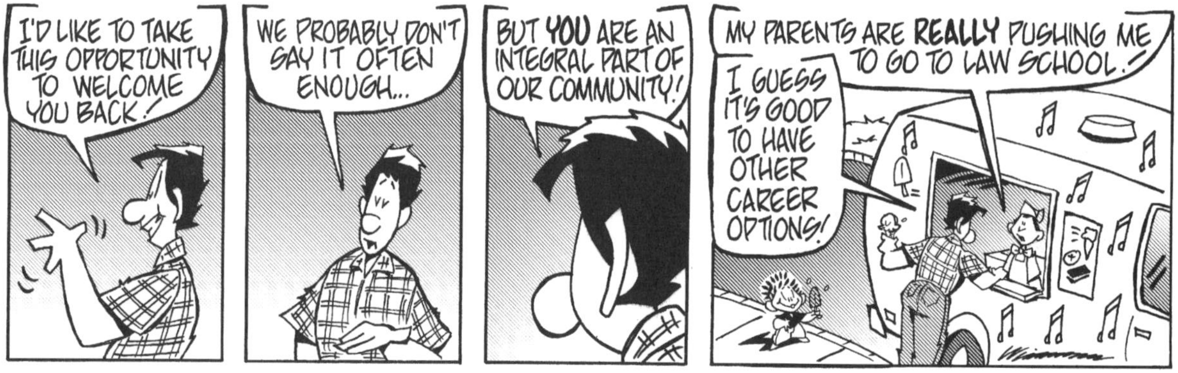
I'D LIKE TO TAKE THIS OPPORTUNITY TO WELCOME YOU BACK!
WE PROBABLY DON'T SAY IT OFTEN ENOUGH...
BUT YOU ARE AN INTEGRAL PART OF OUR COMMUNITY!
MY PARENTS ARE REALLY PUSHING ME TO GO TO LAW SCHOOL!
I GUESS IT'S GOOD TO HAVE OTHER CAREER OPTIONS!

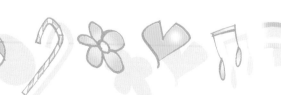

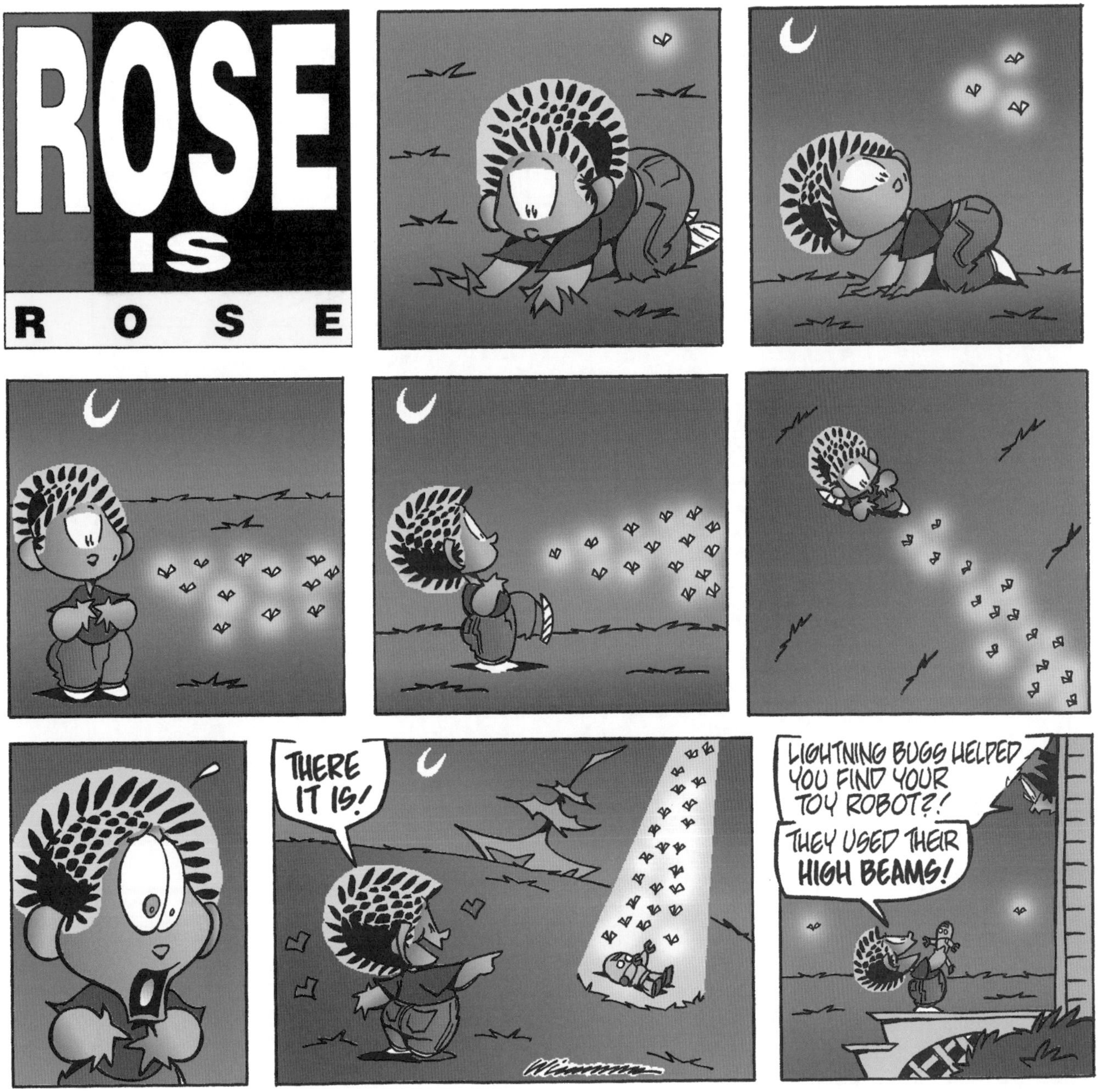
ROSE IS ROSE
THERE IT IS!
LIGHTNING BUGS HELPED YOU FIND YOUR TOY ROBOT?!
THEY USED THEIR HIGH BEAMS!

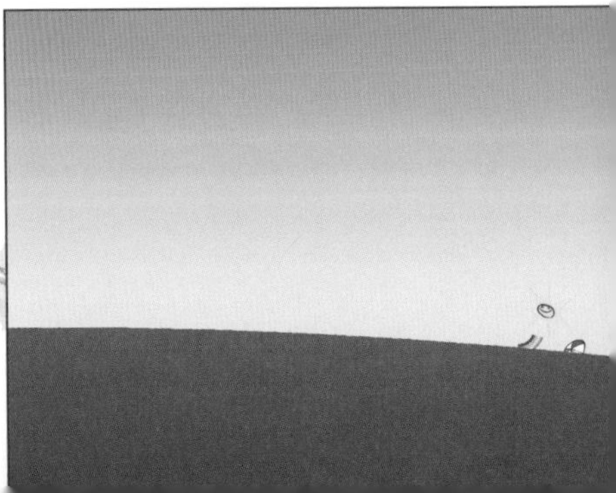

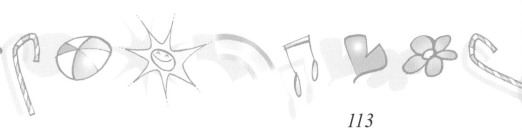

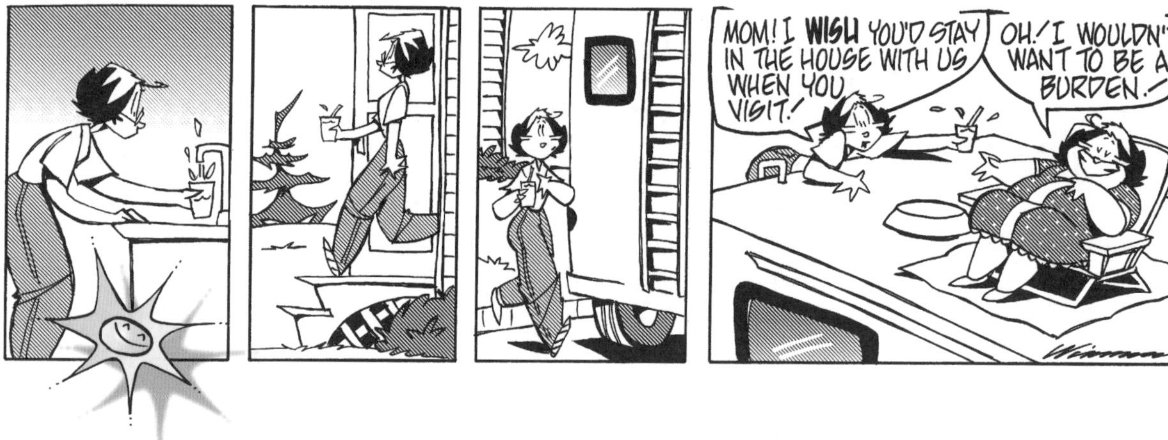
MOM! I WISH YOU'D STAY IN THE HOUSE WITH US WHEN YOU VISIT!
OH! I WOULDN'T WANT TO BE A BURDEN.

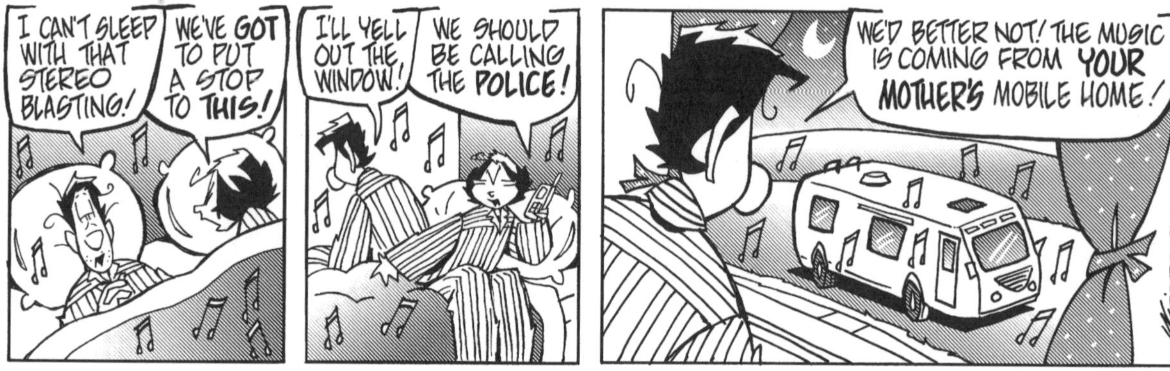
I CAN'T SLEEP WITH THAT STEREO BLASTING!
WE'VE GOT TO PUT A STOP TO THIS!
I'LL YELL OUT THE WINDOW!
WE SHOULD BE CALLING THE POLICE!
WE'D BETTER NOT! THE MUSIC IS COMING FROM YOUR MOTHER'S MOBILE HOME!

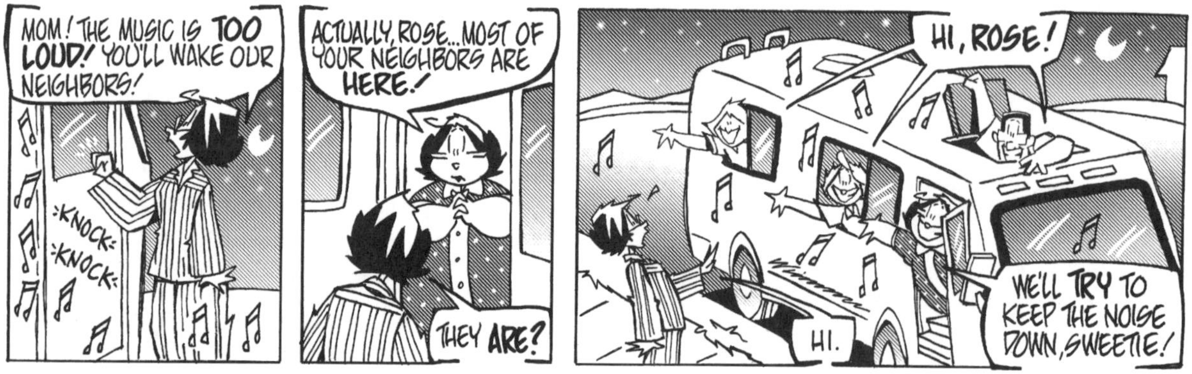
MOM! THE MUSIC IS TOO LOUD! YOU'LL WAKE OUR NEIGHBORS!
KNOCK
KNOCK
ACTUALLY, ROSE... MOST OF YOUR NEIGHBORS ARE HERE!
THEY ARE?
HI, ROSE!
HI.
WE'LL TRY TO KEEP THE NOISE DOWN, SWEETIE!

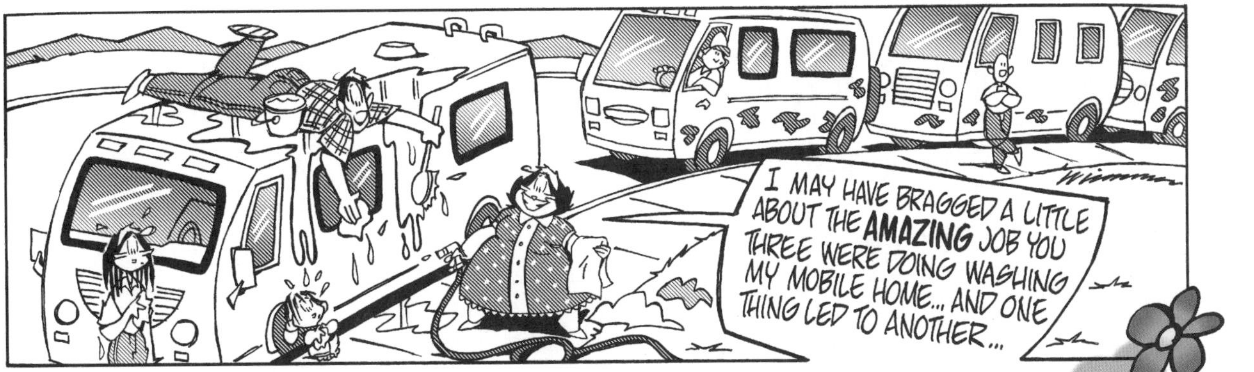
I MAY HAVE BRAGGED A LITTLE ABOUT THE **AMAZING** JOB YOU THREE WERE DOING WASHING MY MOBILE HOME... AND ONE THING LED TO ANOTHER...

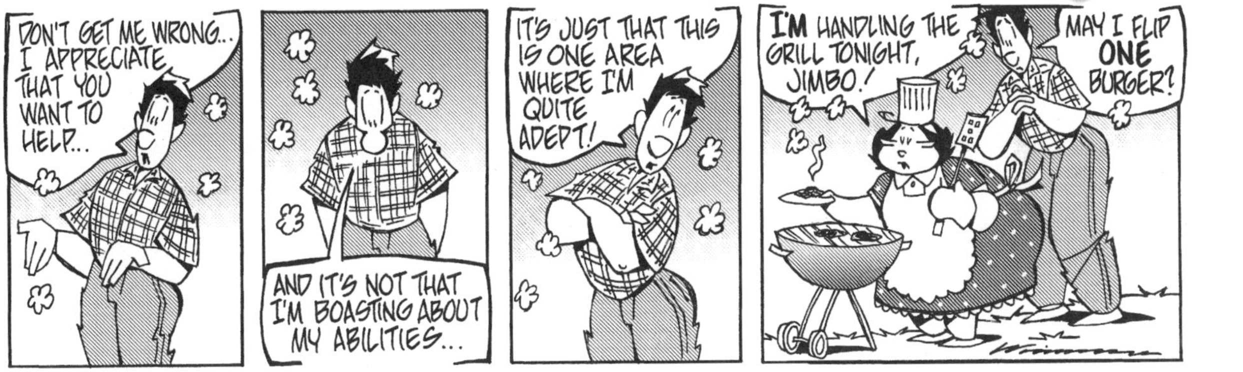
DON'T GET ME WRONG.. I APPRECIATE THAT YOU WANT TO HELP...
AND IT'S NOT THAT I'M BOASTING ABOUT MY ABILITIES...
IT'S JUST THAT THIS IS ONE AREA WHERE I'M QUITE ADEPT!
I'M HANDLING THE GRILL TONIGHT, JIMBO!
MAY I FLIP **ONE** BURGER?

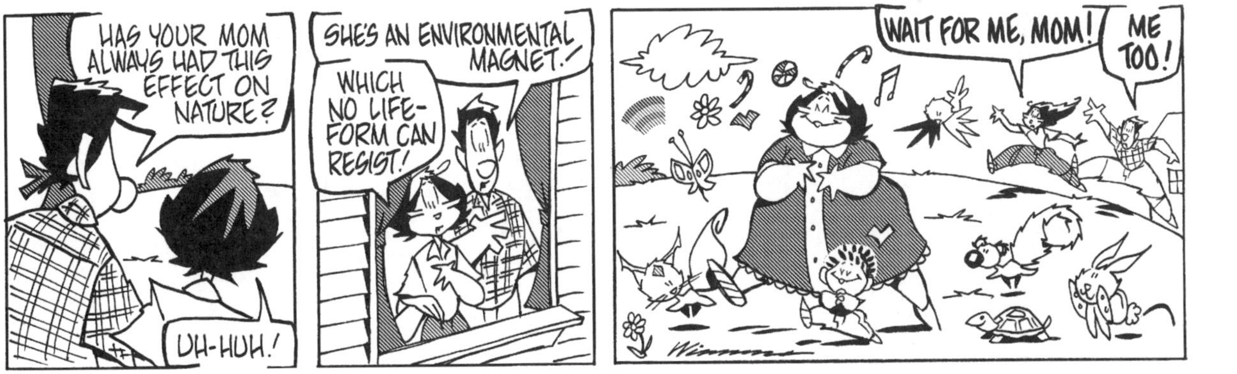
HAS YOUR MOM ALWAYS HAD THIS EFFECT ON NATURE?
UH-HUH!
SHE'S AN ENVIRONMENTAL MAGNET!
WHICH NO LIFE-FORM CAN RESIST!
WAIT FOR ME, MOM!
ME TOO!

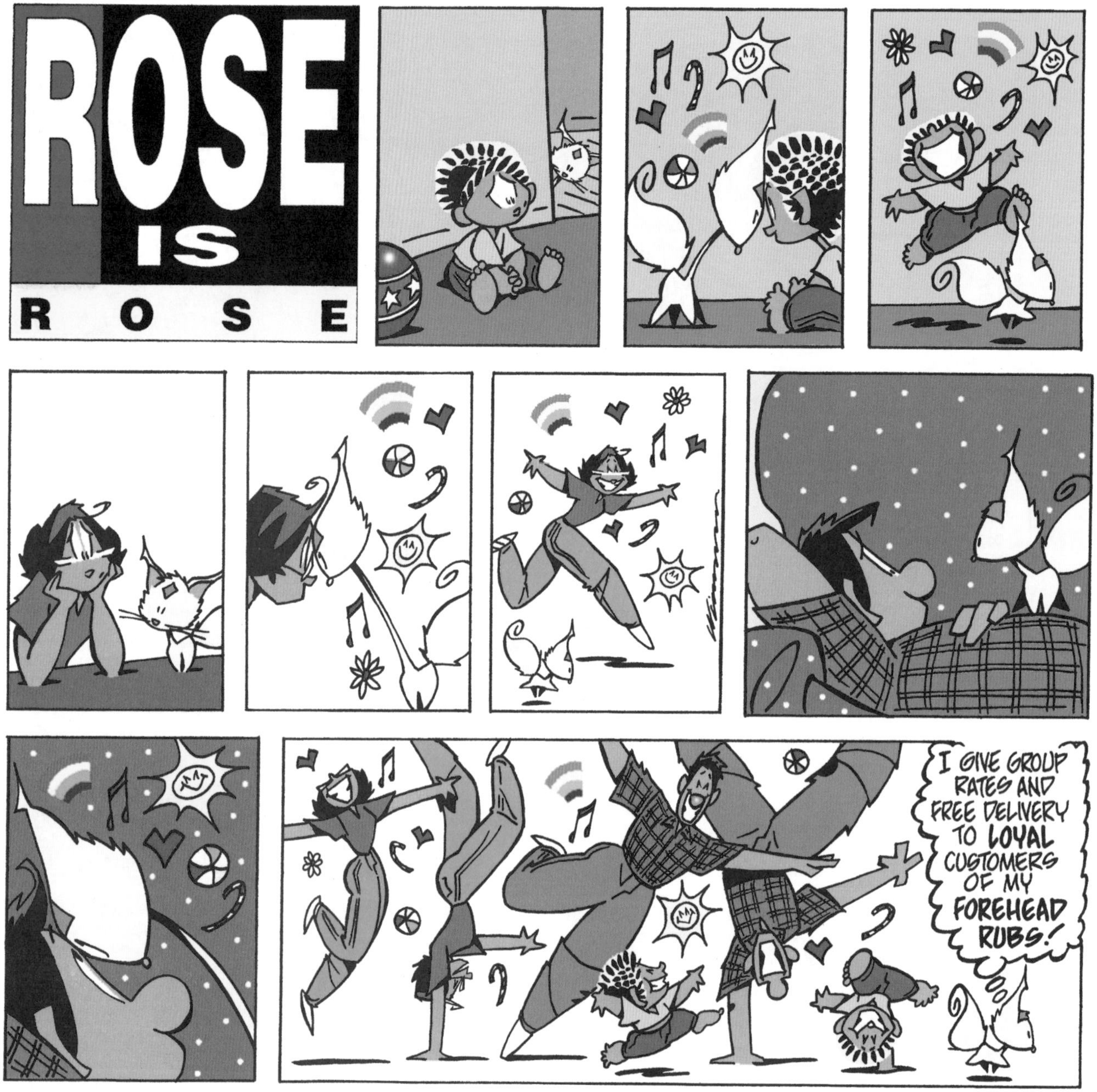
ROSE IS ROSE
I GIVE GROUP RATES AND FREE DELIVERY TO LOYAL CUSTOMERS OF MY FOREHEAD RUBS!

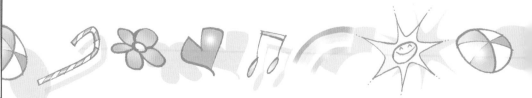

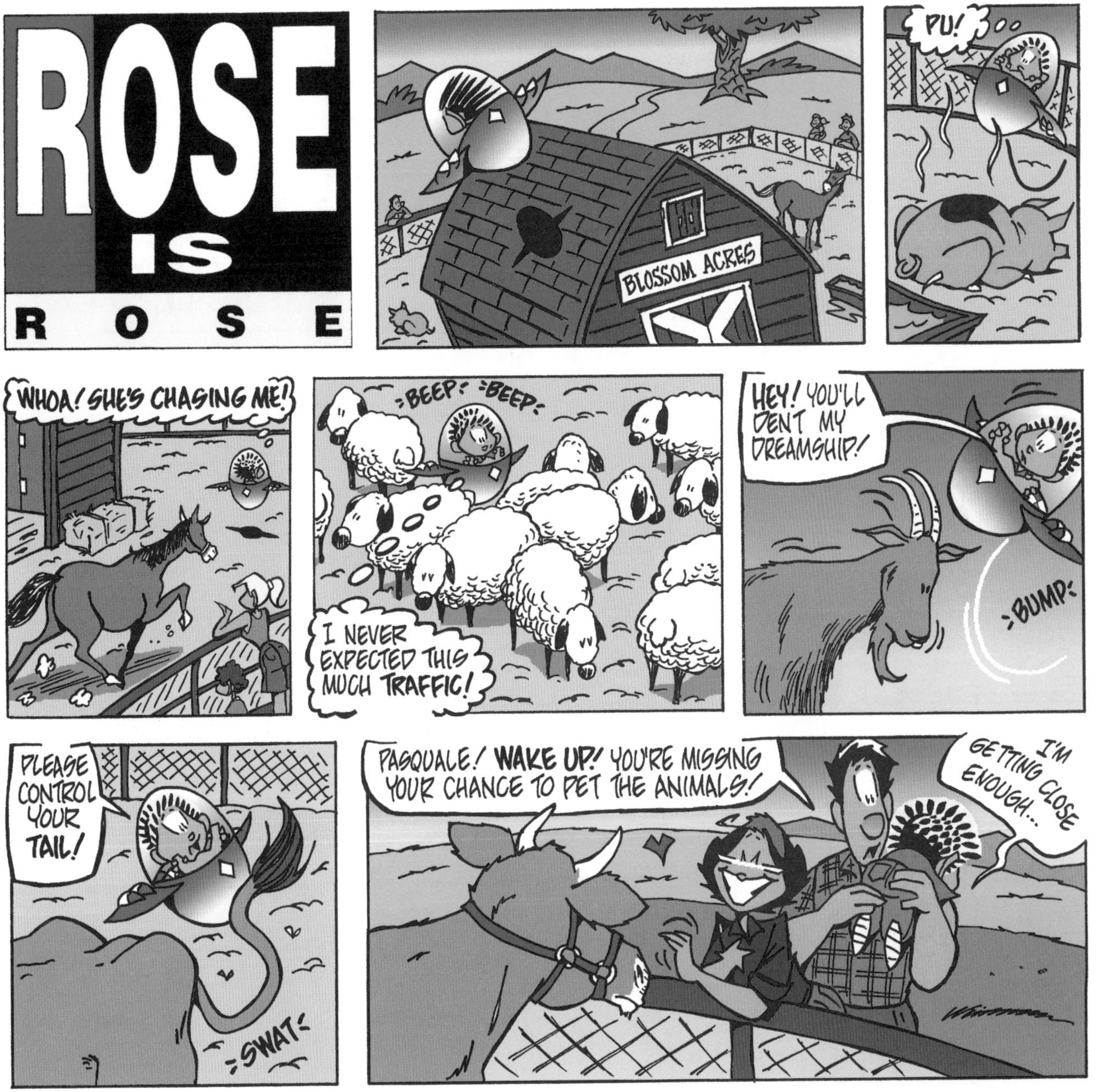
ROSE IS ROSE
BLOSSOM ACRES
PU!
WHOA! SHE'S CHASING ME!
BEEP BEEP
I NEVER EXPECTED THIS MUCH TRAFFIC!
HEY! YOU'LL DENT MY DREAMSHIP!
BUMP
PLEASE CONTROL YOUR TAIL!
SWAT
PASQUALE! WAKE UP! YOU'RE MISSING YOUR CHANCE TO PET THE ANIMALS!
I'M GETTING CLOSE ENOUGH...

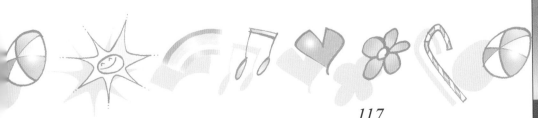

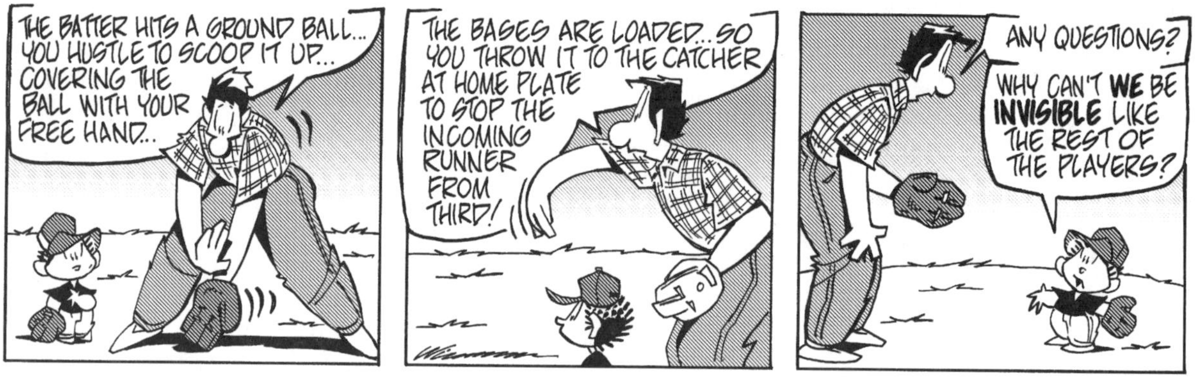
THE BATTER HITS A GROUND BALL... YOU HUSTLE TO SCOOP IT UP... COVERING THE BALL WITH YOUR FREE HAND...
THE BASES ARE LOADED... SO YOU THROW IT TO THE CATCHER AT HOME PLATE TO STOP THE INCOMING RUNNER FROM THIRD!
ANY QUESTIONS?
WHY CAN'T **WE** BE **INVISIBLE** LIKE THE REST OF THE PLAYERS?

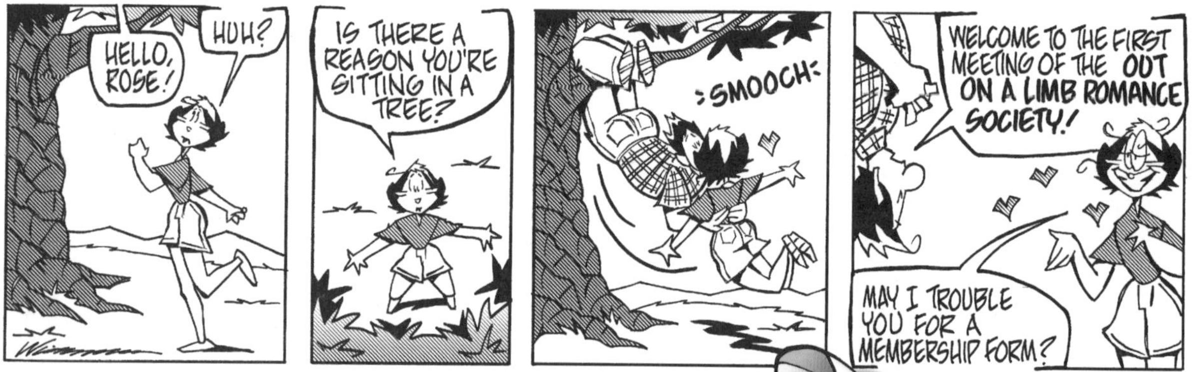
HELLO, ROSE!
HUH?
IS THERE A REASON YOU'RE SITTING IN A TREE?
:SMOOCH:
WELCOME TO THE FIRST MEETING OF THE **OUT ON A LIMB ROMANCE SOCIETY**!
MAY I TROUBLE YOU FOR A MEMBERSHIP FORM?

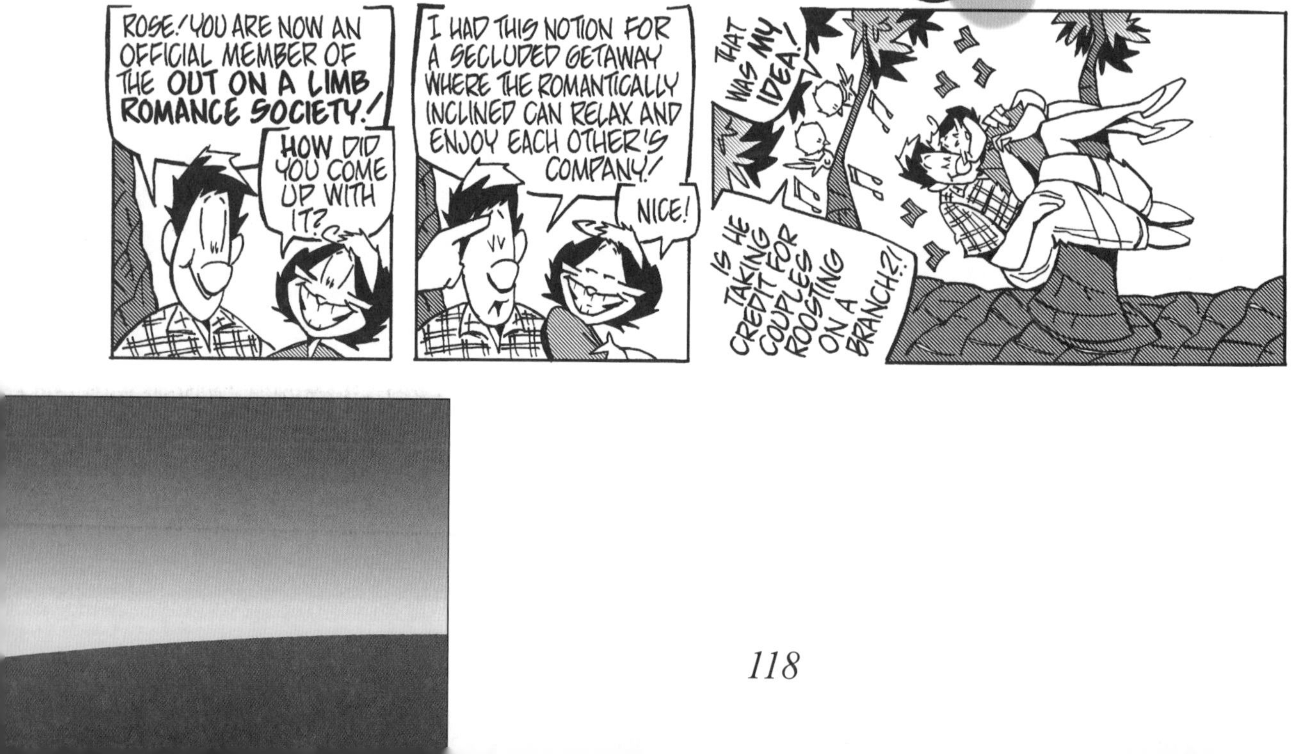
ROSE! YOU ARE NOW AN OFFICIAL MEMBER OF THE **OUT ON A LIMB ROMANCE SOCIETY**!
HOW DID YOU COME UP WITH IT?
I HAD THIS NOTION FOR A SECLUDED GETAWAY WHERE THE ROMANTICALLY INCLINED CAN RELAX AND ENJOY EACH OTHER'S COMPANY!
NICE!
THAT WAS **MY IDEA**!
IS HE TAKING CREDIT FOR COUPLES ROOSTING ON A BRANCH?!

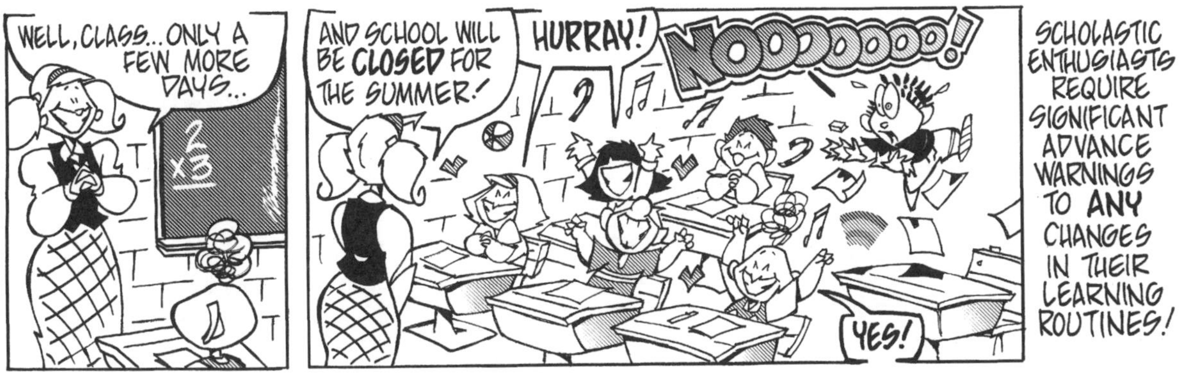

WELL, CLASS...ONLY A FEW MORE DAYS...
2 X3
AND SCHOOL WILL BE CLOSED FOR THE SUMMER!
HURRAY!
NOOOOOOOO!
YES!
SCHOLASTIC ENTHUSIASTS REQUIRE SIGNIFICANT ADVANCE WARNINGS TO ANY CHANGES IN THEIR LEARNING ROUTINES!

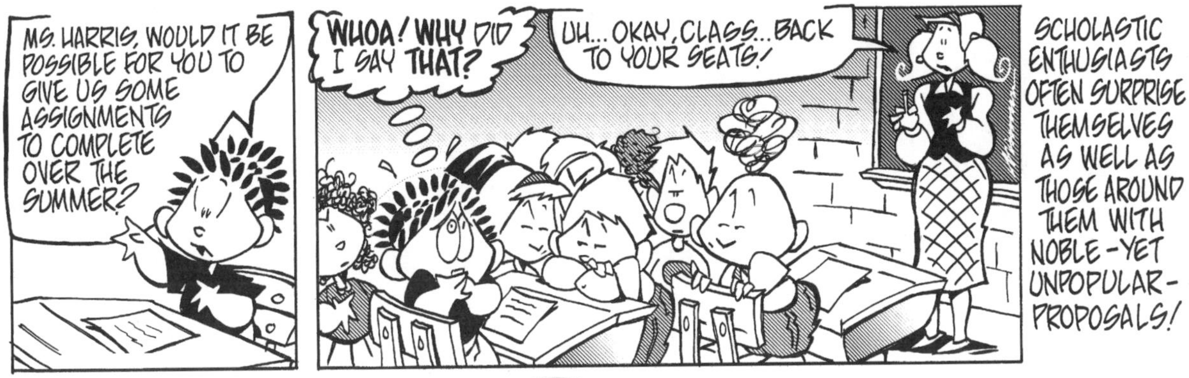

MS. HARRIS, WOULD IT BE POSSIBLE FOR YOU TO GIVE US SOME ASSIGNMENTS TO COMPLETE OVER THE SUMMER?
WHOA! WHY DID I SAY THAT?
UH... OKAY, CLASS... BACK TO YOUR SEATS!
SCHOLASTIC ENTHUSIASTS OFTEN SURPRISE THEMSELVES AS WELL AS THOSE AROUND THEM WITH NOBLE-YET UNPOPULAR-PROPOSALS!

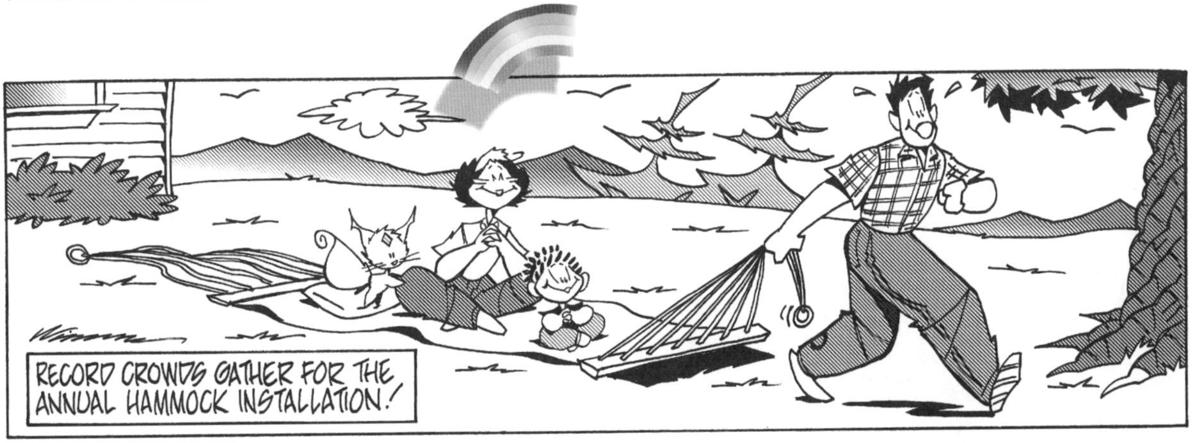

RECORD CROWDS GATHER FOR THE ANNUAL HAMMOCK INSTALLATION!

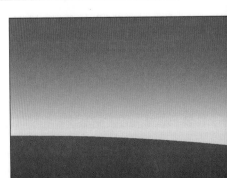

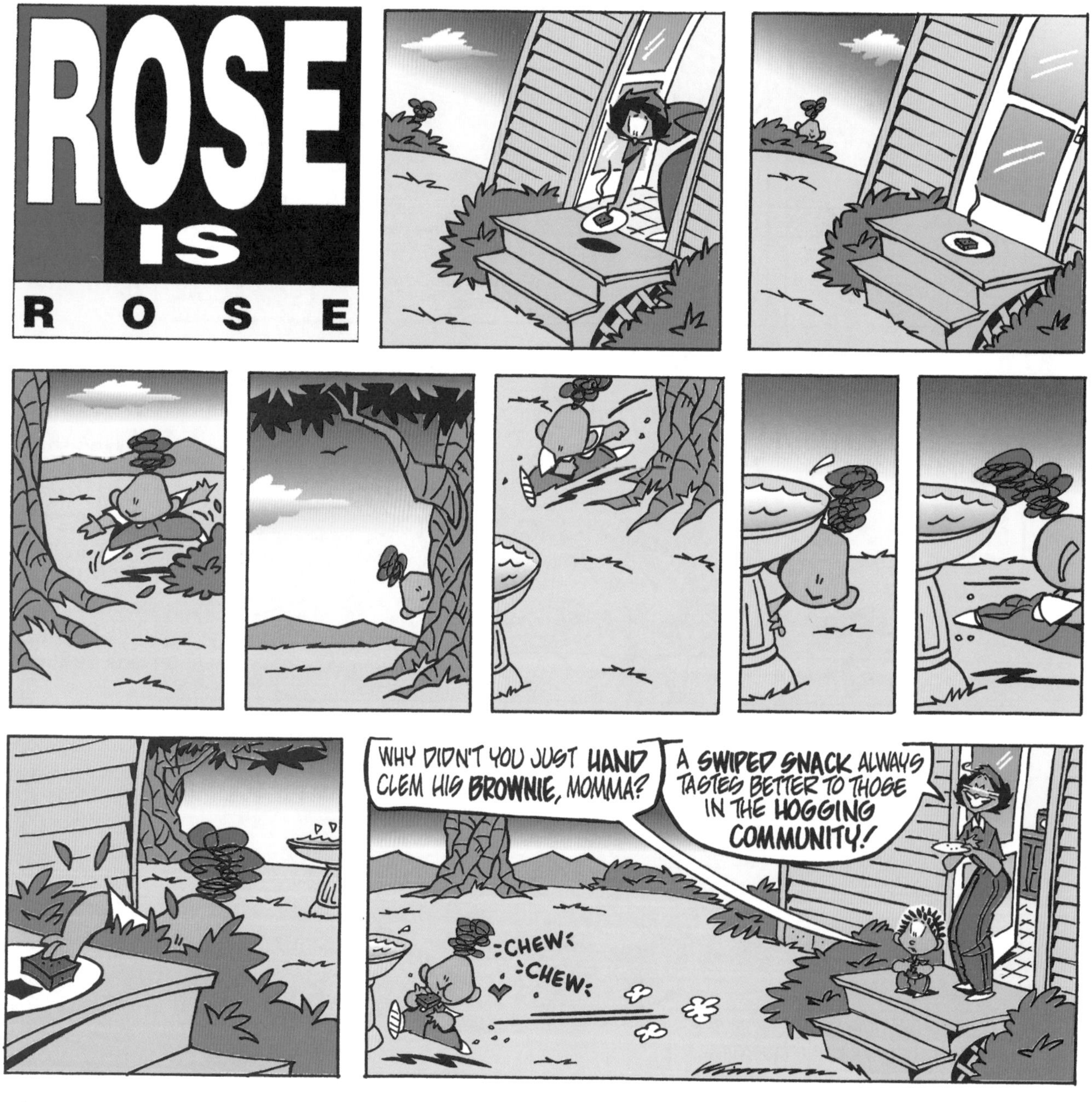
ROSE IS ROSE
WHY DIDN'T YOU JUST HAND CLEM HIS BROWNIE, MOMMA?
A SWIPED SNACK ALWAYS TASTES BETTER TO THOSE IN THE HOGGING COMMUNITY!
CHEW
CHEW

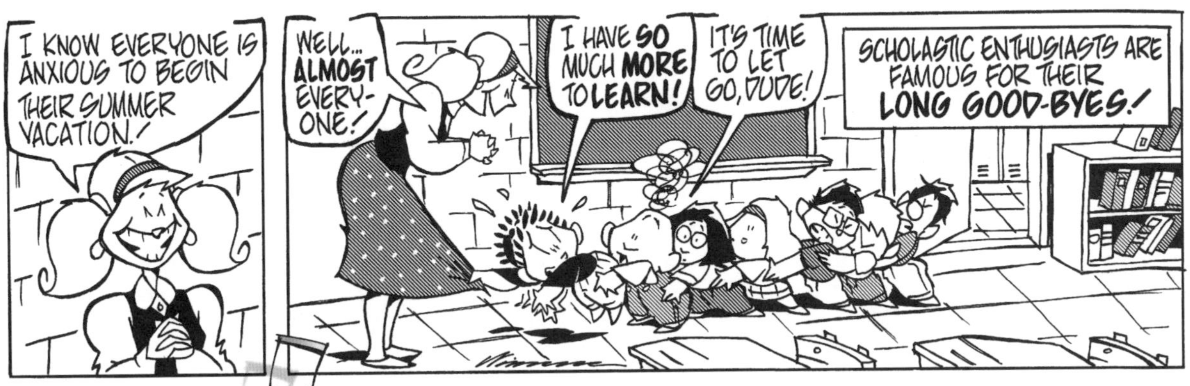
I KNOW EVERYONE IS ANXIOUS TO BEGIN THEIR SUMMER VACATION!
WELL... ALMOST EVERY-ONE!
I HAVE SO MUCH MORE TO LEARN!
IT'S TIME TO LET GO, DUDE!
SCHOLASTIC ENTHUSIASTS ARE FAMOUS FOR THEIR LONG GOOD-BYES!

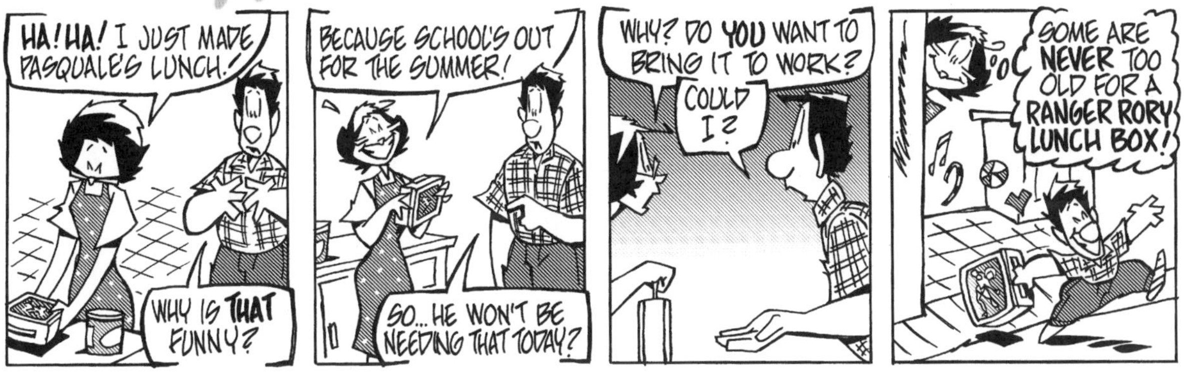
HA! HA! I JUST MADE PASQUALE'S LUNCH!
WHY IS THAT FUNNY?
BECAUSE SCHOOL'S OUT FOR THE SUMMER!
SO... HE WON'T BE NEEDING THAT TODAY?
WHY? DO YOU WANT TO BRING IT TO WORK?
COULD I?
SOME ARE NEVER TOO OLD FOR A RANGER RORY LUNCH BOX!

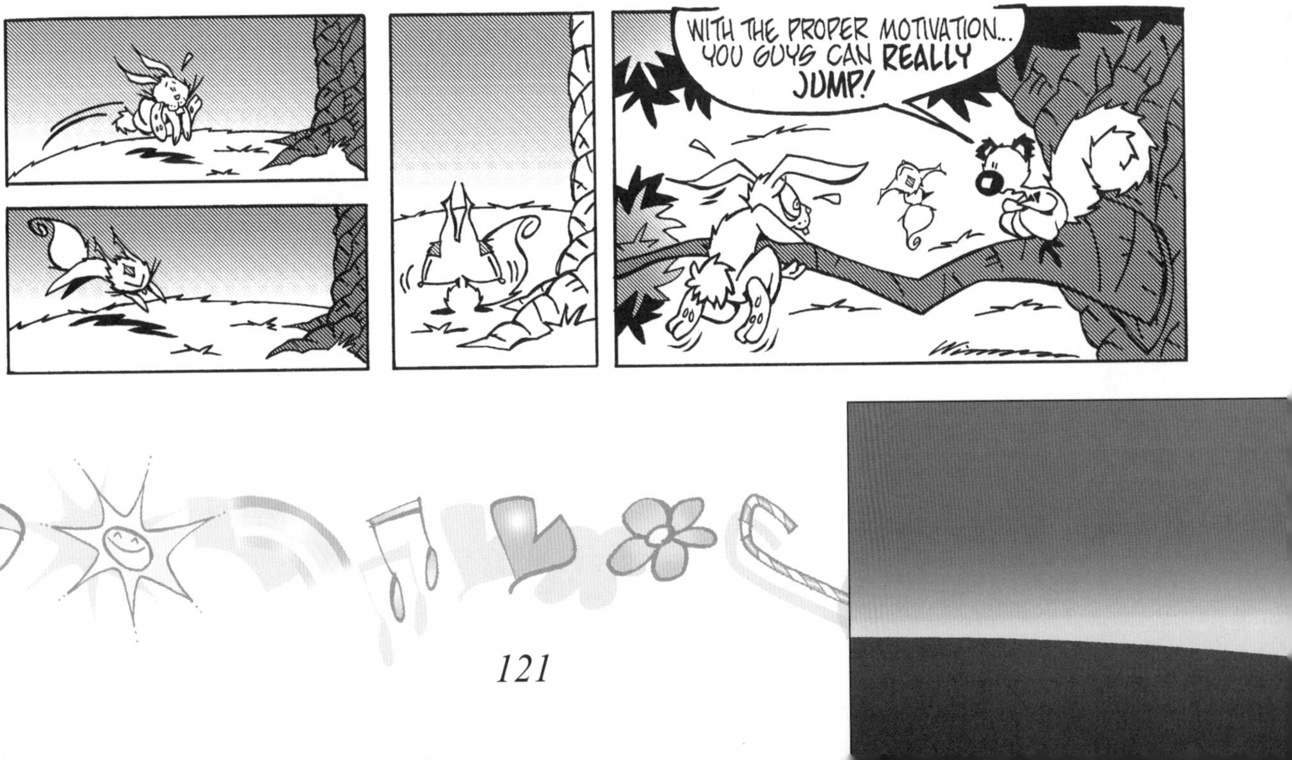
WITH THE PROPER MOTIVATION... YOU GUYS CAN REALLY JUMP!

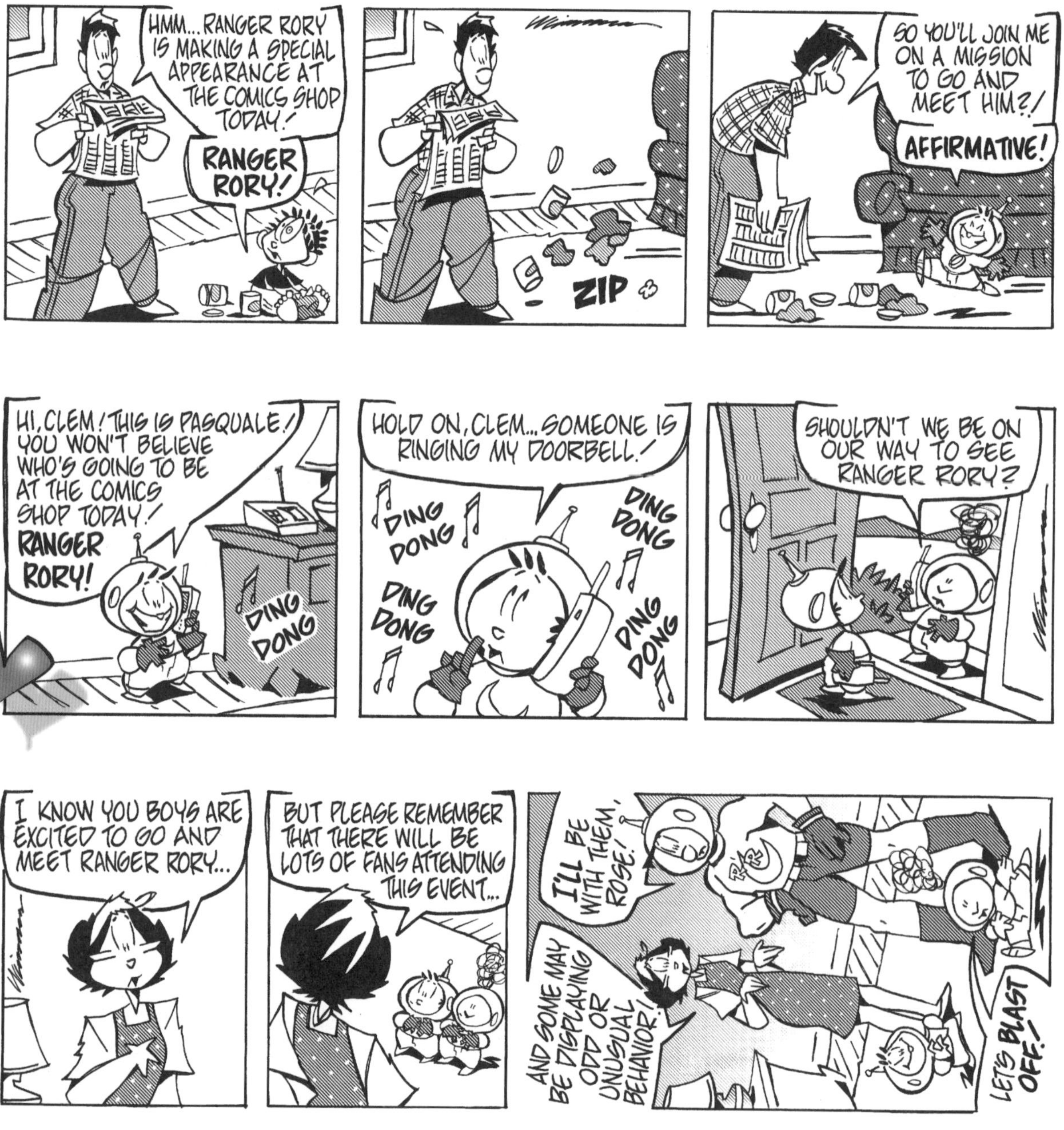
HMM... RANGER RORY IS MAKING A SPECIAL APPEARANCE AT THE COMICS SHOP TODAY!
RANGER RORY!
ZIP
SO YOU'LL JOIN ME ON A MISSION TO GO AND MEET HIM?!
AFFIRMATIVE!
HI, CLEM! THIS IS PASQUALE! YOU WON'T BELIEVE WHO'S GOING TO BE AT THE COMICS SHOP TODAY! RANGER RORY!
DING DONG
HOLD ON, CLEM... SOMEONE IS RINGING MY DOORBELL!
DING DONG
DING DONG
DING DONG
DING DONG
SHOULDN'T WE BE ON OUR WAY TO SEE RANGER RORY?
I KNOW YOU BOYS ARE EXCITED TO GO AND MEET RANGER RORY...
BUT PLEASE REMEMBER THAT THERE WILL BE LOTS OF FANS ATTENDING THIS EVENT...
AND SOME MAY BE DISPLAYING ODD OR UNUSUAL BEHAVIOR!
I'LL BE WITH THEM, ROSE!
LET'S BLAST OFF!

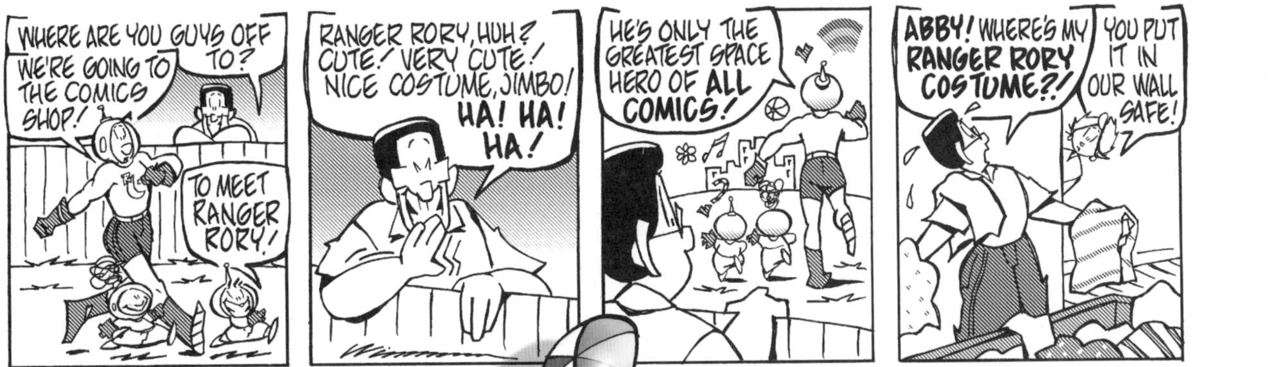
WHERE ARE YOU GUYS OFF TO?
WE'RE GOING TO THE COMICS SHOP!
TO MEET RANGER RORY!
RANGER RORY, HUH? CUTE! VERY CUTE! NICE COSTUME, JIMBO! HA! HA! HA!
HE'S ONLY THE GREATEST SPACE HERO OF ALL COMICS!
ABBY! WHERE'S MY RANGER RORY COSTUME?!
YOU PUT IT IN OUR WALL SAFE!

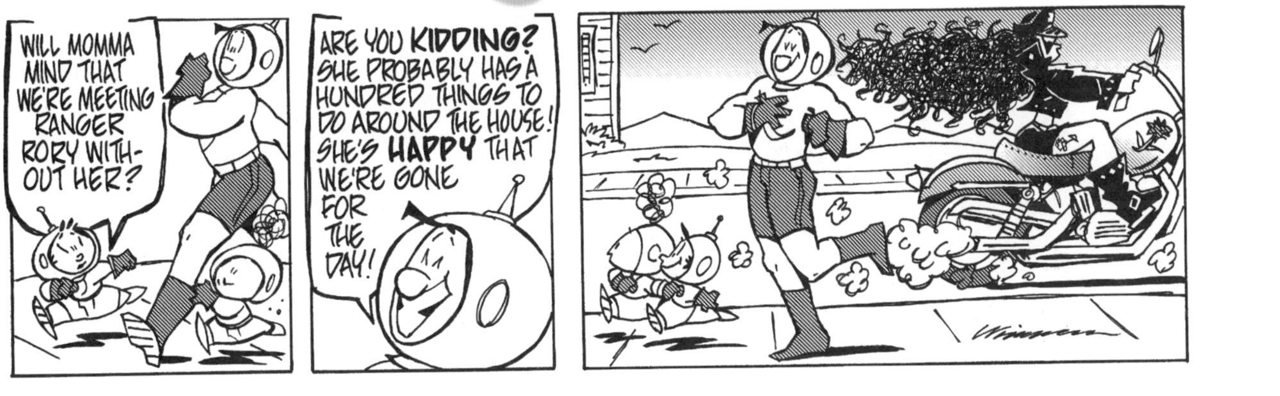
WILL MOMMA MIND THAT WE'RE MEETING RANGER RORY WITHOUT HER?
ARE YOU KIDDING? SHE PROBABLY HAS A HUNDRED THINGS TO DO AROUND THE HOUSE! SHE'S HAPPY THAT WE'RE GONE FOR THE DAY!

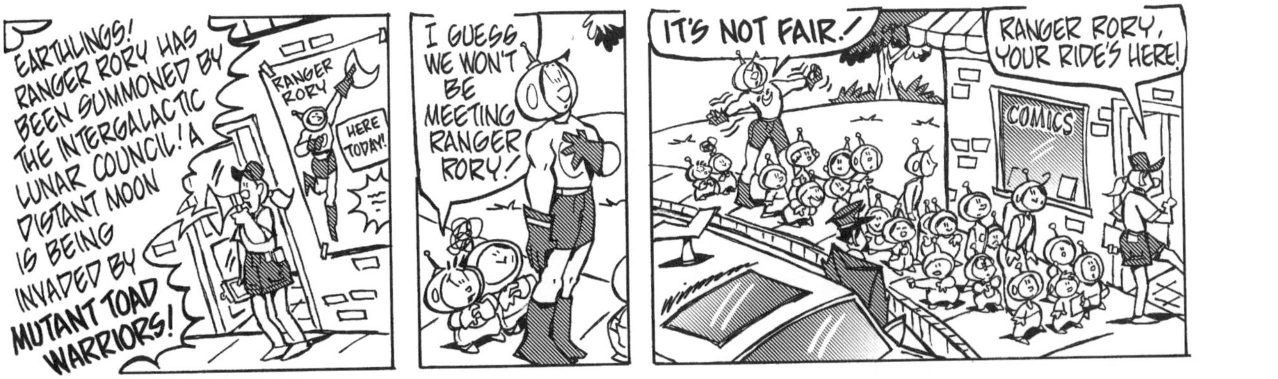
EARTHLINGS! RANGER RORY HAS BEEN SUMMONED BY THE INTERGALACTIC LUNAR COUNCIL! A DISTANT MOON IS BEING INVADED BY MUTANT TOAD WARRIORS!
RANGER RORY
HERE TODAY!
I GUESS WE WON'T BE MEETING RANGER RORY!
IT'S NOT FAIR!
RANGER RORY, YOUR RIDE'S HERE!
COMICS

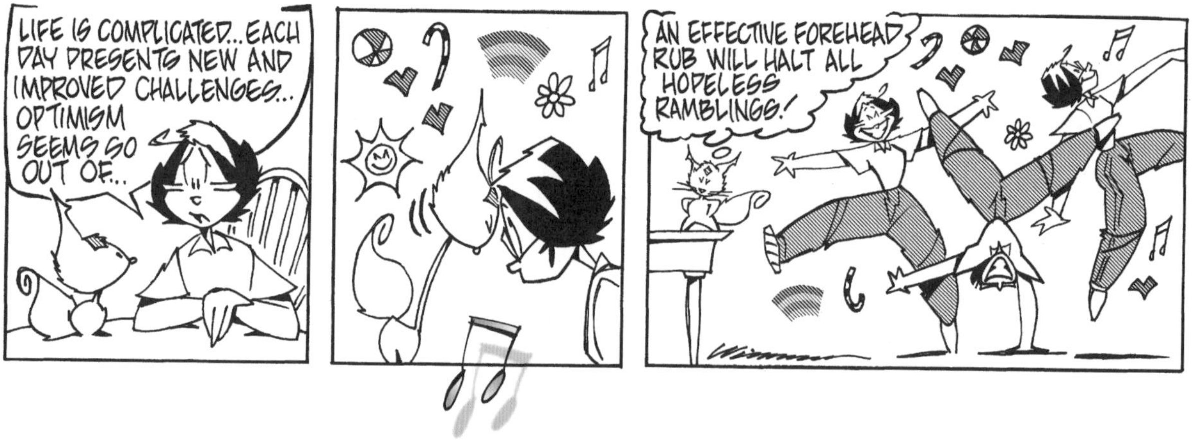
LIFE IS COMPLICATED... EACH DAY PRESENTS NEW AND IMPROVED CHALLENGES... OPTIMISM SEEMS SO OUT OF...
AN EFFECTIVE FOREHEAD RUB WILL HALT ALL HOPELESS RAMBLINGS!

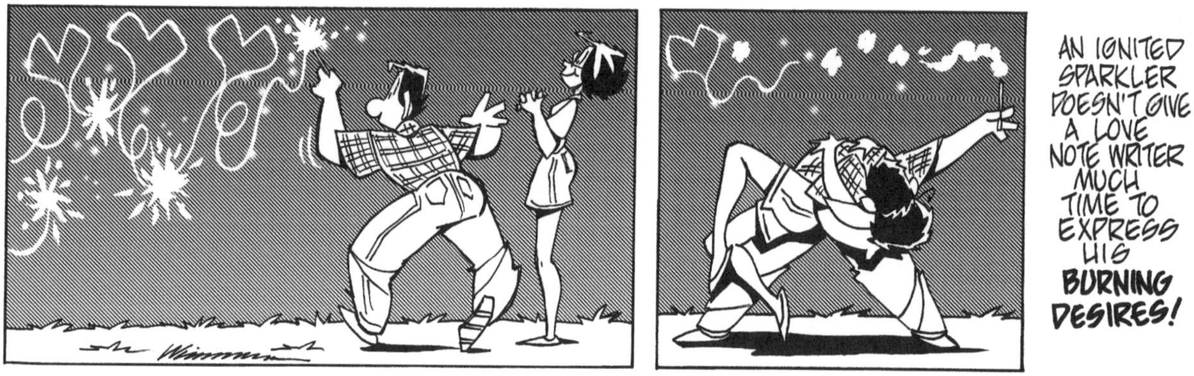
AN IGNITED SPARKLER DOESN'T GIVE A LOVE NOTE WRITER MUCH TIME TO EXPRESS HIS **BURNING DESIRES!**

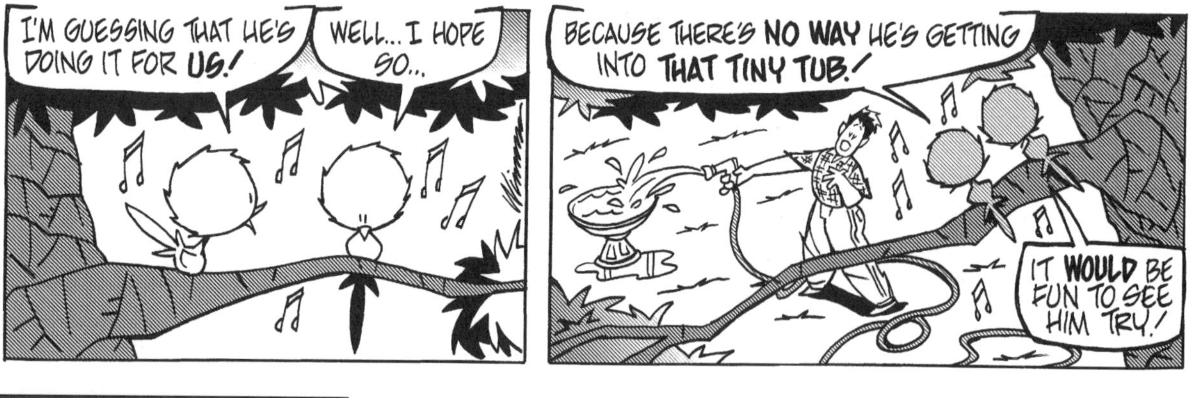
I'M GUESSING THAT HE'S DOING IT FOR **US!**
WELL... I HOPE SO...
BECAUSE THERE'S **NO WAY** HE'S GETTING INTO **THAT TINY TUB!**
IT **WOULD** BE FUN TO SEE HIM TRY!

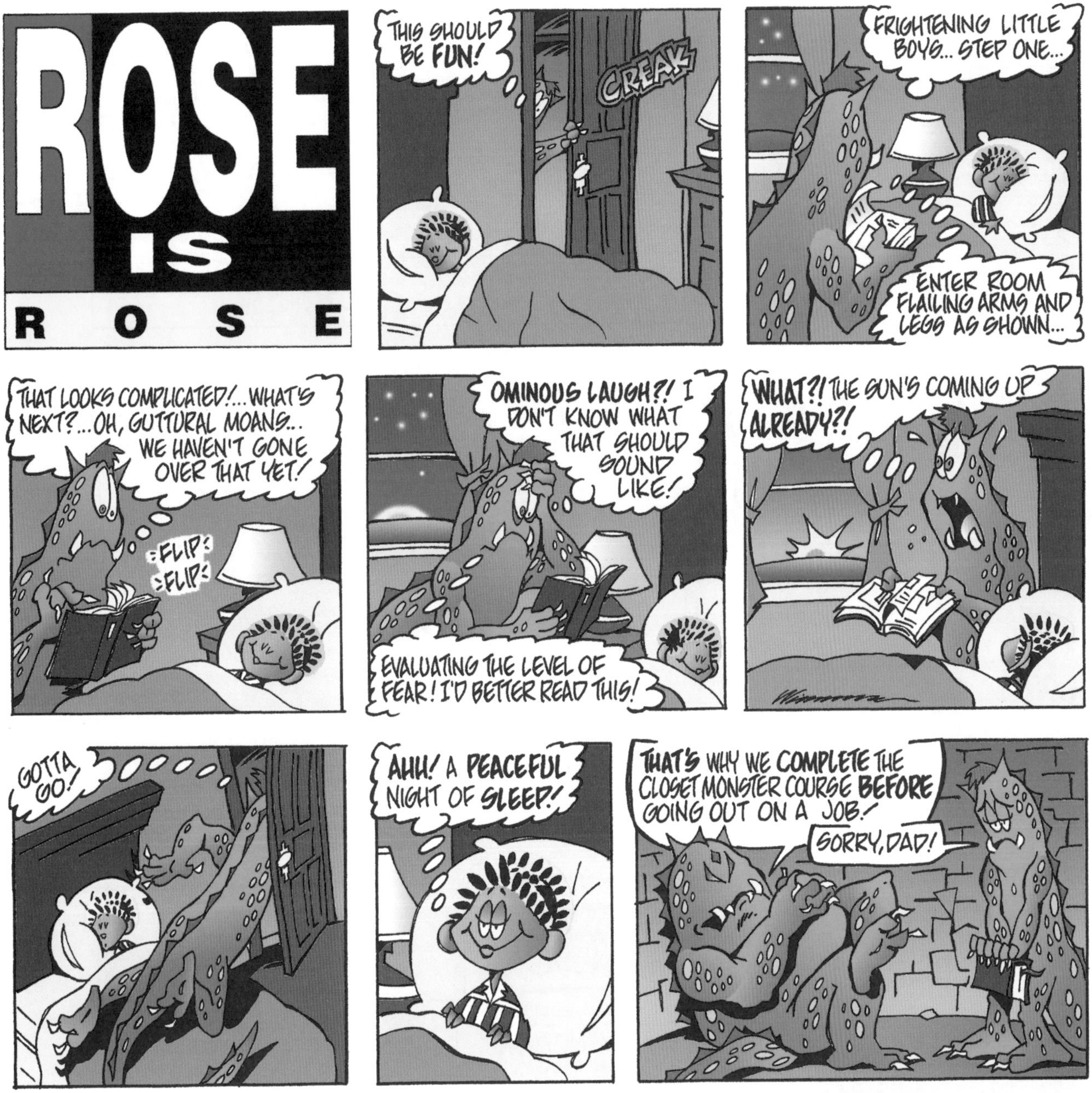
ROSE IS ROSE
THIS SHOULD BE FUN!
CREAK
FRIGHTENING LITTLE BOYS... STEP ONE...
ENTER ROOM FLAILING ARMS AND LEGS AS SHOWN...
THAT LOOKS COMPLICATED!... WHAT'S NEXT?... OH, GUTTURAL MOANS... WE HAVEN'T GONE OVER THAT YET!
FLIP FLIP
OMINOUS LAUGH?! I DON'T KNOW WHAT THAT SHOULD SOUND LIKE!
EVALUATING THE LEVEL OF FEAR! I'D BETTER READ THIS!
WHAT?! THE SUN'S COMING UP ALREADY?!
GOTTA GO!
AHH! A PEACEFUL NIGHT OF SLEEP!
THAT'S WHY WE COMPLETE THE CLOSET MONSTER COURSE BEFORE GOING OUT ON A JOB!
SORRY, DAD!

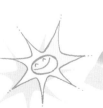

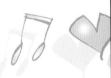

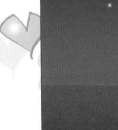

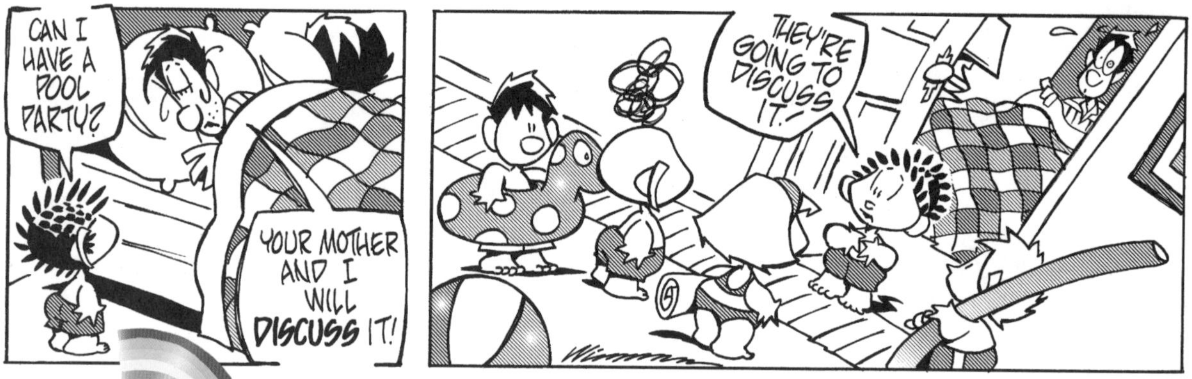
CAN I HAVE A POOL PARTY?
YOUR MOTHER AND I WILL **DISCUSS** IT!
THEY'RE GOING TO DISCUSS IT!

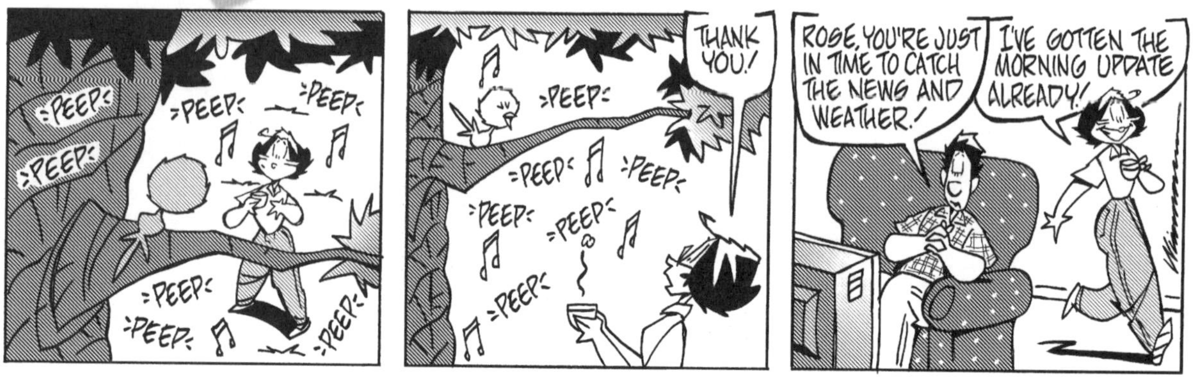
PEEP PEEP PEEP PEEP PEEP PEEP PEEP
PEEP PEEP PEEP PEEP PEEP PEEP
THANK YOU!
ROSE, YOU'RE JUST IN TIME TO CATCH THE NEWS AND WEATHER!
I'VE GOTTEN THE MORNING UPDATE ALREADY!

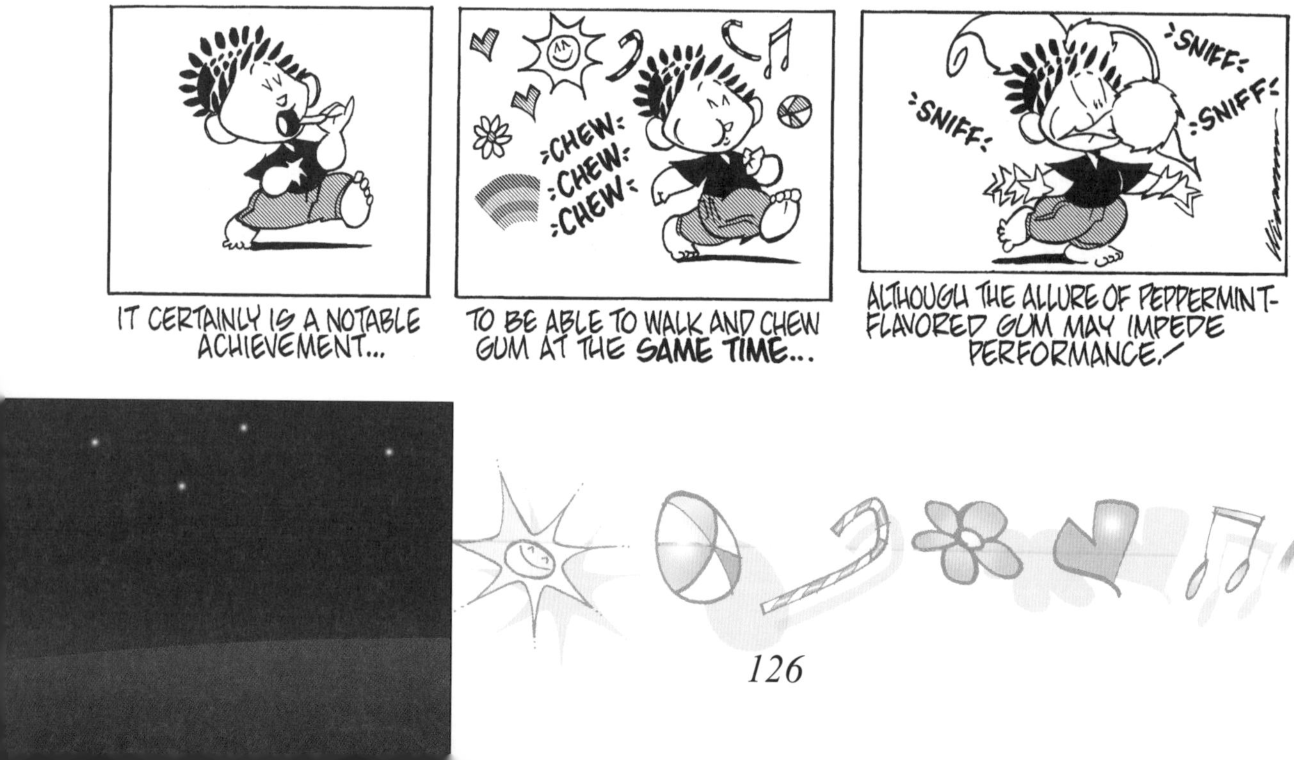
CHEW CHEW CHEW
SNIFF SNIFF SNIFF
IT CERTAINLY IS A NOTABLE ACHIEVEMENT...
TO BE ABLE TO WALK AND CHEW GUM AT THE **SAME TIME**...
ALTHOUGH THE ALLURE OF PEPPERMINT-FLAVORED GUM MAY IMPEDE PERFORMANCE!

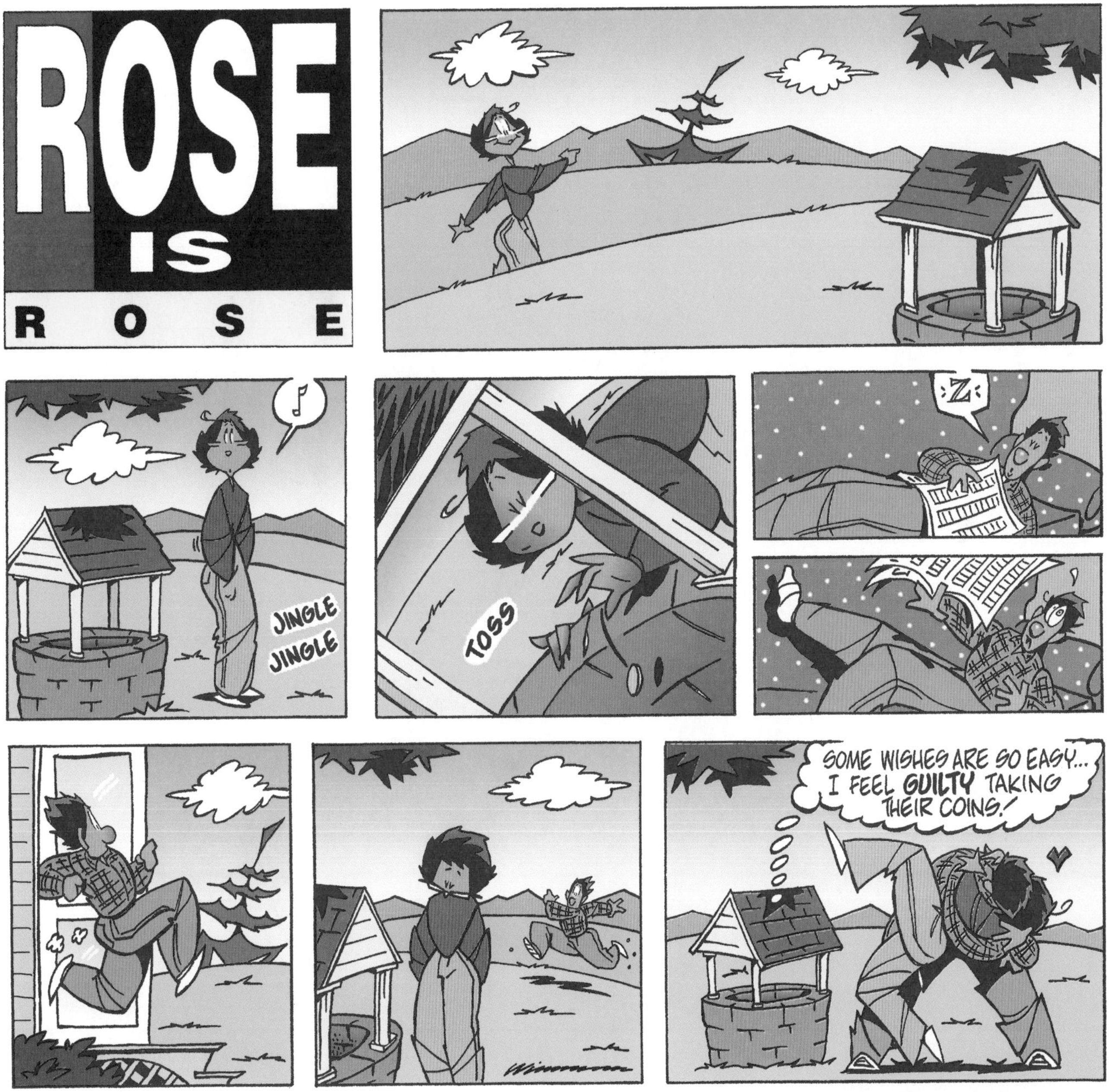
ROSE IS ROSE
JINGLE JINGLE
TOSS
Z
SOME WISHES ARE SO EASY... I FEEL **GUILTY** TAKING THEIR COINS!

FLIP THE PAGE CORNERS FROM FRONT TO BACK AND WATCH BOTH SIDES TOGETHER!

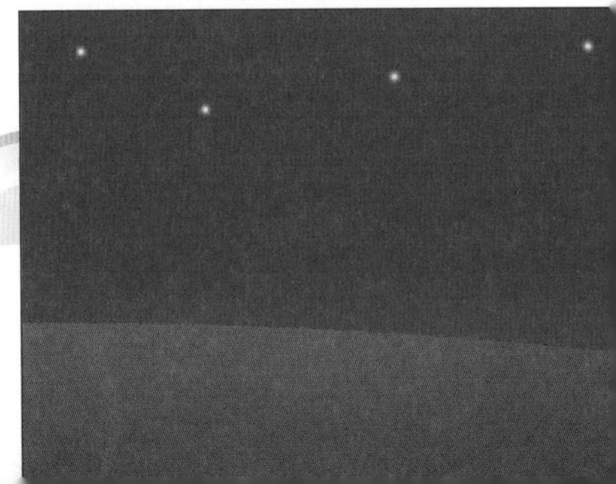

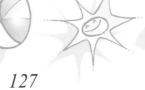